Case Preparation

Case Preparation

Inns of Court School of Law
Institute of Law, City University, London

OXFORD
UNIVERSITY PRESS

OXFORD

UNIVERSITY PRESS

Great Clarendon Street, Oxford OX2 6DP

Oxford University Press is a department of the University of Oxford.
It furthers the University's objective of excellence in research, scholarship,
and education by publishing worldwide in

Oxford New York

Auckland Cape Town Dar es Salaam Hong Kong Karachi
Kuala Lumpur Madrid Melbourne Mexico City Nairobi
New Delhi Shanghai Taipei Toronto

With offices in

Argentina Austria Brazil Chile Czech Republic France Greece
Guatemala Hungary Italy Japan Poland Portugal Singapore
South Korea Switzerland Thailand Turkey Ukraine Vietnam

Oxford is a registered trade mark of Oxford University Press
in the UK and in certain other countries

Published in the United States
by Oxford University Press Inc., New York

British Library Cataloguing in Publication Data
Data available

Library of Congress Cataloging in Publication Data
Data available

Typeset by Newgen Imaging Systems (P) Ltd., Chennai, India
Printed in Great Britain
on acid-free paper by
Ashford Colour Press, Gosport, Hampshire

ISBN 0-19-928148-3   978-0-19-928148-0

1 3 5 7 9 10 8 6 4 2

FOREWORD

It is a privilege to write this Foreword, following the tradition set by my predecessor, the Hon. Mr Justice Elias.

The Bar Vocational Course (BVC) bridges the gap between completion of a university degree and the start of a professional working life, whether by way of pupillage preliminary to a career at the Bar, or otherwise. These Manuals are geared to the practical and professional approach that is central to the BVC. Updated and revised, the Manuals form an integral part of the student's vocational training; as such, they are an important ingredient in the constant drive to raise standards in the public interest.

The Manuals are written by staff at the Inns of Court School of Law (ICSL). The range and coverage of the Manuals have grown steadily. They are intended to provide a useful resource for all concerned in the training of legal skills, hopefully at whichever validated institution such training takes place.

Legal vocational training does not stand still; the ICSL and authors would welcome feedback from any source, which may assist to improve the Manuals in the future. Any such comments should be addressed to the BVC Course Director at the ICSL.

Finally a word of thanks is appropriate to the publishers for their enthusiasm and efficiency in arranging production and publication of the Manuals.

The Hon. Mr Justice Gross
Chairman, Advisory Board of the Institute of Law,
City University, London,
October 2004

OUTLINE CONTENTS

DETAILED CONTENTS

PREFACE

This Manual explains and demonstrates, in the context of the work of a barrister, the underlying skills of legal research and fact management which will ensure that a case has been thoroughly prepared so that every relevant consideration has been taken into account before the client is given any advice, any document is drafted or any case presented in court. Its purpose is to assist those who read it to develop effective techniques which, it is hoped, will ensure that the advice they give is sound, and the arguments they put forward are convincing.

The development of professional legal skills training with its emphasis on the ability to perform lawyers' tasks has underlined the need to develop case preparation skills to a high standard. If relevant law or fact is not identified, or if there is only a superficial assessment of the strength of evidence, the advice given is unlikely to be sound, and the argument presented in negotiation or before a tribunal is unlikely to succeed.

The experience of those studying and teaching on the Bar Vocational Course has identified the need to provide clear guidance on how to carry out legal research efficiently and to identify, analyse and present relevant facts to ensure the best outcome for the client. The methods and techniques adopted in this Manual are the outcome of our experience over many years and our discussions with the many practitioners and academics who have kindly contributed to the debate about how best to develop effective case preparation skills.

The advice given in this Manual is not intended to be prescriptive. The aim is to provide practical advice and to demonstrate through the inclusion of worked examples how particular techniques can be applied to the preparation of a case. It is hoped that this will provide a framework which will assist each individual to develop his or her own intellectual skills in order to carry out the task of preparation competently and professionally.

Students will find that they will have opportunities to apply these techniques throughout the Bar Vocational Course. Some of the case papers will be used in specific classes. In particular, the sections assisting you with legal research and fact management processes will be invaluable when you are working with sets of papers for the skills exercises and should be particularly useful in preparing for assessment and later when you enter practice.

Preparation: a forensic skill

The image of successful barristers suggests that their success depends on the ability to think on their feet, to use words persuasively, to mesmerise by their fluency, and to impress by their very presence and charisma those whom they address. Certainly those skills help. However, the real basis for their confidence is effective preparation for the task they are undertaking so that they know the facts of the case thoroughly and, having considered the potential relevance of all the facts to their legal context, can respond effectively to any point made, and, having thought through and planned their argument beforehand, they can deliver it clearly and address in a convincing way all the relevant questions which must be decided.

The work of a barrister (more fully dealt with in **Chapters 12** and **13** below) although more varied than many realise, is focused on answering one question. If the case came before a court, how likely is it that the client would win? The only way that this question can be answered is for the barrister to address the underlying question which is: how can the case be presented so that evidence can be put before the court which will prove on the facts that the client is legally entitled to a finding in his or her favour? This is why case preparation is a forensic skill.

In order to answer this underlying question the barrister will need to look closely at the facts of the case to see what the client's problem is and what the client hopes to achieve from any legal claim. The barrister will then need to research the law to see whether there is a legal principle which will give the client a right to the outcome being sought. The facts of the case will then need to be analysed to determine whether they can be presented in such a way that all the component parts of the legal principle can be shown to be fulfilled. The barrister will also need to consider whether there are witnesses who can be called to give evidence which, if believed, will prove the facts on which the argument is based and which, it is hoped, will persuade the court of the client's entitlement to a finding in his or her favour.

This analytical process can be demonstrated in graphical form as in Table 1.1 below.

Table 1.1 **Initial analysis of a case**

Legal framework	Facts in support	Evidence
Insert below each element of the crime, cause of action and/or defences	Insert below in relation to each legal element, facts which establish that element	Insert below in relation to each fact the evidence which proves that fact

By identifying every element of the legal principle which is relied on and the facts and evidence which support it, the barrister can test whether there is sufficient available evidence of the facts which establish the legal basis of the case. Even then the preparatory work will not be completed, for the barrister, before being able to advise on the likely success of a case, will have to consider all the arguments about fact and law which the other side might raise, and whether and how they can be countered. Only then will the barrister be able to answer, with any hope of that answer being justified, the question whether the client will win, or be able with confidence to present the case convincingly to the court.

The aim of this Manual is to explain and demonstrate some methods of legal research and fact management which, in the context of the work of a barrister, will assist in developing effective case preparation skills.

Chapters 2 to **11** show how legal research can be made more efficient by increasing familiarity with the basic sources of information and by outlining some of the main techniques of research.

Chapters 12 and **13** provide an overview of the stages of first a civil and then a criminal case. The Bar is predominantly a referral profession and a barrister may be consulted at various stages of a case; it is therefore always important that any preparation is focused on the particular instructions that have been received. As particular aspects of the case may require different emphasis at different stages it is always important to tailor one's preparation to the stage that the case has reached.

Chapter 14 describes the intellectual processes and the analytical skills which are required for effective fact management. The acronym C.A.P. (Context, Analysis, Presentation) has been adopted to summarise the process by which the preparation of a case progresses from an initial understanding of the legal and factual context of a case to a detailed analysis of the issues and the evidence and finally to the construction of a persuasive and pertinent argument which can be presented to whatever audience is appropriate, be it the client or a tribunal.

The chapter also illustrates some of the possible techniques which can be used to ensure that the C.A.P. process is carried out rigorously and may help you to develop your own analytical skills. One technique has already been displayed above at Table 1.1. Once that table has been completed in relation to any set of facts it should provide both an overview and a detailed analysis of the interrelation of the law, facts and evidence issue by issue. This should make it possible not only to assess the likelihood of success in establishing your client's case but also to carry out your specific instructions more precisely.

For instance if your advice is sought, whether in a conference or as a written opinion, the completion of Table 1.1 should make obvious whether there is a prima facie case so that a preliminary assessment of potential success or advice on further steps necessary can be given. If the instructions are to draft a statement of claim the centre column will have identified the material facts which should be included. Moreover the inability to complete the table fully will, of itself, identify what further information may be needed.

If a similar analysis is also done of the case for the other side this should assist, once the strength of all the available evidence has been considered, in providing the basis for planning any negotiation or piece of advocacy and in answering the basic questions: How likely is it that the client will win? How can the case be presented most effectively?

Chapters 15, 16 and **17** explain and demonstrate the practical application of the C.A.P. approach by showing how, in relation to a civil and a criminal case, the process and some of the techniques discussed in **Chapter 14,** can be applied to the preparation of realistic sets of papers. The papers for the civil case, *Lowe v Mainwaring*, and the accompanying preparatory notes showing the C.A.P. approach in action are contained in **Chapter 16.**

The papers for the criminal case, *R v Costas Georgiou*, and its accompanying notes are contained in **Chapter 17**.

Chapters 16 and **17** demonstrate with examples how fact management techniques can be applied by following through a civil and a criminal case and showing the detailed approach to preparation at each stage.

The remainder of the Manual sets out particular aspects of fact management such as dealing with figures and using information technology before providing a set of papers for self-assessment which can be used to put into practice some of the methods of preparation demonstrated in the Manual.

2

Introduction to legal research

2.1 The barrister as legal expert

If you think that the highest function of the barrister is in court-room advocacy, think again. Barristers are 'learned' counsel. This is no formal compliment (like, eg 'Right Honourable Member'). They have earned their traditional title, and not by their in-court resourcefulness but by being the specialists of the legal profession, lawyers whom other lawyers consult.

The ability to provide counsel's opinion, based on researches into the darker areas and novel aspects of the law, is the first requisite of the barrister — first also because it comes long before advocacy, or even drafting of statements of case, in the particular case. There is of course a close connection between all of these functions; the opinion given is one which the barrister knows he or she must be prepared to make stand up in court. It must therefore be well-founded on thorough research, to which the argumentative skills of the advocate can then be applied. It is in their ability to find the law and their facility to adapt and apply it in their client's cause that the most able barristers can be recognised.

If you ask any barrister how he or she learned to research in law, the chances are that they will say by trial and error, jumping in at the deep end, or various other vague expressions. Many will say that they have never actually 'learned' to do it at all. Until recently, the professional law schools have never attempted to teach the technique of systematic legal research. As for the universities, they expect their law students to absorb large amounts of legal doctrine and to apply it; but almost all of this is presented to them by textbooks and lectures, and the further reading these indicate. Not often are students set to find out for themselves. Even if they are, the academic law libraries do not have the materials a practitioner needs to use.

The result is that young barristers and solicitors have arrived at their first job without any real training in one of its most essential functions. They are then expected to 'pick it up' as best they can. Some never do, and perhaps never need to if they find a niche for themselves in areas of practice where research plays little part. If such limited practice is possible at the Bar, it consigns one to the least interesting and stimulating work. At all events, every aspiring barrister should as a matter of self-respect and professional pride want to acquire skill in research and to merit that title of 'learned'.

2.2 From theory to practice

There is of course a traditional answer from the profession to this criticism of lack of training. Seasoned practitioners may say that this, like most other vocational skills, can only be learned by doing it in practice. (But then they once said this about English law itself!) Whether this is true or not, you can't even begin to research in law without some preliminary acquaintance with the sources of legal knowledge and the technique of tapping them. What follows seeks to guide you in that direction, providing sufficient information to start you off in acquiring the necessary skill for yourself.

2.3 Legal research and the pupil barrister

From the day you start in chambers, you will be faced with questions, points of law, procedure, tactics, etc, which are quite new to you. This does not mean that the cases and papers you will see are likely to be bristling with complex legal problems. On the contrary, to a seasoned practitioner, there may be very little 'law' involved, everything turning on the facts as the court eventually finds them. But when everything is new and unfamiliar you must have the facility to know how to find out. To start with you need to know what people are talking about. At a more advanced level, when you are given papers to prepare an opinion, you must know how and where to get at the law.

Some answers will come readily from your pupil master, from sharing experience with other pupils, or from picking the brains of other barristers. That is part of the comradeship of the Bar. But if they say, 'It'll be in *MacGillivray*', it does not extend to taking you by the hand and showing you what that is. You are assumed to know how legal knowledge is organised on the library shelf: statute and case law, reference works, the main practitioners' textbooks, the cumulations and indexes: and how they all cite, classify, fit together and cross-refer. These are things you can and must equip yourself with before you even set foot in chambers. So if you did not learn it all at university, you must do so now. (If you did, or think you did, quaere!)

Before setting off for the library and starting your legal research, make sure that you know exactly what information your pupil master wants and when he or she wants it.

2.4 Order of treatment

2.4.1 The lawyer's traditional sources

Chapter 3 is concerned first with the basic materials of English and EU law which you can expect to find on the shelf in a practitioners' library. This is part of the essential knowledge of our legal literature that you must now start to acquire. Without this familiarity you cannot even begin to research. You must get a general understanding of the way in which legal knowledge is organised, visually and spatially, in general and in your particular library. Most chambers' libraries have the basic sources only. For deeper research you will need to go to one of the Inns' libraries or further afield. But do not wait until a problem forces you to wander hopefully or despairingly round the shelves. Get to know the library, its contents and arrangement. Find the books described in **Chapter 3** and browse through them to see the features indicated.

2.4.2 The growing electronic dimension

Recent years have seen a whole array of electronic tools offered to the law-seeker. These are mentioned in **Chapter 3** alongside each category of hard-copy to which they relate. There are cross-references to **Chapter 8** where we look in detail at the on-screen sources, their types and scope, advantages and disadvantages. Meanwhile acquaint yourself with all the various electronic services. If introductory courses are offered, take advantage of these. Browsing on-line can be an expensive pastime, but at least browse any CD-ROMs which your library holds.

2.4.3 Problem-solving

Chapters 4 to **7** of this Manual, are about finding and applying these lawyer's tools to specific problems. The sequence adopted here is to start with problems in areas of law with which you must be familiar from your studies so far; going on to research in unknown territory; and then the technique of following-through to make sure your answer is completely up-to-date, which entails knowing how to access very recent law generally.

2.4.4 The diagrams

Chapter 9 shows in graphic form a suggested sequence for researching. If these are to be useful, it can only be after you have read and understood the related sections of the text.

2.4.5 Repetition

In this treatment of the tools and methods of research, you will find some things repeated. This may be where materials previously described as static apparatus are then deployed in problem-solving. Repetition has the virtue of reminding you of earlier explorations and explanations, or of sending you back to remind yourself. In any case, familiarity and skill only come with repetition.

Getting to know the lawyer's tools

3.1 Introduction

This chapter assumes that you have responded to the exhortation in the previous one: that although you have not yet begun or have just begun in pupillage, you have already explored your Inn's library. You have found out what it has and where it has it. What follows is a guide to delve the shelves and scan the screens. We have to generalise, since no two libraries' holdings and arrangement, databases and software, are the same. What are the same are the types of material they hold.

3.1.1 Exercises

Merely looking at the books, and perhaps flicking through a few pages, will not do much for you. Do the simple exercises at the end of each section so as to get some dexterity with each of the sources in turn. You should then be able to tackle the problems which are set in the research technique section.

3.2 Essential parts of a law library

An English law library has at least five different sorts of materials: statutes, reports, journals, textbooks, and general reference works such as encyclopaedias, digests, etc. Of these, statutes and law reports are our primary sources because their content, legislation and precedent, is The Law; whereas the other secondary sources, though they may sometimes be highly regarded, are only their writers' opinion of what the law is. It may have sufficed in the classroom to rely on a statement in a textbook but it will rarely do so in court.

3.3 Legislation

3.3.1 Primary legislation

Legislation may be primary or secondary. In the UK, primary legislation takes the form of Acts of Parliament. Acts are either Public General Acts, Local Acts, or Private and Personal Acts. For everyday practice the important ones are the Public General Acts. These make up what is sometimes called the 'statute book'. Some of the other Acts may be found in the Inns' libraries. Local Acts for each year since 1992 are included in *Current Law Statutes* (see (b) at **3.4**), and since 1997 on the Stationery Office website (see **8.4.3**).

3.3.2 Secondary legislation

Secondary legislation, referred to as 'subordinate' or 'delegated', consists of law which has the full force of statute but which has been laid down not in Parliament but by lesser bodies authorised by Parliament. Thus local authorities and public utilities are often given power to make by-laws. (For how to find these, see Local Government Act 1972, s 236 as amended.) But for present purposes we need consider only the regulations made by government departments and published in the form of statutory instruments (see **3.5**).

3.4 Acts of Parliament

Acts appear in the library in three main forms:

(a) *Queen's Printer's copies*: these are the officially-issued Acts in the form in which they were passed by Parliament. Each new Act on getting the royal assent is published in A4 format by the Stationery Office under the authority of the Queen's Printer of Acts of Parliament. On the library shelf, these Acts will be found in smaller format in bound volumes with either 'Public General Acts and Measures' or 'Law Reports Statutes' on their spine. Inside, both these series are identical, Queen's Printer's copies. On screen, the Stationery Office website gives the text of every Act since 1988. These are unamended versions, exactly as passed.

   For citation and use in court, the Queen's Printer's are the versions of Acts which the judges prefer. From the point of view of the researcher who wants to understand the legislation, they are of little use. We should always go to one of the annotated series.

(b) *Annotated statutes*: *Current Law Statutes Annotated* (*CLSA*), from 1950, are issued in annual volumes. Very recent Acts arrive in loose-leaf parts during the year. The annotations, by specialist editors, give much helpful and often critical comments with information about, for example, the legal and legislative background, references after each section to cases, regulations, or other sections or other statutes affecting that section; and often just a general running commentary. *CLSA* have always given some *Hansard* references, and in recent years these are full and complete. (See **Chapter 7**.) Note that *CLSA* appear only in print, not on-screen; and the annotations are not updated, so as they get older they may be superseded by later events.

(c) *Classified annotated statutes*: *Halsbury's Statutes* (not to be confused with *Halsbury's Laws*) are not only annotated but arranged in alphabetical order of subject-headings. This set organises in its many volumes the entire statute law of this country, of whatever date, which is still to any extent in force. Individual volumes are re-issued from time to time when the amount of new material warrants it. Also, the whole set is kept up-to-date to the beginning of the present year by an annual cumulative supplement. For still more recent developments there is a loose-leaf Noter-Up volume. Several more loose-leaf volumes contain the texts of very recent Acts.

An index volume is isssued annually containing (in addition to a subject index) alphabetical and chronological lists of all the statutes in the bound set; or, marked with letter S, in the loose-leaf volumes. The annotations are more formal and less informative than those in *CLSA*; but have the advantage of being updated, which *CLSA* are not. Since 1993 *Halsbury's Statutes* give *Hansard* references. (See **Chapter 7**.)

The electronic equivalent of *Halsbury's Statutes* is *Legislation Direct* on the Butterworths website (see **8.3.1**). These, with a 'stop press' section, are kept very up-to-date, well in advance of the printed version. However, they do not have the full annotations of the printed version.

Annotations take time to prepare. (The publishers meantime issue an unannotated version on coloured paper.) So it may be a while before the *CLSA* or *Halsbury* version of an Act arrives, and their respective publishers' websites do not contain annotations. During that delay you may have to do your own interpreting unaided; though often there will have been some professional commentary on a Bill during its passage, which can be found in the practitioners' journals. See for these **3.16**.

3.4.1 Citation of statutes

Every modern Act of Parliament has a short title and calendar year (eg Theft Act 1968), and a unique 'chapter' number (eg 1968 c 60). Before 1963, chapter numbers were based on the regnal year or years during which the Parliament sat. So, for example, 15 & 16 Geo 5 c 20 is an old friend of yours. Local Acts have their own series with chapter numbers in Roman numerals (Port of London Act 1968 is 1968 c xxxii. Personal Acts have their chapter number in italic eg c *12*.

3.4.2 Looking up statutes

(a) *You know the short title*: In the annual bound volume or volumes of official versions (see (a) at **3.4** above) you will find an alphabetical index of the year's Acts giving the chapter number of each. The Acts are bound in chapter number order. Or you can do the same with the much more useful *CLSA* annual volumes. In these always look for the index in the last volume for the year. The on-screen services set out the Acts under their years.

(b) *You know the short title but aren't sure of the year*: (eg when was the Data Protection Act?) The index volume to *Halsbury's Statutes* will give it in the alphabetical index if it is still in force and tell you where it is in the set. Alternatively, *Current Law Legislation Citator* (see **3.4.3.2**) has at the beginning an alphabetical list of statutes which have been in any way active since 1947 (on-screen since 1989). For a more complete alphabetical list, *CLSA* service file (the one with Current Awareness on the spine) in its Table of Statutes lists every extant Act since 1267 which has received any attention in modern times; as does the final volume for each year. For the most complete alphabetical listing, with full texts, Justis UK Statutes (see **8.3.3**) has almost every Act since 1235.

(c) *You don't know the short title, but do know the year and chapter number*: This is a bit unlikely but may happen with older statutes. If a calendar year, you can find it as in (a) above. If a regnal year and you have the official bound volumes (see (a) at **3.4**) you should be able to find any Act of the past 140 years by looking at the spines of the volumes where the regnal years are given. Failing that, and for older Acts (eg 7 Will IV and 1 Vict c 26, another very old friend), check the chronological index in *Halsbury's Statutes* index volume.

3.4.3   Is the Act in force?

Once you have found your Act, the next most important step is to find out its current legislative status. This poses two distinct questions: Is it yet in force?; and Is it still in force?

3.4.3.1   Has the Act come into force?

Many Acts have a delayed commencement and may hang around awaiting activation, sometimes for years. Look first at the commencement section. In almost all modern Acts this will be found at the end of the Act proper (ignoring any schedules — pronounced 'shedule') which are often appended at the end of Acts. The last sections of an Act will give the short title, the extent (geographical) of operation, and the date of commencement. This may be the date of enactment (which you can find in a bracket at the beginning of the Act after the long title); or a stated period after that; or it may be left to the government department concerned (nominally 'the Secretary of State' or 'Her Majesty in Council') to bring it into operation. If the last, this is done by commencement order made in a statutory instrument (see **6.3.3**).

A simple way to check whether the Act, or the particular bit you want, is in force, is to check the paperback *Is It In Force?* volume which is part of the *Halsbury's Statutes* set. This gives every statute passed in the last 25 years, with its current status ('not in force', 'repealed', etc). The volume is up-to-date to about the beginning of the present year, so you must check the loose-leaf Noter-Up which has an *Is it In Force?* section in the binder. If you find the commencement information this way, all well and good. If there is no such information you may have missed a very recent bringing into force, so it is advisable to check the more up-to-date *Legislation Direct* on the web. This has an *Is It in Force?* service, or you can check against the particular section of the Act itself.

Acts not yet in force but for which a date has been set (even years ahead) are listed in *Current Law* latest monthly part. You should now be up-to-date. The *New Law Journal* gives each week's commencement orders. The Stationery Office publish weekly and daily lists. These are on their website, are summarised by Lawtel, and are included in the CLI 'Leg and Reg Dev Index' or LRDI on Westlaw (see **8.3.6**)).

3.4.3.2   Is it still in force?

There is nothing more embarrassing than finding you have based your reasoning on an Act which has unknown to you been repealed or substantially amended, or on which there has been an important case. There is no way of telling this from the Act itself in the bound volume. *Halsbury's Statutes* plus cumulative supplement plus noter-up should give you the present status of the Act. So will *Legislation Direct*. Any amendments or additions to the Act should appear here in full text. For all subsequent happenings to an Act, section by section, you have the choice of hard copy: *Current Law Legislation Citator* together with the present year's citator in *CLSA* service file; or Halsbury's *Statute Citator* volume. On-screen the same information can be found on the CLI/Westlaw service for happenings to statutes since 1989. A further or alternative source for case law on statutes is in the *Law*

Reports ten-year indexes (see **3.6.7**) of 'Statutes Judicially Considered', which can trace every important happening to any statute from 1950 to the present.

3.4.3.3 Older Acts

Old Acts, no matter how old, that are still in force will be found in *Halsbury's Statutes* and *Legislation Direct*. You will not often have to research old repealed Acts. If you do and are unsure about the reference, check in the two-volume *Chronological Table of the Statutes* published by the Stationery Office. This gives every statute since 1235 in bold type if extant or in italics if defunct. It is not however kept up-to-date, but assuming you are tracing an old repealed Act, it will give you the reference to find it in one of two official collections:

- *The Statutes Revised*; or if not there,
- *The Statutes of the Realm*, huge volumes covering 1235 to 1713.

Neither set is easy to find, but they are the required versions of Acts for citation in court: see Interpretation Act 1978, s 19. You are as likely to find one of the unofficial collections called *Statutes at Large*. These are reasonably accurate, and in size and coverage more useful as well as more available. The edition by Ruffhead is offered by Justis UK Statutes, which continues with subsequent Acts to the present.

3.4.3.4 Repealing Acts

It is important to remember to check any citation of an Act which repeals the Act you are considering, to see if the repealing Act in turn has been brought into force (or repealed!).

3.4.4 Other sources of statutes

Other collections of statutes may be found in the library, mainly where Acts relevant to a particular subject or jurisdiction are provided in works written for that area of practice, eg *Stone's Justices' Manual, Paterson's Licensing Acts*, and the many encyclopaedic textbooks (Planning Law, Highway Law, etc many of which are now appearing on-line and on CD-ROM).

EXERCISE 1   STATUTES

1. What are the short titles of the following statutes?
   - (a) 21 Geo 3 c 49.
   - (b) 1997 c 55.
   - (c) 59 & 60 Vict c 14.
2. Are the following in force?
   - (a) Employment of Children Act 1973.
   - (b) Suppression of Religious Houses Act 1539.
   - (c) Smoke Detectors Act 1991.
3. What is the punishment prescribed by Piracy Act 1837, s 2 as amended?
4. What conduct is made illegal by the Chartered Associations Act?
5. Which marriages are made void by the Royal Marriages Act?
6. What is the heading to part VIII of the Law of Property Act 1925?

3.5 Delegated legislation: the statutory instruments

3.5.1 Publication

The statutory instruments are a vast series. There are currently about 14,000 in force, with a constant flow from Whitehall of new arrivals, revocations and amendments. The official texts are published as Queen's Printer's copies by the Stationery Office. Often these are just one sheet of paper. If the library takes these they will have to be carefully filed in sequence and boxed. In more durable form the statutory instruments will be found in one of three places:

(a) *Annual volumes*: As with the statutes, the Stationery Office publishes annual volumes of statutory instruments in sequence. These fill several large blue A4 volumes each year. Few libraries have the shelf space for these. Also, by the time they arrive many have been revoked or lapsed.

(b) *Halsbury's Statutory Instruments*: This set of volumes, arranged alphabetically by subject-matter, lists all the statutory instruments in force. But it prints the full texts of only a few, selecting the ones which the editors believe to be those most needed by lawyers and which (unlike eg the Civil Procedure Rules or Magistrates' Courts' Rules) are not likely to be found elsewhere in the library. The keys to the set are in the Index and Service volumes. To find a statutory instrument:

  (i)   *by subject-matter*: there is an alphabetical subject-index in the limp-bound Consolidated Index, revised annually, and kept up-to-date in the current year by the monthly index at the back of the loose-leaf Service Volume 1;

  (ii) *by its SI number*: the front of Service Volume 1 has a numerical list, and this is updated monthly, also in the same binder;

  (iii) *by its short title*: check the alphabetical list in the Consolidated Index.

(c) *Older statutory instruments*: If still in force, they should at least be mentioned in *Halsbury's Statutory Instruments*. For the texts of the older ones, the major law libraries have the HMSO blue annual volumes going back many years, and the Statutory Rules & Orders (red) volumes which preceded these. In addition you may find the set of *Statutory Rules and Orders and Statutory Instruments Revised*. This is a reorganised version of all the instruments in force in 1948. There are indexes at the end of the last volume, and the *Table of Government Orders* in a separate volume shows the impact of subsequent instruments.

(d) *On-screen*: Researching has been made easier by the Stationery Office website and CD-ROM which has every statutory instrument since 1987, but only in its original form. Lexis has a file which shows the statutory instruments together with their parent Acts. The complete statutory instruments, starting with the 1948 revision, are on Justis CD-ROM updated quarterly, and weekly on the Web.

We will try to penetrate further into statutory instruments in **Chapter 6**.

3.5.2 Citation of statutory instruments

Every statutory instrument is given a unique number in its year, shown as 2002/1234, or more fully as SI 2002 No 1234. The earlier series before 1948 are cited as eg, SR & O 1923 No 752.

Statutory instruments also have short titles, eg, Prison Rules 1964 (SI 1964/388); Misuse of Drugs Regulations 1973 (SI 1973/797).

EXERCISE 2   STATUTORY INSTRUMENTS

1.   The Access to Personal Files Act by s 3 empowers the Secretary of State to make regulations enabling individuals to see files about them held by various bodies, and to make corrections and erasures, etc. Have any such regulations been made so far? If so, find the actual text of any.
2.   In a work on property law you find a reference, Rule 301 of SR & O 1925 No 1093. What is this? Is it in the library? Have there been any recent cases on it?
3.   What is the date of the earliest piece of subordinate legislation that is still in force?
4.   How many statutory instruments were issued in 2002?

3.6 Law reports

Your library will have various series of reports, some general, covering all courts and subjects; some specialised, covering a limited jurisdiction or area of practice. There are now many specialised series, some of which are included in a practitioners' periodical. Many are now also provided by commercial publishers on-line and archived on CD-ROM (see **Chapter 8**).

3.6.1 Citations

The first problem you may encounter is decrypting the various initials used in citations. You will be familiar with WLR, All ER, Cr App R, and other commonly occurring references. For any initials you are not sure of, check in one of the following:

- French, D., *How to Cite Legal Authorities*;
- Raistrick, D., *Index to Legal Citations and Abbreviations*;
- *Current Law Cases Citator*;
- *Halsbury's Laws* Volume 1;
- *The Digest*, Annual Supplement volumes;
- Sweet & Maxwell's *Guide to Law Reports and Statutes*.

3.6.1.1   Brackets, [Square] and (Round)

Both square and round brackets are used in year-citations. Where the year is given in square brackets thus: [2001] 1 WLR 270, it is part of the reference. The year is like a volume number. Most of our standard series now use this method. Where a date appears in round brackets, it is useful information as to the actual year of the decision, but non-essential; because in such series the publishers give each volume its own number in sequence in the set. For example (1985) 80 Cr App R 117. This volume-number method is now mainly confined to journals and some series which may overlap different years. In Commonwealth and US reports the volume-number method is still quite common.

3.6.1.2 Citation of law reports on the Web

Many current law reports now appear on the Web, and well before they appear in the pages of any of the standard series of reports. The use of these electronic sources in court has been officially approved. However, it calls for a system of 'neutral' citation, not only because citation by series, volume and page number no longer applies but also because citations have to be uniform and recognisable whichever medium or provider or publisher has been used for a particular report. So each judgment when transcribed is given a unique case number, with paragraph numbers instead of page numbers. See *Practice Note* [2001] 1 All ER 293, and *Practice Direction* [2002] 1 WLR 346.

The following citations are used:

UKHL	House of Lords
UKPC	Judicial Committee of the Privy Council
EWCA Civ	Court of Appeal Civil Division
EWCA Crim	Court of Appeal Criminal Division
EWHC Admin	High Court Administrative Court
EWHC	High Court

For example, *White v White* [2001] EWCA Civ 955 [1] indicates case number 955 in the Court of Appeal, first paragraph; *Lewisham LBC v Hall* [2002] EWHC Admin 960 [22] is case 960 in the Administrative Court, QBD, at paragraph 22.

3.6.2 *The Law Reports*

Our major, semi-official series, published by the legal profession under the name of the Incorporated Council of Law Reporting, are called simply *The Law Reports*. They started in 1865 before the reforms of the Judicature Acts, when there were a multiplicity of old courts for each of which the *Law Reports* set up separate series. Today there are just four series:

(a) *Appeal Cases* cited as AC: has the reports of the House of Lords and Judicial Committee of the Privy Council.

(b) *Chancery* cited as Ch: contains reports of all matters heard in the Chancery Division and in the Court of Appeal therefrom.

(c) *Queen's Bench* (and formerly *King's Bench*) cited as QB or KB: contains reports of cases on all matters heard in that Division, including its ordinary, commercial, maritime, appellate, and administrative jurisdictions, and in the Court of Appeal (Civil Division) therefrom; and also decisions of the Court of Appeal (Criminal Division).

(d) *Family* cited as Fam: containing reports of the Family Division in its ordinary and appellate jurisdiction, and in the Court of Appeal therefrom. Before 1971 it was called the Probate, Divorce and Admiralty Division and its reports were cited in a P series.

3.6.3 The Authority of *The Law Reports*

These are our senior series. They are checked by the judges concerned prior to publication. In addition to the usual headnotes, facts and judgments, they usually give a summary of counsel's arguments. This is very helpful in ascertaining the arguments and authorities which the court must have considered, but which may not appear in its judgment. For all these reasons, this is the preferred series for citation in court (see **3.6.9.1**). Their corresponding disadvantage is that they take time to arrive on the shelf or on the screen.

3.6.4 *The Law Reports* on screen

All the main websites offer the whole of *The Law Reports* in full text. Lexis, Butterworths, Westlaw, and Justis; the last on both CD-ROM and on-line.

3.6.5 The weekly series

To fill the interval while we wait for the full edited *Law Reports* versions, the Incorporated Council since 1953 have put out a junior series, the *Weekly Law Reports*. These arrive in paper parts within a month or so of the case being decided. They are grouped into three volumes a year: volumes 2 and 3 contain cases intended to appear in *The Law Reports*. Volume 1 has cases which are not intended to get that full treatment. Each paper part may contain cases destined for volume 1 as well as for volumes 2 or 3. Look carefully at the paper cover to see the exact content. The full texts of the WLR are available on-line from Justis (see **8.3.3**).

Since 1936 Butterworths have provided us weekly with the *All England Law Reports*. The All ER are in most respects comparable to the WLR. There are now four volumes a year, but these are merely consecutive. Further volumes, containing commercial cases and European cases, have recently been added to the series. Butterworths offer the set on-line in *All England Direct*, together with very recent unreported cases and transcripts (see **8.3.1**).

3.6.6 Indexes to all these reports

The Law Reports publishes during the course of each year a cumulative index in a pink booklet. This very helpfully includes not only *The Law Reports* and other series published by the Incorporated Council, but also the All ER, Cr App R, Lloyds, LGR, STC, and other best-selling series. See the front cover for the list. At the end of each year these indexes are conflated with those for past years, becoming the red paperback indexes; and every ten years these are made up into a case-bound red index volume. The usefulness of all these indexes is much increased by their inclusions of citators of statutes, cases, statutory instruments, etc, which have appeared in cases reported in the years covered (see **6.1**).

3.6.7 Older reports

The older reports can be divided into the following:

(a) *Continuous series*: Several journals in the 19th century included regular law reports. These reports were separated and variously bound into volumes: *Law Journal Reports*, *Law Times Reports*, and *Times Law Reports*, respectively LJ, LT and TLR. These series contain cases not reported elsewhere. They continued to the mid-20th century. One such series is still going strong: the *Justice of the Peace Reports*, which began in 1837.

(b) *Named reporters*: Until *The Law Reports* were established in 1865, reporting was left to private individuals, barristers or judges, who made their own collections of cases. These eventually got published, sometimes long afterwards. They are recognisable by their names, eg Coke's Reports; Vesey Senior; Best and Smith; and their corresponding initials, and they are sometimes called the nominate reports. They span about 350 years. Some older libraries may have some of these in their ancient quarto- or folio-size bound volumes. However they have been more conveniently collected into 176 uniform volumes as the *English Reports* (ER). They can be accessed in one of the following ways:

(i)   if you have a case name with a pre-1865 date and some cryptic initials for the reference, it is probably in the ER. At the end of the set there are two volumes with an index of case-names. These give the original reporter's name, ER volume and page;

(ii)   if you have a reference but not the case name (eg 2 M & W 123) there is a chart with the ER set that lists all the reporters by name and initials, and gives the courts in which they reported. Look at the spines of the volumes listed and see at the foot of the spine which includes your reporter's volume reference;

(iii) citing the *English Reports*: strictly, we do not cite them. The ER is just a rationalised reprint. We pretend we still have the original old leather tomes before us and cite the reporter's name, volume and page. For this purpose you will find the original pagination preserved in the midst of the ER pages by numbers in brackets in the text;

(iv)   a CD-ROM edition of the whole of the ER has been published by Juta-Hart, which some libraries may have.

(c) *The All England Law Reports Reprint (All ER Rep)*: This rather misleadingly-named series selects older cases from the LJ and LT and the named reporters ((a) and (b) above) which still have practical importance. So it is a useful alternative source in libraries which do not have these older series in the original.

(d) *The oldest reports*: The anonymous law reports known as the year books run from the late 1200s to the 1600s. 1535 was the last year to be printed. These are very rarely needed in modern litigation, but for the curious they also are now summarised on a free website: www.bu.edu/law/seipp.

3.6.8 The most recent reports

Almost every day in *The Times*, the *Independent*, the *Scotsman* and *Lloyd's List* there are citable law reports. There have also been daily law reports in the *Daily Telegraph*, the *Guardian* and the *Financial Times*. More usefully, they are included with the rest of the newspaper on Lexis/Nexis. They will be summarised on Lawtel and in *Current Law* monthly part. Some of the more significant cases may be reprinted after two weeks or so in one or both of the main practitioners' weeklies: *New Law Journal* and *Law Society's Gazette*. If the law report editors select the case for a full report, this will appear in the WLR and All ER in print and on-line (see **Chapter 8**). However, many such newspaper reports never get reported further and the paper's version itself or at best the practitioners' weekly may remain the only record. For this purpose *Daily Law Reports Index* ran from 1988 to 1999, digesting every newspaper report, and keying it in several possible ways: parties, subject-matter, statute, etc, involved. The whole database is now available on-line, and kept up-to-date, in *Current Law Cases* on the CLI and Westlaw websites (see **8.3.2** and **8.3.6**).

Many cases start off as unreported cases but are soon reported in a newspaper law report and eventually make it to one or more of the main commercial series of law reports. Very current unreported cases can be found on most electronic databases and are a particular feature of the Lawtel UK database.

3.6.9   To cite or not to cite

The great increase in the number of reports and transcripts now available and the possibility of 'total recall' by electronic searching, has led to the courts being inundated with citations. To stem this flow, the courts have issued practice directions with rules restricting indiscriminate citation of cases, both reported and unreported. In *Practice Direction (Citation of Authorities)* [2001] 1 WLR 1001, the Court of Appeal directed that advocates must:

(a) state, in their list of authorities and skeleton arguments, the proposition of law which each demonstrates; and

(b) cite a case only if it clearly indicates that it establishes a new principle or extends the law; or

(c) justify the citation of any case not within (b);

(d) justify citing more than one authority for a given proposition;

(e) justify the citation of any authority from outside England, the European Court of Justice and the European Court of Human Rights.

Note that this practice direction does not apply to criminal courts, including the Court of Appeal, Criminal Division; nor to the House of Lords, which issues its own practice directions.

3.6.9.1   Reported cases: preferred series

The *Law Reports* are our officially authorised reports and take precedence over all other series for citation. In the practice directions referred to in paragraph **3.6.1.2**, the Court of Appeal emphasised that where a case has been reported in the *Law Reports* it must be cited from that report. If the case has not, or not yet, appeared in the *Law Reports*, the earlier *Practice Direction (Court of Appeal: Citation of Authority)* [1995] 1 WLR 1096 requires that it be cited from the WLR or All ER version. Only if it is not reported in any of these series may one of the authoritative specialised series be cited. This 1995 ruling, though expressed only as for the Court of Appeal, must now be taken as applying in all the civil courts.

3.6.9.2   Unreported cases

In so far as an unreported case may be citable, the 1995 *Practice Direction* stated that the only acceptable version is the official transcript. This was re-emphasised in *Hamblin v Field* The Times, 26 April 2000, where the use of a Lawtel summary (see **Chapter 8**) was disapproved. But the prospect of such reported cases being cited has added to the courts' apprehension. In principle unreported cases have the same precedent value as reported cases; but the assumption is that every judgment of any importance has been or will be reported. The restrictions on citation outlined in paragraph **3.6.9** therefore apply with special force to unreported cases. Many years ago the House of Lords pointed the way in *Roberts Petroleum Ltd v Bernard Kenny Ltd* [1983] 2 AC 192 directing that leave must be sought before the transcript of an unreported Court of Appeal case was cited to the Lords. It seems therefore that unreported cases cited acceptably in future are likely to be those very recent cases that will soon appear in a law report, with neutral citation meanwhile (see **3.6.1.2**).

3.7   To find a specific case

If you have absorbed the above information you should be able with a little practice to find a report of any case to which you have the reference. Where you have the case-name only, or the citation seems to be wrong, you need a comprehensive case index. In hard copy and on-line, there is the *Current Law Cases Citator*.

3.7.1   Current Law Cases Citator

This lists every case — of *whatever* date — which has had any happenings (decided, followed, not followed, distinguished, overruled, etc) in the years since 1947. Every report of the case is given, with all its subsequent citings, and a reference to its digested version in *Current Law Year Book*. For any happenings in the present year, the latest monthly part of *Current Law* lists every new case digested this year (in capitals) and every older case cited this year (in small type). The whole of the *Citator* is offered on-line by CLI, and on the Westlaw site as 'Case Locators'. (See **8.3.2** and **8.3.6**.)

3.8   To find case law in general

A point may be reached in your researches where you can confidently say that if there is anything to be found, it will be in case law: that it is that sort of topic and problem area, rather than a legislated one. If you are right, a sensible place to start would be the practitioners' textbook, where all the relevant cases should be at least in the footnotes. Alternatively, if you want just cases since a definite date, you could search in *Current Law Year Book*(s) and the current year's latest part's index; or the equivalent *Halsbury's Laws* Annual Abridgment volumes and noter-up; or their on-line CLI or *Halsbury* equivalents. These have good subject-matter and keyword indexes. However, for the widest trawl by subject through the case law of any date, use *The Digest*.

3.8.1   The Digest

This is a multi-volume encyclopaedia of case law, organised under alphabetical subject-headings. It digests case law from the entire common law world except for the USA. It now also includes EU cases and human rights cases from outside UK. It also goes well back into history. It is slightly complicated to use because of its several index volumes, supplements, and its system of numbering cases. Also one has to use it with care where, for example, it gives without comment, cases which (in England at least) have been made obsolete by statute, or whole bodies of law which are practically defunct like copyhold. Nevertheless it is a most valuable extension to the library, geographically and historically, once you have learned how to use it; and to repeat, once you are right in thinking it is case law you need to find. It also saves some leg work, where, for example, you have a case from the Commonwealth in the footnotes of a textbook or law report: there is a good chance it will be digested here.

Many of *The Digest's* cases are included on Butterworth's *Case Search* site (see **8.3.1**), with a useful system of 'traffic lights' which indicate in order of importance subsequent happenings affecting a case. However, these are limited to case-law happenings and, like the printed volumes, do not indicate where a case has been affected by later legislation. Nor can one search easily on-line by general subject area, overviewing all the related cases throughout the world. To do this one has still to go to the volumes on the shelf.

EXERCISE 3   CASES

1. What are BCLC, BWCC, WWR, Co Rep, WN, NILR, Com Cas, EG, STC? Which of them does your library have?
2. How many reports are there of *Street v Mountford* in the House of Lords?
3. Find the most recent cases in the library on:
    (a)   trishaws;
    (b)   whether the Court of Protection can seal a will if the testator is already dead;
    (c)   the attitude of courts to TV crews accompanying police operations;
    (d)   whether the prosecution are obliged to reveal their witnesses' previous convictions to the defence.
4. What types of goods were involved in *Hurry v Mangles* (1808)?
5. Find a case reported in 1989 that says that for canon law purposes there is no difference between a corpse in a grave and cremated ashes.
6. Using *The Digest*, find:
    (a)   a case from Australia on whether the ringing of church bells on a Sunday morning could be a nuisance;
    (b)   a case involving Switzerland which says that a corporation has no right to freedom of conscience or religion.

3.9   Words and phrases

It has been said that about 90% of all legal problems boil down in the end to the meaning of words: words in statutes, statutory instruments and other official documents to be construed and applied; words in contracts, leases, specifications, etc; new coinages like the language of high-tech and e-commerce; and of course defamatory, threatening, fraudulent and other utterance which may involve criminal liability. In some cases it will be vital to discover whether any meaning has been placed on a particular word or phrase by the law in the past. A law library must have several tools for ascertaining such past definitions or interpretations.

3.9.1   Dictionaries of words and phrases

These very useful multi-volume compilations with supplements try to give us every word or phrase to which any judicial, legislative or other recognised legal meaning has been attached. In doing so they give detailed citations and cross-references, examples of usage, and other helpful information. For example:

(a)   *Stroud's Judicial Dictionary*, published by Sweet & Maxwell, gives many entries, mostly in just a line or two, with citations.

(b)   *Words and Phrases Legally Defined*, published by Butterworths, give fewer entries for each word, but gives them fully in the context of the judgment or other authoritative statement.

Because of their different aproach, it is always wise to consult both works.

3.9.2   *Halsbury's Laws* Index

Volume 56 contains the second half of the alphabetical index, I–Z. Surprisingly, the publishers do not tell us that after letter Z there are some 200 columns of words and phrases, singled out by the Halsbury editors as appearing somewhere in the set in a definitive context. These sometimes give a phrase missed by the dictionaries. Updating is by the Annual Abridgment volumes, which have a separate section of words and phrases listed near the beginning, and then by the loose-leaf Current Service.

3.9.3   *The Law Reports* Pink and Red Indexes

The ten-year, cumulated, and current year's indexes (see **3.6.7**) have a section of words and phrases as defined in any cases in the many reports series covered. It is located under the letter 'W' as though subject-matter. It makes it possible to trace the interpretation of a particular expression over the years or decades, should this be helpful. An electronic version of these indexes is on Justcite (see **8.3.3**).

3.9.4   Current Law

The latest monthly part cumulates all the words and phrases for the year. The Year Books have the whole of the collection for each year. See table of contents for its location.

3.9.5   Lexis

Although we think of Lexis and other databases as containing enormous amounts of law, what they really contain is merely words. Lexis is literal rather than conceptual and we have to approach it in the same way. When it comes to looking for words, however, Lexis and other such databases are very useful indeed. You can just look for occurrence of a word or phrase, but unless it is a very unusual expression you will get far too many unhelpful instances. To find if the word has been given any sort of interpretative consideration by a court, try [the word] w/10 constr! or defin! or mean! or interpret! The same approach can be used on other databases, remembering that different connectors may be required (see **Chapter 8**).

3.9.6   General dictionaries

Do not forget that it is quite proper and sometimes necessary to have one or more standard dictionary definitions available for words where no applicable legal definition has been found. A good law library should have at least the two-volume *Shorter Oxford Dictionary*.

3.10   Foreign legal vocabulary

Nowadays we can expect to have to translate legal terms from and to other European languages. There are professional legal translators who specialise in this work for big transactions, court documents, etc. However, where it is just a term or concept in, say, a letter to or from a lawyer on the continent, it may suffice to refer to a foreign legal dictionary. These may be two-way, or they may be polyglot, giving legal equivalent terms across several languages. Most law libraries have such dictionaries, covering at least the major European languages. Check to see which your library has. As for the new legal language of Eurospeak, some libraries have the *Eurovoc Thesaurus*, in which terms used in Community law are rendered into the languages of member States — including English. That brings us finally to EU documents in general.

EXERCISE 4   WORDS AND PHRASES

1. Find the most recent judicial explanations of:
   (a) 'car park';
   (b) 'reasonable time';
   (c) 'family life';
   (d) 'past known address'.
2. Has it been held defamatory to describe a lawyer as 'a dunce'?
3. An Act requires a notice to be 'displayed outside' premises. Is it sufficient to stick it to the inside of the window of the building so that it is visible outside but remains inside?
4. A recent will left a large legacy 'to X, if he returns to England'. X has returned from Australia, where he lives, and is claiming the legacy. He says that he intends to go back as soon as he has it. The executors say this isn't what the testator meant. Are they right?
5. What do *'purger une hypothèque'* and *'Übertragung einer Schuld'* mean in foreign legal documents?

3.11   European Union legal documents

The legal literature of the EU is vast and ever-increasing. A few official and university libraries in member States have been designated European Documentation Centres and so receive automatically all official publications of the various EU bodies. The larger firms of solicitors and some chambers holds a selection of EU materials. The selection tends to vary greatly, so see what your library has. You will find that it has unofficial publications put out by commercial publishers; these are usually more helpful than the EU's own sources. Also, find out where your nearest documentation centre is; it will be listed in the *Directory of EU Information Sources* which major reference libraries have.

The EU produces various types of law, corresponding broadly to the categories of UK domestic law: primary legislation, secondary legislation, case law, and of course journals and serial literature.

3.12   EU legislation

3.12.1   Primary

This consists of the founding treaties (EEC or Rome, ECSC, Euratom); the treaties of accession of the various later joiners; the Single European Act; and amending treaties such as Maastricht, Nice, etc. There is an official edition of these: *Consolidated Treaties*. However, in most libraries they may be found in one of the many UK publications such as

Sweet & Maxwell's *Encyclopedia of European Union Law*. On the Web they are all included in CELEX (see **3.12.5**).

3.12.2   Secondary

It is the EU's secondary legislation that we are more often looking for. This consists of regulations, directives and decisions. (For their nature as law and their differences, see Article 249 (formerly 189) of the EEC Treaty.) These are cited by their year and running number: year second in regulations as 123/99; and year first for directives and decisions: 99/123.

3.12.3   The Official Journal of the European Union

All EU secondary legislation, including draft legislation, and recommendations, opinions, and much other day-to-day information, is published in the *Official Journal* (OJ), the EU's main publication and official gazette. There are two series: the 'L' series has the secondary legislation and other hard law; the 'C' series has everything else, including draft legislation.

3.12.4   Finding secondary legislation

Finding a particular instrument in the OJ ought to be straightforward if one has the subject or reference. In practice, it is not easy. There is no overall index to the OJ, only a monthly index (not cumulated) and an annual index. Even if you know the month or year, the alphabetical list of subjects follows European classifications rather than terminology we are used to. The methodological table is easier if you know the instrument by number and type. As for the text, not many libraries have the whole OJ on the shelf. The English edition alone runs to more than 40 volumes a year. It was published on microfiche down to 1999 and some libraries have this. However, we mostly rely now on CD-ROM or the Web, taking just the current year's paper parts, which arrive almost daily.

3.12.5   EU legislation on screen

The EU's own database is CELEX. This is accessible officially on the Eurlex part of their vast Europa website (see **8.4.3**). It can also be accessed by various commercial services, eg Lexis/Nexis, and Justis which also issues a CD-ROM version.

3.12.6   Is it in Force?

Finding the text of an instrument will not necessarily tell you its current validity. EU secondary legislation is constantly amended and supplemented. As with UK legislation you must check to see its present state. The EU publishes twice yearly a *Directory of Community Legislation in Force*. This can be accessed via the Europa website Eurlex section. Its arrangement and use is best understood from a glance through the printed version. This consists of a very large volume I containing an Analytical Register, classifying by subject-matter. A smaller volume II has a Chronological Index, and a broad subject-category Alphabetical Index, which is useful for getting into the headings in volume I. If you know the instrument number you want, you should go to the beginning of volume II, to see how it has to be encoded for finding in volume I. Your reward for persistence is that volume I will give you not only the OJ reference of your instrument, but of all the others in force which are connected with it in subject matter.

Lawtel EU gives all secondary legislation in force, with its current status. There is also a subscribers' telephone service for information and copies of official EU documents.

3.12.7 Implementation of Directives

Directives tell member States to legislate and give them a target date, but leave it to them to do it in their national way. In UK almost all implementation is done by statutory instruments. Just occasionally, for a major change, an Act of Parliament is required, such as the Consumer Protection Act 1987 for the Product Liability Directive. At the other extreme, a directive relating to banking practice, for example, may need only an internal circular from the Bank of England to the clearing banks. And no implementation at all is called for where the government consider that the scope of a directive is already covered by existing UK law.

It may be easy enough to find a directive, but hard to find if or how it has been put into law by the UK, or if such implementation is pending. Lawtel EU lists directives, giving for each the UK instrument of implementation, if any.

The latest monthly part of *Current Law* lists all of the present year's statutory instruments which have implemented directives, as well as statutory instruments assisting EU regulations to achieve their intent in the UK.

With a recently-arrived directive, the legal section of the government department concerned may be able to say whether or when it will be implemented. For up to date information on implementation by other member States, CELEX is the best source.

3.12.8 EU draft legislation

Generally speaking the procedure is that the Commission proposes new directives and the Council eventually approves them. But the progress can be tortuous. The Commission's proposals appear first in their numbered COM series. These 'Com docs' will be noted in the various current news services and on the CLI *Leg and Reg Dev Index* (LRDI). The proposals may go to the European Parliament and also to the Economic and Social Committee, and their discussion of them will appear in the OJ 'C' Series. When finally adopted the directive will appear in the 'L' series. The Europa website (Eurlex 'Legislation in Preparation') enables us to observe this whole law-making process.

3.13 EU law reports

3.13.1 ECR

Decisions of the European Court (ECJ) and the Court of First Instance (CFI) at Luxembourg are reported in an official series, the purple-covered European Court Reports (ECR). Within these reports are three series: Court of Justice, Court of First Instance, and Staff Cases. The ECR are slow to appear. Preceding them, paper copies of decisions arrive first in the form of their *Transcript Series*, which some libraries take regularly or selectively. Later come the *Proceedings Series* which however only provide summaries. Quicker than these are the summaries provided on-line: eg Lawtel, *Current Law Cases* and Lexis. The whole of the ECR are archived on CD-ROM from Justis. All transcripts of cases since June 1997 are in full text on the Court's Curia website (see **8.4.3**).

3.13.2   CMLR

The official reports from the EU are not much like law reports of the sort we are used to. More familiar in style are the home-grown *Common Market Law Reports* (CMLR) and they include relevant cases from UK and other member States as well as those of the ECJ.

3.13.3   Finding EU cases

The case law of the EU may be accessed in various ways: by case-names (which, however are often unpronounceable, or unmeaningful: *Commission v UK*, for example); by their docket-number (C series for the Court, and T series for the CFI); or by their area of law, treaty article, regulation, directive, etc, involved. This information, formerly in Butterworths one-volume *EC Case Citator*, now discontinued, is supplied by the Lawtel EU service. Citations are given to ECR and CMLR, and otherwise to the transcript with OJ reference. Butterworths also have a subscribers' phone service with current information.

3.14   EU periodical literature

The various organs of the EU produce a large number of official periodicals and serials. The most general one is the *Bulletin of the European Union*. Various law publishers produce their own general journals: *Common Market Law Review, European Law Review, Journal of Common Market Studies*, etc. Significant articles on EU law relevant to the UK are listed each month in *Current Law* (see **6.4.2**) and the *Legal Journals Index* combined database. These are accessible on the CLI and Westlaw sites.

3.15   Current awareness of EU legal developments

Such is the ferment of EU law-making, proposals and commentaries, that various publishers offer monthly, weekly or even daily information on paper and on-line. On the shelf almost every library will have *Current Law*. This has a 'European Union' subject-heading but happenings affecting UK are digested under the appropriate UK law headings. Its off-shoot, *European Current Law*, is valuable as it covers every country in Europe, not just the EU. It works in the same way as *Current Law*, cumulating through the year and ending as a year book. Neither publication is available on-line. However *EU Direct* from Butterworths, Lawtel's EU module, and *Rapid* (from Justis, giving each day's EU press releases) are all very up-to-date with EU developments.

3.16   Legal journals

Practitioners' libraries may have some periodicals which you will recognise from your academic studies, but the emphasis will be on the specialised journals which now cover just about every aspect of practice. The three general weeklies *New Law Journal, Solicitors Journal* and *Law Society's Gazette* keep up a running commentary on current and pending legal happenings, professional news and opinion. A browse through one of these each week should now become a habit for you in order to be well-informed. You will of course want to scan the specialised journals which are of immediate relevance to you. However, at the same time you should try to keep some continuing acquaintance with all the areas of law you have studied but no longer employ from day to day.

It is now virtually impossible to keep up with all the vast outpouring of periodical literature and professional intelligence, even in your own field of practice. The usefulness of *Current Law* in listing the articles and books for each month (**6.4.2**) was mentioned earlier. However, these are only a small selection. The on-line services scour each new edition of the journals and give us a lead to what the legal luminaries are saying on any given subject. They also help by decoding the eye-catching but uninformative titles which writers often give to their articles.

3.16.1   Lawtel

Lawtel keeps an eye on a large number of journals in its Articles Index and gives useful summaries of very recent articles (see **8.3.4**).

3.16.2   Legal Journals Index

For the most comprehensive survey of everything published in UK and Irish journals (and European journals in English) going back to 1986, there is *Legal Journals Index* and its stable-mate *Financial Journals Index*. These are accessible on the CLI and Westlaw sites. Indexing is by subject-keywords (several for each article); author's name; case-names for case notes; and statute, bill, statutory instrument, treaty, etc, names for articles or cases on these. It makes it easy to get at the latest thinking on any topic of lawyers' concern. Also, the publishers will send subscribers a copy of any article on the database, if necessary by fax.

3.16.3   Index to legal periodicals

Legal Journals Index has two limitations, which for most purposes are not serious: it started only in 1986 and it is almost confined to UK publications. On the rare occasions when you may need to cast the net wider, use the *Index to Legal Periodicals*. This is an American publication but it includes a number of leading journals from the rest of the English-speaking world; and it started in the 1920s. It is therefore useful for current thinking in the wider common law world and for international law. It is on CD-ROM and Lexis/Nexis as well as in hard copy in major reference libraries.

3.16.4   Full texts of articles

Once you have located the reference to the article you are seeking (or a reference to one that sounds interesting) you have to be able to find the thing itself. Major law libraries have sets of the most used journals and you should have no difficulty in finding articles in the mainstream serials on the shelf. For any which are not readily available, Westlaw has the full text of most of Sweet & Maxwell's journals; Lexis/Nexis has many of Butterworths' and other publishers. Best of all, subscribers to CLI get *Legal Journals Index* and with it their extra service of supplying the full text of almost any article on the database back to 1986, and even by fax if it is urgently needed.

EXERCISE 5   JOURNALS

1. Find an article in 1988 about pupillage in chambers being more like unpaid labour than education.
2. Find the most recent article you can on: (a) *Romalpa* clauses; (b) lawyer-client confidentiality; (c) vibration white finger.
3. How many articles did H. W. Wilkinson publish in 2000?

4

Starting to research

Having now surveyed the apparatus of the law, we have to bring it to bear in solving specific problems. This and the following chapters aim to show how this is done. The order adopted here is to start with searching in more familiar areas of law; then going on to research in unknown territory; then to updating and to accessing very recent law; some further thoughts on construing words and phrases; the approach to *Hansard*-researching; and the scope of and techniques for on-screen research. Exercises are set for each section. In **Chapter 9** there are some diagrams presenting a suggested sequence in graphical form.

Although reference to **Chapter 3** may be necessary, some of its content has been repeated from a problem-solving standpoint as a reminder.

There are a few preliminary observations which need to be kept in mind throughout:

(a) *The right way*:   There is no one invariable or correct way to research in law. There are almost always several parallel routes to the same destination. With experience and instinct practising barristers know where and how to look up the law (or whose brains to pick). Many a pupil must have had the experience of sweating for two or three days to produce an opinion on some seemingly esoteric point. Their master scans it with a faint smile and then dictates a full (and very different) opinion off the cuff. But this need not discourage you. In legal research everyone makes mistakes, misclassifies, follows false trails to dead ends. The important thing is to learn from mistakes and to develop an approach which avoids them. For the beginner there *is* one right way: to know all the alternative routes, the short-cuts and the exhaustive searches, so as to be able to choose the one most suited to the research in hand.

(b) *Subject-headings*:   The most usual point of entry into the law books is by way of the subject-matter of the problem, which you have first to recognise and classify. An initial difficulty here is that legal labelling tends to vary from one period to another and from one law publisher to another. For example, if you have a matrimonial dispute to advise on, do you look under 'husband and wife', or 'divorce', or 'family law' or 'domestic relations'? Similarly with what used to be called 'master and servant' and is now called 'employment law' (or is it 'labour law', 'industrial law', 'trade union law', 'equal opportunities', 'discrimination', or whatever?) One discovers with experience, trial and error, which category is used by which publisher.

(c) *The end-product*:   The pupil barrister's ultimate purpose is to produce an opinion which is a well-constructed statement of thoroughly-researched law applied to the essential facts. The proper approach to opinion-writing, described elsewhere in the Manual, has to affect the way you research. Counsel's opinions are not broad and discursive overviews of an area of law such as might have won you high marks in university law school. They have to be clear, concise, realistic, reliable, client-oriented applications of the law to the facts as stated. If you bear this in mind it will help to keep your feet on the ground and to ensure that your research does not pull you in all directions. Be resourceful but not perfectionist.

(d) *Finding nothing*:   The problems set in the exercises which follow all have more or less 'correct' and ascertainable solutions in the law. That this should be so is necessary, or at any rate desirable, for learning purposes. However, to some extent this may give a false picture of law in practice, where sometimes there is no clear-cut answer, and sometimes no discoverable law at all. finding nothing, no case on the point, no legislation, nothing written about it, is not necessarily failure. Always provided you have done your researches thoroughly, it is success. If there is really no authority, you are free to construct what arguments or analogies you can. But of course your instinct should tell you when and where there is likely to be some relevant law on the point and should prompt you to search more widely or thoroughly before accepting a nil finding. Anyway, in the accompanying exercises there will always be something to find. In one situation, finding 'nothing' is quite normal, and usually good news: in the process of following-through. See **4.4** below.

(e) *Further reading*:   There are several books dealing with aspects of legal research. These include:

(i)   Knowles, J. & Thomas, P.A., *How to Use a Law Library*, 4th edn (London: Sweet & Maxwell 2001).

(ii)   Holborn, G., *Butterworths Legal Research Guide*, 3rd edn (London: Butterworths 2003).

But no amount of book-learning will give you the skill necessary for effective research in law. So read and absorb these pages, do the exercises and learn from your successes and failures.

4.1   Finding familiar law

Although in pupillage you will be thrust into areas of law totally strange and new to you, there will be occasions when the ground seems slightly familiar, where you recognise the legal context (contract, tort, crime, procedure, etc) even though you do not know the actual answer.

EXERCISE 6

Consider how you would go about looking up the law on these:

(a)   What is the maximum fee on counsel's brief allowable in a 'fast track' trial where the claimant recovered £10,000?

(b)   What is the maximum fine for an offence under the Tattooing of Minors Act?

(c)   While on holiday in France, John, an Englishman, found some valuable jewellery in the hotel. He kept it and brought it back to England. The jewels (in his possession) have now been identified as stolen and on these facts he has now been charged in London with handling stolen goods, How would you advise him?

ANALYSIS

However blank you may feel about any of these, you do actually know enough at least to set off in the right direction. A moment's reflection should suggest that the answer to (a) will be some-where in the Civil Procedure Rules. For (b) you will have first to find the Act: either by knowing or discovering its date, or by reference to a comprehensive work on criminal law. These will not necessarily give you the answer, but will point you in the right direction. You must have realised that for (c) you will have to go first to the relevant sections of the principal statute, and that you will then have to see if there has been any case law to interpret them.

4.2 Use of textbooks

Where you recognise the area of law involved and have some acquaintance with it, it makes sense to go straight to the known appropriate source: the Act or case itself, if you know it; or, better, the general secondary source, the textbook. Until now textbooks for you have meant students' textbooks. These may still be a useful starting-point, but do remember that you need to switch to the corresponding practitioners' works, with their detailed indexes, comprehensive coverage, multiplicity of decisions cited, updating supplements and general in-court citability. Academic books have the advantage when it comes to speculation about uncertainties in the law, answering difficult questions as yet unresolved in litigation, perhaps drawing inspiration from other jurisdictions. For this purpose some of the major academic works in, for example, criminal law and evidence, are cited from time to time in court. But it will usually suffice to get leads from these rather than to cite the writers' opinions verbatim.

You need to familiarise yourself with what is the practitioners' text in each area of law you are likely to have to research.

EXERCISE 7

Can you name the main practitioners' books in the following fields?

> contract, conveyancing, company law, civil procedure, landlord and tenant, evidence, custody of children, defamation, licensing, town planning, damages, jurisdiction of magistrates, insurance, motor vehicles, industrial tribunal cases, professional ethics of barristers

Now check Chapter 10 and see how many you got right.

If you were correct in your guess at the subject area of your problem, you should make intelligent use of the appropriate textbook index (or table of contents), plus the supplement, and have obtained one or more useful references. Find these in the law reports, statutes or wherever and see if they are what you want.

Can't find them? If your difficulty is in decoding the reference itself, you may need to refer to one of the legal citation manuals. You have been reminded in Chapter 3 how we cite and find statutes (short title, regnal/calendar year, etc) and the more common series of law reports (round and square brackets, etc). More cryptic initials are explained in any of:

- *Current Law Case Citator;*
- *Halsbury's Laws* volume 1;
- *The Digest,* Supplement Volume;
- Raistrick, D., *Index to Legal Citations and Abbreviations,* 2nd edn (London: Bowker-Saur, 1993);
- various law dictionaries.

EXERCISE 8

What do the following commonly used legal abbreviations stand for?

LGR, CLY, OFT, FSR, SI, SFO, CPS, H & N, RPC, CCR

4.3 The right case or Act?

In law reports a quick scan of the lines of catchwords which are provided between the case name and the headnote may help to eliminate unwanted cases. Statutes do not have catchwords but the annotated series (*Current Law Statutes Annotated* and *Halsbury's Statutes*) offer introductory notes, explanations of sections and cross-references which may be helpful for the same purpose. (Unfortunately neither series has these annotations fully in its equivalent on-line.) Annotated statutes are much more useful for the researcher than the official Queen's Printer's versions. Remember, however, that it is the official version that is preferred for citation in court.

4.4 Following through

Never be satisfied with what you have found until you have checked that it is still extant, unoverruled, unrepealed etc. A glance at a supplement taking only a few seconds may transform what the body of the book says. We will look at this more closely in **Chapter 6**.

4.5 Other members of the Bar as a resource

Other barristers can be a very useful research resource in many cases. It is a strong tradition of the Bar that one barrister will help another, and it is natural to talk informally to other members of chambers when you have a problem. This point is fairly obvious and will only be dealt with briefly here. Of course, consulting others should not replace doing proper research yourself, but it can be a valuable addition in many circumstances.

Amongst the circumstances in which you might wish to consult another member of the Bar are the following:

(a) Where an aspect of a case involves an area of law you are not entirely familiar with, you might consult a person who regularly practises in the area. (If the whole brief is in an area with which you are not familiar, you should consider returning it to the solicitor.)

(b) Where you wish to check you are up-to-date on a particular point.

(c) Where you are aware that another barrister has recently acted in a similar case to the one you are presented with.

(d) Where you have a legal or factual hypothesis about your case and you wish to try it on someone.

Ethical considerations must be kept clearly in mind if you do wish to discuss a case. The case is the client's and the client has a right to privacy. Names should not be used and personal details should not be revealed. If it is valuable to discuss points in a case with another practitioner only relevant facts without names should be given, and points may usefully be discussed in an impersonal or hypothetical way, for example, 'I'm appearing for a man who . . .' or 'If a person does not know that . . .'.

EXERCISE 9

1. Mary was left property by the will of her husband, Tom, who died in June. Tom's will, made in November 1982 when Tom and Mary were engaged, stated that Tom was looking forward to marrying Mary. He did marry her in March 1983. Mary wants advice on her rights under the will. She has been told by Tom's family that her marriage to Tom revoked it.

2. Percy, a company director, wants to borrow £20,000 from the bank. He has offered his company as guarantor. The bank manager has agreed, 'if it's allowed'. Can the company guarantee the loan?

3. Daphne employed a firm of heating contractors to replace the central heating system in her house. She warned them of the special need to take care of art treasures in the house. One of the workmen using a blowlamp set fire to a priceless tapestry. The fire was soon put out and little damage was done but Daphne suffered nervous shock. The contractors' insurers have agreed to pay for the damage but not for the nervous shock, since Daphne was admittedly not in fear for her own safety but only for her property. Can she nevertheless claim against the contractors for nervous shock?

5

Cold-starting

You can be set a legal problem that has no obvious starting point. The area of law may be just about recognisable, or not even that. This rarely happens to an experienced lawyer. If it does, he or she will apply some thoughtful analysis to the facts, consider the source or origin of the problem, probe the client for background knowledge, do some brain-picking etc, until some pointers emerge sufficient to indicate the right approach.

5.1 Unfocused problems

Sometimes one is starting cold not so much because the area is unrecognisable as because the problem is unfocused, ie you are asked to advise generally in a situation where no actual problem has yet arisen, in order to forestall any problem. If a client comes with a summons in his or her hand you know broadly what the issue is and will seek out the facts and then the law. If, however, he or she says 'I am thinking of doing so-and-so. Is that all right?', you may have to pose problems to yourself in thinking of all foreseeable snags which might arise.

5.2 Keywords

Obviously any problems set for you here as an exercise have to be hypothetical, so you cannot do any of these things except the first: analysis. This involves a careful examination of the facts, attempting to identify the area of law involved and/or to establish what keywords the facts provide. Keywords are any terms which are legally significant and therefore index-worthy. The broadest general index in the law library is in the index volumes to *Halsbury's Laws*. It descends to factual subjects, not just legal categories. When you have no idea where to begin, begin here. *Halsbury's Laws of England* is a legal encyclopaedia and provided you use it properly (index, volume, cumulative supplement, noteup service) and see where it tells you to go, it is one of your best friends in the library. The whole set (though not the index volumes) is accessible on-line as Halsbury's Laws Direct on Butterworths' website (see **8.3**).

EXAMPLE

A Bar students' magazine wants to run a competition. Readers are asked to guess the number of Bar exam candidates this year who pass in all subjects. Entry is free. Only one entry is allowed per reader, who must be a BVC student. If no one gets exactly the right figure, the prize (new edition of the Civil Court Practice) will go to the closest guess. Some officious BVC lecturer says he thinks the magazine ought to get legal advice in case there are any restrictions or regulations applicable. You are asked to check.

ANALYSIS

Can there be any legal objection to this? What area of law would it be? It doesn't look like wagering or betting. No money is involved. It's not a lottery with tickets. Indeed, some skill is involved. Freedom of the press? Competition law? Prize law? (Surely they mean something quite different?) But maybe 'competition' or 'prize' could be worth trying as keywords.

Assuming that you have succeeded in finding the answer, it is worth noting that the above problem could have been formulated without using the actual words 'prize' or 'competition'. The point is that you must not expect that the keyword which unlocks the law will always be explicit and obvious. You may have to find synonyms or paraphrases before the particular index you are using will respond. A good index will usually give cross-references (drunkenness — see intoxication; drug — see narcotic, pharmaceutical, prescription). But not all indexers are so helpful. You will often have to use your imagination, stretch your vocabulary, and translate from plain lay terms to legal concepts to arrive at the vital keyword.

EXERCISE 10   SIMPLE KEYWORD PROBLEMS

1. When is the close season for snipe?
2. Must London taxis have meters?
3. In what circumstances may a coroner hold an inquest on a Sunday?
4. Why are there quarter-mile posts along the railway track?
5. Where exactly is high-water mark?
6. Are there any age limits applicable to the appointment of bishops?
7. North Sea gas is odourless but when it comes into our houses it smells. In legal terms, why is this so?
8. When did Parliament decide to have 366 days in the year 2000?
9. How old must one be to get a licence to operate a CB radio?
10. Are the winnings of a successful gambler or the earnings of a prostitute subject to income tax?

5.3 Concealed keywords

The keyword approach will not work if, for example, the statutory source we need uses a precise and narrow word which we tend to widen or paraphrase in ordinary usage.

EXAMPLE

Henry, a landlord, granted tenancies of rooms in a newly converted house on weekly terms. To avoid giving security of tenure under the Rent Act he installed a free coffee-machine in the basement kitchen so that his tenants can help themselves in the mornings. Henry would like you to confirm that his tenants are thus not protected.

ANALYSIS

The landlord's thinking is that if he is providing more for his tenants than merely lodging, they are, like paying guests, outside the Act. This is an inevitable distinction which the Acts have always recognised. So a trawl through one of the standard textbooks should eventually reveal how far the law allows it to be pushed. Alternatively, we could try 'food' or 'drink' as keywords. But the books don't respond to these (and they are too general for word-searching on-line). The real keyword is 'board', but no one not knowing it would be likely to guess it. That, however, is the Act's word, and all the cases are based on it, including a House of Lords case in 1988 which you will need to find.

5.4   Red herrings

There may be a plethora of keywords in a problem. Some careful analysis is called for to identify the narrow issues and focus on them to the exclusion of all else.

EXERCISE 11   LESS OBVIOUS KEYWORDS

1. Charles's house was badly damaged in a severe gale last night. The upper part is in danger of falling. Charles's surveyor says it must be pulled down and made safe without delay. Workmen are standing by to do the necessary. But the house is a listed building and no authorisation has been obtained. Can Charles go ahead?

2. Peter, Paul and Mary want to go carol singing for charity on Christmas Day. They intend to stand together, each with a collecting box, in Trafalgar Square. They have also trained their dog to carry a collecting box. Any advice?

3. Waxmell owns a newspaper with a daily circulation of nearly half a million copies. He wants to buy another paper, a local with a circulation of about 20,000 and falling, which its owner, Burdock, wants to sell. Advise Waxmell if he can go ahead or if there are legal steps he has to comply with.

4. The City Council is divided equally between Conservative and Labour members. The mayor, who presides, is a Labour member. Whenever the Council votes on what is a politically loaded matter, the result is a tie. So the mayor, who has already voted with the Labour side, then purports to vote for that side again, tipping the balance. The Conservatives wish to challenge his right to do this. Will they succeed?

5. Clients are a firm of auctioneers. Their sale catalogue described a piece of furniture as Georgian. An experienced dealer purchased it at the auction. He says (and they now agree) it is Victorian and that this amounts to a false trade description. The auctioneers point out that their catalogue conditions state that being merely auctioneers, they are not responsible for vendors' statements of authenticity, origin, date, etc, of any article. They also say that anyway the purchaser is himself an expert who did not rely on their description. They therefore say that they are not liable for false trade description. Are they right?

6. While eating in your local café you see the owner put up a notice 'Waitress Wanted. Mornings Only. Good Wages'. What advice would you give him? What may happen if he doesn't heed your advice?

6

Following through

Just as you should not be discouraged if at first you do not succeed, so conversely you should not be satisfied when you find what seems to be the right case, section, regulations or whatever. Because until you have checked its current status you cannot be sure you have found the last word on the point of law. You must get into the habit of searching cumulatively, right up-to-date.

6.1 Statutes

The first question we ask of any statute is: Is it operative? We saw in **3.4.3** that this is really two distinct questions: Is it yet in force?; and Is it still in force?

6.1.1 Activation

Do not assume because it has been hard-bound for years on the library shelf, or hot from the Queens' Printer, that it has been brought into legal effect. Look first at the commencement section. Nowadays this is always to be found at the end of the Act proper. (Or almost always: see, however, Local Government Act 1985.) Does the commencement section indicate that the bit you want has a delayed start, waiting for the Secretary of State to name the day? If so, you can search the printed sources or on-line.

6.1.1.1 The hard copy methods

Check *Is It In Force?* and follow through to that section in the loose-leaf noter-up of *Halsbury's Statutes*. Or the *Current Law Legislation Citator* and follow through to the citator part of the *Current Law Statutes* service file ('Current Awareness' on the spine), and then the latest monthly part of *Current Law* for the table of all of this year's announced commencement dates. For any more recent announcements, check the Stationery Office's Weekly List.

6.1.1.2 The electronic methods

Halsbury's Legislation Direct will give the Act and using either the *Is It In Force?* tab, or going to the sections themselves, you will find the details of a commencement, if any. The CLI LRDI service covers all 'grey' matter (government and official publications) and this includes the Weekly and Daily Lists, which include the latest statutory instruments. Lawtel gives all the most recent developments.

6.1.2 Survival

It may have been fully in force once, but is it still? You cannot tell from the Act itself what subsequent treatment it has received from Parliament or the courts. *Is It In Force?* on the shelf or the screen will give every Act of the last 25 years. It may say 'whole Act repealed' (or the sections you are considering). If so there is no need to look further. The main *Halsbury's Statutes* version of the Act, plus cumulative supplement and current service, should give every significant happening to the Act up to the present month. Similarly *Current Law Legislation Citator* gives legislative history, amendments, statutory instruments, etc, and case law interpreting the Act. Also, it gives every Act, of whatever date, which has had any such happenings in the last half-century. A similar listing of case law effects, going back to 1950, can be found at the back of the pink and red indexes to *The Law Reports* as 'Statutes Judicially Considered'.

On-line, this information may be found on Halsbury's Legislation Direct, on Justis's Justcite, and on CLI's Legislation Citator. But some of this is confined to legislative events; not all give cases.

6.1.3 Cumulative checking

In all researches, by whatever methods, this cumulative checking is essential. It is easy enough with the sets which have supplements, and on-line with the providers' 'stop press' or other updating. It takes hardly any extra time, and especially when there are no subsequent entries to affect the main information one started with.

6.2 Subsequent happenings in general

It may be helpful to consider the way that law develops: from the researcher's point of view how established law is affected by later legal events. There are four main ways in which law as we know or discover it can be changed:

- statutes affecting earlier statutes (for simplicity we omit the possibility of statutory instruments amending statutes);
- cases interpreting earlier statutes;
- cases affecting earlier case law;
- statutes affecting earlier case law.

Of these, the first two methods of checking have been considered. Checking for cases affecting earlier case law is done with *Current Law Cases Citator* which gives every case, of whatever date, which has been followed, not followed, overruled, approved, distinguished, etc, in the past half century. You must then follow through to the latest monthly part of *Current Law* whose list of cases will include in small type any past case cited this year. On-line the same can be done in one action by checking the CLI or Westlaw sites.

6.2.1 Statutes affecting cases

It is statutes affecting earlier case law which is the most difficult to ascertain. A case or well established body of case law may have been overthrown by recent legislation. The statute, if a considered reform measure from, for example, the Law Commission, will in the annotations to CLSA give this background. But it may be an incidental side-effect on previous case law. The previous case law reports, in whatever medium, do not become annotated to take account of later legislation. One might have thought *Current Law Cases Citator* or *The Digest*, or their on-line equivalents, would indicate when a case they cite has been overturned by Parliament, but they do not.

Examples of this process quickly lose their point, as the text writers and annotators catch up with the effect of the statute. But to illustrate the general point we could consider two examples of common situations on which you may be asked to advise.

EXAMPLES

Fred wants to do some repair work on his house. The part needing attention can only be reached from the next door property owned by Tom. But Tom has refused to allow Fred and his builders to come on to Tom's property. Tom now says that Fred can enter if he pays Tom £500 a day for the duration of the work.

Loveless stalked Dawn, a fashion model, wherever she went. This affected her health and she lost work as a result.

ANALYSIS

A search in *The Digest* will give cases on facts similar to these. For each situation there are makeshift common law remedies. *The Digest* will not mention that the cases it gives are to a large extent superseded by, respectively, the Access to Neighbouring Land Act 1992 and the Protection from Harassment Act 1997. Of course with new editions of the standard text books these effects are noted; and especially as they were specific law reform measures. Until that happens, and for less obvious effects, a search by keywords in *Legal Journals Index* (see **8.3.5**) and on the journals file of Lexis should reveal any contemporary discussion of current shortcomings in the law, reforms officially proposed and actually in progress.

6.3 Statutory instruments: a closer look

Statutory instruments are a law unto themselves, with their great bulk and constant flow, their manner of creation, amendment and revocation, their separate literature, their low profile (for the general public, at least), and the complications of accessing them. At **3.5** we noted the various ways they are located and updated in the library. Lexis groups them with their parent Acts, which can be very helpful. They are archived on CD-ROM and supplied by Justis, Westlaw's LRDI, and Butterworth's Legislation Direct. So with a little practice you should be able to find any statutory instrument by its number, or parent Act, or subject-matter, on the shelf or on the screen. But it may be helpful if we first look a little more closely at the nature of statutory instruments as this impinges on research.

6.3.1 What are statutory instruments for?

Statutory instruments have three main purposes:

- commencement orders to bring Acts into effect;
- regulations, rules, etc, to fill out the often technical detail which Parliament has left to a government department's expertise;
- in recent years, to bring into UK law directives and regulations from the EU.

6.3.2   Are statutory instruments as good as statutes?

The answer is yes. They are made under authority of Parliament and affect all of us, as citizens, not just as lawyers, in many everyday activities. They are cited and construed in the same way as statutes. However, there is one respect in which they are not as good as a statute: they can be attacked as *ultra vires*, where it is alleged that a statutory instrument has gone further than its parent statute authorised.

6.3.3   Why might you be looking for a statutory instrument?

(a) *You have an Act which is to commence on an appointed day, and want to know if there has been a commencement order, and, if so, what it says*: If that is all you want, do not bother to look for the statutory instrument (if any). Follow the suggestions in **3.4.3**. If you feel you must see the full text, it should be in the Current Law Statutes service file and on any of the sites mentioned in **3.5.1**.

(b) *You have a section of an Act which provides for regulations, etc, to be made and want to know if there have been any*: Any of the statute citators mentioned in **3.4.3** will give at least the SI number of any such regulations, Order in Council, etc.

(c) *You have been referred to a statutory instrument by its number*:

    (i) The first loose-leaf service volume of *Halsbury's Statutory Instruments* has a chronological (ie numerical) list of all those in force. This will tell you its name and under which title in the main volumes of the set the statutory instrument is located. If your statutory instrument has a higher number than the last one listed, check the Monthly Index at the back of the service volume. The same procedure broadly applies if you are searching Legislation Direct on-line.

    (ii) If the number is missing from the above lists, this suggests that either your statutory instrument is a local one; or more likely, that it is no longer in force. You can discover its fate in *Halsbury's Statutory Instrument Citator*. This gives almost every statutory instrument back to 1801 (over 50,000 of them!) both alphabetically and in reverse chronological order, with its current status.

(d) *You have been referred to a statutory instrument by its name only*: (For example, the Road Vehicles (Construction and Use) Regulations of uncertain date.) Both *Halsbury's Statutory Instruments* and Legislation Direct have a comprehensive alphabetical index of short titles. Or if you know that the statutory instrument belongs to the present year, *Current Law* latest monthly part will list it, and the same applies for past years in CLY and *Halsbury's Laws* Annual Abridgment. For specialised subject-areas, some of the looseleaf encyclopaedic textbooks and their equivalent CDROMS have tables of statutory instruments arranged by titles.

(e) *You think your problem is in a typical statutory instrument-type area of law but you do not know more than that*: For example, are there any regulations about the limit of allowable aeroplane noise, or the movement of hazardous chemicals by road, or protected birds' eggs? It may be inadvisable to start your researches here, before clearing the ground more thoroughly. The Consolidated Index to *Halsbury's Statutory Instruments* has a good alphabetical index of subject-matter. However, a more methodical approach is to start from the broadest angle and gradually refine the search. Either try an appropriate practitioners' textbook or *Halsbury's Laws*.

(f) *You have found the statutory instrument but do not know if it has been considered in any cases*: Hard copy sources are on the whole better at this than the on-line services. *Current Law Statutory Instrument Citator* notes all happenings to statutory instruments of whatever date that have occurred since 1993. It is continued for the current year by the Statutory Instrument Citator section in the CLS service file. Double check by looking through the pink and red indexes to *The Law Reports*, at the back of which is a list of Statutory Instruments Considered. We have noted that these indexes cover not only *The Law Reports* themselves but several of the other major series. Nevertheless bear in mind that statutory instruments are often concerned with minute areas of technical law too specialised to be reported in any of these series. So check the specialised textbook dealing with this area or any specialised series of reports which may have an index. On-line the most useful search will be in Lexis's Cases file. The SI number, name, or key words, suitably specified, will produce that citation in the context of any cases in which it has appeared.

(g) *Your statutory instrument on close reading is ambiguous*: Could its purpose have been explained during Parliamentary scrutiny? Very few statutory instruments are debated. A trip to *Hansard* may be necessary, both the main ones for each House and the debates in the Standing Committee on Delegated Legislation. See **Chapter 7**.

(h) *What you are looking for, although published as a statutory instrument, is better known in another form*: The best examples are the various rules of procedure of the courts: the Civil Procedure Rules, the Magistrates' Courts' Rules, etc. These are more conveniently found in commercial publications: the *Civil Court Practice, Stone's, Archbold*, etc.

Finally, when dealing with statutory instruments, it is well to be reminded that when dealing with such an active and prolific series, whatever answer you may have found must be checked to ensure it is right up-to-date. A statutory instrument of last week may have been revoked or lapsed today. If your library subscribes to *Halsbury's Statutory Instruments* or Legislation Direct, the publishers offer a telephone service, and will supply a copy of any statutory instrument if it is only summarised in their volumes.

EXERCISE 12   STATUTORY INSTRUMENTS

1. What is the daily maximum fine for breach of the Insolvency Act 1986, s 109(2)? Has the Secretary of State increased it since the Act was passed?
2. When you have contact lenses fitted, to what after-sales service are you legally entitled?
3. After an evening out, Reg drove his girlfriend Gloria home. They parked outside her house talking in the car. As it was a cold night, Reg kept the engine running, revving it from time to time. PC Killjoy was pushing his bike along the pavement, approaching the parked car from the rear. As he drew level with the car, Gloria opened the front passenger door to get out. The door struck the PC's bike but he managed to take evasive action and no damage was done. PC Killjoy told Gloria that she would be prosecuted for not looking before opening the door. He also told Reg that he would be reported with a view to prosecution for keeping his engine running. Reg and Gloria say they have never heard of such offences and ask you to advise them.

6.4   Current awareness

More perhaps than any other professional, the practising lawyer is subject to a very exacting discipline: to be completely up-to-date: this morning's law reports, this afternoon's debate in the Commons. But it does not stop there. We have to be aware of the foreseeable future: bills in Parliament, proposals for EU directives, cases awaiting appeal, and to foresee their possible implications.

In the big law firms the librarians each day prepare and circulate to members all manner of current legal, financial and commercial news. These circulars are filed and may even be indexed. Few chambers offer any such service, other than by subscribing to the legal week-lies. How, then, may you keep on top of the most recent and pending happenings?

6.4.1   On-Line topical news services

Lawtel, Westlaw and *Law Direct* all offer the latest legal news, updated daily or even more frequently. Summaries of cases (as yet unreported), statutory instruments, new legislation, newly activated legislation, and all manner of events affecting the legal world are provided, with citations. If you do not subscribe to any of these services, however, you can find many free services on the internet. The ePolitix website www.epolitix.com has a legislation watch following the progress of all Bills before Parliament, with links to the full texts of associated official documents and media reports. The Daily Telegraph site www.telegraph.co.uk provides a selection of law reports from Westlaw, updated every Thursday. In many areas of practice there are specialised news services, some on subscription, some free. For these try a subject gateway, such as www.venables.co.uk or www.infolaw.co.uk (See also **8.4.3**.)

6.4.2   Updating with *Current Law*

The advent of electronic services has not diminished the importance of the hard copy sources. *Current Law* in particular remains a most important source for each month's happenings; and not least because it is not available on-line. Each issue appears early in the month following. It tries to capture and digest the month's legislation, cases, articles, books, committee reports, etc, under subject headings. Make yourself familiar with its contents, layout and classification scheme. As previously mentioned, note that its indexes cumulate throughout the year. You only need to look at the latest month's index to survey the whole of the current year to the end of that month. There is also a newsletter, *Current Law Week*, which anticipates the monthly parts.

At the end of the year those monthly parts are superseded by an annual volume or volumes: *Current Law Year Book* (CLY). CLY is fully indexed for the year. This gives us yet a further approach to research. For example, if you know that the case, statutory instrument, committee report, etc, which you need to track down was in 2001, you could start here. Or where, for example, your textbook goes up to the end of 2000 or early 2001, the 2001 and 2002 CLY subject headings, plus the latest monthly index, should cover all developments in that subject since. *Current Law* as a whole does not exist on-line. (Neither does *European Current Law*.) *Current Law Cases*, as its name states, has digests of cases (but only cases) from the CLY, the monthly parts, and the daily newspapers. So for recent legislative developments we have LRDI and the services mentioned in **6.4.1**.

6.4.3 Updating with Halsbury's Laws

The *Halsbury's Laws* Current Service, in a looseleaf binder, keeps the main volumes and supplement up-to-date to the current month. These monthly parts are similar in coverage to the *Current Law* parts. And they are similarly gathered into a year book, called the Annual Abridgment. The equivalent on-line service is Halsbury's Laws Direct. This mirrors the hard copy noter-up with latest material at the foot of the screen, awaiting incorporation into the main database. Remembering the virtues of this encyclopaedic work (see **5.2**), the virtues of these frequent updatings, whichever version is used, will be obvious.

6.4.4 Updating with *Legal Journals Index*

Although LJI seems merely a listing of current legal writing, we should remember that such articles represent thinking and comment on just about every legal happening, in the immediate past, present and pending. The many ways in which one can search (case names, authors, legislative instruments, and especially subjects and keywords), make this a very useful resource for getting up to the minute with professional and academic opinion. LJI is an indirect source for the law itself, for example in commenting on unreported cases, some of which may never appear elsewhere.

6.4.5 Newspaper reports

We mentioned earlier that some librarians cut these out day by day and mount them in a file. If your library has these, it may be the place to look first when someone says 'there was a case about this a week ago in *The Times*' (or other daily). But often such recollection will be unreliable in content and date, and the library's scrap-book is unlikely to be indexed. Still it can be a starting point. More methodical searching will be the digests in *Current Law Cases*. This like its stable-mate LJI can be accessed in many different ways, especially by subject-matter, case and statute name.

EXERCISE 13

Find the following:
- (a) The largest award so far this year for personal injuries.
- (b) A ruling in 1989 about barristers who accept two briefs for trials starting the same day.
- (c) Any recent decision on the Insolvent Debtors Relief Act (2 Geo II c 22).

Find the most recent article on:
- (d) Barristers' liability for negligence.
- (e) The police leaking high-profile cases to the media.

7

Researching words and phrases

Sometimes a legal problem comes down to the precise meaning to be given to a word or words. The uncertain words may be in an Act or regulations; or they may occur in a contract, insurance policy, lease etc, between the parties. Or, conversely, you may be at the drafting stage and trying to find an expression which will have the legal effect you want without any risk of unwanted side-effects. What follows deals mainly with the first type of situation: the expression is already there, imposed on you by the document, and you need to know how strictly or flexibly the law allows it to be interpreted. Where you are drafting and have a free hand, the research process is ultimately the same: checking against future problems instead of present ones.

You already know something of the interpretation of statutes and documents, the various approaches (literal, mischief, etc) and subrules (*eiusdem generis*, etc). Those may be needed if at the end of all your researches and interpretative efforts, you are left with ambiguity. However, the initial question is whether the law has already defined the term used, giving it an authoritative interpretation. How is this discoverable?

7.1 Stages of inquiry

There are four stages of inquiry here. It is really only stage (c) which concerns us for present purposes but to be methodical we need to glance at all stages.

(a) Does the Act or document provide its own definitions? Look for these. If the expression is defined, that should end doubt. But it may not be, eg, where it is an inclusionary definition, or where it is expressly subject to exception 'where the context otherwise requires'. Even a definition section may sometimes need interpreting.

(b) Does the Interpretation Act 1978 help? It lays down some very basic clarifications (eg masculine includes feminine, singular interchangeable with plural, England includes Wales, etc). It only applies to statutes, however.

(c) Has any other statute or case provided a definition? (See below.)

(d) Would dictionaries help? They are quite often produced in court to assist in establishing the accepted meaning of words, on the assumption that Parliament (or the parties) had that in mind. An example is *R v Fulling* [1987] QB 426 which shows this can be done even where there is a definition in the statute, provided the definition is not exhaustive.

7.2 Definitions of the term in other contexts

The task for the legal researcher: to find whether the law has defined the word already. Research is necessary to find out if the word or expression has been given any authoritative construction elsewhere in the law. This could be a definition in another statute, or in a case. But before commencing the search, consider whether what you may find will be relevant to the legal context from which you are starting:

(a) Other statutory definitions. To make what should be an obvious preliminary point, one cannot mechanically import a definition of the same word from one statute to another. A definition of, say, 'child' in an Act dealing with succession is unlikely to be thought applicable to the construction of the same word in a statute on, say, employment conditions or education. On the other hand Acts on the same subject (tax, theft, road traffic etc) have to be read together, including their definitions, so that, for example, 'income', 'deception' and 'motor vehicle' have a consistent meaning throughout. Between these two obvious extremes lie Acts which to varying extents may be arguably *in pari materia*, ie on legally comparable or equivalent subject-matter. If so, their definitions may be worth borrowing for the purposes of your argument. The index to *Halsbury's Statutes* may be a helpful place to start looking.

(b) Precedents of interpretation. More commonly the situation is that you are faced with an undefined word in an Act and you want to know if it has been previously defined judicially, either in the same context or more generally.

EXAMPLE

A new Act of Parliament allows compensation for disturbance to property in certain circumstances. The disturbance must be shown to be of 'significant proportion or degree'. The Act does not define this expression. You are consulted by a (slightly) disturbed client. How would you advise him?

ANALYSIS

The problem is the word 'significant'. The dictionaries do not help; it can mean substantial, appreciable, more than negligible, or just showing signs. Has it perhaps been defined in any other statute and been construed by a court? Where do we look?

Reference works for words and phrases: some of these were mentioned in 3.9.1. Most libraries have Stroud's Judicial Dictionary and Words and Phrases Legally Defined. These are multi-volume works. They not only give the words and their established judicial meanings, but full references to the cases and statutes involved. They are kept up to date by supplements. But for more recent information the indexes to the Law Reports, the WLR and All ER all have a section of 'words and phrases'. Then, following through, we go to the latest Current Law monthly part where there is a list of all the words and phrases construed this year so far, with references.

So if you now return to your quest for 'significant' you should find a case about a sex shop. See what it says and use your judgment whether, notwithstanding that it is far from being in pari materia, it could be applied to your case.

While on the subject and in that part of the library, take the opportunity to look at the other, general, law dictionaries. You will probably find Jowitt's Dictionary of English Law, Wharton's Law Lexicon, and the Oxford Companion to Law. They cover a wider field, including all manner of legal terms, maxims, concepts and institutions, with references. It is no shame not to know the meaning of some technical expression or piece of lawyers' Latin on the first occasion it confronts you. You have less excuse on subsequent occasions.

---

1. The police called at the office of Snoop, a private detective, and found there a bugging device for listening in to telephone conversations. Snoop was charged under a statute which makes it an offence to use such apparatus without a licence. His counsel made a submission that, since there was no evidence of his actually using the device he could not be found guilty of the offence. The magistrates rejected this saying that he must have had the device for use. Snoop was convicted. Advise him if he should appeal.

2. Peter insured his factory against damage from 'flood, bursting or overflowing of water tanks, apparatus or pipes'. While moving some office furniture, his employees dropped a heavy metal cabinet on to a water pipe which fractured, flooding the office and causing extensive damage to the firm's records. Peter's insurers say this loss is not within the insured perils. Advise him.

3. Fred took out holiday insurance. While on holiday in Spain he got heat-stroke and died. His policy covered him against 'accidental bodily injury caused by outward visible means'. His widow is claiming against the insurers. Advise them if they should pay her claim. They think there was litigation on a similar clause a few years ago but can't find any report of it.

7.3   Unresolved legislative ambiguity: using *Hansard*

If you have to construe an enactment and no help is found in the sources above, the decision of the House of Lords in *Pepper v Hart* [1993] AC 593 permits recourse to *Hansard* to see what was said during the passage of the Bill through Parliament. As a pupil you may well find yourself being delegated to carry out the task of researching *Hansard*.

7.3.1   The decision in *Pepper v Hart*

In *Pepper v Hart* [1993] AC 593 at 640, Lord Browne-Wilkinson sets out the three criteria which have to be met if *Hansard* is to be used as an aid to statutory construction. They are:

- legislation is ambiguous or obscure, or leads to an absurdity;
- the material relied upon consists of one or more statements by a Minister or other promoter of the Bill together if necessary with such other Parliamentary material as is necessary to understand such statements and their effect;
- the statements relied upon are clear.

The first of these three criteria, if strictly applied, means that the ambiguity must be patent before any recourse to Parliamentary material is made. A provision is ambiguous if it is fairly capable of more than one meaning; obscure if it is not capable of any clear meaning; and absurd if the clear meaning makes the provision nugatory, or self-contradictory or would subvert fundamental legal principle (eg, no confiscation without compensation, no retrospective effect). Having said that, whether a provision meets this criterion is often very much in the eye of the beholder.

The second criterion means that what is said by someone other than the Minister, or other promoter of the Bill, such as a backbencher in the case of a private member's Bill, is not admissible. Thus, strictly speaking, a statement by an opposition MP in moving an amendment would be inadmissible (though what the Minister said in opposing the amendment might be admissible).

The third criterion is designed to prevent the statements being themselves subject to minute construction.

In *Pepper v Hart* [1993] AC 593, the House of Lords described the circumstances in which recourse to *Hansard* as an aid to statutory interpretation *may* now be made, but in practice once there is a possibility of the first of these three criteria being met, *Hansard* research *ought* to be undertaken. Indeed, it would be negligent not to do so. If a matter is urgent and counsel has not had the time to carry out full *Hansard* research in a case where a point of statutory interpretation arises, any advice given by counsel (whether given in the form of a written opinion or in conference) should make that clear.

7.3.2 The subsequent application of the decision by the courts

The decision has since been subject to voluminous commentary and to frequent application by the courts. The House of Lords, however, has been particularly concerned to keep the decision within bounds, conscious of the dangers, originally highlighted by Lord Mackay in his dissenting judgment in the case itself, of unnecessarily adding to the costs of litigation. An early shot across the bows was *Melluish v BMI (No 3) Ltd* [1996] 1 AC 454. Lord Browne-Wilkinson re-iterated the strictness of his three criteria, and warned that counsel might be liable for wasted costs if they introduced material outside their scope. He further held that it was only permissible to use statements from *Hansard* that were directed to the particular statutory provision in issue, not to other, albeit similar or related, provisions.

Moreover, in a series of recent decisions of the House of Lords, an alternative view of the true ratio of *Pepper v Hart* seems to be gaining ground. This view finds difficulty with loose treatment of *Pepper v Hart* not merely on the pragmatic grounds of cost, but on conceptual and constitutional grounds. Its main proponent is Lord Steyn, who delivered an influential lecture, '*Pepper v Hart*: a re-examination', published in (2001) 21 OJLS 59–72. He first referred to it judicially in *R (Westminster City Council) v National Support Asylum Service* [2002] UKHL 38, [2002] 1 WLR 2956, in discussing, at [1]–[6], the separate (but logically related) question of the admissibility of Explanatory Notes to Bills as aids to statutory interpretation (see **7.3.6.1**). And now in *McDonnell v Christian Brothers Trustees* [2003] UKHL 63, [2004] 1 AC 1101 he has had the opportunity to state it judicially in the specific context of *Hansard*. He puts it thus, at [29]:

It is permissible to use *Hansard* to identify the mischief at which a statute is aimed. It is, therefore, unobjectionable to use ministerial and other promoters' statements to identify the objective background to the legislation. To the extent that *Pepper v Hart* . . . permits such use of *Hansard* the point is uncontroversial. A difficulty, however, has arisen about the true ratio of *Pepper v Hart*. It is certainly at least authority for the proposition that a categorical assurance by the Government in debates as to the meaning of the legislation may preclude the Government vis-à-vis an individual from contending to the contrary. This may be seen as an estoppel or simply a matter of fairness. This view of *Pepper v Hart* restricts its ratio to the material facts of that case. There is, however, a possible broader interpretation of *Pepper v Hart*, viz that it maybe permissible to treat the intentions of the Government revealed in debates as reflecting the will of Parliament. This interpretation gives rise to serious conceptual and constitutional difficulties which I summarised elsewhere . . .[ie in his lecture]. In my view the narrower interpretation of *Pepper v Hart* ought to be preferred.

Lord Steyn then proceeds to say that accordingly the appellant in the case had used *Hansard* for an illegitimate purpose. (Lord Bingham too thought its use dubious; he reluctantly looked at it 'de bene esse', but found it inconclusive on the relevant point [20].)

Other law lords have expressed support for Lord Steyn's view that *Pepper v Hart* is properly regarded as an estoppel on the executive, rather than as a means of divining 'the phantom of Parliamentary intention'. It has been mentioned in at least four cases since his lecture and before *McDonnell:* by Lord Hope in *R v Secretary of State for the Environment, Transport and the Regions, ex p Spath Holme Ltd* [2001] 2 AC 349 at 407–408, and in *R v A (No 2) (Complainant's Sexual History)* [2001] UKHL 25, [2002] 1 AC 45, at [81]; by Lord Hoff-mann in *Robinson v Secretary of State for Northern Ireland* [2002] UKHL 32, [2002] NI 390, at [40]; and by Lord Nicholls in *Wilson v First County Trust Ltd (No 2)* [2003] UKHL 40, [2004] 1 AC 816, at [59]. While all these cases evidence a growing judicial aversion to the citing of *Hansard*, in one respect a different light is cast on the limits that Lord Browne-Wilkinson was trying to impose in his very first criterion. For it is apparent that the benign 'unobjectionable' and 'uncontroversial' use of *Hansard* identified in the quotation from *McDonnell* above does not depend on there necessarily being an ambiguity of language as such. As Lord Steyn explains in the *National Asylum Service* case, at [5]:

The starting point is that language in all legal texts conveys meaning according to the circumstances in which it was used. It follows that the context must always be identified and considered before the process of construction or during it. It is therefore wrong to say that the court may only resort to evidence of the contextual scene when an ambiguity has arisen.

For an illustration of the circumstances where *Hansard* might be used exactly in the way that Lord Steyn would regard as unobjectionable, see *Three Rivers District Council v Bank of England (No 2)* [1996] 2 All ER 363, a case where unusually leave to cite *Hansard* was the subject of a separate interlocutory application (usually the material is simply included in counsel's list of authorities — see **7.3.4** — and any issues of admissibility dealt with during argument at trial). The reasoning as reflected in the headnote to that case suggests that *Hansard* can only be used to establish the object or purpose of the statute as a whole where the statute implements an EC Directive (as in the case) or an international convention. But there seems no reason in principle, as is implicit in the views of Lord Nicholls in *Wilson v First County Trust (No 2)* discussed below, why such use of *Hansard* should be so confined.

Persuasive though Lord Steyn's comments in *McDonell* and *National Asylum Support Service* are, a definitive ruling of the House Lords will have to be awaited before the original decision in *Pepper v Hart* can be consigned to that category of precedent that is confined to 'its own material facts', or is overruled altogether. But three specific points on the admissibility of *Hansard* do also arise from these recent House of Lords decisions. First, in *Spath Holme* it was held that *Pepper v Hart* applied only to resolving an ambiguity in statutory words, not to any ambiguity as to the ambit of a statutory power, which in the case was an enabling power to make regulations by statutory instrument (see further **7.3.3**; *Spath Holme* is also relevant to construing consolidation Acts — see **7.3.7.1**). Secondly, *Hansard* is not generally to be used in deciding compatibility issues under the Human Rights Act 1998: *Wilson v First County Trust (No 2)* (see especially Lord Nicholls at [51]–[67]). Its use in such cases is not ruled out altogether. Though Lord Nicholls thought it would seldom arise, the court is entitled to look at statements made in Parliament, just as it is entitled to look at extra-Parliamentary materials, in examining the background to the policy objective of the legislation, in the same way that it may look at such material to establish the 'mischief' in an ordinary case of statutory interpretation. But it cannot use such statements to infer the objective intention of Parliament as expressed in the language of its enactments: 'the proportionality of a statutory measure is not to be judged by the quality of reasons advanced in support of it in the course of parliamentary debate, or by the subjective state of mind of individual ministers' (Lord Nicholls at [67]). Thirdly, a settled authority of the House of Lords decided before *Pepper v Hart* cannot be disturbed on the basis that had the court been able to look at *Hansard* it would have decided it differently: *McDonnell* (Lord Bingham at [20]), though the House of Lords has retrospectively applied *Pepper v Hart* to overrule a lower court decision, eg *Stubbings v Webb* [1993] AC 498.

In addition to any chilling influence on citing *Hansard* that may result from these recent House of Lords decisions, it should also be borne in mind that, even where a liberal view of its admissibility has been taken (usually on the pragmatic ground that it is simpler to look at it just in case, rather than argue the toss on admissibility), cases where the court has in fact found the material to be of any great assistance are relatively few; cases where the material has been decisive of the outcome scarcer still (though for a rare example see *A.E. Beckett & Sons (Lyndons) Ltd v Midland Electricity plc* [2001] 1 WLR 281). Unfortunately, of course, once the ambiguity has been detected (on the conventional view of *Pepper v Hart*), whether *Hansard* will be admissible and of assistance will only be discovered in a particular case after all the effort of research has been expended.

7.3.3   Application to statutory instruments

Pepper v Hart was concerned with a statute. Before that decision the House of Lords had already ruled that *Hansard*, in certain circumstances, was admissible when construing a statutory instrument (*Pickstone v Freemans plc* [1989] AC 66). But of course many statutory instruments, by their nature, receive no debate in Parliament. Only if the Act under which it is made provides that the statutory instrument must be approved by a resolution of both Houses of Parliament will there definitely be some debate (albeit usually very short), but that procedure is reserved for particularly important statutory instruments — perhaps one in ten. For a greater number the enabling Act provides that once the statutory instrument is made, a motion to annul it may be brought before either House within a certain period, but Parliamentary time is rarely allocated to debate such negative resolutions. The majority of statutory instruments are subject to neither the affirmative resolution nor the negative resolution procedures — they are simply 'laid' before Parliament after they are made, which is a formal procedure entailing no debate.

Particularly given this usual absence of any Parliamentary debates, guidance might also be sought in any debates on the enabling provision in the Act under which the statutory instrument was made. There might possibly be statements on how it was envisaged that the regulation-making power would be exercised. Indeed *Denny v Yeldon* [1995] 3 All ER 624 is an example where the court used *Hansard* in that way. However, different considerations apply where the question is whether a statutory instrument has been made ultra vires, rather than merely where a statutory instrument, accepted as valid, falls to be construed. In *Spath Holme* (see **7.3.2**), where the vires of the Rent Acts (Maximum Fair Rent) Order 1999 was challenged, the majority of the House of Lords, having found the words of the enabling Act unambiguous, held that it was not proper to use *Hansard* to identify the scope of the discretionary power thus conferred. Nevertheless, of the majority, Lord Bingham and Lord Hope did concede that if, improbably, a minister gave a categorical assurance that a power would not be exercised in a particular way, the statement would be admissible. This very much echoes the estoppel ratio of *Pepper v Hart* discussed above (**7.3.2**). And again the improbability of there having been such a statement does not diminish the research effort in having to look for one in appropriate circumstances.

7.3.4   Putting extracts from *Hansard* before the court

The procedure to be followed if you were going to cite Hansard in court was originally set out in the *Practice Direction (Hansard: Citation)* [1995] 1 WLR 192. As far as *criminal* cases are concerned its provisions are now to be found in the *Consolidated Criminal Practice Direction*, www.hmcourts–service.gov.uk. cms pds.htm and in *Blackstone's Criminal Practice* (2005 edn, appendix 8)) at paras II.20 (Court of Appeal) and IV.37 (Crown Court). The requirements are:

- a copy of the extract together with a summary of the argument which relies on the extract must be served on the other parties and the court;
- the extract must be from the Official Report (ie *Hansard* itself);
- service must be five clear working days in advance of the first day of the hearing, whether or not it has a fixed date;
- three copies should be sent to the Registrar of Criminal Appeals or the chief clerk of the relevant Crown Court centre, as the case may be.

As far as *civil* cases are concerned there is no longer any express provision in the practice directions accompanying the CPR. The editors of *Blackstone's Civil Practice* (2004 edn, para 71.44) merely suggest that reasonable advance notice must be given to the other parties and the court. In the case of civil appeals the extracts should be included in the bundle of authorities, which now normally needs to be lodged seven days in advance of the hearing (CPR PD52, as revised 30 June 2004, para 15.11).

One small point to note when making copies from *Hansard* for use in the court is that they should be taken from the officially published bound volumes, not from the loose daily or weekly parts, which are published first in unrevised form (see **7.3.6.1**). The bound volumes form the official record and contain editorial (though not, in theory, substantive) revisions. Furthermore the column numbering is often adjusted.

7.3.5   Parliamentary procedure

To find your way around *Hansard* and to use the material found effectively it is essential to have some grasp of Parliamentary procedure and how a Bill gets to the statute book. There is not space here to cover more than the basic procedure as it relates to a typical government Bill that ends up as a public general Act. For the numerous complications and exceptions that can arise, for procedure on private members' Bills, private Bills and statutory instruments, and for further guidance generally refer to Holborn, Guy, *Butterworths Legal Research Guide*, 2nd edn, London: Butterworths, 2001, chapter 4 '*Pepper v Hart* research and the background to legislation'. The two main textbooks on Parliamentary procedure are *Erskine May's Treatise on the Law, Privileges, Proceedings and Usage of Parliament*, 23rd edn, London: Butterworths, 2004, and Griffiths, J.A.G., and Ryle, Michael, *Parliament: Functions, Practice and Procedures*, 2nd edn London: Sweet & Maxwell, 2003. If you are stuck, the House of Commons Information Office can be very helpful (contact details on www.parliament.uk).

7.3.5.1   Pre-Bill

Before a Bill is published the government will often issue a green paper for consultation and then a white paper outlining firm proposals in light of consultation. Or, the proposals may have their origin with the Law Commission, which again usually first issues a consultation paper and then a final report, often with a draft Bill attached. Government consultation papers may also take the form of, or include a draft Bill. But there is new pre-Bill procedure, first used experimentally in 1998, and now becoming common, whereby a draft Bill is considered by a Select Committee of the House of Commons or House of Lords or by a Joint Committee of both Houses. The purpose is to improve pre-legislative scrutiny, so that the Bill proper is in a better or more acceptable state when it starts its passage, thereby ensuring that the best use is made of scarce Parliamentary time. A particular advantage that such a Select Committee has over each House in its legislative capacity (even at the Committee stage proper — see **7.3.5.5**), is that it can take evidence, orally or in writing, from outside experts and other interested parties. The reports and proceedings of such Select Committees are published as House of Commons or House of Lords Papers, not in *Hansard* (see **7.3.6.1**). All these documents may of course be admissible, apart from *Pepper v Hart*, under the mischief rule of statutory interpretation, but they are often useful to consult in any case because they may be referred to by the Minister and may come under the category of 'other Parliamentary material' in the second *Pepper v Hart* criterion.

7.3.5.2 Which House first?

A Bill may be introduced in either House, but most major government Bills and all Finance Bills start in the Commons. If a Bill starts in the Lords '[HL]' appears after its title, and such Bills will include those for which the Lord Chancellor (or in future the Secretary of State for Constitutional Affairs) is the Minister responsible, eg, 'law reform' Bills, and consolidation Bills; but it is now the practice, for timetabling reasons, for a few government Bills each session to start in the Lords. A Bill will go through the same stages wherever it starts. Incidentally, where a speaker in one House refers to the other, the convention is that it is not called 'the Commons' or 'the Lords' but 'another place'.

7.3.5.3 Some procedural differences between the two Houses

Unlike the Commons, there is no guillotine or other formal method of curtailing debate in the Lords. It is very frustrating to wade through Commons *Hansard* only to find that they never reached your clause because of a guillotine motion — at least there might be something in the Lords. There is also no selection of amendments for debate in the Lords, so there is greater chance of a particular point being aired.

These differences, together with the facts that the Lords are notably conscientious in their revising role and are more free of party political considerations, often make their debates more fruitful hunting grounds for *Pepper v Hart* material than the Commons' debates.

7.3.5.4 Parliamentary sessions

Unless a general election intervenes, a Parliamentary session normally starts with the Queen's Speech at the end of November and continues to the beginning of November the following year. Most business has to be completed by the start of the summer recess, but both Houses return for a short period in the autumn before Parliament is prorogued and many Bills complete their passage in the Lords during this period. A general election may result in a Parliamentary session being unusually short or unusually long, depending when it falls. Bills and most other Parliamentary materials are published and referred to in accordance with the session (eg 1995–96) rather than calendar year. This can occasionally cause confusion, particularly with Finance Bills where there is more than one or where the Parliamentary session is not of standard length, because the resulting Acts are cited and numbered according to the calendar year.

A Bill usually has to complete all its stages within the Parliamentary session, otherwise it falls in its entirety, and if it is to be proceeded with has to be introduced afresh in the next session. Since 1999 a Bill may, exceptionally, with all-party agreement, be carried over from one session to the next.

7.3.5.5 Parliamentary stages of a public Bill: the basic pattern

A Bill introduced in the Commons will go through the stages below. Although some stages are more fruitful than others for *Pepper v Hart* material, it is usually necessary to follow a Bill through its entire passage, not only because a relevant amendment or statement may appear only at a very late stage, but also in case the Minister at a later stage varies what he said at any earlier stage.

Commons introduction and first reading

This stage is purely formal and takes place without debate. The Bill is ordered to be printed and a date is set for the second reading.

Commons second reading

This is a debate on the general principle of the Bill. There are no amendments at this stage. The Bill will normally be introduced by the Minister who will outline its provisions and explain any background, such as green papers and white papers. The debate is usually wound up by the Minister (or often a junior Minister) speaking again in response to points made. Although the Minister, whether in his or her opening or closing remarks, may provide useful elucidation of major clauses, the second reading will rarely include the detailed discussion of a particular clause that is usually needed. But it should be looked at and is useful for the background. The House will have before them the Bill as first printed.

Commons committee stage

This is when detailed clause-by-clause consideration of the Bill is given and amendments are first moved, and so is usually the most fruitful stage. The committee stage is usually taken off the floor of the House in a Standing Committee (lettered A, B, C, etc). However, certain clauses or the whole Bill may instead be taken by a 'committee of the whole House' on the floor of the House. Finance Bills have been split between the floor and Standing Committee since 1968–69 (before that they were taken on the floor in their entirety) and matters of constitutional or similar importance will also be reserved for the floor (the Human Rights Bill, session 1997–98, for example). The practical implication is that only debates on the floor of the House are reported in the main *Hansard*. Standing Committee debates form a different series. The Bill before the Committee is that first printed for the Commons.

Commons report stage

This is also sometimes referred to as the consideration stage. New amendments may be moved, especially government amendments made in response to undertakings given at committee stage. The procedure on making amendments and speaking, however, is more circumscribed than in committee. Usually the House will have before them a fresh print of the Bill as amended in Standing Committee (with corresponding changes to the clause numbers as originally published).

Commons third reading

This provides a chance for final consideration of the Bill. However, no further amendments, other than pure drafting corrections, may be moved. It is usually taken without a gap immediately after the report stage and is generally purely formal with no debate. The Bill is not usually reprinted for this stage.

Lords introduction and first reading

As for the Commons.

Lords second reading

As for the Commons, though it will be introduced by the government spokesperson or a junior Minister in the Lords. His or her brief will the same as that of the Commons Minister and so there will be little difference between what they say, though remarks in the Lords may be modified in light of the debate that took place in the Commons. The House will have before them the first print of the Bill in the Lords series of Bills, which will be the text as amended by the Commons.

Lords committee stage

This, as for the Commons, is the detailed clause-by-clause consideration. Although there may be no debate on a particular clause, each has to be separately moved and agreed. Unlike the Commons, the committee stage is almost always taken by a committee of the whole House on the floor of the House, so the debates will be in the main Lords *Hansard*. However, the Lords in recent years have been experimenting with taking some Bills off the floor of the House as in the Commons. These are taken by a Public Bill Committee, a Special Public Bill Committee (which hears evidence from outside parties), or a Grand Committee (a committee of the whole House off the floor of the House). The last of these has now become quite common and the relevant debates appear in the main Lords *Hansard* but with separate column numbering prefixed with 'CWH'. The first two forms of committee off the floor of the House, however, have proved less popular. When they have been used their debates have been published separately. The Bill at committee stage is that first printed for the Lords.

Lords report stage

As for the Commons.

Lords third reading

Unlike the Commons, this is usually taken separately from the report stage, and further-more substantive amendments may be and frequently are, moved; again, these are often government amendments on undertakings given in committee or at report. The consequence is that a particular section of any Act may have its origin in such a clause that was introduced only at the eleventh hour having bypassed all previous stages. The Bill is usually reprinted as amended at report stage for consideration at third reading.

Commons consideration of Lords amendments

Having gone through the Lords, the Bill returns to the Commons for agreement to the amendments made by the Lords. The whole Bill is not reprinted, but all the amendments made by the Lords are brought together with reference to the Bill as first printed for the Lords. The Commons may disagree with the Lords, in which case it returns once more to the Lords. In theory a bill can yo-yo back and forth indefinitely, but usually an accommodation is reached. In the very rare event of the Lords not conceding, the Bill will fall, but may be reintroduced in a subsequent session and can proceed without the agreement of the Lords under the Parliament Acts 1911 and 1949.

Royal assent

This is the final stage and is recorded in *Hansard*, but is purely formal without debate.

7.3.6 Parliamentary materials

7.3.6.1 Categories

The following are the main categories of Parliamentary publications.

Hansard

Its title proper is *Parliamentary Debates: Official Report*, and it is sometimes referred to as the *Official Report*. It has been the 'Official' report since 1909. The earlier series, produced by the private enterprise of the publisher Luke Hansard, go back to 1803, but they were unofficial and are not necessarily complete or verbatim — the earlier one goes back the less complete they are.

The modern debates are published in two series, one for the Commons and one for the Lords (before 1909 they are in one series).

Both series are issued in daily and weekly unrevised parts, and then in official bound volumes covering, in the Commons, a fortnight. As well as carrying a near-verbatim record of all proceedings on the floor of the House, they include written questions and their answers, which have separate column numbering.

Standing Committee debates

The procedure in the Commons of taking the committee stage in Standing Committee off the floor of the House was introduced in 1907, but their verbatim proceedings were not at first published, so there are no debates for the period 1907–19, but fortunately the use of the Standing Committee procedure did not become a matter of routine until after the Second World War.

The debates are published separately from *Hansard*, in individual parts for each sitting (a morning or afternoon) and then in sessional bound volumes published by HMSO and its successor the Stationery Office, and arranged by Committee letter (though some libraries may bind up the loose parts for themselves). Unlike *Hansard*, the HMSO bound volumes do not contain revised text, but lists of errata are inserted at the front of the proceedings on each Bill. For large Bills there may be 20 or more sittings.

Bills

There are two series of Bills, those printed for the Commons and those printed for the Lords. The distinction between the two series is not to be confused with the House in which the Bill was introduced. A Bill introduced in the Lords (which has [HL] after its title) is printed with the Commons Bills like any other when it comes to that House.

Each series is separately numbered for each session. Fresh prints as amended at various stages get fresh numbers. Amendments to be moved are printed and issued with the Bills in the case of the Lords, but are not issued to subscribers in the case of Commons Bills (they form instead part of the 'vote bundle' issued to MPs which is not otherwise widely available). In the Lords on the day of the relevant debate all the amendments are gathered together and printed as a marshalled list of amendments. If the relevant stage lasts longer than a day, a fresh marshalled list of amendments still outstanding is issued each day. The Lords amendments bear the same number as the print of the Bill to which they refer.

Explanatory notes

From session 1998–99 Explanatory Notes, prepared by the sponsoring government department, have been issued to accompany each government Bill. These replace the Notes on Clauses, which were only made available to MPs and peers, and the rather terse Explanatory Memorandum that formed part of the first print of the Bill in each series. The Explanatory Notes are issued with the first print of the Bill in the Commons, and then again, with any necessary revisions, with the first print of the Bill for the Lords. On Royal Assent they are issued in third and final form as Explanatory Notes on the Act. Their appearance naturally prompted the question whether they would be admissible as aids to statutory interpretation. The first explicit reference to them in a reported case was in

R v A (No 2) (Complainant's Sexual History) [2001] UKHL 25, [2002] 1 AC 45, at [82]. But, as mentioned at **7.3.2**, we now have a full exegesis from Lord Steyn in *R (Westminster City Council) v National Asylum Support Service* [2002] UKHL 38, [2002] 1 WLR 2956, at [1]–[6]. Furthermore in *R v Montila* [2004] UKHL 50, [2004] 1 WLR 3141, at [35], Lord Hope, having cited with approval the *National Asylum* case, remarks that it has now become commonplace for their Lordships to ask to be shown the Explanatory Notes (see also *Attorney-General's Reference (No 5 of 2002)* [2004] UKHL 40, [2005] 1 AC 167, Lord Bingham at [21]). Thus it would seem sensible to treat Lord Steyn's analysis as governing the position. Lord Steyn puts Explanatory Notes in the same logical category as he does *Hansard*. Thus there are two circumstances where they might be used. First, they are always, with or without the presence of an ambiguity, admissible in so far as they 'cast light on the objective setting or contextual scene of the statute, and the mischief at which it is aimed' [5]. Lord Steyn goes on to say that for this purpose they might in fact be more valuable and informative than Law Commission reports, white papers and the like, because their connection is closer to the proposed legislation. Secondly, 'if exceptionally there is found in Explanatory Notes a clear assurance by the executive to Parliament about the meaning of a clause, or the circumstances in which a power will or will not be used, that assurance may in principle be admitted against the executive in proceedings in which the executive places a contrary contention before a court' [6] — in other words, the same estoppel ratio that Lord Steyn would give to *Pepper v Hart*. A third circumstance, not mentioned by Lord Steyn, in which one could see Explanatory Notes being admitted is if a ministerial statement from *Hansard* — one that itself had been properly admitted — referred to the Explanatory Notes. They might then fall into the category of 'other Parliamentary material' in Lord Browne-Wilkinson's second criterion, if they were necessary to understand the statement. One practical point to bear in mind is that it may be necessary to refer to the Explanatory Notes for the *Bill* (either as printed for the Commons or for the Lords), especially if they are being used in tandem with *Hansard*, rather than for the *Act*. These are not available on the internet once the Bill has been passed — see **7.3.6.2** on availability. Also remember that Explanatory Notes are only available for Acts passed from 1999 onwards.

House of Commons papers

This category comprises a great variety of material both emanating from the House and printed for the House, but included are the reports and minutes of select committees (not to be confused with Standing Committees). The papers are not needed routinely for *Pepper v Hart*, but may occasionally be needed for background on a Bill, for certain exceptional categories of proceedings on a Bill, and now also for Select Committee reports on draft Bills. They are numbered each session and cited as, for example, HC (1994–95) 231.

House of Lords papers

These are a similar category to the House of Commons papers. They include the reports, minutes and verbatim proceedings of Special Public Bill Committees, where the committee stage is taken in that form.

Command papers

These are government papers presented to Parliament, and include white papers and Law Commission reports. Green papers are also sometimes command papers, but often they are simply published by the Stationery Office or by the government department concerned. Since 1986 command papers have been published with the abbreviation 'Cm' and a running number. Earlier series have different permutations of the abbreviation.

7.3.6.2   Availability

Consult your librarian as to the best place to go for Parliamentary publications. The biggest problem is with Standing Committee debates as only a handful of libraries in the country have complete sets going back to 1919. All the Inn libraries take some Parliamentary publications, but Lincoln's Inn has a complete set except for Standing Committee debates, which it holds only from 1983–84 with a small selection of volumes for the sessions 1954–55 to 1971–72. The Information Office at the House of Commons can also advise, and the House of Commons Library publishes a list: *Parliamentary Holdings in Libraries in Britain and Ireland* (1993, edited by David Lewis Jones and Chris Pond).

A substantial amount of Parliamentary material is now freely available on the internet (at www.parliament.uk) (see **8.4.3**), but this is only of limited assistance for *Pepper v Hart* research, for the time being at any rate because of the limited retrospective coverage — by no means does *Pepper v Hart* research only arise with recent Acts. Commons *Hansard* starts with session 1988–89 and Lords *Hansard* with session 1994–95, but the Standing Committee debates, without which any research would almost always be dangerously incomplete, only start with session 1997–98. Furthermore, Bills, which are often needed too (see **7.3.7.2**), are replaced with the Act once passed. Likewise the Explanatory Notes to Bills only remain on the Parliament website while the Bill is still in progress, though the Explanatory Notes to Acts (see **7.3.6.1**) are permanently available on the Legislation part of the HMSO site (www.hmso.gov.uk).

7.3.7   Finding debates on a section of an Act

Before embarking on the steps below, be aware that *Pepper v Hart* research can be time-consuming. As a pupil you may well be asked to do the research. If a thorough and competent job is to be done, do not allow your pupil master to set unrealistic deadlines. With all the materials at your fingertips, and if the provision in question is contained in a very short Act, the research might possibly be done in half an hour; much more commonly it will take half a day, or longer.

7.3.7.1   Step 1: Are you looking for debates on the right Act?

Is it a Consolidation Act? Some Acts consolidate a number of previous Acts without changing the law, and the long title of the Act will say that that is its purpose. Under the Consolidation of Enactments (Procedure) Act 1949, Bills for such Acts are referred to the Joint Committee [of both Houses] on Consolidation Bills who have to certify that the Bill contains corrections and minor improvements only and not any change in the law. Consequently, when the Bill goes through each House there is no debate on the substance of the provision, and often no debate at all.

Thus if *Hansard* is to be used it is the debates on the original Act which first introduced the provision that need to be found. Before looking, bear in mind the basic *Pepper v Hart* rule that the provision in the consolidation Act must be ambiguous. In *Ex p Spath Holme Ltd* (see **7.3.2**) the House of Lords recently held that it was ordinarily impermissible to construe a consolidating provision by reference to the enactments it replaced except where (a) the language of the provision was ambiguous, or (b) its purpose could only be understood by examining the context in which it had originally been used. In the case, the majority held that it had been proper for the Court of Appeal to have examined earlier enactments because of exception (b), but not proper to do have done so with the benefit of *Hansard* because the *Pepper v Hart* criteria were not satisfied.

Derivations may usually be found either in annotations to the particular section or in a separate table of derivations in either *Halsbury's Statutes* or *Current Law Statutes*. From 1967 the official annual volumes of public general Acts also include tables of derivations, which will be found in the last, Tables and Index, volume for the year. In the unlikely event of all those sources failing, examine any Acts repealed that are listed in the schedule of repeals at the end of the consolidating Act. Sometimes, for instance with the Companies Acts, it may be necessary to trace the section back through several successive consolidations. Here old editions of standard textbooks are sometimes helpful. The *Justis Statutes* database, which contains the full text of all Public General Acts as enacted, is another possibility, since the same wording is usually, though not invariably, recycled.

It could conceivably arise that the ambiguity in your section has arisen as a consequence of the consolidation process — the drafting of the provisions of the earlier Act may have been recast to some degree. You will need to compare the two versions. If that is the case, light may be shed by the report and minutes of the Joint Committee which will have taken evidence from the drafter of the Bill. The reports are published as House of Commons papers.

Has the section been inserted or amended by a later Act? If the source of your text of the Act is one that reprints text as amended, eg, *Halsbury's Statutes* or a Butterworth's subject handbook, check that the relevant text is as originally passed. Lettered section numbers or text in square brackets point to an insertion. The notes to the section will usually give the source of any amending Act, and your *Hansard* research may then have to be directed to that Act rather than, or as well as, the original Act.

7.3.7.2   Step 2: Look at the Bills

Although in the case of short Bills this step may be skipped, with long Bills it usually saves time in the long run if you look at all the prints of the Bill from both Houses before you start. First, this enables you to establish whether your clause was in identical form throughout its passage and if not at what stage it reached its final form — that stage is then likely to be the most fruitful, though bear in mind the possibility that an amendment that is successful at one stage may have been debated without being agreed at an earlier stage. Secondly, you can note the clause number of your provision at each stage — this may change several times and almost certainly will not be the same as the section number in the final Act. You will find this helps when leafing through the debates to find your bit. Usually there will be two complete prints of the Bill in the Commons and three in the Lords.

7.3.7.3   Step 3: Find the *Hansard* references for each stage

See **7.3.6.1** on *Hansard* and its constituent parts and see **7.3.5.5** on the various stages of Parliamentary procedure.

Typically, there will be eight stages for which *Hansard* references will need to be found: (1) Commons second reading; (2) Commons committee; (3) Commons report and third reading; (4) Lords second reading; (5) Lords Committee; (6) Lords report; (7) Lords third reading; (8) Commons consideration of Lords amendments (see **7.3.5.5**).

There are a number of approaches to this but the safest is to use the sessional indexes to the *Hansard* for each House, bearing in mind that (as described below) the Commons Committee stage will usually have to be sought, as a separate exercise, in the Standing Committee debates. Each series has an index for each session either as a separate volume at the end of the session or in the back of the last volume for the session (usually November but note what is said in **7.3.5.4** about the duration of Parliamentary sessions).

Under the title of the Bill, all stages are given with both dates and volume and column numbers. Ignore those with an asterisk which are formal only without debate.

The sessional indexes, however, are produced slowly and are usually two or three years behind. If the Bill went through in the current session, look at the latest issue of the *House of Commons Weekly Information Bulletin*, taken by many libraries. There is a complete list of public Bills with the dates (though not the volume and column numbers) of each stage. For earlier sessions use the *Sessional Digest* which is an annual cumulation of the *Weekly Information Bulletin*.

For statutes passed from 1993, an equally good alternative to the above sources is *Halsbury's Statutes*. At the start of each Act this now gives full details of each stage with *Hansard* references.

Current Law Statutes may also be used, but there are a couple of caveats. The annotations to the particular section, especially for recent Acts, may well draw attention to any particularly crucial debates on the section (as may sometimes nowadays *Halsbury's Statutes*). This is a helpful short cut, but does not preclude the need to check all of the debates for yourself if you wish to be thorough. *Current Law Statutes* have always included references to the Parliamentary debates at the start of each Act. However, until 1998 these appeared only as a string of *Hansard* references without stating which stage each referred to. Although the recent volumes, certainly since *Pepper v Hart*, give all references, the earlier volumes suffer from editorial laxity and do not necessarily include every stage where there was debate, and are not therefore to be relied upon.

Bear in mind that some editors of textbooks are now taking pity on the *Pepper v Hart* researcher. For example, *Copinger on Copyright* includes a full section-by-section table of *Hansard* references for the Copyright Acts and *Hansard* references or extracts abound in the many books on the Human Rights Act 1998.

When it comes to finding Commons Standing Committee debates on the shelf, it will depend how they are arranged in the library. If they are in the form of the official bound volumes, you will need to know the letter of the relevant Standing Committee (Bills are not assigned to a particular Committee in any order, except that Standing Committee C usually considers private members' Bills). The letter is not given in the sessional indexes to *Hansard*, but all the other sources mentioned above do. Otherwise look at the listing of the individual parts of the debates in the annual *Catalogue of Government Publications* published by the Stationery Office or at the contents list in each volume.

7.3.7.4 Step 4: Find the debates on your clause at each stage

Having noted your *Hansard* references, it is usually then simply a question of leafing through them until you find the debates on your clause, remembering that every stage has to be checked. But with large and complicated Bills it can help if you are aware of the usual order of consideration at each stage, and of what to do if the clauses are not considered sequentially as can sometimes happen.

At the Commons committee stage the usual order of consideration is: each clause in the original Bill and amendments thereto, new clauses not in the original Bill at all, schedules in the original Bill, new schedules. A distinction is thus made between new matter introduced as an amendment to an existing clause and new matter in the form of a separate clause. However, this order may be varied, for example, to take a schedule with its parent section. If the debates do not seem to be going in the usual order, look at the debate for the first sitting where the proposed order will have been agreed. In the official bound volumes of Standing Committee debates there is a usually an index by clause number.

At the Commons report stage, the usual order is different: new clauses, amendments to clauses, new schedules, amendments to schedules. If this order is varied, look at the start of the first day's debate.

The Lords do not distinguish between amendments to clauses and new clauses, so the latter are usually debated where they naturally arise. If a sequential order is not followed, the order of debate can be established either by looking at the marshalled list of amendments with the print of the Bill or by looking at the 'motion for approval' in *Hansard*. These motions to approve the order of consideration appear in advance of the particular stage, not usually with it, but they are indexed in the *Hansard* sessional indexes together with the other stages of the Bill.

Finally, having eventually found your clause at each stage, do not be surprised if it is not debated at all; if it is debated do not be surprised if it is of no assistance whatsoever.

In **Chapter 9** there is a diagram setting out a suggested sequence in which to approach problems on the meanings of words, especially in construing statutes.

8

Using electronic research tools

This chapter offers a practical overview of the main strategies and techniques you will need to employ when researching legal problems using an electronic source. It does not give detailed instructions as to how to use each resource — mastering the mechanics of the databases is best achieved by reading the user guides available online or attending a training session or demonstration given by an experienced user (such as a law librarian).

When searching an electronic legal database you need to be aware of three major issues, all of which are dealt with in greater detail in this chapter:

(a) *Know the precise scope and content of the database you are searching.* The overviews of the major commercial legal databases given in this chapter provide a good starting point. This issue also applies to printed sources of course, but there is a temptation to assume that 'everything' is available on a database. This is not an assumption one would make with a book, nor is it one that applies to electronic sources.

(b) *Learn how to search the database.* The risk of failing to retrieve material simply because you don't know how to use the database correctly is much greater for the untrained user than it is when you use printed sources. The correct formulation of a search strategy is all-important.

(c) *Update your findings.* It is tempting to assume that information available electronically is always more up to date than any printed equivalent. Often this is the case but not always . . . and updated information is rarely incorporated into the main text on the database straight away. You need to learn how each database updates its material.

8.1 Electronic formats

There are three main methods of accessing electronic databases.

8.1.1 Online databases

Now regarded as 'old' technology, the traditional online service required the user to dial up to a remote database, incurring an online charge for conducting a search. Internet technology has now made this type of online database largely obsolete, but the 'pay-as-you-go' approach is still attractive to light users of legal databases. While most providers now require an annual subscription, some (such as Westlaw) have continued with the 'pay-as-you-go' option.

8.1.2   Internet

The internet offers database publishers the ability to combine sophisticated search mechanisms with a technology that allows them to remotely update their databanks on a daily basis. The currency of the information is particularly attractive to those producing and using legal databases. Commercial databases on the internet are usually made available on subscription under licence, the price charged varying depending on the number of users, the type of organisation and how the organisation uses the information retrieved. A large commercial law firm would be charged more than an academic institution, for example.

There are disadvantages to using an internet-based database however. The rush to put data onto the internet has often been at the expense of the user. It is not always clear what information a database contains or how often it is updated and the search engines on many databases lack functionality and user-friendliness.

8.1.3   CD-ROMs

CD-ROMs remain a popular alternative to database provision via the internet. They offer limited storage capacity — they could never hold the Westlaw or Lawtel databases, for example — but searching is usually much quicker and more sophisticated on a CD-ROM, than it is on the internet. Users can search at their leisure as there are no hidden online charges or telephone bills and this makes them more suitable for in-depth legal research. These advantages could well be outweighed by their lack of currency however — updated disks are generally supplied quarterly, or monthly at best. Providers often get round this by supplying the main database on CD-ROM but then allowing users to access updated material on the internet (see **8.3.2.2** and **8.3.7.2**).

8.2   Types of electronic database

It is important that the user knows both the contents and type of database s/he is searching. Electronic legal databases fall into three broad categories.

8.2.1   Full text services

The full text of a document is added to the database. LexisNexis Professional contains the full text of law reports from *The Times*, for example. Full text services offer the user the ability to conduct in-depth research at the desktop without needing to leave the database to search for another source. In this respect, they offer greater flexibility and the possibility of thorough research. In practice, however, they require good searching techniques and a sound knowledge of the database contents. Simply because of the size of these databases, the number of results that are returned tends to be unwieldy whilst, at the same time, the user can never be sure that they are not missing some relevant information. The need for refined search strategies and techniques rapidly becomes apparent on a full text retrieval database.

8.2.2   Abstracting and indexing services

In these, law reports, journal articles, legislation and other documents are summarised by professional indexers and the summaries placed on the database. Keywords identifying concepts are assigned to each abstract and links provided to related summaries and sometimes to the full text of a document. When the user searches the database, s/he is searching the summaries and keywords rather than the full text of the document itself. This allows for much greater precision in searching, reducing the number of extraneous results. Current Legal Information and Legal Journals Index (available via Westlaw or as separate services) and Lawtel, are all abstracting and indexing services.

8.2.3   Bibliographic services

Bibliographic services offer publication details only. The *Index to Parliamentary Papers* CD ROM for example, is a searchable bibliographical database which can help to locate relevant Parliamentary Bills and Bill numbers when carrying out *Pepper v Hart* research (see **7.3**). Some bibliographic databases now offer links to the *Pepper v Hart* full text of documents and this greatly increases their value to the researcher even if the full text of the document itself is not searchable. The gateway web site *UK Official Publications on the Internet* is an example of a searchable bibliographic database that links to the full text of many (though not all) the documents it indexes.

8.3   Commercial legal databases

The databases listed here are the main competitors in the provision of electronic legal information in the UK. There are other legal database providers and the list does not aim to be comprehensive. All are commercial services usually available on subscription. The scope or contents of each database is highlighted and any problems concerning searching and display are briefly summarised.

8.3.1   Butterworths Services

 Butterworths
Services

Major changes are planned in 2005 for the incorporation of the Butterworths suite of databases into the publishers' 'sister' database, LexisNexis. At the time of writing it is not clear exactly what format the new database will take. This text refers to the position as at May 2005.

8.3.1.1   Scope

This is a suite of full text databases that can be searched independently of each other or as a group using a *TotalSearch* option. *Case Search* and *Legislation Direct* cover the primary sources for legal research while the subject-based services offer the full text of many Butterworths publications including textbooks, loose leaf works and practitioner tools. Butterworths Services databases include:

- Case Search — case summaries with links to full text law reports. Includes an archive of case law from 1502 taken from *The Digest*.
- All England Direct — complete archive from 1936 and recent cases in advance of publication in the printed series.
- Halsbury's Laws — full text of the encyclopaedia with cumulative supplement and monthly noter-up.
- Legislation Direct — full text of legislation in force in England and Wales, as amended by later enactments.
- Subject-based services — such as Crime Online, Employment Law Online etc.

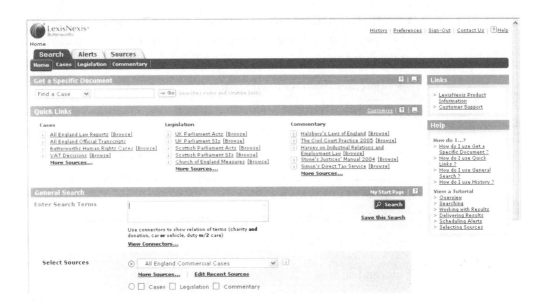

8.3.1.2   Search and display

Searching is straightforward but very exact (in some circumstances, a search returns different results if you use capital letters rather than lower case) and the user must be careful how s/he completes the search boxes. The display, though a little cluttered, emulates a book and is easy to browse and navigate.

8.3.2   Current Legal Information (CLI) databases

8.3.2.1   Scope

This is an abstracting and indexing service. Its excellent coverage of law reports and legal journals makes it an indispensable tool for researching UK case law back to 1947. CLI databases include:

- Current Law Cases — includes all abstracts taken from printed digests appearing in *Current Law Yearbook* and *Monthly Digest* since it began in 1947. It aims to cover all reported cases and unreported cases sent in by barristers and solicitors. Cases are noted-up with the procedural history and subsequent judicial consideration.

- Case transcripts — an index of selected transcripts of judgments from 1999.

- Legal Journals Index — title details and brief abstracts of articles taken from virtually all legal journals published in the UK from 1986. It also indexes articles commenting on cases and cases reported in journals and so is, itself, an excellent source for case law.

8.3.2.2   Search and display

The CLI databases are available in several formats including CD-ROM (Folio Views software), Blackwell's Idealist software (updated fortnightly by disk), on the internet through a Sweet & Maxwell website, and via Westlaw. Searching and display varies depending on the software used. The careful application of keywords to the digests taken from the printed *Current Law* ensures that searching is precise.

8.3.3   Justis

Justis

8.3.3.1   Scope

A suite of full text services focusing on individual resources such as statutes or law reports. The resources are largely for the UK jurisdiction but Justis also offer several services covering

European law. Justis allows for a flexible combination of one-off payments and on-going subscriptions, depending on the product and type of access (internet or CD-ROM). Justis databases include:

- *The Law Reports* (Official Series).
- Law Reports Digest.
- *Times Law Reports* (from 1990).
- *Parlianet* (index to publications and proceedings in Parliament, from 1979).
- Statutes and Statutory Instruments (full text in their *original* form — statutes from 1235; SIs from 1987).
- CELEX (the official database of the European Communities).
- *JustCite*, a legal reference and citation search facility.

8.3.3.2   Search and display

Search Wizards guide you through constructing your searches using step-by-step prompts and drop-down menus. Data has clearly been transferred from CD-ROM onto the internet and searching 'fields' in this way presents some restrictions in terms of searching and display. Justis products are suitable for obtaining an electronic version of a resource (law reports, for example), but they are not an alternative to the other online databases listed here.

8.3.4   Lawtel

8.3.4.1   Scope

An abstracting and indexing service for UK law, owned by Sweet & Maxwell. The strengths of the main Lawtel UK database lie in its coverage of unreported cases and the speed with which decisions are placed on the service. The main database, Lawtel UK, is supplemented by separate, specialist databases such as Lawtel Personal Injury and Lawtel Civil Procedure. Lawtel UK databases include:

- Case law abstracts from 1980. Comprehensive coverage of decisions from the House of Lords, Court of Appeal, Privy Council and the High Court, many with links to full text transcripts.

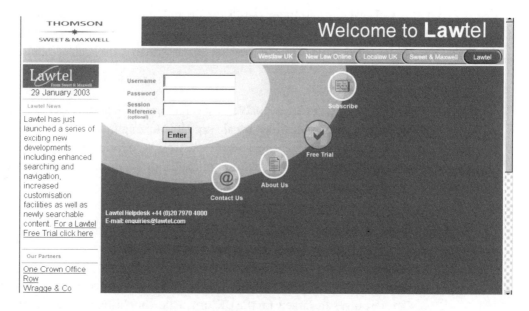

- Legislation. Full text UK legislation in its *original* form. Statutes from 1984, Statutory Instruments from 1987. Tables of commencement, amendments, repeals etc but the text itself is not amended.

- Articles Index. Summaries of articles from over 50 legal journals many of which discuss cases unreported elsewhere.

8.3.4.2   Search and display

Searching is relatively simple and the display of results is intuitive and user-friendly.

8.3.5   LexisNexis professional

Major changes are planned in 2006 for the incorporation of the Butterworths suite of databases into the publishers' 'sister' database, LexisNexis. At the time of writing it is not clear exactly what format the new database will take. This text refers to the position as at May 2005.

8.3.5.1   Scope

Full text service with an international scope. Excellent UK, European and Commonwealth databases of case law and legislation, many with links to the full text of law reports and journals. LexisNexis databases include:

- Case law — a database of case law benefiting from the full text of many series of law reports (though principally Butterworths products as there are no Sweet & Maxwell publications on this database). Includes unparalleled retrospective coverage of transcripts of unreported cases back to 1980.

- Legislation — full text statutes and statutory instruments currently in force, as amended.

- Journals — full text of around fifty UK legal journals, but retrospective coverage is limited. Legal Journals Index on CLI offers more in terms of journal coverage despite its lack of full text content.

8.3.5.2   Search and display

The excellent coverage of the LexisNexis database was in the past marred by complicated search techniques that could defeat all but the most experienced user. The move to a web-based service and the introduction of a more user-friendly search screen has eased these

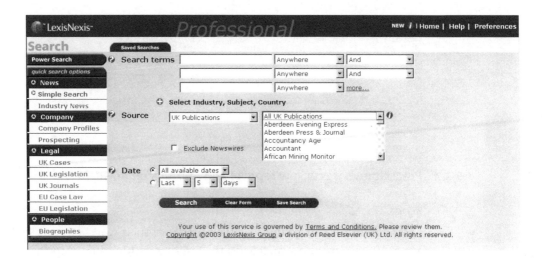

problems substantially. The service can still prove daunting, simply because a search on a database of this size produces so many results — the need for a tightly controlled search becomes imperative. Training is available — free to academic institutions but a chargeable service for commercial users.

8.3.6   Westlaw UK

Westlaw UK

8.3.6.1   Scope

Formidable and rapidly growing full text database that has very quickly established a leading market position in the UK to match that of its principal rival, LexisNexis. The full text of many Sweet & Maxwell journals and loose leaf works are available online. This service is available by subscription or on a 'pay-as-you-go' basis. Westlaw UK databases include:

- Current Legal Information databases (see above) with links to the full text of many law reports and journals (though these are limited to mostly Sweet & Maxwell publications).
- Legislation — full text statutes and statutory instruments currently in force, as amended.
- Journals — full text of around thirty Sweet & Maxwell journals, but retrospective coverage is limited. Legal Journals Index on CLI offers more in terms of journal coverage despite its lack of full text content.

8.3.6.2   Search and display

Reasonably user-friendly but the display could do with improvement. The service boasts the full text of many publications but they are neither advertised online nor are they easy to find.

8.3.7   Practitioners' texts, law reports and journals on CD-ROM

8.3.7.1   Scope

Legal publishers still produce a large number of their works electronically on CD-ROM. Many of these are also available via the internet within some of the online services listed above. The CD-ROM version is particularly useful for expanding a law collection piece-meal without the need to buy and store printed copies or to pay an annual subscription for an expensive service such as LexisNexis or Westlaw. A fuller listing of works provided on CD-ROM is available in **Chapter 10**.

8.3.7.2   Access

Many CD ROMs are supplied free with the printed publications. Others such as *Kemp & Kemp Personal Injury Practice CD-ROM* require separate annual subscriptions. Discs are usu-ally supplied on a regular basis (usually monthly or quarterly) to update the work or the user might download updates from an internet site with a password.

8.3.7.3   Search and display

The software for CD-ROMs varies considerably but searching is generally faster than the internet. The material can also be downloaded in a format suitable for word processing. Publications such as *Atkins Court Forms* and the *Encyclopaedia of Forms and Precedents* work well with CD-ROM technology for this reason, as users need to complete forms and preced-ents before printing them. Many CD-ROMs also offer additional interactive tools such as damages calculators and the ability to save searches, cases and related data and return to work with them at a later date.

8.4   Free legal information on the internet

The internet is a rich source of free legal information with many web sites offering a range of legal databases and documents of great use to practitioners. A few of the most useful web sites are listed in the table at **8.4.3**. It is very tempting to see the internet as *the* source for all legal information. In fact, any web sites you find on the internet should be used with extreme caution, particularly for legal information where currency and accuracy are so important — the quality of a web site is crucial when using the internet for legal research. This makes it necessary to search in a controlled way for the information you need and to evaluate every web site you find, in terms of the currency and quality of the information it offers.

8.4.1   Searching the internet for legal resources

8.4.1.1   Search engines

These are best used when you want to search the internet for a *specific resource* — for example, to find the Court Service home page or to see if there is a transcript of a particular case available for free on the internet. There are many search engines to choose from but if you need legal resources from the UK, then you should use a UK-based search engine: one of the best is *Google* www.google.co.uk.

Other search engines include *AltaVista* http://uk.altavista.com, *All The Web* www.alltheweb.com and the 'natural language' search engine, *Ask Jeeves* www.ask.co.uk.

8.4.1.2   Directories

These allow you to *browse* a list of categories and sub-categories to narrow down the area of the search until you find what you are looking for. *Yahoo!* www.yahoo.co.uk is a good UK-based directory search engine: click Social Science to access listings under Law.

8.4.1.3   Legal Gateways

These offer links to good quality legal resources on the Internet and are of most use when you wish to *browse* the internet for authoritative web sites. The more general legal gateways such as Delia Venables *Portal* or *SOSIG — Law* offer a short description of the linked web site, evaluating its contents for the quality and currency of information.

Other gateways offer links to resources in a particular area of law, such as employment law or company law often combined with a free current awareness service or newsletter and occasionally an additional database or priced services. Several legal gateways are listed in the table at **8.4.3**.

8.4.2   Evaluating the contents of a web site

Once you have found a web site offering legal information, you must ascertain how good it is. Currency and accuracy are vital in legal research. When viewing any legal web site, ask yourself the following series of questions:

- *WHO* is providing the information and *WHY*? Are they reliable and authoritative?
- *WHEN* was the web site, or the database it hosts, last updated? How often is it updated? Does it include all amendments? Is it likely to be there tomorrow?
- *WHERE* is the website published? Which jurisdiction? UK law or US law? England or Scotland?

For example:

What is the close season for snipe?

If you were to search for the keywords 'close season snipe' on a search engine such as Google, the first few results would look something like this:

- *WHO?* — the first two links are official documents, the web addresses betraying their origin. Both web sites are from respected sources. The third link is a gamekeeper's personal website which authoritatively displays close seasons. Is the author up-to-date with the law?
- *WHEN?* — none of these web sites display a date! You might deduce some likely dates for the Act and Bill by following the links on the web sites for the first two results but even official web sites are notoriously bad at providing dates. Legislation provided

on the internet is, in any case in its original format and there is no full text legislation available prior to 1988.

- *WHERE?* — the first two results relate to Northern Ireland legislation rather than that for England and Wales.

Conducting this search has supplied us with a date for the close season for snipe — but we must check it on a more authoritative database. Why not use a legal database from the start? If you do use the internet for legal research, use well-established web sites available through legal gateways or use the resource in the same way as you would use an encyclopaedia — to find background information which you would then check with a more authoritative source.

8.4.3   Free legal information on the internet

The table below lists some of the legal materials available for free on the internet. It is not a comprehensive listing. Web addresses are subject to change but all these web sites (and many others) can be found through a legal gateway such as *Delia Venables Portal* or *SOSIG — Law*.

LEGAL GATEWAYS	Gateway sites with links to free legal resources on the internet	
British Employment Law	Free area with 1,200 fact cards and locator map of employment lawyers.	www.emplaw.co.uk
Company Law Club	Excellent gateway to company law. Free on registration. Database of company law topics, links to company-related web sites, newsletter and bulletin board.	www.companylawclub.co.uk
Delia Venables	*Legal Sites and Resources in the UK.* Very practical pages of links regularly updated by Delia Venables.	www.venables.co.uk
Electronic Immigration Network	Immigration, refugee and nationality law. Gateway site with links to relevant organisations, case law, tribunal decisions and databases; UK and international law.	www.ein.org.uk
Intellectual Property	The Patent Office website hosts a wealth of information concerning intellectual property issues in the UK and EU (patents, designs, trade marks and copyright).	www.patent.gov.uk
Law Society	Latest offerings on policy, law reform and education and links to legal resources in the UK, Europe and abroad.	www.lawsociety.org.uk

Social Science Information Gateway — Law	*SOSIG — Law* catalogues a host of legal internet sites with evaluative abstracts of web site content and links to the homepages.	www.sosig.ac.uk/law

CASE LAW	*Transcripts, law reports and summaries of cases*	
BAILII	UK portal, the *British and Irish Legal Information Institute* offering access transcripts of cases from the High Courts and Court of Appeal, from 1996.	www.bailii.org
Court Service	Database of selected High Court judgments (full text transcripts from 1998 and links to tribunals, many with their own judgments); full text of Practice Directions from July 2000; extensive array of Court forms, leaflets and guidance.	www.courtservice.gov.uk
European Court of Human Rights – HUDOC database	Full text judgments and decisions from 1959. Aims to be comprehensive but there are omissions. Includes pending cases, text of European Convention and Rules of the Court.	www.echr.coe.int
European Court of Justice	Full text judgments of the European Courts of Justice and First Instance from 17 June 1997.	www.curia.eu.int
House of Lords	Full text transcripts of all judgments delivered from 14th November 1996.	www.parliament.uk
Recent, Current & Forthcoming Law Reports (ICLR)	Summaries of cases in *The Law Reports*, *Weekly Law Reports* and *Industrial Cases Reports*. Also access to *Daily Law Notes*, offering briefs of forthcoming cases.	www.lawreports.co.uk
Swarbrick Law Index	Index of cases principally from the Times and Law Society Gazette abstracts. View by date, legislation, subject or court.	www.swarb.co.uk

LEGISLATION	*Acts, SIs, Parliamentary material, EU legislation etc*	
Acts of Parliament and SIs	In their ORIGINAL form. Full text statutes from 1987, SIs from 1996 published by *The Stationery Office*.	www.hmso.gov.uk
Civil Procedure Rules 1998	Full text, updates and related materials are available on the Lord Chancellor's Department web site.	
Eurlex	Full text of all EC legislation currently in force, preparatory legislation, consolidated texts and Treaties. Latest 45 days of the Official Journal (C and L series).	http://europa.eu.int/eur-lex/en/index.html
Government Information	Links via to central and local government departments, agencies and services and to some NGOs.	www.ukonline.gov.uk
Parliament	Full text of parliamentary materials including Bills, Weekly Information Bulletin, recent Hansard debates, etc from 1997.	www.parliament.uk

PUBLICATIONS	*Online versions of major publications*	
Bar Code of Conduct	. . . and other Rules and Guidance.	www.barcouncil.org.uk
Bar Directory	The official directory, searchable by barrister or chambers.	www.smlawpub.co.uk/bar/index.cfm
Crown Prosecution Service	Publications including Code for Crown Prosecutors, the Victims and Witnesses Charter and recent CPS reports.	www.cps.gov.uk
Electronic Law Journals	Gateway to UK law journals, electronic and paper. Some with links to full text, abstracts and contents pages.	http://elj.warwick.ac.uk
Law Commission for England & Wales	Click *Library* for summaries or full text of recent reports, consultation papers, annual reports and *Law Under Review*.	www.lawcom.gov.uk
Ogden Tables	From the Government Actuary Department.	www.gad.gov.uk
UK Official Publications on the Internet	Links to full text of UK official documents including White papers, Command papers, research briefs etc. Search by title, date, publishing department or category.	www.official-documents.co.uk

8.5 Search strategies using electronic resources

8.5.1 First principles

Searching an online legal database requires a different approach to that which many users employ when searching the internet. On the internet we tend to type any combination of keywords into the search box and click *Search*. In fact 80% of searches carried out on the internet use just one keyword. Another common approach is to type a sentence into the search box, much as you would when using the 'natural language' search engine, *Ask Jeeves*.

We adopt this approach because whatever we search for on the internet, we nearly always obtain a large set of results: *recall* is very high. We often find, however, that the *relevance* of many of these results is actually very low. If we were to search again using slightly different keywords, we would be very likely to find other web sites that did not appear when we first searched: our original search has not been very *precise*.

When conducting legal research we need to adopt a more accurate and controlled approach to searching electronic legal sources — we cannot afford to miss any relevant results but nor do we have time to plough through a large set of results to find what we need. To do this we need to devise a search strategy that uses carefully selected keywords combined in such a way as to maximise *recall*, *relevance* and *precision*.

8.5.2 Basic search strategies for electronic sources

Legal research technique is dealt with in more detail in **Chapter 9**. What follows here relates more specifically to searching electronic databases.

8.5.2.1 Analyse the problem: what *exactly* are you looking for?

Spend some time identifying clearly the information you are trying to find. Is the solution likely to be found in case law, legislation or is it a procedural matter? This will help you to decide which database to search and the keywords you might use.

8.5.2.2 Choose which database you are going to search

It is very important to know the contents of the legal databases you have access to. There is little point in searching for a case dating from 1977 on Lawtel for example, as the case law database began in 1980. Similarly if you wanted the full text of a law report in *Criminal Appeal Reports* you will only find it on Westlaw as it is a Sweet & Maxwell publication and will not appear on LexisNexis, a Butterworths product.

Which database is the best to use? It depends what you need. A good method for finding out which database to use is to ask yourself what *type* of question you are faced with. Is it legislative or procedural? Might it involve finding case law? If you are faced with a very general problem and you don't know where to begin, then use a general source. An encyclopaedia of law — *Halsbury's Laws* — is an excellent starting-point.

EXAMPLE

When during the year, does the law prohibit one from shooting snipe?

The word 'prohibit' hints that the answer is probably to be found in legislation and we might therefore use a legislative database but as there may be case law or procedure involved, it is probably best to start with a general source such as *Halsbury's Laws Direct*.

8.5.2.3   Select the keywords

Search engines will find all occurrences within the text, of the words you enter into the search box. If you enter a word that does not exist on the database or you misspell a word, you will get no results. If you enter too common a word, you will get too many results. Selecting the correct combination of keywords is crucial.

Which words define the problem you are researching? These might be:

- words offered to you by the problem itself (*shooting, snipe*);
- alternatives to those words (*shoot, bird, wild bird*);
- concepts behind those words (*game, close season, licensing*).

Search engines are good at finding facts, names and concrete entities; they are poor at classifying problems into concepts. Try to convert the problem into equivalent concrete keywords — the name of a case, the title of a statute, etc.

8.5.2.4   Combine the keywords in a 'controlled' search

After selecting our keywords we need to combine them in a search that will maximise recall, relevance and precision (see **8.5.1**). To do so we make use of a range of tools.

Boolean operators (or 'connectors') AND, OR and NOT

Search phrase	*. . . will find . . .*	*Use it to . . .*	*Notes*
shoot AND *snipe*	. . . records containing the words *shoot* and *snipe*	. . . combine keywords, **narrowing** the search	Many databases assume an AND if no connector is entered. (eg, *close season* will find *close* AND *season* rather than the phrase *close season*).
snipe OR *game* OR *bird*	. . . records containing the words *snipe* or *bird* or *game*	. . . search for alternative keywords, **widening** the search	Useful for searching for alternative concepts (eg, *copyright* OR *patents* OR *designs* OR *intellectual property*).
snipe NOT *bird*	. . . records containing the word *snipe* provided it does *not* contain the word *bird*	. . . exclude keywords, **narrowing** the search	Use rarely and with caution as it excludes records that may actually prove relevant.

Most databases allow several operators to be combined into one search. *Brackets* may be needed to group complex phrases and refine the search even further.

eg, *shoot AND (snipe OR bird)*
eg, *shoot AND (snipe NOT bird)*

Wild card characters / truncation

Wildcards such as the asterisk * or the exclamation mark !, allow the user to search for different permutations of a word ending. Most databases use an asterisk but some use other characters such as an exclamation mark !, a question mark ?, a percentage sign % or a dollar $.

8.5.2.5   Ensure the search form is completed correctly before clicking *Search*

Database providers have made their products easier to search by providing search forms but one of the most common user errors is not completing the form correctly. On the Butterworths Services search form illustrated below, for example, you must complete the *Search Where* and *Search How* boxes. The system defaults to *words next to each other in order* (ie, a phrase). If your keywords do not form a phrase you will not retrieve any results.

Search phrase	. . . will find . . .	Use it to . . .	Notes
licen*	. . . records containing the words *licence, licensing, licensed, licensee* etc.	. . . replaces one or more letters, searching for alternative keywords, **widening** the search	Particularly useful for obtaining plurals to words (though some databases do this automatically).
licen?e	. . . records containing the words *licence* or *license*	. . . search for alternative keywords, **widening** the search	Allows for uncertain spelling (US v UK English, in this example). Might also be used where a hyphen may appear in the text, eg, *self? incrimination*

8.5.2.6   Display a list of results . . . and search again!

After performing a search, databases usually display the results as a list of 'hits' with links to the full text of the record. If the result list you have retrieved is too big (or too small) or you cannot find the information you need, you should go back and search again. Think about your keywords:

- too many results? *Narrow* your search. Add another keyword using an AND;

- too few? *Widen* your search — think of alternative keywords the text might use and add them using an OR;

- results not relevant? Find a result from the list, that is relevant, select keywords from that record and combine them in a new search.

8.5.3   Updating your findings

After finding an answer on the database, you must check that the information you have found is up to date. Changes to legislation, case law and commentary are rarely incorporated into the online text immediately and you are usually required to check elsewhere on the screen for updating information. The availability of updates also varies from one database to another and it may be necessary to 'migrate' to a different source to check that the law is current. You need to consider:

(a) *How the service actually displays updated material.* Is the updated information included in the text (Lawtel UK case database) or do you need to scroll to the bottom of the screen (Halsbury's Laws Direct)? Do you need to click a *stop press* button (Legislation Direct) or a coloured flag (Westlaw)?

(b) *How often the service is updated.* If the database is updated daily, does this apply to the WHOLE database or just a part of it? Case law on Lawtel is updated daily but articles are added on a weekly basis for example.

As a general rule, case law and legislation are usually updated on a daily basis or regularly (ie, 'within a few days') on an online service. Practitioner texts and loose leaf works available online are usually only updated when the printed text is published. The online service may offer frequent *commentary* but this does not form part of the text of the work and it does not mean the online version is more up to date.

CD-ROMs are updated infrequently. Check the front screen when you first log on for information about when the disk was last updated.

EXAMPLE

How do you go about changing a child's surname when the name was first registered incorrectly and where the divorced parents are in dispute as to what the correct form should be?

Stage of legal research: the question	*The answer . . .*
1. Analyse the problem: what *exactly* are you looking for?	The *procedure* for changing a minor's surname. Any relevant *legislation* and *case law.* The question assumes we *CAN* change the name but we must check *IF* we can.
2. Choose which database you are going to search.	The procedure may involve *legislation* and *case law.* Faced with such a general question *Halsbury's Laws Direct* might be best placed to offer an answer . . .
3. Select keywords. What words most accurately define the problem you are researching? (i) words offered to you in the written text (ii) alternatives to those same words (iii) concepts behind those keywords	Keywords we could search on here might be: (i) child, changing, surname (ii) children, change, changes, name, forename (iii) registration of names; divorce
4. Join keywords using appropriate connectors and wildcards . . .	Join keywords with AND connector to narrow the search down; use a wildcard to search for variations on the keywords: *child* AND chang* AND name**
5. Ensure search form is completed correctly before clicking *Search.*	Complete *Search where* box to search all of *Halsbury's Laws.* Complete *Search how box* to search 'words in any order' in the same paragraph.
6. Display a list of results . . . and search again! (i) too few results? (ii) too many results? (iii) not relevant?	Around 20 results are returned in the 'hit list.' The keywords for each result indicate that paragraph 1274 within the title *Children* may offer an answer. However you could: (i) widen the search by using the OR connector in place of an AND; or search on fewer keywords by removing one (ii) narrow the search by adding another connector and keyword. eg: *AND parent** (iii) choose keywords from a results that is more relevant and search again
7. Update your findings	Scroll to the bottom of the paragraph; the update information for *Halsbury's Laws Direct* appears at the bottom of the screen and incorporates the text of the Cumulative Supplement and monthly Noter-up. The service is updated monthly.

8.5.4 More advanced searching

8.5.4.1 Fields

Databases are made up of 'records' — a case summary on Lawtel or the full text of a law report on LexisNexis, for example. Usually those records are further divided into 'fields' (such as case name, citation, etc) that are themselves searchable. If you retrieve too many results searching the full text, try *narrowing* your search by confining it to a specific field (such as the 'catchwords' field for case law or the statute title field for legislation) where the words would only appear if they were pertinent to the main text.

8.5.4.2 Proximity searching

Searching for several keywords joined by an AND can be a problem on a full text database as one keyword may appear at the beginning of the record and the other, in an entirely different context, right at the end. Proximity searching allows the user to define how close together the keywords should be, thereby *narrowing* the search. On LexisNexis, to find the phrase *close season* in close proximity to *snipe* (say within twenty words), enter the search: *"close season"* w/20 *snipe*

8.5.4.3 Phrases

Databases vary in how they search for phrases. If you were to enter *close season* into LexisNexis or Justis, it would find records containing the exact phrase. On Butterworths Services, it would search for *close* AND *season*, unless you specified otherwise. On Westlaw, it would assume an OR between the words. Each search produces different results so if you wish to search for a phrase (or an exact word and no other variations of it), always use double quotation marks " " around the keywords. For example, *"consumer protection"* finds only documents in which these two words appear next to each other rather than anywhere within the text of a database record.

You can also combine the use of the asterisk wildcard and double quotes to search for derivatives of words next to each other — *"unfair*dismiss*"* finds *unfair dismissal* and/or *unfairly dismissed*.

8.5.5 Problematic searches

There are a few situations in which you should be aware of the limitations of electronic searching and the foibles of the particular database you are searching.

8.5.5.1 Hyphenated words

Databases vary as to whether they treat a hyphen as a space or a character. Use an OR to ensure you retrieve all variations, eg, *trademarks* OR *trade marks* OR *trade-marks*

8.5.5.2 Stop words

Most databases will not search for very common words such as *the, is, of* or *have*. Thus *breach of confidence* will produce a syntax error; use double quotation marks around the phrase.

8.5.5.3 Section numbers

When searching for a particular section of an Act, it is usually better to search on a specific field (see above). If you must search the full text avoid using the word 'section' or the abbreviation, 's'. Those terms may or may not be used in the text and inputting the section number alone will suffice. Trying to specify sub-sections is similarly counter-productive.

Use proximity searching, as the section number might appear before or after the title of the act. eg: *employment* w/4 *1998* w/15 *7*) to find s 7 of the Employment Act 1998.

8.5.5.4   Capital letters

While many databases are not case-sensitive, some (such as Butterworths Services), do retrieve different results if you enter your keywords entirely in capital letters. This can be useful for organisation names and abbreviations but is otherwise confusing. It is good practice to enter keywords in lowercase and the Boolean operators AND, OR and NOT in capitals. You can then see immediately if you've entered your search terms and connectors incorrectly.

	Butterworths Services	Lawtel	Westlaw	LexisNexis
Distinguish between search phrase with and without AND? (eg *firearms offence* or *firearms* AND *offence*)	Yes	No (assumes AND)	No (assumes AND)	Yes
Connectors allowed	AND, OR, NOT	AND, OR, NOT	AND, OR, NOT	AND, OR, NOT
Assumes plural? (eg looks for *vehicles* as well as *vehicle*)	No	No	Yes	Yes
What wildcards are used?	* truncates word ? replaces single character () eg (*dog* OR *animal, firearm* AND *ammunition*)	* at start or end of word (eg **legal* would search for illegal, legality, etc) ? replaces single character " " allows exact phrase searching eg "*professional negligence.*" () eg (*dog* OR *animal*), (*firearm* AND *ammunition*)	* replaces single character ! truncates word " " allows exact phrase searching	* replaces single character ! truncates word
Possible to search for words in proximity?	Yes, but limited. Possible to search for words in any order, in same paragraph.	No	Yes. w/n (where n is a number) searches for terms within that many words of each other. eg *alcohol w/4 bloodstream*	Yes. w/n (where n is a number) searches for terms within that many words of each other. eg *alcohol w/4 bloodstream*

Legal research technique

9.1 Diagrams

The diagrams which follow are meant to offer suggested methical sequences for tackling basic research. They are necessarily very generalised and introductory. After a few exercises you will able to dispense with them.

The diagrams are not self-sufficient or self-explanatory. They presuppose that you have read the relevant sections of the text of the preceding chapters, and have some familiarity with the sources there described.

The emphasis in the diagrams is on research using books rather than electronic sources. Generally speaking, when starting cold on unfamiliar law, it is better to start with hard-copy than going straight to the screens. Browse the indexes which lead into and open up the subject. Then browse the subject-area to get a good initial grasp of its scope and makeup, its criteria and policy.

Suggested technique

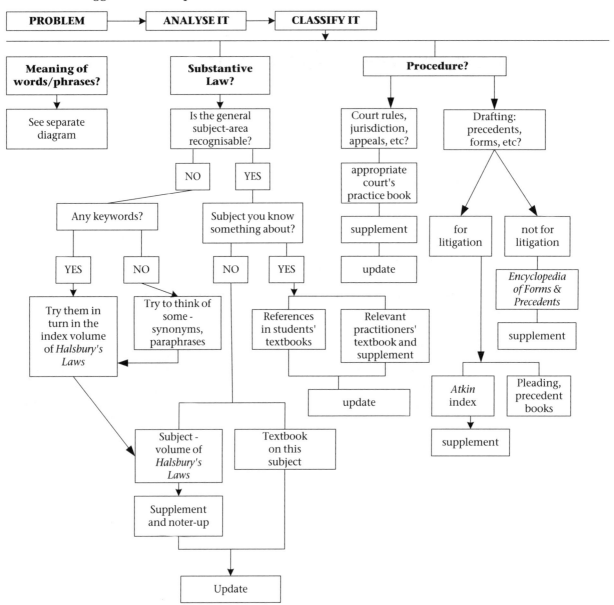

Notes

1. This diagram is only a rudimentary outline, indicating the main directions you might usefully follow in problem-solving. In so far as you find it states the obvious, you must already have some skill or instinct for basic research.

2. Paper sources are in rectangles; electronic sources are circled. As explained, the emphasis is on paper sources as being the more useful at this stage, and also to avoid overloading the diagrams.

3. If you follow a particular line and the result or lack of result suggests that your original classification was incorrect, go back and start again at the appropriate heading.

4. 'Update' means you must go through the appropriate updating sources, some of which are indicated in the 'Law Known' line. Which particular method of updating you should use will depend on the case(s), statute(s), SI(s) or whatever you have found to be the source of the law.

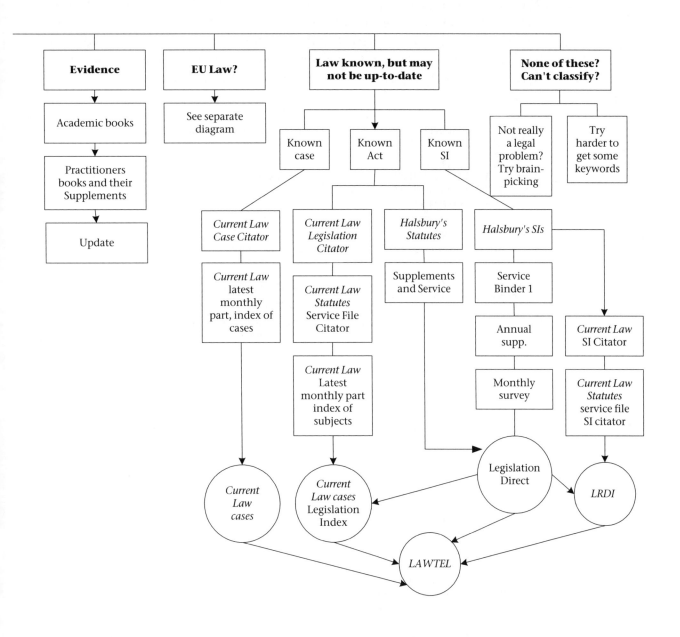

5. The distinction between *Atkin's Court Forms* and *Encyclopedia of Forms and Precedents* as being litigious/non-litigious is not clear-cut. It is sometimes helpful to look in the index to the other set if you draw a blank with the set indicated.

Words and phrases in statutes, etc

There follows a suggested sequence for construing their meaning. It may also be used for construing documents, by analogy; and when drafting your own. The sequence may not need to be followed through every stage if a definition or interpretation is revealed early, eg, in the annotations to a statute. Similarly, if a meaning before or after a specific date is sought, CLYB or Halsbury's Annual Abridgment may be a useful approach.

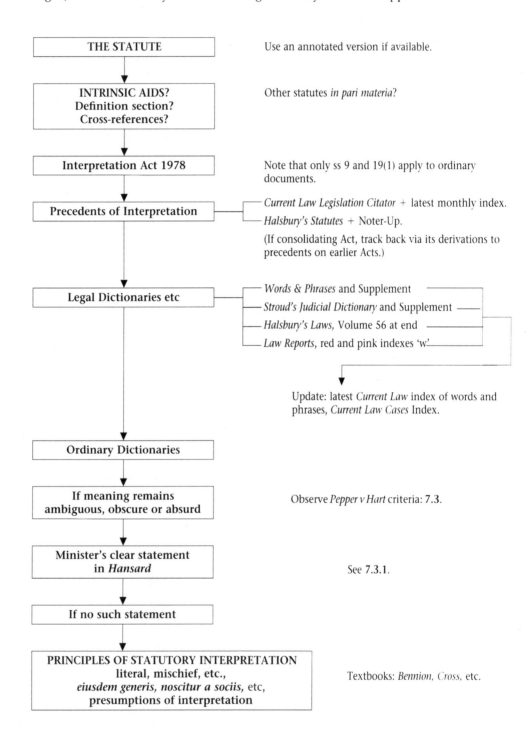

THE STATUTE — Use an annotated version if available.

INTRINSIC AIDS?
Definition section?
Cross-references? — Other statutes *in pari materia*?

Interpretation Act 1978 — Note that only ss 9 and 19(1) apply to ordinary documents.

Precedents of Interpretation
— *Current Law Legislation Citator* + latest monthly index.
— *Halsbury's Statutes* + Noter-Up.
(If consolidating Act, track back via its derivations to precedents on earlier Acts.)

Legal Dictionaries etc
— *Words & Phrases* and Supplement
— *Stroud's Judicial Dictionary* and Supplement
— *Halsbury's Laws,* Volume 56 at end
— *Law Reports,* red and pink indexes 'w'.

Update: latest *Current Law* index of words and phrases, *Current Law Cases* Index.

Ordinary Dictionaries

If meaning remains ambiguous, obscure or absurd — Observe *Pepper v Hart* criteria: 7.3.

Minister's clear statement in *Hansard* — See 7.3.1.

If no such statement

PRINCIPLES OF STATUTORY INTERPRETATION
literal, mischief, etc.,
***eiusdem generis, noscitur a sociis,* etc,**
presumptions of interpretation — Textbooks: *Bennion, Cross,* etc.

Researching European Community Law

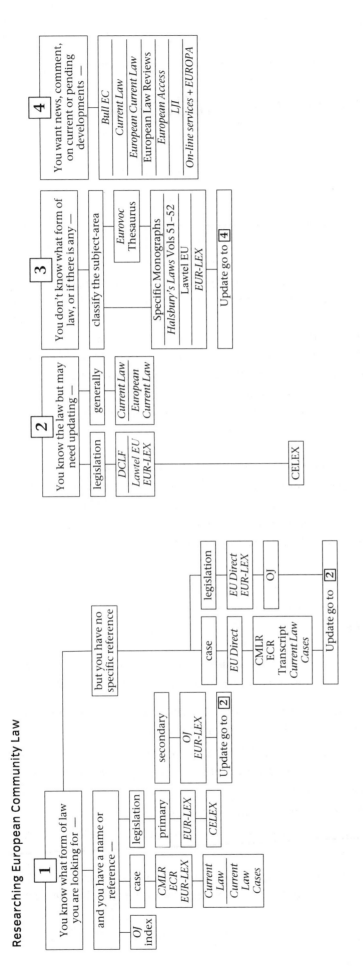

KEY

Bull, EC	Bulletin of the European Communities (official publication).
CMLR	Common Market Law Reports.
Current Law	the English monthly (Sweet & Maxwell).
Current Law Cases	CLI on line.
DCLF	Directory of Community Legislation in Force (Official publication).
ECR	European Court Reports (official publication).
Encyclopedia	Encyclopaedia of European Community Law (Sweet & Maxwell).
EU Direct	Butterworths on-line.
EUR-LEX	http://europa.eu.int/eur-lex
EUROPA	http://europa.eu.int
European Current Law	English monthly (Sweet & Maxwell).
Eurovoc	Eurovoc Thesaurus (official publication).
LJI	Legal Journals Index — on-line.
OJ	Official Journal of the European Communities.

10

Legal sources for the practitioner

10.1 Introduction

Legal textbooks such as *Street on Torts* or the popular *Blackstone's Guides* are excellent for students but they are rarely used in practice and are usually not authoritative enough to cite in court. Practitioners use more specialist and practical texts in their legal research. Similarly, students are introduced to a plethora of online legal databases whilst in the academic community but few chambers will take more than one of the major legal databases described in **Chapter 8**. Many chambers do not have access to the larger legal databases at all, except through their Inn library.

For these reasons alone, it is important that during the course, you become familiar with the leading printed texts and online services and begin to use them in your practical work for the course and thereafter in pupillage. In conducting your legal research, you will need to call on a variety of different sources available in both printed and electronic formats. In practice, you will not have the option of relying solely on electronic databases or indeed solely on printed works. That said, many chambers do have good libraries and all will have at least a core collection of primary and secondary legal materials, drawing on the Inn libraries for more specialised legal texts and databases.

10.2 Types of legal sources

The main sources for practitioners' legal research can be classified into the following types. Many of these can often be accessed in both printed and electronic format:

- *legal encyclopaedias* such as *Halsbury's Laws, Current Law*, etc are excellent and authoritative tools and a good starting point for legal research;
- *legal dictionaries* such as *Stroud's Judicial Dictionary* or *Words and Phrases Legally Defined* combine statutory and case law definitions of words in one reference work — a quick shortcut in legal research;
- *law reports* provide detailed analysis of individual cases;
- *journals* offer discussion of recent case law, legislation and legal practice in general, or in specific subject areas;
- *practitioner texts and loose-leaf works* (or their electronic equivalents) provide more indepth coverage of the law and it is these texts that form the 'meat' of the practitioners' legal resources.

10.3   Updating legal sources

10.3.1   Printed texts

Books are out of date as soon as they are printed and most practitioner texts are not published annually. Always use the latest edition of any printed text and check to see if it has itself been updated by another publication. Publishers update their texts using a combination of one or more of the following:

- *cumulative supplements:* hardback volumes for legal encyclopaedias such as *Halsbury's Laws, Atkins Court Forms* etc; paperback supplements for practitioner works (eg, 1st supplement to *McGregor on Damages*, 4th supplement to *Stroud's Judicial Dictionary* etc);
- *loose-leaf noter-ups:* loose sheets housed in a separate hardback binder (eg, *Halsbury's Laws*);
- *loose bulletins, inserts or newsletters* (eg, *Wilkinson's Road Traffic Bulletin*);
- *online updates* using an internet service — a relatively recent means of updating but it may become more common in the future (eg, *Blackstone's Criminal Practice — Monthly Update* via *Crime Online*).

It is also important to know whether the law within the printed text is up-to-date. Consider the following:

- *new editions and/or supplements:* check for a statement '*the law is as stated at . . . [date]*' or '*up to date to . . . [date]*', usually located at the end of the preface or shortly after the title page;
- *loose-leaf noter-up:* look at loose-leaf issue numbers and the filing record located to the front or rear of the first or last volumes in the set;
- *online updates:* look for a statement when you log on to the publisher's web page.

Note that if the commentary within the practitioners' text refers to legislation or case law, you may need to bring those authorities more up to date using an electronic database or another printed source.

10.3.2   Electronic sources

You should be aware that not all electronic services are updated as frequently as you might think — just because it is online does not mean a source is any more up-to-date than its printed equivalent. Updating electronic sources is dealt with in more detail in **Chapter 8** at **8.5.3**.

10.4   Legal sources for the practitioner: a bibliography

The list of books, law reports, journals and electronic sources that follows, offers a subject guide to some of the leading sources within each field of law. It is by no means a comprehensive list and there are many excellent practical legal works that are not listed here.

Works usually updated by one or more supplements before the publication of a new edition are indicated in the text. Most of the loose-leaf works referred to, are available on CD-ROM or by subscription via an online service — more details can be obtained direct from the publisher. The main commercial legal databases are described in more detail in **Chapter 8** at **8.3**; a guide to free legal resources on the internet is at **8.4.3**.

10.4.1   Legal encyclopaedias

Atkins' Encyclopaedia of Court Forms in Civil Procedure, 2nd edn (LexisNexis). Updated by reissued volumes and loose-leaf noter-up.

Current Law Cases and *Current Law Statutes* (Sweet & Maxwell). Includes *Yearbooks* and *Citator*. Updated by *Current Law Monthly Digest*. Available online via Westlaw.

The Digest: annotated British, Commonwealth and European cases, 3rd edn (LexisNexis). Updated by regular reissued volumes, annual *Cumulative Supplement* and quarterly *Survey*.

The Encyclopaedia of Forms and Precedents, 5th edn (LexisNexis). Updated by reissued volumes and loose-leaf noter-up. Available online via Butterworths Services.

Halsbury's Laws of England, 4th edn reissue. (LexisNexis). Updated by regular reissued volumes, annual *Cumulative Supplement* and monthly *Current Service Noter-up*.

Halsbury's Statutes of England and Wales, 4th edn (LexisNexis). Updated by regular reissued volumes, annual *Cumulative Supplement* and monthly *Current Service Noter-up*.

10.4.2   Legal dictionaries

Stroud's Judicial Dictionary of Words and Phrases, 6th edn (Sweet & Maxwell). Updated by supplement.

Words and Phrases Legally Defined, 3rd edn (LexisNexis). Updated by supplement.

10.4.3   Law reports

The principal series of 'general' law reports are listed below. For a more detailed analysis of the key series of law reports, refer to **Chapter 3** at **3.6**. Other law reports are listed by subject matter at **10.4.5**.

All England Law Reports, 1936–. (LexisNexis).

The Law Reports (The Incorporated Council of Law Reporting for England and Wales). Known as *The Official Series*. For details of individual series, see the table below.

The Law Reports	*Citation*	*The Law Reports*	*Citation*
Admiralty & Ecclesiastical	LRA & E	Exchequer Division	Ex D
Appeal Cases	AC	Family Division	Fam
Chancery Appeals	Ch App	King's Bench	KB
Chancery Division	Ch D	Privy Council	LR PC
Common Pleas	CP	Probate & Divorce	LR P&D
Common Pleas Division	CPD	Probate Division	PD
Crown Cases Reserved	LR CCR	Probate Division	P
English & Irish Appeals	LR HL	Queen's Bench	QB
Equity	LR Eq	Queen's Bench Division	QBD
Exchequer	LR Ex	Scotch & Divorce Appeals	Sc & D

Weekly Law Reports, 1953–. (The Incorporated Council of Law Reporting for England and Wales).

10.4.4 Journals

Key journals of a general legal nature are listed below. These will keep the reader up to date with legal news and current legal issues. Other journals are listed by subject matter at **10.4.5**.

Counsel: incorporating Bar News. (Bar Council).
The Law Society's Gazette. (Law Society). Available online at www.lawgazette.co.uk
The Lawyer. Available online at www.the-lawyer.co.uk
Legal Week. (Legal Week). Available online at www.legalweek.net
New Law Journal. (LexisNexis). Available online via LexisNexis.
Solicitors' Journal. (Sweet & Maxwell).

10.4.5 Legal sources — by subject area

Administrative Law
See also: **Civil Litigation**
See also: **Criminal litigation**
Administrative Court Digest, law reports (Sweet & Maxwell).
De Smith, Woolf & Jowell, *Judicial Review of Administrative Action*, 6th edn (Sweet & Maxwell, 2002). Updated by supplement.
Fordham, *Judicial Review Handbook*, 4th edn (Hart Publishing, 2004).
Lewis, *Judicial Remedies in Public Law*, 3rd edn (Sweet & Maxwell, 2004). Updated by supplement.
Supperstone & Goudie, *Judicial Review*, 3rd edn (LexisNexis, 2005).
Wade & Forsyth, *Administrative Law*, 9th edn (Oxford University Press, 2004).

Agency
Bowstead & Reynolds, *Law of Agency*, 17th edn (Sweet & Maxwell, 2001). Updated by supplement.

Arbitration
Arbitration Law Monthly, journal (Informa Publishing).
Lloyds Arbitration Reports, law reports (Lloyds).
Mustill & Boyd, *The Law and Practice of Commercial Arbitration in England*, 2nd edn (Butterworths, 1989). Updated by companion volume (2001).

Banking
Banking Law Direct, online service (Butterworths Services).
Byles, *Bills of Exchange*, 27th edn (Sweet & Maxwell, 2001).
Encyclopaedia of Banking Law, loose-leaf. (LexisNexis). Available online via *Banking Law Direct*.
Guest, *Chalmers & Guest on Bills of Exchange*, 16th edn (Sweet & Maxwell, 2005).
Hapgood, *Paget's Law of Banking*, 12th edn (Butterworths, 2002). Available online via *Banking Law Direct*.

Bankruptcy and Personal Insolvency
Dennis, *The New Law of Insolvency* (Law Society, 2003).
Bankruptcy and Personal Insolvency Reports, law reports (Jordans).

Insolvency Law Direct, online service (Butterworths Services).

Muir Hunter on Personal Insolvency, loose-leaf (Sweet & Maxwell).

Totty & Moss, *Insolvency*, loose-leaf (Sweet & Maxwell). Available online via Westlaw.

Building

Construction Law Direct, online service (Butterworths Services).

Construction Law Journal, journal (Sweet & Maxwell).

Construction Law Reports, law reports (LexisNexis).

Emden's Construction Law, loose-leaf (LexisNexis).

Keating on Building Contracts, 7th edn (Sweet & Maxwell, 2003). Updated by supplement.

Charities

Tudor, *Tudor on Charities*, 9th edn (Sweet & Maxwell, 2003). Updated by supplement.

Children

See also: **Family Law**

Child & Family Law Quarterly, journal (Jordan).

Childright, journal (University of Essex).

Clarke, Hall & Morrison on Children, loose-leaf (LexisNexis). Available online via *Family & Child Law Direct*.

Hershman & McFarlane, *Children Law and Practice*, loose-leaf (Jordans).

Civil Litigation

See also: **Administrative Law**

See also: **Costs**

Blackstone's Civil Practice, annual (Oxford University Press). Available online via Lawtel.

Bullen & Leake & Jacob's Precedents of Pleadings, 15th edn (Sweet & Maxwell, 2004). Available online via Westlaw.

Butterworths Civil Court Precedents, loose-leaf (LexisNexis).

The Civil Court Practice ('The Green Book'), annual (LexisNexis). Updated by supplements and regular reissues. Available online via *GreenBook.co.uk*.

Civil Procedure Online, online service (Butterworths Services).

Civil Procedure ('The White Book'), annual (Sweet & Maxwell). Updated by supplements and regular reissues. Available online via Westlaw.

GreenBook.co.uk, online service (Butterworths Services).

Lawtel Civil Procedure, online service (Lawtel/Sweet & Maxwell).

Practical Civil Court Precedents, loose-leaf (Sweet & Maxwell).

Rose, *Pleadings without tears: a guide to legal drafting under the Civil Procedure Rules*, 6th edn (Oxford University Press, 2002).

Westlaw UK Civil Procedure, online service (Sweet & Maxwell).

Company and Commercial Law

All England Law Reports: Commercial Cases, 1996–. (LexisNexis).

British Company Law and Practice, loose-leaf (CCH).

British Company Cases, law reports (CCH).

Butterworths Company Law Cases, law reports (LexisNexis).

Butterworths Company Law Service, loose-leaf (LexisNexis).

Butterworths Corporate Law Service, loose-leaf (LexisNexis). Available online via *Corporate Law Direct*.

Company Lawyer, journal (Sweet & Maxwell).

Corporate Law Direct, online service (Butterworths Services).

Gore-Browne on Companies, 44th edn loose-leaf (Jordans).

Journal of Business Law, journal (Sweet & Maxwell).

Law, *Company Formation*, loose-leaf (Butterworths Tolley).

Palmer's Company Law, loose-leaf (Sweet & Maxwell). Available online via Westlaw.

PLC Magazine, journal (Practical Law for Companies)

PLC Competitiion, Corporate, Property, database services (Practical Law for Companies).

Roberts, *Law Relating to Financial Services*, 5th edn (Financial World Publishing, 2003)

Westlaw UK Corporate Business, online service (Sweet & Maxwell).

Competition Law

Bellamy & Child, *European Community Law of Competition*, 5th edn (Sweet & Maxwell, 2001).

Butterworths Competition Law, loose-leaf (LexisNexis).

Common Market Law Reports, law reports (Sweet & Maxwell).

Common Market Law Review, journal (Kluwer).

European Competition Law Review, journal (ESC Publishing).

Korah, *An Introductory Guide to EC Competition Law and Practice*, 8th edn (Hart Publishing, 2004).

Sweet & Maxwell's Encyclopedia of Competition Law, loose-leaf (Sweet & Maxwell).

Whish, *Competition Law*, 5th edn (Butterworths, 2003).

Conflict of Laws

Cheshire & North, *Private International Law*, 13th edn (Butterworths, 1999).

Dicey & Morris, *Conflict of Laws*, 13th edn (Sweet & Maxwell, 2001). Updated by supplement.

Contract

Chitty & Beale, *Chitty on Contracts*, 29th edn (Sweet & Maxwell, 2004). Updated by supplement.

Goff & Jones, *Law of Restitution*, 6th edn (Sweet & Maxwell, 2002). Updated by supplement.

Conveyancing

See also **Real property**

Emmet & Farrand, *Emmet on Title*, loose-leaf (Sweet & Maxwell).

Encyclopedia of Compulsory Purchase, loose-leaf & CD-ROM (Sweet & Maxwell).

Fisher *Fisher & Lightwood's Law of Mortgage*, 11th edn (Butterworths, 1999). Updated by supplement.

Ruoff & Roper, *Law and Practice of Registered Conveyancing*, loose-leaf & CD-ROM, (Sweet & Maxwell).

Silverman, *The Law Society's Conveyancing Handbook*, annual (Law Society).

Sweet & Maxwell's Conveyancing Practice, loose-leaf (Sweet & Maxwell).

Coroners

Burton & Mathews, *Jervis on the Office and Duties of Coroners: with forms and precedents*, 12th edn (Sweet & Maxwell, 2002). Updated by supplement.

Costs

See also: **Civil Litigation**

See also: **Criminal litigation**

Butterworths Costs Service, Loose-leaf(LexisNexis).

Cook on Costs, annual (LexisNexis).

Crime

See also: **Sentencing**

Archbold, *Criminal Pleading, Evidence and Practice*, annual (Sweet & Maxwell). Updated by supplement. Available online via Westlaw.

Blackstone's Criminal Practice, annual (Oxford University Press). Available online via *Crime Online*.

Crime Online, online service (Butterworths Services).

Criminal Appeal Reports, law reports (Sweet & Maxwell).

Criminal Law Review, journal (Sweet & Maxwell).

Westlaw UK Crime, online service (Sweet & Maxwell).

Wilkinson's Road Traffic Offences, 21st edn (Sweet & Maxwell, 2004). Updated by supplement.

Criminal Litigation

See also: **Administrative Law**

See also: **Costs**

Anthony & Berryman, *Magistrates' Court Guide*, annual (LexisNexis).

Archbold, *Criminal Pleading, Evidence and Practice*, annual (Sweet & Maxwell). Updated by supplement. Available online via Westlaw.

Blackstone's Criminal Practice, annual (Oxford University Press). Updated by online monthly update. Available online via *Crime Online*.

Stone's Justices' Manual, annual (LexisNexis). Available on CD-ROM and online via Butterworths Services.

Damages

See also: **Personal Injury**

Allen, *APIL Guide to Damages*. (Jordans, 2004).

Bell, *Guidelines for the assessment of Damages in Personal Injury Cases*, annual (Judicial Studies Board / Oxford University Press). Available online via Lawtel.

Kemp & Kemp Quantum of Damages in Personal Injury and Fatal Accident Claims, loose-leaf & CD-ROM (Sweet & Maxwell).

Lawtel Personal Injury, online service (Lawtel / Sweet & Maxwell).

McGregor, *Damages*, 17th edn (Sweet & Maxwell, 2003). Updated by supplement.

Personal Injury and Quantum Reports, law reports (Sweet & Maxwell).

Wilde, *Facts and Figures: tables for the calculation of damages*, annual (Professional Negligence Bar Association / Sweet & Maxwell, 2003).

Data Protection

Carey, *Data Protection Handbook*, (Law Society, 2004).

Encyclopedia of Data Protection, loose-leaf (Sweet & Maxwell).

E-Commerce

See: **Information Technology**

Ecclesiastical Law

Hill, *Ecclesiastical Law*, 2nd edn (Butterworths, 2001).

Education

Hyams, *The Law of Education*, 2nd edn (Jordans, 2004).

The Law of Education, loose-leaf (LexisNexis). Available online via *Local Government Law Direct*.

Employment Law

See also: **Health and Safety**

Employment Law Journal, journal (Legalease).

Employment Law Online, online service (Butterworths Services).
Encyclopedia of Employment Law and Practice, loose-leaf (Sweet & Maxwell).
Employment Law Journal, journal (Legalease).
Harvey on Industrial relations and Employment Law, loose-leaf (LexisNexis).
Available online via *Employment Law Online*.
Industrial Cases Reports, law reports (Incorporated Council of Law Reporting).
Industrial Relations Law Reports, law reports (LexisNexis).

Environmental Law
Encyclopedia of Environmental Health Law and Practice, loose-leaf (Sweet & Maxwell).
Encyclopedia of Environmental Law and Practice, 2nd edn loose-leaf (Sweet & Maxwell).
Environmental Law Reports, law reports (Sweet & Maxwell).
Garner's Environmental Law, loose-leaf (LexisNexis). Available online via *Local Government Law Direct*.

Equity and Trusts
Snell, *Equity*, 31st edn (Sweet & Maxwell, 2004). Updated by supplement.
Underhill & Hayton, *Law Relating to Trustees*, 16th edn (Butterworths, 2002).

European Community Law
See also: **Competition Law**
All England Law Reports: European Cases, 1983–. (LexisNexis).
Encyclopedia of European Community Law, loose-leaf (Sweet & Maxwell).
European Law Review, journal (Sweet & Maxwell).
Vaughan, *Law of the European Communities*, loose-leaf (LexisNexis).

Evidence
Cross & Tapper, *Evidence*, 10th edn (LexisNexis, 2004).
Dennis, *The Law of Evidence*, (Sweet & Maxwell, 2002).
Keane, *The Modern Law of Evidence*, 6th edn (Butterworths, 2005).
May, *Criminal Evidence*, 5th edn (Sweet & Maxwell, 2004).
Phipson, *On Evidence*, 6th edn (Sweet & Maxwell, 2004). Updated by supplement.

Family Law
See also: **Children**
Bird, *Ancillary Relief Handbook*, 4th edn (Jordans, 2003).
Butterworths Family Law Service, loose-leaf (LexisNexis). Available online via *Family & Child Law Direct*.
Family and Child Law Direct, online service (Butterworths Services).
Family Court Reports, law reports (LexisNexis).
Family Law, journal (Jordans).
Family Law Reports, law reports (Jordans).
Jackson, *Matrimonial Finance and Taxation*, 7th edn (Butterworths, 2002). Available online via *Family & Child Law Direct*.
Practical Matrimonial Precedents, loose-leaf & CD-ROM. (Sweet & Maxwell).
Rayden & Jackson's Divorce and Family Matters, 17th edn, loose-leaf. (LexisNexis). Available online via *Family & Child Law Direct*.
Singer & Parker, *Essential Family Practice*, annual (LexisNexis). Updated by supplement. Available online *Family & Child Law Direct*.

Forms & Precedents
See also: **Civil Litigation**

See also: **Criminal litigation**

See also: Individual subject areas

Atkins' Encyclopaedia of Court Forms in Civil Procedure, 2nd edn (LexisNexis). Updated by reissued volumes and loose-leaf noter-up.

The Court Service, online service at www.courtservice.gov.uk (Court Service).

The Encyclopaedia of Forms and Precedents, 5th edn (Butterworths). Updated by reissued volumes and loose-leaf noter-up. Available online via Butterworths Services.

EveryForm, online service at www.everyform.co.uk or via Butterworths Services.

Kelly, *Kelly's Draftsman*, 18th edn (Butterworths, 2003).

Health & Safety

See also: **Employment**

Encyclopedia of Health and Safety at Work Law and Practice, loose-leaf (Sweet & Maxwell).

Hendy, *Redgrave's Health and Safety*, 4th edn (Butterworths, 2002). Updated by supplement. Available online via HSE Direct.

HSE Direct, online service (Butterworths Services).

Housing Law

Arden & Partington, *Housing Law*, 2nd edn, loose-leaf (Sweet & Maxwell).

Dowding, *Dilapidations: the modern law and practice* 3rd edn (Sweet & Maxwell, 2004).

Encyclopedia of Housing Law and Practice, loose-leaf (Sweet & Maxwell).

Housing Law Reports, law reports (Sweet & Maxwell).

Human Rights

Emmerson, *Human Rights and Criminal Justice*, 2nd edn (Sweet & Maxwell, 2004).

European Human Rights Reports, law reports (Sweet & Maxwell).

Human Rights Direct, online service (Butterworths Services).

Human Rights Practice, loose-leaf (Sweet & Maxwell). Available online via Westlaw.

Lester & Pannick, *Human Rights Law and Practice*, 2nd edn (LexisNexis, 2004). Available online via *Human Rights Direct*.

Westlaw UK Human Rights, online service (Sweet & Maxwell).

Immigration Law

Butterworths Immigration Law Service, loose-leaf (LexisNexis). Available online via *Immigration and Asylum Law Online*.

Immigration and Asylum Law Online, online service (LexisNexis).

MacDonald, *Immigration Law and Practice*, 6th edn (LexisNexis, 2004). Available online via *Immigration and Asylum Law Online*.

Information Technology

Computers and law, journal (Society for Computers and Law).

Encyclopedia of Information Technology Law, loose-leaf (Sweet & Maxwell).

Journal of Information Law and Technology, journal (University of Warwick). Available online at http://elj.warwick.ac.uk/jilt

Lloyd, *Information Technology Law*, 4th edn (Oxford University Press, 2004).

Insolvency

See: **Bankruptcy and Personal Insolvency**

Insurance

Birds, *Birds' Modern Insurance Law*, 6th edn (Sweet & Maxwell, 2004).

Birds, *MacGillivray on Insurance Law*, 10th edn (Sweet & Maxwell, 2002).

Encyclopedia of Insurance Law, loose-leaf (Sweet & Maxwell).

Lloyds Law Reports: Insurance and Reinsurance, law report(Lloyds).

Intellectual Property

Copinger & Skone Jones on Copyright, 15th edn (Sweet & Maxwell, 2005). Updated by supplement. Available online via Westlaw.

Cornish, *Intellectual Property Patents, Copyright, Trademarks and Allied Rights*, 5th edn (Sweet & Maxwell, 2003).

Encyclopedia of United Kingdom and European Patent Law, loose-leaf (Sweet & Maxwell).

Fleet Street Reports, law reports (Sweet & Maxwell).

Intellectual Property and Technology Direct, online service (Butterworths Services).

Kerly's Law of Trade Marks and Trade Names, 14th edn (Sweet & Maxwell, 2005). Available online via Westlaw.

Laddie, *Modern Law of Copyright*. 3rd edn (Butterworths, 2000). Available online via *Intellectual Property and Technology Direct*.

Merkin & Black, *Copyright and Designs Law*, loose-leaf (Sweet & Maxwell).

Terrell on the Law of Patents, 16th edn (Sweet & Maxwell, 2000). Available online via Westlaw.

Westlaw UK Intellectual Property, online service (Sweet & Maxwell).

Landlord and Tenant

See also: **Housing**

Commercial Property Law Direct, online service (Butterworths Services).

Hill and Redman's Law of Landlord and Tenant, loose-leaf (LexisNexis). Available online via *Commercial Property Law Direct*.

The Landlord and Tenant Factbook, loose-leaf (Sweet & Maxwell).

Landlord and Tenant Reports, law reports (Sweet & Maxwell).

Smith, *The Law of Landlord and Tenant*, 6th edn (Butterworths, 2002).

Westlaw UK Landlord and Tenant, online service (Sweet & Maxwell).

Woodfall's Law of Landlord and Tenant, loose-leaf (Sweet & Maxwell). Available online via Westlaw.

Legal Profession

Birds & Weir, *The Law, Practice and Conduct of Solicitors* (Waterlow, 1989).

Boon & Levin, *The Ethics and Conduct of Lawyers in England and Wales* (Hart, 1999).

Code of Conduct of the Bar of England and Wales, 8th edn (Bar Council, 2004).

The Consolidated Regulations of the Inns of Court and the General Council of the Bar. (Bar Council, 2003).

Cordery on Solicitors, loose-leaf (LexisNexis).

The Guide to the Professional Conduct of Solicitors, 8th edn (Law Society, 1999).

Solicitors' Accounts Manual, 9th edn (Law Society, 2004).

Legal Skills

Beardsmore, *Opinion writing and drafting in tort* (Cavendish, 1996).

Bennion, *Statutory Interpretation: a code*, 4th edn (Butterworths, 2002). Updated by supplement.

Blake, *A Practical Approach to Effective Litigation*, 6th edn (Blackstone/Oxford University Press, 2005).

Fridd, *Basic Practice in Courts, Tribunals and Enquiries*, 3rd edn (Sweet & Maxwell, 2000).

Holborn, *Butterworths Legal Research Guide* (Butterworth, 2001).

Hyam, *Advocacy Skills*, 4th edn (Blackstone, 1999).

Munkman, *The Technique of Advocacy* (Butterworths, 1991).

Libel

Carter-Ruck, *Libel and Slander*, 5th edn (Butterworths, 1997).

Gatley, *Libel and Slander*, 10th edn (Sweet & Maxwell, 2003). Updated by supplement.

Licensing

Entertainment and Media Law Reports, law reports (Sweet & Maxwell).

Hyde, *Licensing Procedures and Precedents Manual*, loose-leaf (Sweet & Maxwell).

Licensing Law Online, online service (Butterworths Services).

Paterson, *Paterson's Licensing Acts*, annual (LexisNexis).

Local Government

Bailey, *Cross on Principles of Local Government Law,* 3rd edn (Sweet & Maxwell, 2004).

Cross on Local Government Law, 8th edn loose-leaf (Sweet & Maxwell).

Encyclopedia of Local Government Law, loose-leaf (Sweet & Maxwell).

Encyclopedia of Rating and Local Taxation, loose-leaf (Sweet & Maxwell).

Lawtel Local Government, online service (Sweet & Maxwell).

Local Government Direct, online service (Butterworths Services).

Ryde on Rating and the Council Tax, loose-leaf (LexisNexis). Available online via *Local Government Direct*.

Maritime Law

Baughen, *Shipping Law,* 3rd edn (Cavendish, 2004).

Carver on Bills of Trading, 15th edn (Sweet & Maxwell, 2005).

Hill, *Maritime Law*, 6th edn (LLP, 2004).

Lloyds Law Reports, law report (Lloyds).

Lloyds Maritime and Commercial Law Quarterly, journal (Lloyds).

Sassoon & Merren, *CIF and FOB Contracts*, 4th edn (Sweet & Maxwell, 1995).

Scrutton on Charterparties and Bills of Lading, 20th edn (Sweet & Maxwell, 1996).

Thomas, *Modern Law of Marine Insurance* (LLP, 2004).

Medical Law

Grubb, *Principles of Medical Law*, 2nd edn (Oxford University Press, 2004).

Lloyds Law Reports: Medical, law report (Lloyds).

Malsher, *Medical Records for Lawyers* (EMIS, 2002).

Montgomery, *Health Care Law*, 3rd edn (Oxford University Press, 2005).

Palmer, *Medicine for Lawyers* (Royal Society of Medicine, 2004).

Powers & Harris, *Clinical Negligence*, 3rd edn (Butterworths, 1999).

Mental Health

Mental Health Services: law and practice, loose-leaf (Shaw & Sons).

Heywood & Massey, *Court of Protection Practice*, loose-leaf, 13th edn (Sweet & Maxwell).

Journal of Mental Health Law, journal (Northumbria Law Press).

Lush, *Cretney & Lush on Enduring Powers of Attorney*, 5th edn (Jordans, 2001).

Negligence

See: **Torts**

Partnership

Encyclopedia of Professional Partnerships, loose-leaf (Sweet & Maxwell).

Lindley & Banks, *Lindley & Banks on Partnership*, 18th edn (Sweet & Maxwell, 2002). Updated by supplement.

Personal Injury

See also: **Damages**

Buchan, *Personal Injury Practice: the guide to litigation in the County Court and High Court*. 4th edn (LexisNexis, 2003).

Butterworths Personal Injury Litigation Service, loose-leaf (LexisNexis). Available online *PI Online*.

Curran, *Personal Injury Pleadings,* 2nd edn (Sweet & Maxwell, 2000).

Journal of Personal Injury Law, journal (Sweet & Maxwell).

Lawtel Personal Injury, online service (Lawtel / Sweet & Maxwell).

Personal Injury and Quantum Reports, law reports (Sweet & Maxwell).

PI Online, online service (Butterworths Services).

Solomon, *Personal Injury Practice and Procedure*. 11th edn (Sweet & Maxwell, 2005).

Planning Law

Butterworths Planning Law Service, loose-leaf (LexisNexis). Available online via *Local Government Law Direct*.

Encyclopedia of Planning Law and Practice, loose-leaf (Sweet & Maxwell).

Estate Gazette Law Reports, law reports (Estates Gazette).

Journal of Planning and Environmental Law, journal (Sweet & Maxwell).

Planning Law Reports, law reports (Estates Gazette).

Property, Planning and Compensation Reports, law reports (Sweet & Maxwell).

Rating
See: **Local Government**

Real Property
See also: **Conveyancing**

Butterworths Property Law Service, loose-leaf (LexisNexis).

Encyclopedia of Compulsory Purchase, loose-leaf (Sweet & Maxwell).

Estates Gazette Law Reports, law reports (Estates Gazette).

Megarry & Wade, *The Law of Real Property*, 6th edn (Sweet & Maxwell, 2000).

Property Planning and Compensation Reports, law reports (Sweet & Maxwell).

Sara, *Boundaries and Easements*, 3rd edn (Sweet & Maxwell, 2002).Updated by supplement.

Road Traffic Law

Bingham & Berryman's Motor Claims Cases, 11th edn (Butterworths, 2000). Updated by supplement.

Butterworths Road Traffic Service, loose-leaf (LexisNexis).

Encyclopedia of Highway Law and Practice, loose-leaf (Sweet & Maxwell).

Encyclopedia of Road Traffic Law and Practice, loose-leaf (Sweet & Maxwell).

Road Traffic Reports, law reports (Sweet & Maxwell).

Wilkinson's Road Traffic Offences, 21st edn (Sweet & Maxwell, 2003) Updated by supplement.

Sale of Goods & Consumer Law

Atiyah, *Sale of Goods*, 11th edn (Pearson/Longman 2005).

Benjamin, *Sale of Goods*, 6th edn (Sweet & Maxwell, 2002). Updated by supplement.

Butterworths Law of Food and Drugs, loose-leaf (LexisNexis). Available online via *Local Government Law Direct*.

Butterworths Trading and Consumer Law, loose-leaf (LexisNexis). Available online via *Local Government Law Direct*.

Encyclopedia of Consumer Credit Law, loose-leaf (Sweet & Maxwell).

Encyclopedia of Consumer Law, loose-leaf (Sweet & Maxwell).

Goode, *Consumer Credit Law & Practice*, loose-leaf (LexisNexis).

Miller, *Product Liability and Safety Encyclopaedia*, loose-leaf (LexisNexis). Available online via *Local Government Law Direct*.

O'Keefe, *Law of Weights and Measures*, loose-leaf (LexisNexis). Available online via *Local Government Law Direct*.

O'Keefe & Smith, *Law Relating to Trade Descriptions*, loose-leaf (LexisNexis).

Sentencing
See also: **Crime**

Criminal Appeal Reports (*Sentencing*), law reports (Sweet & Maxwell).

Magistrates Bench Handbook: *a manual for lay magistrates*, loose-leaf (Waterside).

Thomas, *Current Sentencing Practice*, loose-leaf (Sweet & Maxwell). Available online via Westlaw.

Thomas, *Sentencing Referencer* (Sweet & Maxwell, 2004).

Wasik, *Emmins on Sentencing*, 4th edn (Blackstone Press, 2001).

Shipping
See Maritime law

Social Security and Welfare Law

Encyclopedia of Social Services and Child Care Law, loose-leaf (Sweet & Maxwell).

Journal of Social Welfare and Family Law, journal (Routledge).

Social Security and State Benefits Handbook, annual (LexisNexis Tolley).

Wikely & Ogus, *Law of Social Security*, 5th edn (Butterworths, 2002)

Taxation
See also: **Local Government**

Bramwell, *Taxation of Companies*, 8th edn loose-leaf (Sweet & Maxwell).

British Tax Review, journal (Sweet & Maxwell).

Butterworths Orange Tax Handbook, annual (LexisNexis).

Butterworths Yellow Tax Handbook, annual (LexisNexis).

De Voil's Indirect Tax Service, loose-leaf (LexisNexis).

Foster's Inheritance Tax, loose-leaf (LexisNexis).

Simon's Direct Tax Service, loose-leaf (LexisNexis). Available online via *Tax Services* (Butterworths Services).

Sumption, *Capital Gains Tax*, loose-leaf (LexisNexis).

Tax Services, online service (Butterworths Services).

Taxation, journal (LexisNexis).

Whiteman, *On Capital Gains Tax*, 4th edn (Sweet & Maxwell, 2003). Updated by supplement.

Whiteman, *On Income Tax*, 3rd edn (Sweet & Maxwell, 1989). Updated by supplement.

Torts

Charlesworth & Percy on Negligence, 10th edn (Sweet & Maxwell, 2001). Updated by supplement.

Clerk & Lindsell on Torts, 18th edn (Sweet & Maxwell, 2000). Updated by supplement.

Jackson & Powell on Professional Negligence, 5th edn (Sweet & Maxwell, 2002). Updated by supplement.

Lloyds Law Reports: Professional Negligence, law reports (LLP/Informa).

Maddison, *Bingham's Negligence Cases*, 5th edn (Sweet & Maxwell, 2002).

Pittaway, *Professional Negligence Cases* (Butterworths, 1998).

Wills, Probate and Succession

Butterworths Wills, Probate and Administration Service, loose-leaf (LexisNexis).

Available online via *Trusts and Estates Direct* (Butterworths Services).

Theobald on Wills, 16th edn (Sweet & Maxwell, 2001) Updated by supplement.

Sherrin, *Williams on Wills*, 8th edn (Butterworths, 2002). Updated by supplement.

Sherrin & Bonehill, *Law and Practice of Intestate Succession*, 3rd edn (Sweet & Maxwell, 2004). Updated by supplement.

Tristram & Coote, *Probate Practice*, 29th edn (Butterworths, 2002). Updated by supplement.

Trusts and Estates Direct, online service (Butterworths Services).

Walker, *Administration of Estates*, 3rd edn (Financial World Publishing).

Williams & Mortimer, *Executors, Administrators & Probate*, 18th edn (Sweet & Maxwell, 2000). Updated by supplement.

Practical legal research

11.1 The purpose of this chapter

The preceding chapters of this Manual have set out in detail the legal research process. This chapter is intended to serve two purposes: to summarise the key points contained in the earlier chapters, and to emphasise the distinction between academic research and practical research.

11.1.1 What is 'practical' legal research?

The important hallmarks of a practitioner's research are these:

(a) A practitioner may start the research with a textbook, but will base the advice to the client on primary sources (that is, cases, statutes or statutory instruments) unless there is no primary source which adequately answers the question.

(b) Research carried out by a practitioner has a very narrow focus: the practitioner will only search for the law which is needed to answer the specific questions which have to be answered in order to deal with the specific matters on which the client needs advice. As **Chapter 6** of the *Opinion Writing Manual* makes clear, the law is a means to an end, not the end itself.

(c) A practitioner's research must be quick ('time is money') but it must also be accurate (since getting it wrong may well amount to negligence).

11.1.2 Identifying the issues

The first step is, of course, to digest the facts of the problem. Once you have done this, the next step is to identify the issues which need to be researched. In some cases, your instructing solicitor will already have done this, and your instructions will contain a series of questions for you to answer. Even if this is so, you should consider whether there are any other questions which the solicitor should have asked you. In other cases, the solicitor will seek general advice and so you will have to identify the specific questions yourself.

Remember that some problems with which you may be faced might involve basic principles of law and so need little or no legal research, or the problems may raise purely factual questions which actually involve no law.

11.1.3 What sources should I use?

If the problem is one where you need to do some legal research, you must first decide what source(s) you are going to use.

In most cases, there will be more than one starting point to solving the problem. It will often be the case that another user of the library has got the source you wish to consult or the web site you want to use is down, and so you will have to think of an alternative. All libraries have lists (usually on computer), arranged according to subject-matter, of the titles they hold. There is also the list of practitioner books in **Chapter 10**.

11.1.4 Textbooks

If you are unfamiliar with the area of law in question, you will probably want to use a text-book. You should use textbooks written for practitioners, not those written for students. For example, *Chitty on Contracts, Clerk and Lindsell on Torts, Charlesworth on Negligence* or 'looseleaf' works (such as *Harvey's Industrial Relations and Employment Law* and *Butterworth's Family Law Service*). These may look rather off-putting at first, but they function in exactly the same way as ordinary textbooks. If you cannot identify an appropriate practitioners' text, or the one you want is not available, *Halsbury's Laws of England* is often a good starting point.

Unless you are looking for commentary on a particular case or a particular statutory provision (in which case you will use the table of statutes or table of cases in whichever book you are using), the best starting point in any textbook is the index. This is the essential tool which enables you to find the part of the book you are looking for. To use an index you need to be able to formulate the question which you are trying to answer by using words which are likely to be found in the index. This involves identifying 'keywords'. If you cannot find the word(s) you are looking for, try to reword the question. To take a rather trite example, you might have to look for 'taxi' instead of 'cab'.

11.1.5 Primary sources

In some instances, you might want to bypass textbooks and go straight to the 'primary' sources (in other words statutes, statutory instruments, or cases). You might know, for example, that the basic law governing a particular subject is statutory, and so the statute is likely to provide the starting point you need. For example, the statutory provisions relating to unfair dismissal are in the Employment Rights Act 1996, so you might decide to start your research there.

If you want to find a statute, you should choose an annotated version, since this will give you assistance in interpreting the Act. *Current Law Statutes Annotated* contain commentary written when the statute was first enacted (including references to Parliamentary debates for *Pepper v Hart* research). However, *Halsbury's Statutes* has two advantages over *Current Law*. First, the volumes are periodically reissued; this means that where the statute has been amended, the amended version is shown and the footnotes take account of cases decided after the enactment of the statute. Secondly, there is a very useful Cumulative Supplement which gives up-to-date information about the statutes printed in the main volumes and in the loose-leaf binders which contain more recent statutes. Many text-books also reprint statutes, although the commentary will often be in the main body of the text and not in the form of annotations to the statute itself. When you are trying to find your way around a statute, remember that the list of sections (headed 'Arrangements of Sections') at the start of each Act will help you to find the section(s) you need.

If you are looking for case law, the starting point will often be to use a textbook. When reading cases themselves, it is best to use the official law reports published by the Incorporated Council for Law Reporting (the *Weekly Law Reports, the Appeal Cases* etc) or the *All England Law Reports*. However, do not forget that there are several very useful 'specialist' series of law reports. For example, the *Industrial Relations Law Reports*, the *Family Law Reports*, the *Criminal Appeal Reports* and the *Justice of the Peace* reports.

11.1.6   Electronic resources

You should also be aware of the range of electronic databases available for legal research. Quite a lot of information is available free of charge on the Internet, including statutes from 1996 and statutory instruments from 1997 (via the HMSO web site), House of Lords decisions from 1996 (via the Parliament web site), Court of Appeal and Administrative Court decisions from 1996 (via the SmithBernal web site) and a selection of cases from the Court of Appeal and the High Court (via the Court Service website, http://www.courtservice. gov.uk/judgments/judg_home.htm). A useful link to freely available legal information is http://www.bailii.org. There is also an ever-increasing range of CD-ROMS: many series of law reports (including the 'official' law reports and the *All England Law Reports*) are available in this format. Finally, there are various on-line subscription services, such as *Butterworths' Direct* (which includes an electronic version of the *All England Law Reports*, *Halsbury's Laws of England* and *Halsbury's Statutes*), LEXIS, *Westlaw* and *Lawtel*.

If you are using an electronic resource, you have to decide what words you are going to ask the computer to search for. Each database has its own rules regarding how the search should be phrased, but all search engines perform the same basic function of looking for words or phrases. You can specify where in the database the search should take place (often called a 'field'). Remember too that if you ask the computer to look for negligen* (the * is called a 'wildcard') it will look for 'negligent', 'negligently', 'negligence'.

Bear in mind that if you are searching through an electronic law reports database, each case begins with a series of 'catchwords' (which list the keywords to which the case relates), and a headnote. If the case is going to be really helpful, the word or phrase you are looking for is likely to be in either or both of these. It is therefore sensible to confine your search to the catchwords and/or head notes.

Searching for combinations of words will also make your research more focused. For example, if you are trying to find cases on sentencing in theft cases, you will get far too many hits if you just look up 'theft' or if you just look up 'sentencing'. If you confine your search to the catchwords or to the headnotes and search for theft AND sentenc* you should get a far more manageable number of hits.

Another way of defining your electronic search to get a more manageable number of hits is to ask the computer to look for words within a specified distance from each other. For example, if you are looking for cases involving theft in breach of trust, you could ask the computer to look for 'theft' within 10 (say) words of 'trust'.

11.1.7   Finding relevant material

Once you have found the law you are looking for, you must be able to sort through it. You will generally find more law than you need to answer the particular question you are dealing with. You therefore need to be able to distinguish between what is relevant and what is irrelevant. The acid test of relevance is whether the source you have found actually helps you to answer the question or whether it is merely background material.

If when you are giving your advice you cite a case, be clear what proposition you derive from it. It is a mistake to cite cases without making it clear what proposition of law is to be derived from each case you are citing.

11.1.8   Interpreting the law

In some cases, the law will be so clear that only one interpretation is possible. However, this will not always be so.

If the language of a particular statutory provision is obscure, look to see if there is a definition section and/or relevant case law on that section.

In an area governed by case law, you may well have to distil the relevant legal principles from dicta in a series of cases.

It may be necessary to consider whether the facts of the case upon which you are advising can be distinguished from the facts of the authorities you have found. If there are conflicting authorities, it may be necessary to predict which is more likely to be followed.

If you cannot find a clear answer to the problem you are researching, it may well be that you can find a case (or series of cases) setting out a narrow principle which you can then use to establish a wider principle.

Textbooks (or the commentary in *Halsbury's Laws of England*) will often show how various authorities relate to each other, pointing out any inconsistencies and suggesting ways in which apparently conflicting case law can be reconciled.

11.1.9   Following through between sources

You must also be able to 'follow through' from one source to another. For example, if a textbook sets out a proposition of law which seems to answer the question you are researching, and the book cites a particular case as authority for that proposition, you should ensure that the case really does say what the textbook asserts. It is rarely sufficient (although very tempting!) to rely on what textbooks say about primary sources.

11.1.10   Updating

For the practitioner, one of the most important stages of the legal research process is the updating stage. Giving advice, or making submissions to a court, based on out-of-date law may well amount to negligence on the part of the researcher. It is therefore essential that you take all reasonable steps to ensure that your answer is current.

Where you have found the primary sources upon which your answer is based through use of a textbook, check how up-to-date the textbook is and whether there is a supplement to it (this will give you an idea of the period which your subsequent updating should cover).

If your answer is based on a statute, make sure that the statute was in force at the relevant time (ie that, at the relevant time, it had been brought into force and had not been repealed) and that it has not been amended. Doing statute-based research in *Halsbury's Statutes*, it is important to remember to check not only the hardback cumulative annual supplement but also the loose-leaf noter-up service binder.

If your answer is based on case law, it is important to check the status of the case(s) on which your answer is based (for example, that the case on which your advice is based has not been overruled, or distinguished in a case that is similar to the one in which you are advising). If you are doing the research in a paper source, you can check *Current Law* and/or the 'Cases Judicially Considered' section of the Law Reports Index.

If you are doing research electronically, remember that you still have to do some updating. Exactly what you have to do depends on how up-to-date the particular source is and whether it contains an up-dating facility. *Halsbury's Laws Direct* includes an 'update' window which contains all the text that is in the annual cumulative supplement and in the loose-leaf noter-up service binder which updates the supplement. *Legislation Direct* is kept up-to-date, showing the amended version of statutes and statutory instruments quite soon after the changes are enacted; there is a 'stop press' button which gives brief information about changes which have not yet been incorporated.

A useful electronic source for checking the currency of case law is *Westlaw*, which includes a 'history' section in each case summary: this includes references to cases in which the case you are looking up has been considered, applied, distinguished or even overruled. It is important to carry out such checks even if you are using a source that is regularly updated such as *Lawtel* (which has new cases added quickly but does not indicate in a case summary whether that case has subsequently been applied or overruled).

11.1.11   Using the law that you have found

Once you have done all this, you need to be able to summarise the relevant law and apply it to the facts of the case you are dealing with, so that you can give accurate and succinct advice to your client.

A barrister does not carry out abstract legal research. The purpose of the research is to give the best advice you can to your client, or to ensure that the strongest possible case is put before the court on behalf of your client. You must therefore apply the law to the facts of the case in a realistic and practical way. Your advice must not be an essay on the law: it must be specific to the case in which your advice is sought.

You must attempt to answer all the questions or issues raised in your instructions. It may or may not be possible to give a definite answer. If you are unable to give a categorical answer, you must try to assess the likely result and the degree of probability that the court will come to the conclusion you suggest.

Each answer you reach must be 'satisfactory' in the sense that it has a reasonable prospect of being upheld by the court.

11.2   Notes to pupil master

In most cases, your pupil master will not require you to produce a full opinion, but rather the notes which could form the basis for an opinion. The notes must be clear, concise and accurate. The following guidelines may help you:

(a) You may write in note form (rather than writing complete sentences which conform with the rules of grammar) if you wish to do so, but do remember that the result must be intelligible to another reader (ie your pupil master).

(b) Your answers must be satisfactory, in the sense of being sustainable given the present state of the law which applies to the questions you are answering.

(c) Your answers must be supported by relevant authority (usually, statutory or case law):

   (i)   Only cite relevant authority, as the citation of irrelevant sources adds to the length of your notes and tends to create confusion. Something is relevant if it actually makes a difference to your answer.

   (ii) Show how the authority you cite is relevant. This will involve relating that authority to the facts of the case upon which you are advising. When you are

citing precedent, you will normally find it easier to show its relevance by referring to a particular dictum rather than simply referring to the case as a whole.
If you do not set out your legal reasoning, your pupil master cannot check the
soundness of your reasoning.

(iii) Correct citations must be given for each primary source to which you refer.
For example, a statutory instrument should be cited thus: the Tax Credits
(Appeals) Regulations 2002 (SI 2002/2926). A case should be given its full citation, *Arthur J S Hall & Co (a firm) v Simons* [2002] 1 AC 615 (and where a particular
dictum in referred to, it should be located: for example, at p 704 per Lord
Hoffmann). If you do not give the correct citation for the authority which
supports your conclusion, your pupil master will not be able to find that
authority quickly.

(iv) Verbatim quotation of statutes and judgments should be kept to a minimum.
If the passage upon which you wish to rely is very short, or the precise words
are crucial, then you will have to write it out in full. Otherwise, you should
simply distil the essentials, which will involve paraphrasing the material
rather than copying it out.

(v) You should always cite 'primary' sources (ie statutes, case law, etc) in preference to 'secondary' sources (textbooks, articles etc). However, if there is no
authority, or there are conflicting authorities, then it may be appropriate to
cite academic opinion. In that case, you should wherever possible refer to a
source which could be cited in court (that is a textbook written for practitioners rather than students, or an article in a publication which is aimed,
at least in part, at practitioners).

(d) Finally, some guidance on the incorporation of background detail in your notes. If
you are unfamiliar with an area of law, it may well be that you will have to do a certain amount of background reading before you can put the questions which you
have to answer into context. However, your notes should contain only reasoned
answers to the questions which are posed (expressly or by implication) in your
instructions. Otherwise you will find that you are writing a legal essay, not the notes
which form the starting point for an opinion.

11.3 Summary

To summarise, these are the basic steps of legal research:

(a) Analyse the issues raised by your instructions so that you can identify what questions of law (if any) have to be answered.

(b) Classify the questions (eg magistrates' court procedure, criminal law, tort, high-
ways). This will help you to decide what source(s) to look for. Remember that if the
source you want is unavailable, there is almost certain to be another one that you
could use.

(c) Decide what word(s) you are going to look up in the index or on the database ('keywords' or 'catchwords'). To do this, you must be able to formulate the question(s)
you are trying to answer and then see what keywords appear in that formulation.

If the word you are looking for is not in the index or database, try to think of another one.

(d) If you have found what you are looking for, distil what you have found. Set out the statement of law and the authority for that statement.

(e) Ensure that the law you have found is up-to-date. Is the statute in force? Has the statute been amended? Has the statute been repealed? Has the case you have found gone on appeal to a higher court? Has the case been considered, followed, distinguished or overruled by a later case?

(f) Check that you have answered the question(s) completely. If not, look for other relevant sources, distil the contents and check that what you have found is up-to-date.

(g) Summarise the relevant law, apply it to the facts of the case you are dealing with, and advise the client.

11.4 Criteria by which you may assess your legal research

To assess the standard of your performance in carrying out a legal research exercise, you may use or adapt the following basic criteria. In carrying out legal research, you should be able to:

- identify the legal issues raised by your instructions (whether expressly or by implication) correctly and completely;
- identify relevant primary sources and materials;
- show, clearly and concisely, the route by which that answer was reached;
- ensure that the law found is current and up-to-date;
- produce a satisfactory answer to each question.

There now follows a worked-through example demonstrating the legal research process from beginning to end.

11.5 A sample exercise in legal research

There is no single 'right' way of conducting legal research. However, we now consider one way of approaching a particular exercise. It is not the only approach that is possible.

So that the rest of this chapter has the greatest general value, we are going to assume that specialist books are not available and that the researcher has access only to *Halsbury's Laws of England* and *Halsbury's Statutes* or to the online versions (*Halsbury's Laws Direct* and *Legislation Direct* on the Butterworths web site). It should be borne in mind that the method of research would be very similar using other sources.

RE JOHN AND JANE HAYWARD

Instructions to Counsel to Advice

Counsel is instructed on behalf of Mr and Mrs Hayward. They recently purchased the freehold of a plot of land in Kent. This land has been used as an apple and pear orchard for over 100 years. Together with their two children (Emily and Rachael), they moved into a large mobile home which they brought onto the land.

Shortly after the mobile home was moved into the orchard, the local authority wrote to Mr and Mrs Hayward saying that this represented a change in the use of the land (by introducing a residential element onto land which should be used for wholly agricultural purposes). However, Mr and Mrs Hayward have refused to remove the mobile home. They say that they could not afford to buy a house as well as the orchard and so they have no choice but to live in the orchard.

The local authority have now issued proceedings in the County Court seeking an injunction requiring Mr and Mrs Hayward to remove the mobile home from the orchard.

Counsel is instructed to appear at the hearing of this application and to use best endeavours to prevent the granting of the order being sought by the local authority.

Before going to the hearing, you need to know what approach the court will take to this application.

For the purposes of considering the legal research aspect, we will focus on just one particular question — namely whether, in dealing with the application for an injunction, the court applies the usual 'balance of convenience' test (the *American Cyanamid* test) or applies a different test that is specific to the subject-matter of the application.

The starting point is to classify the problem. It could be civil procedure/civil litigation, or it could be planning law. If it is the former, the research process could start in a textbook such as *Blackstone's Civil Practice* (either using the paper version or, for those who subscribe to it, the electronic version on the Lawtel web site). If it is the latter, the starting point would be a textbook on planning or, if a specialist text is not to hand, *Halsbury's Laws of England* (or the electronic version *Halsbury's Laws Direct* on the Butterworths web site).

Another way of classifying a problem is to consider whether the answer is likely to be found in statute law (an Act of Parliament or a statutory instrument) or in case law. If the former, the research could be done in a source such as *Halsbury's Statutes or Halsbury's Statutory Instruments* (or the electronic version *Legislation Direct* on the Butterworths web site). If the latter, a search in the Law Reports Index or a search of a case law database (such as *All England Direct* on the Butterworths web site or Westlaw or Lawtel) could be employed.

Let's assume that we are going to classify this as a problem of planning law, and that we are going to carry out the research using Halsbury's Laws.

If we are using the paper version, the best starting point is the two-volume Consolidated Index. When using an index, we have to try to think in the same way as the people who compiled the index. In other words, a series of words: the main keyword, followed by a sub-keyword, followed by sub-sub-keywords. We must be prepared to try different orders for the words. For example, we may find the answer by looking up 'planning — injunctions — criteria', or it may be 'injunctions — planning — criteria'.

In fact, in the Consolidated Index of Halsbury's Laws, you will find:

PLANNING

> Breach of planning control
>> Injunction restraining: 46,684

These keywords thus take us to paragraph 684 in volume 46.

Using an electronic source, the order of the words does not matter unless we select a search option which requires that the search terms appear in a particular order.

Let's try *Halsbury's Direct*. We begin by searching for 'planning AND injunction*' (the * makes sure that we search for the plural as well as the singular). We could narrow the search by searching only the volume that deals with planning, but let's see how many 'hits' a search of the entire database produces. The search results in 30 hits. Scrolling down, we come to Town and Country Planning (the volume title) — Enforcement — injunctions. Clicking on that hit takes us to para 684 of the relevant volume.

The text contains the following:

---

684. INJUNCTIONS

Where a local planning authority(1) considers it necessary or expedient for any actual or appre-hended breach of planning control(2) to be restrained by injunction, it may apply to the court(3) for an injunction, whether or not the authority has exercised, or is proposing to exercise, any of its other statutory powers(4) relating to enforcement(5). On such an application the court may grant such an injunction as the court thinks appropriate for the purpose of restraining the breach(6). Rules of court may provide for such an injunction to be issued against a person whose identity is unknown(7).

1   For the meaning of 'local planning authority' see para 2 note 1 ante.
2   For the meaning of 'breach of planning control' see para 654 ante.
3   For these purposes, 'the court' means the High Court or the County Court: Town and Country Planning Act 1990s 187B(4) (added by the Planning and Compensation Act 1991 s 3).
4   I.e. any of its powers under the Town and Country Planning Act 1990 Pt VII (ss 171A–196C) (as amended): see para 654 et seq ante and para 685 et seq post.
5   Ibid s 187B(1) (added by the Planning and Compensation Act 1991 s 3). For general guidance as to injunctions to restrain breaches of planning control see Department of the Environment Circular 21/91 Annex 4 (paras 1–8). As to injunctions generally see INJUNCTIONS; and as to injunctions in relation to Crown land see para 658 note 3 ante. The functions of a local planning authority under the Town and Country Planning Act 1990 s 187B (as added) are exercisable by any body having the functions of taking enforcement action in respect of the breach in question: s 1(5)(c), Sch 1 para 12A (added by the Planning and Compensation Act 1991s 32, Sch 7 paras 8, 53(7)). The Town and Country Planning Act 1990 Sch 1 para 12A (as so added) does not, how-ever, apply in Greater London: Sch 1 para 21(1). For the meaning of 'functions' see para 2 note I ante; for the meaning of 'taking enforcement action' see para 654 ante; and for the meaning of 'Greater London' see para 10 note 3 ante.
6   Ibid s 187B(2) (added by the Planning and Compensation Act 1991 s 3).
7   Town and Country Planning Act 1990s 187B(3) (added by the Planning and Compensation Act 1991s 3). As to the procedure for obtaining an injunction against a person whose identity is unknown see RSC Ord 110 and PRACTICE AND PROCEDURE.

Local planning authorities will nevertheless need to identify, to the best of their ability, the person against whom the injunction is sought; and the following may be used in support of the authority's submission to the court: (1) photographic evidence of the person concerned; (2) affidavit evidence sworn by the local planning authority's officers; (3) reference to chattels on the land known to belong to, or to be used by, that person, eg a registered motor vehicle; or (4) other relevant evid-ence, such as a name by which the person is known, even though it is not his given name: Department of the Environment Circular 21/91 Annex 4 para 8.

At the bottom of the screen there is an 'Update' window. It contains the following text:

UPDATE

NOTES — RSC replaced by Civil Procedure Rules 1998, SI 1998/3132 ('the CPR').

See generally PRACTICE AND PROCEDURE.

See *Kettering BC v Perkins* [1999] JPL 166.

NOTE 2 — See *Wealden DC v Krushandal* [1999] JPL 174, CA.

NOTE 5 — Under the 1990 Act s 187B the court has jurisdiction to grant interlocutory injunctions and mandatory injunctions to enforce actual breaches of planning control: *Harwood v Runnymede BC; Croydon LBC v Gladden* [1994] JPL 723, CA (applied in *South Hams DC v Halsey* [1996] 3 PLR 38, CA). Once an injunction has been granted, it cannot be discharged except where there has been a significant change of circumstances since the order was made: *Salisbury DC v Le Roi* [2002] EWCA Civ 1490, [2002] 1 P & CR 501, CA. A local planning authority is not prevented from using the enforcement procedure in the 1990 Act s 178 even though it has been granted an injunction to restrain a continued breach of planning controls pursuant to s 187B: *R (on the application of Lee) v Nuneaton and Bedworth BC* [2004] 18 EG 101 (CS).

NOTE 6 — The 1990 Act s 187B(2) confers an original, not a supervisory, jurisdiction to be exercised as the court thinks just and proportionate in all, including the personal, circumstances of the particular case: *South Buckinghamshire DC v Porter, Chichester DC v Searle*; *Wrexham BC v Berry*; *Hertsmere BC v Harty* [2003] UKHL 26 [2003] 2 AC 558; considered in *Tonbridge and Malling BC v Davis* [2004] EWCA Civ 194, [2004 All ER (D) 426 (Feb) (hardship of travelling show people, using land in designated special landscape area in breach of planning controls, outweighed by serious environmental damage caused and their conduct); and *Warwick DC v West Midlands International Airport Ltd* [2004] EWHC 1636 (QB), [2004] 25 EG 170 (CS). See *Hillingdon LBC v Guinea Enterprises Ltd* (1998)76 P & CR 338 (multiple defendants).

NOTE 7 — See *South Cambridgeshire DC v Persons Unknown* (2004) *Times*, 11 November (1990 Act s 187B empowered court to grant injunction to restrain breach of planning control against persons unknown).

This information in *Halsbury's Direct* is also contained in the paper version of *Halsbury's Laws*, using a combination of the updates for Vol 46, para 684, in the 2004 *Cumulative Supplement* and the *Noter-up* section of the *Current Service Noter-up* looseleaf binder. Limiting the search to just the Town and County Planning volume, reduces the number of 'hits' to 19.

From this we learn that there is a specific injunctive power in relation to planning matters (footnote 5 reveals that the power is contained in s 187B(1) of the Town and Country Planning Act 1990 (added by the Planning and Compensation Act 1991, s 3)) and, from the Update section, that there is a highly relevant case called *South Buckinghamshire District Council v Porter*.

The summary of the case is rather terse in *Halsbury's*, so we need to look at the case itself. If we are using the online version of *Halsbury's* and there is a hyperlink, we could jump straight to the All England report of the case. If not, we would have to search for the case by name. Or we could simply go to the paper version and read the case there (using the citation in *Halsbury's* or finding the citation in, for example, *Current Law* or the *Law Reports Index*).

This is the headnote to the report of *South Bucks District Council v Porter* [2003] 2 AC 558 (this is the most authoritative report of the case, although it should be noted that the headnotes in the *All England* reports may be slightly fuller). It reads as follows:

Planning — Planning control — Breach — Local authority's application for injunction — Gipsies occupying mobile homes on own land in breach of planning control — Whether court obliged to consider likely effect of injunction and any penalties for infringement on gipsies' right to respect for home and family life — Whether environmental considerations outweighing gipsies' human rights — Town and Country Planning Act 1990 (c 8), s 187B (as inserted by Planning and Compensation Act 1991 (c 34), s 3) — Human Rights Act 1998 (c 42), s 6(1), Sch 1, Pt 1, art 8.

In three cases local planning authorities applied successfully to the court under section 187B of the Town and Country Planning Act 1990 for injunctive relief against the defendants, who were gipsies, to prevent them from living in mobile homes and caravans on land acquired by them for that purpose but for which planning consent had been refused. The defendants appealed on the ground that in granting the injunctions the court had failed to consider, in addition to any relevant planning considerations, the likely effect of the orders on their human rights in accordance with section 6(1) of the Human Rights Act 1998 and the Convention scheduled to that Act. The Court of Appeal allowed their appeals. On appeal by the local planning authorities —

Held, dismissing the appeals, that section 187B of the 1990 Act conferred on the court an original and discretionary, not a supervisory, jurisdiction, to be exercised with due regard to the purpose for which it was conferred to restrain actual or threatened breaches of planning control; that it was inherent in the injunctive remedy that its grant depended on the court's judgment of all the circumstances of the case; that, although the court would not examine matters of planning policy and judgment which lay within the exclusive purview of the authorities responsible for administering the planning regime, the court was not obliged to grant relief because a planning authority considered it necessary or expedient to restrain a planning breach; that the court would have regard to all, including the personal, circumstances of the case, and, since section 6 of the 1998 Act required the court to act compatibly with a Convention right as so defined, and having regard to the right guaranteed in article 8, the court would only grant an injunction where it was just and proportionate to do so; and that, accordingly, the planning authorities' applications would be determined on that basis (post, paras 20, 27–31, 37–42, 49–50, 53, 55–59, 63–67, 71, 73–74, 75–77, 84–89, 92–93, 95, 98–104).

Mole Valley District Council v Smith (1992) 90 LGR 557, CA and *Hambleton District Council v Bird* [1995] 3 PLR 8, CA distinguished.

Decision of the Court of Appeal [2001] EWCA Civ 1549; [2002] 1 WLR 1359; [2002] 1 All ER 425 affirmed.

This headnote confirms the relevance of the case and points to the paragraphs of the judgment which set out the court's reasoning.

We found this case through the updating process using *Halsbury's Laws* and so it is likely to be the up-to-date answer. However, it is worth double-checking. Electronically, we could use a source such as *Westlaw*. Again, we know the name of the case, and so we can search for that specific case either using keywords from the name of the case or else the citation of the case. The case summary on *Westlaw* includes a 'history' section; this section includes details of instances where the case in question has been subsequently considered.

Entering the name of the case on *Westlaw* and then clicking the 'history' button (or scrolling down to the 'history' section) reveals only that the House of Lords upheld the decision of the Court of Appeal. It is of course unlikely that a decision of the House of Lords would be reversed (since the House only departs from its own earlier decisions in exceptional circumstances). However, it is always worth checking the 'History' of a case (even a House of Lords case, since that decision may well have been applied, or distinguished, in a case similar to the one in which you are instructed). Where a decision has been overruled a red flag usually appears on the *Westlaw* page for that case; the 'History' section of the page gives fuller details of cases where the present case has been considered.

If the updating were to be done using paper sources, *Current Law* would be a good choice. Searching for cases reported in the current year requires you to look at the *Cumulative Table of Cases* in the latest monthly part (research for previous years can be done in the *Current Law Case Citators*).

11.5.1   Analysis of the sources

It is often the case that the researcher finds a lot of material which ends up being discarded. But it is important to be thorough in the research process or you might miss material that is highly relevant.

Porter was decided after the commencement of the Human Rights Act 1998 and takes full account of the rights conferred by the European Convention on Human Rights (were this not so, some further research might be necessary to ensure that the human rights perspective is properly considered).

The next stage is to reduce the material you have found into more manageable proportions by summarising the key points.

The *Porter* case sets out a number of factors to be taken into account:

(a) The judge should not grant injunctive relief unless he would be prepared, if necessary, to enforce the order by committing the defendant to prison in the event of a breach of the order.

(b) The judge must therefore consider the question of hardship to the defendant and his family if they are required to move.

(c) This has to be set against countervailing considerations, such as the need to enforce planning control in the general interest and the planning history of the site.

(d) The degree and flagrancy of the alleged breach of planning control might well prove critical.

(e) If conventional enforcement measures have failed over a prolonged period of time to remedy the breach, the judge will be readier to grant an injunction; on the other hand, an injunction may not be appropriate where enforcement action has never been taken, unless there is some urgency in the situation which justifies the pre-emptive avoidance of an anticipated breach of planning control.

(f) The extent to which the planning authority can be shown to have had regard to all the material considerations and to have properly posed and approached the Article 8(2) questions as to necessity and proportionality before seeking injunctive relief.

(g) The degree of environmental damage resulting from the breach and the urgency or otherwise of bringing it to an end.

The final stage is to apply the law you have found to the facts of the case in which you are advising, so that you can produce an answer. That answer might be along the following lines:

Section 187B of the Town and Country Planning Act 1990 (inserted by s 3 of the Planning and Compensation Act 1991) empowers a local planning authority to seek an injunction to restrain an actual or threatened breach of planning control. It has this power whether or not it has exercised, or is proposing to exercise, any of its other statutory enforcement powers. The exercise of this power was considered by the House of Lords in *South Buckinghamshire District Council v Porter* [2003] UKHL 26; [2003] 2 AC 558. In that case, it was held that the judge should consider a number of factors. These factors include consideration of the hardship which would be caused to the defendants and their children if they are required to move from what is now their home (a factor made all the more weighty by the operation of Article 8 of the European Convention on Human Rights).

Detailed evidence from Mr and Mrs Hayward about the question of alternative accommodation (or the lack of alternative accommodation) would therefore be very useful. The hardship to the defendants and their family has to be balanced against other considerations, such as the need to enforce planning control as a matter of public interest. The judge will also consider the degree and flagrancy of the alleged breach of planning control (and so it might be relevant how prominent the mobile home is in the orchard). Although s 187B specifically provides that there is no requirement that the planning authority must have tried using other enforcement methods before seeking an injunction, the judge may be more reluctant to grant an injunction where the local authority has not tried other methods first.

11.5.2 A further exercise

The instructions in the case of Mr and Mrs Hayward may well require you to research a number of other issues. Even if the immediate threat of an injunction can be averted, how should Mr and Mrs Hayward go about applying for planning permission to have a mobile home in their orchard? What criteria will the local planning authority use when determining that application? Try to answer these questions using either a planning text or *Halsbury's Laws* (online or paper). Remember that your answer should identify, and be based upon, relevant primary sources (ie cases, statutes, or statutory instruments) and that you should apply the law you find to the facts of the case in which you are advising.

11.6 And finally, some useful tips

You might find this non-exhaustive list of tips helpful in carrying out your legal research. You may like to add to the list as you do your own research and discover for yourself useful shortcuts.

11.6.1 Paper sources

(a) If you are unfamiliar with an area of law, it is often best to start with a paper source rather than an electronic source: it is easier to browse through a paper source to get an overview of a subject.

(b) Once you have formulated the legal question(s) you are trying to answer and you have found an appropriate textbook, it is usually best to start with the index at the back of the book rather than the contents pages at the front.

(c) Do not forget to go through the up-dating process: eg, check to see if the textbook you are using has a supplement. Remember that even if there is a supplement it is likely to be at least a little out-of-date, so check the supplement to see when it was issued and update from then; similarly, even loose-leaf publications can be out-of- date, so check to see when the publication was last updated.

(d) If your answer is based on a statute or statutory instrument, check that it was in force at the relevant time.

11.6.2 Electronic sources

(a) Remember that in most databases you can make your search more efficient by the use of 'Boolean searches', ie using connectors such as AND, OR, NOT.

(b) Sometimes the use of brackets is needed in a search, eg, '(transfer OR transaction) AND illegal' if you are not sure whether the appropriate noun is 'transfer' or 'transaction'.

(c) You can narrow your search by using 'proximity searching', eg, looking for one word within (say) 10 words of another word, eg solicitor w/10 negligence.

(d) Truncation (use of 'wildcards') enables you to look for words with a common stem; with most databases the symbol to use is an asterisk (*), with others it is an exclamation mark (!). For example, neglig* would find negligent, negligently, negligence.

(e) When searching a case law database, it is often wise to confine your search to a specific field, eg, 'catchwords' or 'headnote': that is likely to ensure that only relevant case law is produced.

(f) The best way of searching for a particular section of a statute, eg, s 246 of the Insolvency Act 1986, is usually best to search for: 246 AND insolvency AND act AND 1986.

(g) If you want to find out whether a particular word appears in the file you have currently opened, click on 'edit' — 'find' and type in the word you are looking for.

(h) If you do not know the web address for the site you want to use for your legal research, try using a link site such as http://www.venables.co.uk/legal or http://library. ukc.ac.uk/library/netinfo/intnsubg/lawlinks.htm or http://www.sosig.ac.uk/law.

(i) Most databases have an 'about' function which will give you further information about what that particular source covers.

(j) If you want to copy information from the Internet or a CD-ROM into a word processing document, highlight the text you want to copy by dragging the cursor over the relevant text with the left-hand mouse button held down; then you have three options: click on 'edit', then 'copy', and then go to your word processed document and click on 'edit', then 'paste' (or click on the paste icon); or press 'ctrl' and the letter 'c' simultaneously, then go to your word processed document and press 'ctrl' and the letter 'v' simultaneously; or press the right-hand mouse button, highlight 'copy' and click with the left-hand mouse button, and when you are in your word-processed document, press the right-hand mouse button, highlight 'paste' and click with the left-hand mouse button. If you want to eliminate formatting from the text you are copying (eg you want to remove hyperlinks) you can select 'edit' — 'paste' — 'unformatted text'.

(k) If you cannot remember how you got to where you are on the Internet (or in most CD-ROMS), you can use the 'history' function to retrace your steps.

(l) Remember that a case reported in one set of reports may be referred to in a later case that is not reported in the same set of reports: *Westlaw* or *Lawtel* are good sources for tracking down the later case.

12

Overview of a civil case

12.1 Introduction

This chapter outlines the different contexts in which you will be working and what may be required of you at the different stages of a case by setting out the main stages in a civil case, explaining the different roles of the solicitor and barrister, the work done by the solicitor at each stage, the stages at which the barrister will generally be consulted and the work done by the barrister at each of these stages.

12.2 Stages in a civil case

12.2.1 Introduction

Civil disputes cover a broad range of cases including those involving general common law, family matters, insolvency, Chancery claims and claims to statutory tribunals such as employment tribunals. The steps set out here relate to those in the most common types of common law cases taken in the High Court and County Courts, eg, suing for debts and damages in tort and contract. This is not a civil litigation manual and does not cover the detailed rules but rather the main stages in a civil case and the work to be done by the lawyers at each stage. The Woolf reforms implemented as the Civil Procedure Rules 1998 (CPR) on 26 April 1999 have made major changes to the terminology used and procedure followed in both courts, simplifying them and attempting to cut the cost and delay of litigation in many cases. This has been done by introducing the concept of 'proportionality' by which the court will attempt to balance the need for disputes to be resolved as quickly and cheaply as possible with the need for cases to be properly prepared and fairly heard. Although the changes have altered what is required or possible at any particular stage of a case, the main stages in the preparation of a case remain the same.

12.2.2 Main stages

The conduct of a civil case through the courts can be divided into seven main areas of work from the time the client first sees a lawyer to the closure of the client's file:

(a) *Before action*: involves analysis of the case and decisions by the client and the lawyer, in particular whether court action is appropriate and how the costs will be paid. In some cases, some urgent action may need to be taken, eg, a tenant claiming to have been unlawfully evicted may seek an injunction to be reinstated pending determination of his or her right to remain by a full trial.

A big change introduced by the Woolf reforms in certain standard cases is the introduction of the concept of 'pre-action protocols', which requires parties to exchange a fair amount of information before initiating proceedings. A number of such 'protocols' have been implemented for specific areas of work, eg, personal injury and clinical negligence. It is envisaged that such 'protocols' will be written for as many standard types of cases as possible. In areas where no protocol exists, parties are required to follow the general spirit of the protocols. The idea is to break down the present adversarial and secretive approach and promote settlement as early as possible.

(b) *Initiating proceedings*: involves deciding which court to use, the drafting and issue of proceedings, and exchange of statements of case by the parties.

(c) *Interim*: involves all the intermediate steps between the exchange of statements of case and the trial, some taken automatically and some requiring applications to the court. These steps are largely concerned with determining what issues will be fought and collecting the evidence to support the allegations by both sides.

(d) *Trial*: involves the preparation immediately before the trial and the actual day(s) of the trial.

(e) *Enforcement*: involves the winning party taking formal steps to force the losing party to obey the order of the court where there is any failure to do so.

(f) *Appeal*: involves any party dissatisfied with the court's judgment or order considering whether an appeal is possible and appropriate and taking the formal steps necessary to appeal.

(g) *Payment of costs*: involves ensuring all costs of the litigation have been assessed, where appropriate, and been paid to the relevant person or authority.

Clearly, the first four of these areas of work occur in succession. However, the parties may decide not to proceed further or to discontinue the case at any time during the process, for example, if the parties agree to settle the case. A case may not involve enforcement or appeal. Payment of the various costs of litigation occur throughout the process.

12.2.3 Civil Procedure Rules

The Civil Procedure Rules 1998 set out in some detail how cases are to be conducted and prepared for trial. Important concepts introduced by these rules in April 1999 which affect the work of both barristers and solicitors are:

(a) The 'overriding objective' which the court and parties must bear in mind throughout. One of the principal concepts is that of 'proportionality' by which the court, parties and lawyers must, throughout the case, deal with the case expeditiously and efficiently and keep the preparation involved proportionate to the value and importance of the case.

(b) The use of pre-action protocols (see (a) in **12.2.2**). These result in the costs of a case being moved earlier as much of the information will have been exchanged before proceedings are even issued. It also sometimes means that barristers are more involved in cases before proceedings are issued (see **12.3.5**).

(c) Case management by the courts. The idea behind this is that the control of the timescale and costs of the litigation should be vested in the courts. This is done partially through tracking of cases (see (d)) where the steps allowed in preparation are kept commensurate with the value and importance of the case. It is also done by 'procedural' judges keeping an eye on cases and, where necessary, having case management hearings with the lawyers to ensure that the case is proceeding in a way which is efficient and cost effective.

(d) Tracking of cases. There are three tracks, each with its own set of rules to ensure that the cost and speed with which the case comes to trial is proportionate to the value and importance of the case. The three tracks are:

(i)   Small claims (basically where the value of the claim is £5,000 or less with some exceptions). The way in which cases are dealt with in the small claims track is very different from the fast track. The procedure is very simple. The hearing is informal and strict rules of evidence do not apply. A party who wins his or her case will not have his legal costs paid. Such cases are therefore frequently conducted by litigants in person.

(ii)   Fast track (basically where the value of the claim is £15,000 or less but over £5000) — slightly more detailed procedure with limited steps to ensure sufficient disclosure of documents, witnesses and expert evidence (where relevant) and a trial date set for 30 weeks after the case has been allocated to this track. In addition, the time for the trial will be limited to one day. These rules attempt to ensure that the case does come to trial as quickly as possible and the costs of preparation are controlled.

(iii) Multi-track (basically where the value of the claim is more than £15,000) — more detailed procedure which allows for more detailed disclosure and preparation of evidence to reflect the greater complexity of the case. In addition, judges are more likely to become actively involved in managing the case through procedural hearings such as 'case management conferences' (held early on to determine the main issues, steps to be taken in preparing the case, etc), 'listing hearings' (to assist the parties and court in the decisions necessary for fixing the date for trial) and 'pre-trial reviews' (to set out how the actual hearing will be conducted — eg the length of time for speeches, witnesses, etc).

Thus the amount of work involved in the interim and trial stages (see (c) and (d) in **12.2.2** above) will vary depending on the 'track' to which the case is allocated and the specific requirements of the individual case.

12.3 Roles of solicitor and barrister

12.3.1 The bar is a referral profession

Although there are now some cases where clients have direct access to barristers, the Bar is a referral profession which, generally, gets its work from solicitors. A solicitor will use counsel for specialist advice or advocacy either because the solicitor lacks the relevant expertise or rights of audience or because it is more cost-effective for the solicitor to use a barrister than to do the research or advocacy personally. It is the solicitor who decides when to use a barrister and if he or she fails to instruct counsel when it is necessary, the solicitor may be liable to the client in negligence.

12.3.2 Solicitors' work

The level of expertise and specialisation of solicitors' firms varies enormously, from a firm which offers a broad range of legal services, from drafting wills to acting for defendants in criminal cases, to one which specialises, eg, doing largely personal injury work. In any firm, work will be done by the partners, who must be solicitors, employed solicitors and paralegals who are often qualified legal executives. Most firms will assign the contentious and non-contentious work to different people. The litigation department may also be divided into criminal, family and civil, with solicitors specialising in one or two areas, eg, personal injury and housing. In many firms, the litigation department has people with expertise in numerous areas ranging over commercial, landlord and tenant, employment, family, financial services etc. Paralegals usually do the more routine aspects of civil litigation such as service of documents or sitting behind counsel and taking notes in a hearing.

Technically a client instructs a firm of solicitors to act. Barristers may be instructed directly by those clients authorised under the BARDirect rules which includes largely professionals (eg, accountants, valuers). All correspondence and instructions or briefs to counsel will be in the firm's name. Once the other side has been notified that solicitors are acting, it is improper for any other lawyer to communicate with the client directly (although there is nothing wrong with the parties dealing with each other directly). When court proceedings are issued, the firm (but not the individual solicitor) is on the record at court as acting for the client in the particular proceedings and will remain so until this is altered or the case is concluded or withdrawn. Although the firm as a whole technically acts for the client, an individual solicitor will usually conduct the case. Most firms will try to ensure that the solicitor who first sees the client takes the case on and sees it to completion.

The individual solicitor with conduct of the case will decide when to consult a barrister. Within the seven areas of work set out above, barristers will frequently be involved in pre-action, initiating proceedings, interim work, the trial and appeals. In addition, they need to be able to justify costs where the court assess costs summarily at the end of the hearing rather than doing a detailed assessment later. This is likely to happen where interim applications are made prior to the hearing. However, barristers are rarely involved in enforcement.

12.3.3 Dealing with costs

Prior to taking any steps, including instructing counsel, the solicitor must explain the costs of litigation to the client and ascertain how they will be paid.

12.3.3.1 Ascertaining the costs

The bulk of the costs will be the fees to cover the work done by the solicitor and any barrister involved. The bulk of the solicitor's fees will usually be calculated on the basis of an hourly charge, with even small firms charging at least £100 an hour. Barristers' fees are usually calculated on a piecework basis, for a particular opinion or statement of case or court appearance. The level of the fee depends on the seniority of the barrister doing the work and its complexity, and is agreed between the solicitor and the barrister's clerk, but the minimum charge even for a junior barrister on a short application would be £100. In addition to the 'legal fees', expenses are incurred such as court charges and the costs of obtaining expert reports. The client must be made aware of the fact that every consultation with the solicitor, and every step taken in the case, adds to the costs. The solicitor must also make clear that if the case is lost the client may be liable for the other side's costs because courts rarely order the loser to pay all the winner's costs.

12.3.3.2   Methods of payment

The method of paying costs in civil litigation is changing rapidly. The client may simply pay privately, ie pay the costs from his or her own pocket. He or she may be asked to pay 'on account' (ie a sum upfront calculated to cover a certain amount of work) and/or pay as he or she receives the invoices for work done by the solicitor. Expenses other than solicitor's fees (eg barrister's fee, court fees, experts fees, etc — called 'disbursements') are paid by the solicitor and the money recouped from the client. If the client wins his or her case, the other side may be ordered to pay his or her costs. However, this may not be ordered so the client may still be liable for all of his or her own costs, and in any event, will almost certainly have to pay some of his or her own costs.

Alternatively, the client and solicitor may enter a conditional fee agreement (CFA) whereby, if the client loses no legal fee will be charged by the solicitor, but if the client wins the solicitor is entitled to payment of the usual rate plus a success fee. Such agreements with the solicitor will cover only the solicitor's fee and not 'disbursement' costs such as expert's fees or the barrister's fees which the client will pay in the normal way. A client conducting litigation on a conditional fee basis remains potentially liable for the other side's costs if the claim is unsuccessful, but this liability can often be covered by insurance. Some people have legal expenses insurance whereby the costs are met by the insurance company. This is called 'before the event' insurance, and is increasingly common as part of motor insurance and household insurance policies. Even if no such insurance has been arranged before the event that results in litigation, 'after-the-event' insurance is available and increasingly popular. It can be obtained even during the litigation process. The premium payable will depend on the risk taken by the insurance company (ie the amount of cover sought and the strength of the case).

Finally, some people qualify for public assistance by way of legal aid or its replacement, help under the Community Legal Service. The manner in which public funds are made available for litigation is changing dramatically. The new method requires firms to apply to the Legal Services Commission to obtain a franchise. This franchise enables the firm to conduct publicly-funded work on the basis of being given a budget from public funds for each period for which the firm has a franchise. The old method required firms to apply to the Legal Aid Board in each case and often for each step in the case, and if the Board approved the application, a 'legal aid certificate' was issued by the Board. As old cases are completed, this method will gradually disappear.

12.3.4   **Instructing and briefing counsel**

The solicitor with conduct of the case will also decide which barrister to consult and when 'booking' the barrister will officially deal through the clerk to the barrister's chambers. Most solicitors build up a 'stable' of several barristers in any one field of work whom they use regularly because they are good, fast, efficient, get on well with clients or with whom they have a particularly good rapport. Solicitors new to litigation or a particular area of work without such a 'stable' will select on the basis of recommendations of those working in the firm, solicitors working in the same field or, possibly, the clerk of a set of chambers which the solicitor has used. Lacking such recommendations, a solicitor may select on the basis of the specialisation of the chambers which can be obtained from the various directories.

A solicitor will use a range of barristers from very junior barristers for fairly simple matters, generally because it is cost-effective, to very senior Queen's Counsel for their highly specialist knowledge and advocacy skills on particularly complex cases. The cab-rank rule (see paras 601–607 of the Code of Conduct for the Bar) requires barristers not to refuse to do work except for specified reasons which include lack of expertise, inadequate time and opportunity to prepare and lack of proper fee. Within the rule, when taking on work for the barristers in their set, clerks do try to take into account the work preference of the barristers. However, in early years of practice most barristers have no particular area of expertise and will usually take a broad range of cases.

12.3.5 The barrister's involvement

A barrister's involvement in any civil case is limited to doing specific tasks as requested by the solicitor. The three types of tasks which solicitors will usually ask a barrister to undertake are:

- advising on:
  - merit and/or quantum,
  - difficult or obscure points of law,
  - evidence;
- drafting documents, eg, statements of case, affidavits;
- advocacy at:
  - interim hearings,
  - trial.

The solicitor consults the barrister separately on each specific step. Most solicitors will want continuity of barrister throughout a case so, for example, will ask the same barrister who advised on the merits at the beginning to draft the statement of case and do the advocacy at the trial. In the civil brief in **Chapter 16** the same barrister has been instructed at three stages: to draft a Defence; advise on merits; and appear at an interim hearing. However, if the solicitor is not satisfied with the work done at any stage he or she may ask someone else or decide to do the work personally. A solicitor may also use barristers of different call for different aspects of the same case, eg, one of very junior call for simple interim hearings but a more senior barrister for advising on evidence and the trial. Finally, briefs for interim hearings or for trial may pass from one barrister to another because the original barrister briefed is not available, eg, when he or she is 'double booked' because a case is taking longer than expected.

The solicitor is responsible for paying any fee charged by a barrister. The solicitor pays the barrister's fee and recoups the money from the client. If the barrister's fee is not paid, the barrister pursues the solicitor and not the lay client. The traditional way in which a barrister charged the fee was on a piece-work basis (eg a fee for an opinion or a fee for the advocacy at an interim hearing). However, barristers now also enter conditional fee agreements with solicitors which operate on the same basis as conditional fee agreements between lay clients and solicitors (ie no fee if the case is lost but an additional success fee if the case is won). Such an agreement can cover all areas of work done by the barrister or be limited to specific areas of work. This means that the barrister has to do a 'risk assessment' when deciding whether or not to accept instructions from a solicitor. Doing such an assessment can be very complicated and further consideration of this is beyond the scope of this Manual.

12.3.6   Form and content of instructions or brief

Although solicitors may consult counsel by phone on occasion, it is more usual for them to consult in writing or by email. Technically a solicitor 'instructs' counsel to advise or draft documents and 'briefs' counsel to attend hearings. The solicitor will send a fresh set of 'instructions' or 'brief' each time the barrister is consulted. Instructions or briefs from solicitors should include copies of all relevant documents, follow a fairly standard format (see **16.1** for an example) and include:

(a) The heading which sets out the names of the prospective parties if proceedings have not yet been issued or the title of the case as drafted if proceedings have been issued.

(b) The party for whom counsel is instructed or briefed.

(c) A list of the documents enclosed.

(d) The name of the instructing firm and the name, reference and extension of the particular solicitor conducting the case within the firm.

(e) A brief summary of the case which should identify the relevant issues, information and documents and explain the solicitor's opinion, advice to the client and steps taken to date.

(f) Specific directions as to what work the barrister is instructed or briefed to do, for example, to advise on merit and quantum or represent a client at a hearing.

(g) A 'back sheet' which contains the heading, the barrister's name and chambers address, the solicitor's firm name, address, telephone number, fax number and e-mail address, the reference or name of the individual solicitor dealing with the case and the words 'Community Legal Service' if the client is publicly funded, or counsel's fee where briefed to appear on a hearing for a private client. If counsel is instructed on a condition fee basis this will be noted in the brief.

12.3.7   Returning the work and endorsing the brief

The barrister does the work as instructed or briefed and returns the instructions or brief to the solicitor with all the enclosed documents and an endorsement on the back sheet of the work done, the date and the fee. The endorsement is important as it is the statement of the work done. Where an opinion or draft is enclosed with the returned brief (as in the case of *Lowe v Mainwaring* at **16.2**), the endorsement merely signifies the work done, the date and the counsel who did it. Where court hearings are attended, it is important to ensure that the endorsement fully and accurately sets out the order made or the settlement reached. It should contain all the relevant details including the date, the judge, the order made and be signed by counsel. An example of such an endorsement after a hearing in a criminal case is shown at **17.2**. Writing a full attendance note for the solicitor can be very useful and impress him or her.

The barrister usually retains none of the papers once the work under any particular set of instructions or brief has been completed. When solicitors instruct or brief counsel they should include any previous instructions or briefs together with their enclosed documents and any written advice or opinion. However, it is important for a barrister to keep a copy of any written work done for the solicitor and a note of any relevant detail about the case, eg, factual analysis of the case or legal research done, for future reference, as the barrister may be instructed again on the case.

12.3.8   Solicitors and barristers as client's agent

Solicitors and barristers act as the client's representatives and as such the rules of agency apply. The actual authority of the solicitor conducting the case will depend on the instructions of the client and the solicitor should obtain specific instructions from the client before taking any step. The actual authority of the barrister at any stage will be limited to the work required by the current set of instructions or brief. Both solicitor and barrister may be liable to the client if they act outside their actual authority.

The apparent authority of solicitor and barrister to bind the client may be wider or narrower than their actual authority. The solicitor's apparent authority will extend to accepting service on behalf of the client and progressing the case to trial. It will also extend to making admissions and, in certain circumstances, compromising or settling the case. The barrister's apparent authority extends to speaking for the client in court and may also extend to making admissions and settlements on behalf of the client. If either the solicitor or barrister bind their lay client by acting within their apparent authority but beyond their actual authority, they will be in breach of their professional duty to the client and liable to them.

12.4   Pre-claim stage

12.4.1   The barrister's involvement

A barrister's involvement at this stage is usually confined to being:

- instructed to advise on merit and/or quantum; and
- briefed to appear in court to obtain pre-action orders.

In both situations, the solicitor will have dealt with the legal costs and how these will be paid. The solicitor will almost invariably have interviewed the client, should have obtained full details of all relevant matters and sent instructions or a brief to counsel including all the relevant information and documents. How much barristers will become involved with satisfying pre-action protocols (see (a) at **12.2.2**) remains to be seen.

12.4.2   Opinion on merits and/or quantum

12.4.2.1   Generally

The solicitor will seek counsel's opinion if he or she wants a second opinion of the case, feels further legal research or a more expert view is required to assess the case or it is required, eg, by the insurance company where the client has legal expenses insurance.

Prior to seeking counsel's opinion, the solicitor should have obtained full information from the client on personal details, the problem, details of any loss suffered and the solution the client is seeking. The solicitor should have discussed with the client what the best course of action is, given the remedy the client is seeking, taking into account all the relevant factors including:

- the solicitor's provisional view on the merits of the client's case;
- the position of the potential defendant(s) (eg, easily located, in the country, financially good for the sum to be claimed, likely to pay up if proceedings are issued);

- the time it will take to bring proceedings to trial if necessary; and
- whether some other alternative, such as mediation or complaint to an ombudsman, might be more appropriate.

Having reached a provisional view that litigation is at least worth investigating, the solicitor may then seek counsel's opinion by sending instructions setting out clearly all the relevant information, the solicitor's own view and advice to the client to date and any steps already taken, for example, an attempt may have been made to mediate or settle the case which has failed. The instructions should set out clearly what advice is sought from counsel.

The date of receipt of instructions in chambers will be noted on the instructions. Once the barrister has written the opinion, which should be signed and dated by counsel, it will be returned to the solicitor together with the original instructions to counsel with the back sheet properly endorsed with the fee and the date the work was completed. One of the criticisms of barristers is the time taken to return written advice. It is important therefore to ensure you develop efficient methods which enable you to achieve a reasonable turnaround time. With ever more efficient methods of communication being used (eg fax, email) what is a 'reasonable' turnaround time gets shorter and shorter.

Although the instructions to counsel will rarely be shown to the lay client, solicitors frequently do either give or show a copy of counsel's opinion to the lay client. The client will then make a decision on whether or not to issue proceedings. Depending on the type of case and client, the solicitor may call the client in for an interview and give or show the client a copy of the opinion. Alternatively, a copy of the opinion may just be sent to the lay client with a covering letter setting out the solicitor's view and seeking the client's decision.

12.4.2.2   Case analysis: advising on the merits and/or quantum

Context

Even where you are asked to advise before proceedings have been issued, your analysis is focused on what will happen at trial: what issues will be fought and what is the likelihood of success (ie will your client win and, if so, get the remedy he or she is seeking?).

When advice is being sought at this preliminary stage, the solicitor will have been conscious of not taking any steps which might cost the client and be wasted because the advice is not to proceed. Thus the instructions may not contain, for example, expert reports, all the necessary documentation, or much in the way of evidence, eg, proofs from witnesses. The solicitor may also have felt that, in the circumstances, despite the additional cost to the client, a conference with counsel might be advisable prior to any written advice being given. However, if the instructions do not suggest a conference, counsel should advise on the basis of the information in the brief. Clearly if essential information has not been provided, counsel could contact the solicitor to obtain this before advising.

Consider the stage the case has reached. Is there any urgency? For example, is the limitation period about to expire. If it is a case where a pre-action protocol applies, has this been followed? From the tone of the instructions, how knowledgeable about civil procedure is your instructing solicitor? In addition to advising on the merits and quantum, what procedural aspects should you also include in your advice?

Analysis

Your analysis should be focused on the allegations which will be included in the client's statement of case, any possible counter allegations by the potential defendants and how these allegations will be proved in court. On the basis of this analysis, you must evaluate the client's case and form an opinion on the likelihood of the court finding in your client's favour.

You should be considering in as much detail as possible:

(a) What cause(s) of action will form the basis of the client's claim and what facts will be used to support the cause(s) of action? Thus, for example, if the claim is based on negligence, what precisely will you allege are the breaches? In addition, you must consider how the potential defendant is likely to defend the case, eg will he or she simply deny the breaches or also plead contributory negligence by your client? You are thinking forward to how you will draft your client's statement of case, which issues are likely to be disputed in the defence and therefore the issues which the court will have to decide.

(b) What evidence exists to support or counter the allegations which will be contained in the statements of case? Your analysis of the evidence must be thorough, detailed and precise. You need to be clear what evidence the solicitor has already identified and what further evidence should be collected. It is essential that your analysis is firmly focused on the allegations which are likely to be disputed and will need to be proved.

Having done this analysis, you then need to evaluate the case. Consider the allegations which need to be proved. Who bears the burden of proof? How likely is it that the court will find for your client on the allegations? How difficult and/or expensive will it be to collect the evidence? What remedy is your client likely to get if he or she wins?

Finally, consider any procedural points which need to be highlighted for your instructing solicitor, given your analysis and evaluation of the case.

Presentation

The opinion must be practical and accessible to the reader. The lay client will want to know his or her chances of succeeding and what the court will award if he or she does win. The solicitor will want to be able to understand quickly what your conclusions are, why you have reached those conclusions and the action you advise be taken. This means that your opinion must be structured and written in language which clearly sets out:

- *your conclusions*: on the case overall and on the individual issues which will be fought;
- *your reasoning*: identifying the cause(s) of action, the allegations of fact and evidence on which you have relied in your evaluation of the case;
- any advice on further evidence to be obtained;
- any procedural steps of which the solicitor should be advised.

For more information on writing opinions, see the ***Opinion Writing Manual***.

12.4.3 Making applications before issue

There are a variety of orders which can be obtained prior to issue. Most of these are done by application to the court for a hearing at which the matter can be determined on the basis of written evidence. Although solicitors may have the right to appear on such an application, counsel is frequently instructed. The more common of these orders are set out below.

12.4.3.1   Injunctions

A client may require an immediate court order to be protected from an alleged wrong. Thus, for example, the client's neighbour may be doing building work which is undermining the client's house and an application is made to court to order the neighbour to cease the building work until the case can be determined at trial. Another client may fear that property relevant to his claim (eg a pirated video) held by the wrongdoer may be destroyed and a search order will be sought to permit the client to search and seize the property pending trial. A third client who fears that the wrongdoer will dissipate assets or transfer them out of the country so as to render judgment hollow, may seek a freezing injunction to freeze those assets.

12.4.3.2   Orders to assist collection of evidence

In order to ascertain whether or not a client has a sufficiently good case to issue proceedings, it may be necessary to obtain documents or inspect property which is in someone else's possession. If access is refused, an application can be made in certain circumstances for a court order that inspection be given.

12.4.3.3   Making the application

In these situations, particularly where injunctions are sought, counsel may receive extremely short notice of the hearing (eg, an hour), and very little written information from the solicitor (sometimes only the back sheet). The written evidence which forms the basis of the application is that of the client but will be drafted by the barrister or the solicitor. Counsel may be asked to make the application on the basis of the written evidence drafted by the solicitor. Alternatively, counsel may also be instructed to advise in conference (where time is short the whole thing may be done in one telephone call) and/or draft the written evidence (faxed to the solicitor's office). If time is very short, the written evidence may be drafted outside the court door. Indeed the matter may be so urgent that a telephone application can be made for the injunction.

Where a detailed order is also sought (eg, an injunction), counsel should have a draft order ready to present to the court. Again this may have been prepared by the solicitor or by counsel. Clearly care must be taken in the drafting of the order to ensure that it does give the client the protection sought and is within the court's powers.

Those attending court should, in theory, include the barrister, the solicitor and the lay client. However, often the solicitor will not attend. If the case is sufficiently straightforward there may be no representation from the solicitor's firm. Alternatively, the solicitor may send an 'outdoor clerk', ie, a file carrier from the solicitor's office who may be extremely bright and au fait with the client and the case or a part-timer who has no idea about the case and very little, if any, legal knowledge. In addition, there is strictly no need for the client to attend as he or she will have no role to play in the hearing (the evidence being that contained in the written statement). However, if possible it is desirable for the client to attend in case something unexpected arises. Thus the barrister at the hearing may have access to fairly comprehensive information where both the solicitor and the lay client attend. However, he or she may equally have to rely solely on information from the brief including the written evidence.

At court, there may be attempts to settle the matter, either just the immediate application or the whole matter. Although the solicitors may have been negotiating prior to this, once at the court door, negotiations will usually be between counsel. Thus the barrister needs to be aware of the wider context of the case and be ready to receive and process information very quickly indeed. If a settlement is reached, the barrister should ensure that he or she knows exactly what has been agreed and that it is within the client's instructions. Clearly this will be extremely difficult, if not impossible, where the client is not present and the solicitor is represented by an uninformed 'outdoor clerk'.

12.4.3.4 Case analysis: pre-issue applications

Context

As explained above, when instructed on a pre-issue application, you may be instructed to draft the documents which form the basis of the application or be instructed to make the application on the basis of documents drafted by someone else. In either case you need to ensure that all the relevant documents are available for the hearing. What precisely is required depends on the urgency of the application and whether or not it is being made without notice to the other side. You need to check the relevant Civil Procedure Rules as to what documents are required. For most applications, even those made without notice to the other side, the applicant (as the prospective claimant) is required to have a claim form, particulars of claim, application notice, evidence to support the application (either a witness statement or affidavit depending on the type of application) and a copy of the draft order sought in the proper format. Sometimes, eg for injunctions, the draft order is also supplied on disk so that it can be readily adapted by the court.

If you are briefed to make the application on the basis of documents drafted by someone else, check that copies of all relevant documents are included in your instructions and that they are in the required format. If you are instructed to draft relevant documents, ensure you are clear what documents must still be drafted. Generally you will be instructed to draft the order and possibly witness statement/affidavit. However, you may also be instructed to draft the particulars of claim.

Whether just making the application or also drafting the documents, you will need to be clear what the application is for and why it is being made now, what your client's case is and what, if any, prior contact there has been with the (proposed) defendant(s). The instructions may contain minimal evidence about the case as a whole at this stage, eg just that contained in the witness statement or affidavit and exhibits, for much the same reasons as set out above (see **12.4.2**). The information and evidence in the instructions will be focused mainly on that required for the particular application.

Analysis

Your analysis should cover both:

(a) *THE case*: you need to be clear what cause(s) of action your client is relying on, who the defendants are, what facts are alleged by your client which support the cause(s) of action against each defendant and what evidence there is at this point to prove those facts. All these should be clear from the particulars of claim and the witness statements (or affidavits) and exhibits if already drafted. If these have not yet been drafted, the information should be contained in the instructions from the solicitor and documents enclosed (eg statements from the client taken in interview). The extent to which the court will focus on the merits of the main case depends on the type of application being made and the test which the court applies in determining that type of application (see below). However, whatever the application, you must understand why your client's case is pleaded as it is (ie what the allegations of fact are and how they support the cause of action) and the evidence currently available.

(b) *THIS application*: you need to be clear about what the client is seeking; what test the court will apply in determining whether or not to grant the application; whether the application is opposed or not; what, if any, notice has been given to the other side and the reasons why no notice or short notice has been given; and, what evidence is available to the court in the witness statements or affidavits and exhibits on which to determine the application. This should be clear from the witness statements or affidavits and exhibits and the draft order if already drafted. If these have not yet been drafted, the information should be contained in the instructions from the solicitor and documents enclosed (eg statements from the client taken in interview).

Once you have done this detailed analysis, you must formulate the arguments which can be used both for and against the granting of your client's application. In doing this, you must focus on the issues that will concern the court in determining the application. This will include considering every element of the test that the court will apply, being clear which aspects will be disputed and which will be of most concern to the court and will therefore require more attention in your argument. In addition, you need to consider the precise wording of the order very carefully as you will be required by the court to justify the order as drafted.

You also need to evaluate the arguments, ensuring that you are focusing on your strongest arguments and ready to deal with any weaknesses in the case. If necessary, consider what your 'fall back' position will be (ie if you cannot persuade the court to grant the order as drafted, what amendments might you suggest to get the most for your client?).

If the application is without notice to the other side, you need to consider carefully your duty of full and frank disclosure and ensure that you have identified any matters which professional conduct requires you draw to the courts' attention in the absence of the defendant (see *Advocacy Manual* and *Civil Litigation Manual* on this).

Finally ensure that you are prepared to deal with costs if this is necessary. What are the rules on costs on this type of application? Have you all the relevant information from the solicitor (eg a schedule of costs if this is required)?

Presentation

Ensure you know the order in which the judge will hear the submissions and tailor your submission accordingly. Thus, for example, if you are instructed for a defendant to oppose an application for an interim injunction, the judge will hear the applicant first. You need to be ready to both respond to the applicant and make any additional points you feel are important to raise on behalf of your client.

Judges deal with numerous applications, often in a very short time. You must therefore ensure that you present your case clearly and concisely focusing on the decisions that the judge has to make in the order he or she will make them. Thus, for example, if the application is made without notice to the other side, the court will want that issue addressed first to determine whether or not the application should proceed in the absence of the defendant(s). Only then, will the court be interested in considering the test to be applied in determining the application.

Consider which matters may be of concern to the judge and which you wish to draw to the judge's attention and ensure you focus on these. Take very careful note of the arguments which are raised by your opponent and be ready to counter them with your strongest arguments. Alternatively, be clear when a strong argument by your opponent cannot be rebutted and acknowledging this will add credibility to the other arguments on which you do rely.

Skeleton arguments are required in many instances. In any event, a skeleton argument is a useful tool to assist you. If you have time, draft a skeleton argument and have a copy ready to hand to the judge (for further advice on drafting skeleton arguments, see the *Drafting Manual*).

Ensure that you have all the papers in order suitably marked so that you can refer to specific documents quickly.

Once the judge has heard the submissions and states his or her decision on the application, if an order is granted, you must note the precise wording and check that it is within the power of the court to make and is enforceable. You must also make sure that the costs of the application have been dealt with and (where necessary) that a certificate for counsel has been granted. You should also be clear who must draft and serve the order.

Once outside court, you should ensure that the solicitor (or whoever attended from the office) and the lay client (if attending) understand exactly what has been ordered, both in terms of the substantive order and as to costs. The brief should be properly endorsed (see **12.3.7**).

12.5   Instituting proceedings

12.5.1   Introduction

If the client decides to take proceedings on the basis of the solicitor's advice or counsel's opinion, any of the requirements of a relevant pre-action protocol not already satisfied should be completed before issue. Even in cases where no pre-action protocol exists, the spirit of these protocols must be followed (see (a) at **12.2.2**). Failure to follow a particular protocol or the spirit of protocols, may result in the client, even if he or she wins in the end, having to pay costs incurred by the other side which would not have been incurred if the protocol had been followed. At a very minimum a 'letter before action' should be sent to the proposed defendant or his or her solicitors warning that proceedings will be issued if the client's claim is not satisfied. The client will have to pay court costs if no such letter is sent and the defendant satisfies the claim on receipt of the court documents and argues that this would have been done if warned of the impending proceedings. The proper court documents must also be drafted, served and, where necessary, filed with the court.

A barrister will rarely be involved in writing the 'letter before action' but may be consulted on satisfying the pre-action protocol and will frequently draft court documents. In addition, there are a variety of orders which may be sought early in the litigation process and the barrister may be briefed to obtain these (see above).

12.5.2   Court documents

12.5.2.1   The claimant's case

Claims are commenced by issuing a 'claim form' and 'particulars of claim'. The claim form always contains basic information such as the name and address of solicitors acting for the claimant. The particulars of claim set out the facts (but not generally the law or evidence) of the claimant's case sufficient to inform the defendant of the nature of the case which has to be met. The particulars of claim may be set out on the claim form or in a separate document. Whether or not a separate document is needed depends on the complexity of the case, generally only simple cases do not require a separate document.

It is vitally important that the statement of the claimant's case (the particulars of claim) is properly drafted as it sets out the issues which the claimant wishes the court to consider and the remedies being sought. It is usual to instruct counsel to draft the particulars of claim. The instructions from the solicitors should contain all the relevant information and documents. If counsel has already advised on the merits and/or quantum, the instructions seeking this advice and the advice given should be included in the instructions to draft the statement of the claimant's case.

When counsel has drafted the particulars of claim, his or her clerk will then arrange for the instructions together with the draft document to be returned to the solicitor. The solicitor (or a clerk in the firm) will then complete the formal documentation. This includes completing the claim form and the client or solicitor signing a 'statement of truth' verifying the content of the particulars of claim. The solicitor will also arrange for sufficient copies to be sent or taken to the court where they are stamped (the date of issue). Service on the defendants will be arranged by the court or by the solicitor by posting or personal delivery (by clerk or process servers).

Once served, the defendant will have a set period of time to respond by serving a defence. If the defendant fails to respond within the period, the claimant, in many cases, can get 'judgment in default' (ie of the defendant responding). This is a routine step in which the barrister will not be involved. A defendant who does respond may also consult a solicitor, who in turn may instruct counsel to draft the statement of his or her case.

12.5.2.2   The defendant's case

Counsel instructed to draft a response to particulars of claim should receive a proper set of instructions with all the relevant documents and sufficient information for the drafting of a defence and, where appropriate, a Part 20 counterclaim (where the defendant, in addition to a defence, has a claim against the claimant) and/or a Part 20 claim against another person (third-party notice) (where the defendant alleges someone else is wholly or partly responsible for any damages which the claimant may obtain against the defendant). The barrister will return the instructions with the relevant documents which have been drafted to the solicitor who will serve them on the relevant parties. Strict time limits apply and counsel must ensure that the necessary work is done in sufficient time for the solicitor to keep to those limits.

12.5.2.3   Reply by claimant

Where the defendant makes a counterclaim, which is relatively common, the claimant must serve a defence to that claim. If the defendant merely serves a defence, the claimant only needs to serve a 'reply' if the defence raises a good answer to the claimant's claim. The need for a 'reply' is rare. The barrister who drafted the initial statement will almost invariably be instructed to draft the subsequent responses. Again there are time limits for these to be served.

12.5.2.4   The statements of case

The particulars of claim, defence, counterclaim, defence to counterclaim and any reply constitute the 'statements of case'.

If any of the parties consider that the statement of case served on them does not give sufficient information to enable them to prepare their case properly, he or she may request further information. The further information provided will be available at trial.

12.5.2.5   Case analysis: drafting statements of case

Context

The statements of case set out the issues to be determined by the court and the parties are confined to arguing the issues in dispute as set out in the statements of case. Although all statements of case can be amended throughout the litigation process, there are limits on the amendments which can be made and there are cost implications for a party seeking amendments. Thus it is very important that counsel draft the statements of case carefully.

Analysis

In drafting particulars of claim, you must ensure that you have done sufficiently detailed and precise analysis to enable you to draft both the statement of the client's case and the relief sought as strongly and clearly as possible. The analysis is much the same as that set out in **12.4.2** (opinion on merits and/or quantum). Consider whom to join as parties, in particular whom should be joined as defendants and how all the parties should be named on the particulars. Ensure that you have considered all possible cause(s) of action (eg the claim may be brought in contract and tort) and determined which should be pleaded and the allegations of fact to be included to prove each element. Check that you have included all the remedies desired by and available to your client (eg if damages and an injunction are sought, both of these are included). Check that all the requirements on content contained in Civil Procedure Rules are satisfied (eg if your client is seeking aggravated or exemplary damages, the particulars of claim must include a statement to that effect and the grounds for claiming them).

In drafting defences, you must ensure that you have identified each and every allegation made in the particulars. You must then consider very carefully what your client's version of events is. You then need to consider each allegation in turn and decide how the defence will respond to it: admit it (where it is clear from your instructions and the evidence that it is true); deny it (where it is within your client's knowledge that it is not true and he or she has a positive case to the contrary); or require the claimant to prove it (where it is not something on which your client can comment because it is outside his or her knowledge or any evidence to the contrary). Finally you must consider very carefully your client's positive case (ie his or her alternative version of events to that which appear in the particulars of claim) and ensure that you include any additional facts on which the defendant intends to rely. Check that all the requirements on content contained in Civil Procedure Rules are satisfied (eg if your client is relying on the expiry of any limitation period, details must be set out in the defence).

When acting for a defendant, your client may also contend that he or she has a counter-claim or that someone else is wholly or partially responsible for the claimant's losses. Drafting a Part 20 counterclaim or a Part 20 claim against a new person is the same as drafting particulars of claim (see above). If the counterclaim also amounts to a set off, this must be included in the defence.

Presentation

Any statement of case, whether it is particulars of claim, defence, counterclaim or Part 20 claim, must be set out clearly and concisely and comply with the Civil Procedure Rules both in the content and format. Your draft statements of case must be signed and dated by you before you return them to the solicitor. The solicitor must then have the statement of case verified by a statement of truth signed by the lay client or solicitor.

Examples of statements of case can be found in the civil brief in **Chapter 16**. Detailed consideration of this is beyond the scope of this Manual and you are referred to the *Drafting Manual*.

12.5.3   Applications to the court

12.5.3.1   Introduction

In any civil proceedings there are a variety of applications which the parties can make to shorten the process or obtain payment or some form of court order without having to wait for the full hearing. Although some of these can be used at any stage in the proceedings, they will more commonly be employed relatively early in the process and before much of the evidence has been collected.

Applications are usually heard by judicial officers known as Masters (in the High Court in London) and District Judges (in a County Court and the High Court outside London). Although solicitors have rights of audience in these matters, they often instruct counsel. The hearing will generally be in public but often in a smaller room than a courtroom with counsel being invited to sit rather than stand. The Master or District Judge will hear argument from counsel for both parties on the basis of the statements of case served to date and written evidence. Counsel may have drafted the statements of case and also have been instructed to draft the written evidence for the hearing. However, applications often have to be made on the basis of statements of case and written evidence drafted by someone else, whether it be the solicitor or another barrister. The most common of the applications in which counsel may be involved are set out below.

12.5.3.2   Summary judgment

The claimant may apply to the court for 'summary judgment' where there is no real prospect the defence will succeed and therefore no real need for trial. The defendant may also apply for summary judgment where the claimant's case has no real prospect of success. The purpose of this process is to dispose of the case without the expense and delay of a full trial. In drafting the written statements and doing the advocacy at the hearing, counsel will need to balance the need to present the best case for the client with the fact that, as the purpose is to dispose of the case without extra expense, the application will be made at a stage before much of the evidence has been collected.

12.5.3.3   Interim payments

Although there are now procedures to attempt to bring cases to trial much faster than in the past, the interim payment procedure recognises that even this delay may cause hardship to a claimant and allows an application for early payment of at least some of the money being claimed. An interim payment will be ordered only where it is clear that the claimant will be at least partially successful and it would be unjust to delay immediate payment of that entitlement.

12.5.3.4   Security for costs

A defendant who considers he or she has a strong case may be worried that, though he or she will win at trial, the claimant will be unable to pay his or her costs. In certain circumstances, a defendant can apply to the court for an order that the claimant give 'security for costs', usually by paying a specified amount into court. There is no general right to obtain such security merely because an individual is impecunious. The applicant must satisfy the test in the Civil Procedure Rules (see the *Civil Litigation Manual*).

12.5.3.5   Other orders

The orders which can be sought prior to issue can equally be sought after issue and before the full hearing (see **12.4.3** above).

12.5.3.6   Case analysis: applications to court

Context

Given that proceedings have been issued and served, the defendant(s) will be aware of the claim against them and the remedies sought by the claimant. The context varies according to the purpose of the application which range from seeking to stop the claim in its tracks (summary judgment), through getting money up front before the trial (interim payment) to ensuring the claimant can pay the costs if the defendant wins (security for costs). It will also depend on the point in the litigation process at which the application is made. Although most of these applications will be made early on in the process, when little if any evidence has been collected or exchanged, they may also be made later in the process when much more of both sides' cases have been revealed.

Analysis

The process of analysis for these applications is much the same as for those made pre-issue (see **12.4.2.2**). Generally the only difference will be that you are likely to have more information about the case.

Presentation

The considerations in respect of presentation for these applications are much the same as for those made pre-issue (see **12.4.2.2**). The only difference will be that, generally, a court file will exist which contains documents already filed and served. There will be no file available in a hearing before a Queen's Bench Master.

12.6   Interim stage: preparing the evidence

12.6.1   Introduction

Once statements of case have been exchanged, the issues between the parties have been defined and they now move to collecting and preparing their evidence for trial, including any relevant documents, real evidence (eg, goods which are claimed to be faulty), expert reports and witness statements.

The evidence at trial is that of all the parties, and the solicitor for each party must ensure that he or she collects all the evidence relevant to his or her client's case and exchanges evidence and information with the other parties where mutual disclosure is required or appropriate.

12.6.2   Obtaining information from other parties

There are formal steps by which all parties are obliged to exchange information about their evidence. This will be done by the solicitor, sometimes with counsel's assistance. The steps involved include the following.

12.6.2.1   Disclosure

This is the process by which the parties exchange information about the potential documentary evidence which they hold. All parties are obliged within a set time period to make a list of all relevant documents (even those they themselves do not intend to use at the trial) which are or have been in their possession, custody or power and serve the list on the other parties who then have the right to inspect all those still in possession and for which privilege is not claimed. Inspection may be by exchange of photocopies of documents or actual inspection at the solicitors' offices. From this exchange of lists and inspection, both sides collect the documents and information contained in them which may form evidence for or against them. The process, which it is essential to carry out carefully, can be extremely tedious and, fortunately, counsel is rarely involved in it, unless problems occur as in the case of *Lowe v Mainwaring* at **16.3**. Frequently the process is done by each side sending photocopies of their relevant documents to the other side. Theoretically the costs of the copying are borne by the side receiving them. However, to avoid unnecessary bureaucracy, it is also common for each side to undertake to pay these costs and, if the cost is low or comparable on either side, the parties then waive the right to enforce the undertaking.

12.6.2.2 Requests for further information

A party can request 'further information' from other parties on matters which are reasonably necessary and proportionate to enable the party to understand the case he or she has to meet or to assist in the preparation of his or her case. The request could be for clarification/further information of the statements of case (see **12.5.2.4**) or other matters, such as witness statements. The requests and answers form part of the bundle of documents used at trial and counsel is likely to be involved in drafting both.

12.6.2.3 Notice to admit facts

The length and cost of trial will depend to a degree on the number of disputed issues which need to be determined. The statements of case limit the issues to those which the defendant denies or does not admit (ie puts the claimant to proof). A party may attempt to limit the issues further by seeking admissions from the other side through the formal process of serving a notice to admit. A party who fails to admit facts in response to such a notice may have to bear the cost of proving them at trial. Counsel may be asked to draft notices and replies.

12.6.2.4 Exchange of witness evidence

Within a set period parties must simultaneously exchange both witness statements and expert reports of all those they intend to call and are basically confined at trial to the evidence in the statements and reports exchanged. The actual wording of them is therefore very important and counsel will frequently be involved in the drafting of them. The solicitor then arranges the exchange with the other parties.

12.6.3 Advising on evidence

12.6.3.1 Generally

The solicitor may seek counsel's advice on evidence at any stage in the litigation process, either through formal instructions seeking written advice or a conference with counsel, with or without the lay client. Even where this is done in conference, counsel is frequently asked to confirm the advice in writing. Counsel's involvement in collecting and preparing the evidence for trial is usually confined to advising on the strengths and weaknesses of the evidence and what further evidence should be collected.

12.6.3.2 Case analysis

Context

As explained above, you may be asked to advise on evidence at any stage in the proceedings and this will dictate the amount of information you have and the period which the solicitors have to act on your advice. Generally the disputed issues will have been identified and there will be some information on which to gauge the overall strength of the case. Documents may have been inspected and expert reports and witness statements obtained. At this point you are focusing on precisely what evidence will be used, ie what documents to include in the court bundle, whether any additional witnesses are needed, and the precise content and format of witness statements and expert reports.

Analysis

Check that the solicitor has sent you all the relevant materials to enable you to advise properly. From the statements of case, you should determine precisely what issues are disputed and on whom the burden of proof lies to prove the various allegations of fact on those issues. Consider whether any of the issues could be clarified or narrowed by the use of requests for further information or notices to admit. Consider whether any amendments are necessary to the statements of case in light of the evidence.

You then need to review the evidence available on each issue and decide what evidence to tender on each of those issues. It is helpful to make a list of the issues at this point and in respect of each issue, consider the evidence available. Are there any gaps? In particular, identify the matters on which it is essential that evidence is tendered on your client's behalf to make out your case and ensure there are no gaps. Consider what form the evidence will take on the various issues (witnesses of fact, expert opinion, documentary and/or real evidence) and any formalities which need to be fulfilled to be able to tender the evidence in this form.

In respect of potential documentary evidence, consider whether full disclosure has been given by both sides. Do you want the authenticity of any document challenged? Consider which documents relate to which issues. Where documents or real evidence are to be relied on, consider who will produce them.

Consider what matters call for expert evidence, check that the expert instructed has the relevant expertise to give opinion evidence on these matters and that the report contains relevant evidence including copies of any articles, literature etc on which the expert relies for his or her views. Check that the directions in respect of experts has been followed (eg if a meeting was directed, has this happened?) and that the report complies with the Civil Procedure Rules on content and format. If there is a single joint expert or an expert report from the other side, are there matters on which it might be useful to put written questions to the expert?

Consider what witnesses of fact need to be called. Go through the proofs of each witness checking the issues on which he or she can give useful evidence. Note any gaps where the proof does not cover matters on which it appears the witness could give evidence. When you have considered all the proofs, check whether there are any issues on which there is no or insufficient oral evidence. Consider whether or how these gaps can be filled (eg by other existing witnesses or a new witness). Note if there are any particular difficulties in respect of any of the witnesses, eg reluctant to give evidence or may be confused when giving evidence. The solicitor, having taken the original statements from the witnesses may be in a better position to gauge this than you. Where you have been provided with witness statements, ensure they comply with the Civil Procedure Rules on content and format. Check that any directions have been fulfilled, eg, witness statements exchanged.

Having considered what is available, you need then to decide what evidence should be tendered. For example there may be several witnesses who can give evidence on the same facts. Consider whether all of them are needed and, if not, which should be called. Similarly check which documents should be put before the court and what advice you might give on the preparation of the bundles for use at trial.

When advising on the evidence to be collected and the evidence to be available for the hearing, you should be acutely aware of the overriding principle of 'proportionality' (see (a) at **12.2.2**). This involves two aspects. First, the amount of time involved and difficulty in obtaining the evidence. The actual work of collecting the evidence falls to the solicitor who will interview witnesses to obtain statements, ensure all the relevant documents and items of real evidence are assembled and, where necessary, instruct and obtain a report from an expert. You must weigh up the need to have all relevant evidence available for the hearing with the feasibility of the solicitor actually being able to produce it in the time available. Secondly, collecting and preparing the evidence increases the client's costs. The solicitor charges for any work done on the case. In addition there will be 'disbursement costs' incurred which will be passed on to the client where a charge is made to the solicitor to obtain information, copy documents, advice etc from others. Experts will charge for their work as will counsel. You must therefore also weigh up the need for the evidence against the cost of obtaining it.

Presentation

An advice on evidence must be practical and accessible to the solicitor. He or she will want to be able to understand readily what further evidence needs to be collected and why it is needed. He or she will also want to be able to identify readily what evidence you advise should be tendered at court and the reasons for your decisions. This means that your opinion must structured and written in a way which clearly sets out:

- what further evidence needs to be collected;
- what evidence should be tendered at trial;
- any formalities which must be satisfied to ensure the evidence can be tendered;
- any procedural steps which should be followed.

For more information on writing opinions, see the *Opinion Writing Manual*.

12.6.4 Drafting witness statements

12.6.4.1 Generally

Until recently, all witnesses except expert witnesses gave evidence orally at trial. The solicitor drafted statements (or 'proofs' as they were sometimes called) for use by the advocate in court as the basis for questioning in examination-in-chief. These statements or proofs were not revealed to the other side and the evidence of the witness in chief was what was said orally at the trial. Any errors or omissions in the statements or proofs could therefore be rectified by counsel's careful questioning in court.

In virtually all cases now, witness statements must be in a particular format and exchanged prior to the hearing. The statements themselves stand as the bulk of the witness's evidence-in-chief. The actual wording of the witness statements is therefore incredibly important. The witness signs it as an acknowledgement that he or she accepts the truth of its contents and the solicitor should, therefore, ensure that the witness has the opportunity to check and amend the contents prior to signing and exchange.

12.6.4.2   Case analysis

Context

Although the witness statement is technically that of the witness, it is usually drafted by the solicitor or barrister. The Bar's Code of Conduct (para 705) prohibits 'witness coaching' and sets out some guidance for discussing the evidence with witnesses. Generally, you will be instructed to draft statements on the basis of the solicitor's instructions and enclosed documents including records of interviews with the client, letters, client's files and attendance notes by the solicitor. Alternatively, you may be instructed to 'polish' a statement drafted by the solicitor.

Analysis

The statement represents the witness's evidence-in-chief and should cover all the issues in the statements of case on which this witness can give evidence. You therefore need to determine from the statements of case precisely what issues are in dispute and the allegations of fact made by each side. You then need to consider each witness in turn and determine which allegations of fact they can deal with in their evidence. In addition, clarify what first-hand evidence the witness can give and what evidence is hearsay. Although hearsay evidence is now admitted in civil cases and it can be included in the witness statement, the source of it should be set out in the witness statement and you should be conscious that it will be given less weight than first-hand evidence. Finally consider what, if any, documents or real evidence support this witness's evidence and ensure that reference to it is included in the statement. Check that appropriate formalities have or will be fulfilled, eg, hearsay notices served on the other side where appropriate.

Presentation

At trial the witness statement will become the witness's evidence-in-chief. It is therefore written in narrative form in the first person as if written by that witness. Getting the style or tone of the language right in a witness statement can be difficult as, while technically it is supposed to be the words of the witness, generally the language used is slightly more formal than the language many witnesses would use when questioned. Any documents or real evidence which the witness will produce must be formally marked and exhibited to the witness statement. The witness statement must also fulfil the formal requirements as to form and content. For further guidance on drafting witness statements, see the *Drafting Manual*.

12.6.5   Experts and their reports

12.6.5.1   Generally

The success of many cases will depend on the expert evidence. Thus, for example, in personal injury cases, the court will usually determine the extent of the claimant's injuries on the basis of medical evidence. In building disputes, the parties may rely on the opinion of surveyors, eg, as to the extent of disrepair and what is required to rectify it. Expert evidence is basically opinion evidence of a suitably qualified or experienced person. Experts can differ in their opinions. In order to prevent the trial disintegrating into the swapping of numerous expert opinions, parties are usually each confined to a certain number, frequently one or two, experts. In addition, the procedure has for a number of years encouraged the parties to limit as far as possible the need for experts to be called at trial by directing exchange of expert reports and meetings of experts to attempt to limit the issues and have the reports agreed if possible. The Woolf reforms have increased the limitations on numbers of experts, including requiring the appointment of a single joint expert's report (ie no oral testimony) in fast track cases generally.

Obtaining expert evidence can be a complicated task which requires great skill to choose the right experts, instruct them properly and ensure that their evidence is well presented.

A barrister's involvement in obtaining expert evidence will depend on the level of expertise of the instructing solicitor. The solicitor may be new to this area of work and look to the barrister for advice throughout including seeking advice on which expert to instruct. However, most solicitors who specialise will have a 'stable' of experts on which they can rely and will be sufficiently au fait with the area to instruct them. The solicitor will obtain the report and the barrister will have no involvement with the expert prior to the evidence being given in court. The only exception to this is where the expert evidence is complicated or in an area not known to the barrister. In such a case, a conference may be held with the expert for the barrister to ensure that he or she has sufficient understanding of the evidence to deal with it properly at court.

The basis of expert evidence is the reports which the experts will write themselves. The report will be considered by the solicitor, who may also seek the barrister's view of it, to ensure that it covers all relevant matters and does not include irrelevant ones. If an expert report is not favourable, the lawyer (solicitor or barrister) can discuss the contents of the report with the expert. Clearly there are professional conduct issues in the lawyers becoming too involved in the drafting of the report and attempting to 'rework' the opinion of the expert. If the expert's view is genuinely not favourable to the client, the lawyers need to decide whether or not to seek the opinion of another expert. The report of the first expert remains privileged and will not be shown to the other parties. However, if the other parties have discovered that the expert has been consulted there is nothing to stop them from calling that expert to give evidence.

12.6.5.2   Case analysis

Context

As can be seen from the above, the contexts in which you may be instructed to deal with experts and expert evidence are many and varied. The two main areas on which you are likely to become involved are advising on the report and questioning experts in court.

Analysis

In either situation, advising on an expert report or preparing to question an expert in court, you need to check precisely what issues call for expert opinion evidence, that the expert has the relevant expertise (qualification and/or experience) to give the evidence and that the report does cover the issues on which expert opinion is required. You also need to understand fully and in detail what the expert opinion is and the expertise on which it is based. This includes understanding all technical terms used and any diagrams or plans. It also includes understanding the basis of the expert's expertise (ie his or her experience and any other sources which inform his or her view such as journals, custom in the trade, etc) and why he has the opinion he does in respect of this case.

To assist you in dealing with experts, keep information or ensure easy access to information on areas of expertise common to your practice, for example, copies of relevant books, websites and diagrams to assist in deciphering reports, eg, medical dictionaries, surveying terminology, etc.

Once you thoroughly understand the expert evidence fully, identify any gaps and ambiguities in the report and the issues to which they relate. Check that any directions of the court in respect of experts has been or will be fulfilled and that the report satisfies the requirements of the Civil Procedure Rules on both form and content.

Presentation

Advice on an expert report will usually be contained in an advice on evidence generally. See comments above on this. Dealing with experts at trial will form part of preparation for trial. See comments below on this.

12.7 The trial: final preparation and hearing

12.7.1 Introduction

Having gone through the stages of exchanging statements of case to define the issues to be tried, and collecting and exchanging the evidence as required by the rules, the final preparations for trial involve ensuring that all the parties, witnesses and lawyers attend court properly prepared and that the evidence is put into a format which is convenient for all, including the judge.

12.7.2 Trial dates and timetables

Cases assigned to the small claims and fast tracks will almost invariably be given trial dates when allocated to that track. In cases where no trial date has been given (in multi-track cases and some fast track cases) a trial date will have to be obtained from the court. In addition, in both fast track and multi-track cases, a few weeks before the trial date, the court will make directions as to the evidence to be called, the documents to be used (see **12.7.4**), how the trial should be conducted (trial timetable which will include limitations on the amount of time for each step in the trial) and any other matters it considers are required to prepare the case for trial. Where it is intended that counsel act as advocate, he or she should be involved in providing the information to the court on which decisions as to trial date and directions for trial are made (whether done in writing or by way of a procedural hearing at court).

12.7.3 Witnesses

It is the solicitor's duty to ensure that the witnesses attend court on the hearing day. The solicitor should therefore make sure that all the witnesses (and the client, if not also a witness) are given as much information as possible about likely hearing dates and, when it is actually fixed, the precise date. If there is any likelihood that a witness will not attend, the solicitor should consider compelling attendance by issuing and serving a witness summons.

12.7.4 Trial bundles

The claimant's solicitor must, within a set number of days before the date fixed for the trial, prepare and lodge with the court copies of all the documents which will be used or referred to at the trial by the claimant or defendant (the defendant's solicitor having given notice to the claimant's solicitor). The division of labour becomes more complicated where there is a claim and counterclaim (ie the defendant taking on the role of claimant in respect of the counterclaim).

The purpose of preparing and lodging the bundles of documents is to ensure that they have been put into a usable format for the court. The rules set out the number and format (eg, paginating) of bundles to be lodged; the principal documents lodged include:

- the claim form and all statements of case;
- a case summary and/or chronology where appropriate;
- all requests for information and the answers;
- all witness statements with an indication of whether the contents are agreed;
- all expert reports with an indication of whether the contents are agreed;
- all documents which any of the parties wish to have before the court.

The claimant's solicitor will arrange for sufficient copies of the bundles to be provided for all parties (the other parties paying a reasonable fee for their copies). Each party will usually have three or four copies, one for the solicitor, one for counsel, one for the witness and, possibly, one spare.

Ensuring that the bundles contain all the relevant documents and are compiled in accordance with the rules is an extremely important but tedious task. Fortunately, counsel's only involvement in this will be to advise on which statements, reports, documents etc are to be included.

12.7.5   Briefing the advocate

12.7.5.1   The brief

Where the solicitor has decided not to do the advocacy personally, his or her choice of counsel will depend on a variety of factors including the type of case, its complexity and whether counsel has been involved in the preparation stages. Whoever the solicitor decides to use should be properly briefed (see **12.3.6** for general format) and should include copies of the following:

- any bundles lodged at court;
- all previous advice and opinions of counsel;
- any additional proofs of evidence from witnesses (ie updating their statements).

The detail in the brief will depend on counsel's previous involvement. Thus, where counsel has been actively involved, and the documents enclosed include previous opinions and advice, the brief itself may be relatively short as counsel is au fait with all the detail.

12.7.5.2   The brief fee

The barrister's fee for the case will depend on his or her standing and the complexity of the case. It is agreed on the basis of a 'fee' of £x for the first day (a sum which includes preparation time) and a 'refresher' of £y (a lower sum than the fee, a daily charge) for subsequent days. Although technically the full fee is payable once the brief is delivered even if the case settles or folds before then, in practice many barristers agree to accept no fee if, eg, the case settles before a deadline date which is calculated to give them time to prepare.

Where a conditional fee agreement has been made between the barrister and solicitor, the brief will be so marked.

12.7.5.3   Delivery of brief/acceptance by counsel

Ideally, where the trial is of any substance, briefs should be delivered to counsel at least two weeks before the hearing date.

While some solicitors are very professional and do ensure counsel has the brief in adequate time, some more often than not deliver it very late. On the reverse side of the coin, barristers who have been booked to do the hearing may become unavailable, eg, because of being 'part heard' (ie in the middle of a case which has overrun its estimated time). Counsel's clerk should notify the solicitor as soon as the problem arises so the solicitor can choose another barrister to take the brief. Some chambers are very good at notifying solicitors and some delay the notification, hoping the barrister will in the end be free. The clerk may suggest someone else in chambers to take over. The advantage of this is that counsel taking over has more opportunity to discuss the case with counsel who was initially briefed.

12.7.5.4   Preparation for trial by the advocate: case analysis

Context

The brief you receive from the solicitor should contain all the documents set out in **12.7.5.1**. In addition, your instructing solicitor should confirm that all the witnesses and experts have been warned and, where necessary witness summons have been issued to compel attendance.

The focus of your preparation is on your submissions, in particular your closing submission and your questioning of the witnesses. If you are familiar with the case, in particular have given an advice on evidence just prior to trial, you can build on the analysis done at that stage. In addition, you will at this stage have all the evidence on which the opponent relies which you may not have had when you gave the advice on evidence. If you are not familiar with the case, you will need to do the analysis from scratch.

Analysis

Check that you have received all the relevant documents. The analysis will follow much the same lines as that set out in **12.6.3.2**, **12.6.4.2** and **12.6.5.2** but this time it will also include consideration of the other side's evidence (ie identifying the strengths and weaknesses of their evidence).

You must ensure that you are clear which issues the court will have to determine, ie, the issues in dispute and the factual allegations by each side on those issues, and the evidence which will be used by you and your opponent on those issues. Evaluate the strengths and weaknesses of your case on the basis of this analysis.

From your analysis and evaluation, the important areas of the case will have emerged. You then need to work out how you are going to present the case, focusing on the relevant issues, using the strengths and avoiding or neutralising the weaknesses. This is often called developing a 'theory of the case'. Basically it is your client's 'story' told through your submissions and the evidence of the witnesses which gives a logical and convincing account of how the events in the case are likely to have happened in a way which is favourable to your client's case. It must be plausible and firmly based on the legal principles and evidence. However, it will rely on inferences and generalisations to fill the gaps which always exist in cases (given they are generally based on what people remember of an event which occurred sometime in the past). You need to be clear what inferences you wish the court to draw and the generalisations (premises which rest on the general behaviour of people or objects) on which you rely to persuade the court to accept your explanation.

For example, you might have a case where your client, a 65-year-old woman fell while in a fast food hamburger restaurant just after a 19-year-old employee had washed the floor.

She alleges that she slipped on a wet floor. The restaurant allege that she was not paying attention to where she was going. The case turns on whether or not the floor was wet and whether this caused the fall. One could use the 'generalisations' that washing floors is a routine task and that most 19-year-olds would find it boring and that when someone finds a task boring they may not do it properly. The inference you would be seeking the court to find is that the floor was not dried properly in this case.

The 'theory of the case' must be a coherent story which is consistent with the legal principles and all the evidence which will be heard by the court. It should include consideration of both the overall story and the 'characterisation' of any relevant witnesses (as done in the example above).

Having developed a 'theory of the case' you then need to consider the contents of your closing speech, the issues which will concern the court and how you will use your 'theory of the case' to persuade the court to find for you. You then need to consider each witness in turn and determine what you must draw out in questioning, both in examination-in-chief of your own witnesses and in cross-examination of the opponent's witnesses. You must also consider at what point documents and real evidence will be introduced.

Presentation

Determine what speeches are allowed by counsel, eg if you are for the defendant will you be allowed an opening and a closing or just a closing speech (more likely). Decide the contents of both, keeping your submissions/arguments for the closing speech.

Counsel should consider whether a skeleton argument is required. This may have been included in the case management directions, or it may be required by a specialist court guide. Skeleton arguments are generally required for High Court trials (and in the Court of Appeal). Otherwise, it is a matter of professional judgment based on the complexity of the issues. Skeletons should be served on the other side and filed at court 24 or 48 hours before the hearing (except for the Court of Appeal, when they must be lodged early on in the process).

As witness statements generally stand as evidence-in-chief, oral examination-in-chief is severely restricted in civil cases. You will need the court's permission if you wish to expand or introduce new matters which have arisen since the exchange of witness statements. You will also need to inform your opponent. Knowledge of the general practice of the particular court is helpful on this as some courts are more restrictive in allowing oral examination than others.

Consider the witness statement of each of the opponent's witnesses. First consider whether or not you should cross-examine that witness. If there is no purpose to it, don't do it! You must 'put your case'. You must challenge all material parts of the evidence given by a witness which your client (or his or her witnesses) does not accept. Be clear which points you must 'put' to the witness. Then identify the evidence on which you can you build (ie are helpful to your case or neutral and may support your theory of the case) and the areas on which the witness is damaging (eg, evidence which directly contradicts your theory of the case). Then plan the order in which you will cross-examine, building on the favourable before moving on to the aspects with which the witness is likely to disagree.

Finally consider how you will 'tab' the bundle (mark the documents for easy access by you in the trial). Make notes as appropriate to assist you both in the submissions and the questioning. This may include highlighting the witness statements, documents, expert reports, etc. Also plan how you will take notes during the trial, eg, during questioning of witnesses to ensure that you can cross-examine or re-examine effectively and precisely.

12.7.6 The trial

When counsel is instructed as the advocate at trial, there may or may not be a representative of the instructing solicitor's firm present. The representative may be the solicitor, where the case or the client is worth a reasonable amount, or a 'file carrier' who may or may not know anything about the case or the law.

At trial, the advocate has control of and responsibility for the conduct of the case. There are numerous matters which require some attention immediately before going into court, eg, there may be last-minute checking of information, updating of statements, reassuring witnesses who are nervous, ensuring the court has the advocate's name, etc. It is the advocate's duty to ensure the smooth running of the case — that all the witnesses are present, all the documents are before the court and available for those who need them, eg, witnesses when giving evidence, etc. It is also important to make sure that witnesses have read their statements before giving their evidence.

Once the hearing has started, the advocate will be fully occupied either addressing the court or dealing with witnesses. It is an important part of the barrister's duty to take careful notes during the trial even where the attendant solicitor (or representative) is also taking notes. It is the barrister's own notes on which he or she will rely if questions arise later as to precisely what happened. The barrister may cross check with the solicitor. However, it is not possible to turn constantly to the solicitor (or representative) for their notes and the quality of their notes varies enormously.

Once all the evidence has been called and the closing speeches given, the court will deliver judgment. This may be done immediately or, where the case has been long or complex, may be reserved, by an adjournment to the next day or to a much later date where the judge requires more time to consider it. Counsel should take a full note of the judgment and endorse the brief properly (see **12.3.7**). Counsel should also check that any orders are within the court's power, the details are accurate and that he or she understands the judgment or order in detail.

The advocate for the successful party will ask for costs. It is important that the court makes orders on all the costs before it including any which are outstanding from interim hearings. In addition, the court should deal with the summary assessment of costs if it is a fast track trial, or make an order for detailed assessment, including the detailed assessment of any public funding costs.

The judgment and/or order of the court cannot be enforced until it is formally drawn up. This will usually be the task of the court. Counsel must ensure that his or her notes and endorsement are sufficient for the solicitor to check that the court has done the task properly before serving the order on the party against whom it has been made.

12.8 Settlement during the process

A very high percentage of cases never get to trial but settle at some stage along the way. Although there is nothing preventing the parties themselves from negotiating a settlement, once proceedings are issued, negotiations are usually conducted through the lawyer, usually the solicitor. Counsel may be involved in negotiations, most frequently at the court door prior to the full trial or possibly at interim hearings. All such negotiations should be conducted on a 'without prejudice' basis which means that they cannot be revealed to the court if settlement is not reached.

A defendant who wishes to put some pressure on the claimant to settle can use one of two devices. If the claimant's claim is for money (damages or a debt), a 'payment in' (now called a 'Part 36 payment') to court may be made. Under this procedure the defendant pays a sum into court which the claimant can then accept, which ends the matter, or refuse, in which case the case will still go to court. However, if the claimant does not win more than the sum paid in, he or she will have to pay the defendant's costs from the date of the 'payment in'. Where 'payment in' is not possible, eg, the claim is not for money or raising the money would require the sale of an asset which would be unreasonable to do prior to acceptance of the offer, the defendant can make an offer in a 'Part 36 offer'. This procedure may also be used by claimants. The contents of the letter cannot be revealed at trial prior to judgment but will be used in much the same way as a 'payment in' for costs. Counsel may be asked to advise on the level or format of the offer or its acceptance.

12.9 Enforcement

Many parties against whom judgments are given or orders are made comply with them without any further steps being required. However, if a party fails to comply, further formal steps are required to force compliance, eg, the issue by the court of a warrant for possession to instruct the bailiffs to evict a person whom the court has ordered to deliver up possession or a warrant of execution to instruct the bailiffs to seize goods and sell them to obtain money a person has been ordered to pay. All of this falls to the solicitor and the barrister is rarely, if ever, involved.

12.10 Appeal

A party may wish to appeal a decision of the court, eg because judgment has been given against them or because, although an order has been made in their favour, they disagree with the terms set by the court. Counsel will frequently be involved both in advising on whether or not to appeal and in drafting the grounds of appeal.

12.11 Costs

The costs incurred which form the subject of a costs order include court fees, lawyers' fees and other costs such as photocopying costs and expert witness fees. Although the general rule is that 'costs follow the event' which means that the losing party is ordered to pay the winning party's costs, this is not always the case and the court may refuse to make the order, eg, where there has been a 'payment in' which has not been exceeded at trial.

Even where a costs order is made, the winning party will rarely have all of his or her costs paid by the loser. There are three different methods for determining the actual amount which the loser must pay:

(a) Under 'agreed' costs' the parties agree how much of the winner's costs the loser will pay.

(b) 'Summarily assessed' costs are used in 'fast track' cases where, immediately after giving judgment, the court assesses and states the costs payable.

(c) 'Detailed assessed' costs are used where the solicitor whose client's costs are being paid submits a bill of costs to the court and a court officer decides the costs which should be allowed, reduced or disallowed on either a 'standard' or 'indemnity' basis. The 'standard' basis is the usual basis used and allows a reasonable sum in respect of all costs reasonably incurred, any doubts being resolved in favour of the paying party. The 'indemnity' basis, under which all costs are allowed except in so far as they are unreasonable, is far more generous and is ordered against the loser only in exceptional cases.

The solicitor has overall responsibility for keeping a record of all the costs incurred, including the barrister's fees, paying the various expenses, including the barrister's fees, having the bill assessed where a costs order is made and getting payment from the paying party and/or the client and/or the Community Legal Service.

Where a costs order is made, the winning party still has to pay his or her solicitor the full amount of the bill and is reimbursed by the losing party paying what was agreed or assessed. However, the winning party may feel that the bill is too high and have it assessed (which may be done on the indemnity basis). Only the amount allowed on assessment is payable. Counsel's brief fee will generally be what was agreed between the clerk and the solicitor. Although technically still payable by the solicitor to the barrister, the solicitor will only recoup from the client what was assessed as reasonable. In light of this, the barrister needs to decide whether or not to press for the full amount of the assessed amount, particularly where these solicitors regularly instruct the barrister.

A barrister who has entered a conditional fee agreement with the solicitor will be paid in accordance with that agreement, generally nothing if the case is lost and a success fee if the case is won.

Anatomy of a criminal case

13.1 Introduction

The purpose of this chapter is not to act as a textbook on criminal procedure, nor as a guide to criminal advocacy. Rather, its function is to set out the stages of a case in which counsel may be involved so that this involvement can be put in its proper context as regards fact management (or case analysis as it is sometimes called). Further details regarding the procedure adopted by the criminal courts may be found in the Criminal Litigation and Sentencing Manual and in the Advocacy Manual, as well as specialist practitioner texts such as *Blackstone's Criminal Practice*.

The popular picture is of the barrister acting as an advocate in the courtroom. However, counsel's role is invariably much wider than that. This chapter sets out some of the tasks which a barrister instructed in a criminal case may have to perform. You should compare and contrast this chapter with **Chapter 12** (especially **12.3**), which deals with civil cases.

Although counsel may be briefed only for a particular stage in a case, real life does not exist in tidy compartments. For example, counsel may be instructed to apply for bail, but in the course of talking to the client about the bail application may be asked questions about what plea the defendant should enter or (in cases where there is a choice) which court should try the case. It is therefore vital for the barrister to be able to take an overview of the case as a whole.

Although reference is made to the role of the Crown Prosecution Service, most of this chapter is written from the perspective of a barrister representing the defendant. This is because barristers in private practice are generally required to have gained several years' experience in the criminal courts as defence advocates before being instructed to prosecute cases.

13.2 Role of the defence barrister

A barrister only represents a defendant if 'briefed' to do so by a solicitor. Solicitors themselves have complete rights of audience in the magistrates' court, and so there is nothing a barrister can do there that a solicitor cannot.

In the Crown Court, any solicitor may appear at the hearing of an appeal (against conviction and/or sentence) from a magistrates' court and at the sentencing hearing which follows a committal for sentence by a magistrates' court, provided that the solicitor is from the firm of solicitors which represented the defendant in the magistrates' court. Solicitors who have been granted Rights of Audience in the Higher Courts under the

Courts and Legal Services Act 1990 may also conduct a Crown Court trial or appear at hearings in the Crown Court prior to the trial.

If a barrister is instructed, the brief (generally entitled 'Instructions to Counsel') usually consists of a short introduction to the case, written by the instructing solicitor, together with a proof of evidence (ie, a written statement) from the defendant. In the criminal brief in **Chapter 17**, the same barrister has been instructed at three stages of the same case but this will not necessarily be what happens in practice.

At the early stages of a case, the brief sent to the barrister may consist of very little. Indeed, there will be cases where the barrister is the first lawyer the defendant sees in connection with this particular offence. In that case, the brief may consist of only a 'back sheet' (ie, a piece of paper containing the name of the defendant, the court in which that defendant is appearing and the name and address of the solicitors).

When the barrister meets the client it is necessary to go through the proof of evidence (assuming there is one) with the client. It may be that there are things the client wishes to correct or to add. Where the barrister is taking instructions from the client at court (shortly before the hearing), there may only be a short time available and counsel should give priority to eliciting information which is relevant to the hearing which is about to take place. For example, if the reason for the appearance is to make a bail application, then the information which counsel needs to draw out first from the client should relate to matters which are relevant to bail. Other matters can be dealt with after the more important information has been discovered.

By the time the case is ready for trial, counsel should have a much fuller brief which contains not only a proof of evidence from the client, but also statements from any witnesses whom counsel is to call in support of the defence case. In the case of Crown Court trials, defence counsel will also be in possession of the written statements made by the witnesses whom the prosecution intend to call. In the case of magistrates' court trials, counsel for the defence *may* have copies of the witness statements made by the prosecution witnesses; if the offence is one which is triable either way (ie, triable either in the magistrates' court or in the Crown Court), counsel will at least have a summary of the prosecution case.

If the solicitor has not already done so, defence counsel should make sure that the defendant looks through the statements made by the prosecution witnesses and so has a chance to comment on those statements; this may give counsel very useful ammunition with which to cross-examine those witnesses when the time comes.

In the magistrates' court, where counsel has been instructed on behalf of the defendant, no representative from the solicitor's office will be present. If the defendant brings witnesses who have not made statements to the instructing solicitor, counsel will have to take statements from those witnesses.

In the Crown Court, a representative from the instructing solicitor should be present (although this will usually be an 'outdoor clerk', that is, a representative who is not legally qualified).

13.3 Criminal Defence Service

Since April 2001 publicly-funded representation for defendants has been available through the Criminal Defence Service (established by the Access to Justice Act 1999).

Representation through the Criminal Defence Service is granted if it is in the interests of justice. The following factors are taken into account:

- whether the defendant would, if convicted, be likely to lose their liberty or livelihood or suffer serious damage to their reputation;
- whether the determination of any matter arising in the proceedings may involve consideration of a substantial question of law;
- whether the defendant may be unable to understand the proceedings or to state their own case;
- whether the proceedings may involve the tracing, interviewing or expert cross-examination of witnesses on behalf of the defendant; and
- whether it is in the interests of another person that the defendant be represented.

Representation in the magistrates' court is provided by the Criminal Defence Service irrespective of the defendant's means. Where the defendant appears in the Crown Court, that court has the power to require the defendant to pay for some of the costs incurred (including any costs incurred in the magistrates' court) by the Criminal Defence Service acting on his behalf. The defendant's means (disposable income and disposable capital) have to be taken into account by the Crown Court when deciding whether to order the defendant to contribute to the costs of the defence.

13.4   Crown Prosecution Service

At a very early stage in the case, papers are sent by the police to the Crown Prosecution Service (CPS). A Crown Prosecutor will decide whether to proceed with the case.

In the magistrates' court, the CPS is represented by a Crown Prosecutor or by an 'agent' (that is, by a solicitor or barrister instructed by the CPS); in the Crown Court the CPS will usually be represented by a barrister.

In the magistrates' court, the CPS file takes the place of the brief for the prosecutor. In the Crown Court, prosecuting counsel receives a brief which is very similar in form to the brief sent to counsel for the defence. The file or brief, as the case may be, will contain an introduction written by a Crown Prosecutor, copies of written statements made by the witnesses to be called on behalf of the prosecution, and details of the defendant's previous convictions (if any).

In the Crown Court, a representative from the CPS should be available to assist counsel, and the police officer in charge of the case will also be present. In the magistrates' court the prosecutor will be alone, although the police officer in charge of the case will be present for the trial (but not for any hearings which precede the trial).

13.5   Stages of a criminal case: a thumbnail sketch

To help you make sense of the rest of this chapter, this section aims to provide a thumbnail sketch of criminal procedure in so far as counsel may be involved.

Where proceedings were commenced by the issue of a 'written charge' and a 'requisition' requiring the suspect to attend court (the procedure established under s 29 of the

Criminal Justice Act 2003 to replace, in the case of public prosecutions, the laying of an information and the issue of summons as a way of commencing criminal proceedings), counsel is likely to attend only for the trial itself. This is because the question of bail does not arise (and so remand hearings, where the question of bail is addressed, do not take place).

The other method of commencing proceedings is to arrest and charge the suspect. The suspect will be arrested and will usually then be interviewed at the police station. At the police station, the suspect is entitled to legal advice; that advice will invariably be provided by a solicitor, not by a barrister. If the suspect is to be charged with an offence, that will either happen at the police station (the police having first sought advice from a Crown Prosecutor) or else the papers will sent to the CPS, who will decide whether to charge the suspect and, if so, with what offence (in which case, the CPS will commence proceedings through the issue of a written charge and requisition). If the suspect is charged at the police station, he or she may either be granted bail by the police or else be held in custody until the next sitting of the magistrates' court (when the magistrates can be asked to grant bail to the defendant). If police bail is granted, counsel may attend remand hearings but, assuming the prosecution do not subsequently oppose bail, the grant of bail is a formality and so there is little for counsel to do.

However proceedings were instituted, a Crown Prosecutor will decide whether those proceedings should be continued. In coming to this decision, the Crown Prosecutor will have regard to the strength of the evidence against the suspect and to whether it is in the public interest to continue the prosecution. In complex cases, the CPS may seek the advice of counsel.

If proceedings were commenced by the arrest and charge of the suspect, and police bail was withheld, counsel may be instructed to attend the magistrates' court to make an application for bail on behalf of the defendant. In many cases, however, the first bail application will be made by a solicitor. Where the prosecution oppose the grant of bail, the bail application will be opposed by the CPS representative. If that application for bail is unsuccessful, counsel may be briefed to return to the magistrates' court a week later to make a further bail application, as in the criminal brief of *R v Costas Georgiou* at **17.1**.

If bail is withheld by the magistrates after the second application for bail, counsel may be asked to return to the magistrates' court to reapply for bail if there is a material change in circumstances (enabling a further bail application to be made) or there may be an appeal against the refusal of bail by the magistrates; this appeal is to the Crown Court. In the Crown Court, bail will be opposed by a barrister instructed by the CPS.

In addition to the remand hearings in the magistrates' court, counsel may, if the offence is triable either way, be instructed to attend the magistrates' court to represent the defendant at the mode of trial hearing: at this hearing, the defendant is asked to indicate whether he intends to plead guilty or not guilty to the 'either way' offence(s) with which he is charged. If the defendant gives no indication or indicates an intention to plead not guilty, the next step is for the decision to be taken whether the case should be heard in the magistrates' court or in the Crown Court. Again, the prosecution will be represented by a Crown Prosecutor or by a solicitor or barrister instructed by the CPS.

In some cases, prosecuting counsel may be asked to advise on evidence and/or on the question of disclosure to the defence of material which the prosecution have but which they do not intend to use at the trial. Defence counsel may be instructed to advise on the contents of (or even draft) the statement of the defence case which (in the case of Crown Court trials) must be served on the prosecution.

Next, counsel may be instructed to appear at the trial itself. This trial will be in the magistrates' court if the offence is a summary one or if the offence is triable either way but both the defendant and the magistrates agreed (at the mode of trial hearing) to summary trial; if the offence is triable only on indictment, or the mode of trial hearing resulted in a decision in favour of trial on indictment, the trial will take place in the Crown Court. In the magistrates' court, the prosecution will be conducted by a Crown Prosecutor or by a solicitor or barrister instructed by the CPS; in the Crown Court, the prosecution will usually be represented by counsel.

Wherever the defendant is tried, if he or she either pleads guilty or is found guilty, counsel will have to make a plea in mitigation on behalf of the defendant before sentence is passed.

At the conclusion of the case it may be necessary for defence counsel to advise the defendant on the possibility of appeal against conviction and/or sentence. Where the trial took place in the magistrates' court that appeal will normally be heard in the Crown Court (although an appeal on a point of law may be made to the High Court, by way of case stated or by means of an application for judicial review). Where the trial took place in the Crown Court, appeal lies to the Court of Appeal (Criminal Division).

13.6   The stages in greater detail

Having set out an overview of criminal procedure, it is necessary to examine some of the stages in more detail.

13.6.1   Bail application

In most cases, on the first occasion that a defendant appears before the magistrates' court charged with a particular offence, representation will be provided either by a duty solicitor or by a solicitor from the firm which later instructs counsel. An application for public funding may be made at that hearing.

There will be occasions, however, where the barrister is the first lawyer the defendant meets in connection with this offence. It may be, for example, that the defendant agreed to be interviewed by the police without a lawyer being present and, after being charged with an offence and finding that police bail was withheld, contacted a firm of solicitors he or she has used before. If there is insufficient time for a solicitor from that firm to see the defendant prior to the first court appearance, counsel may receive instructions by telephone or fax (or even email) to go to the magistrates' court. In that case, it will be for counsel to take initial instructions from the defendant, to give preliminary advice, to apply for public funding, and to make a bail application.

Even where counsel is in possession of a brief which includes a proof of evidence from the defendant, the role of defence counsel when attending court to make a bail application involves a number of elements: preparation, advice and advocacy.

In particular, counsel will have to:

(a) *Take instructions from the client:* If a proof of evidence from the defendant is included in the brief, it is necessary to check with the client that it is complete, accurate and up-to-date; if there is no proof of evidence, it is up to counsel to elicit all the necessary information from the defendant. In deciding what questions to ask the defendant, counsel should consider the factors set out in the Bail Act 1976, Sch 1 (eg risk of absconding, committing offences while on bail or interfering with witnesses, all of which are assessed in the light of such matters as the nature and seriousness of the present offence, the defendant's previous convictions (if any), the defendant's community ties and record of answering bail in the past).

(b) *Advise the client:* If this is the client's first court appearance, he or she may need reassurance; it may therefore be necessary to explain to the client what will happen in court. It is highly likely that the client will ask counsel to advise on the probable result of the bail application. Furthermore, the client may seek advice about other aspects of the case. Where such advice is given, a short note of that advice should be endorsed on the brief, signed and dated by counsel (so that the solicitor knows what advice has been given).

(c) *Address the court in favour of bail:* The prosecutor addresses the court first and explains to the court why the prosecution oppose bail. Counsel for the defence then replies to those submissions and will try to show that the prosecution objections to the grant of bail have no foundation or that those objections can be overcome by the imposition of conditions on the grant of bail. No witnesses are called (unless a surety comes forward, in which case that person will usually have to give evidence to show that he or she is a suitable surety). The submissions to the court should be based on the matters that the court is required to consider under the Bail Act 1976.

(d) *Advising the client on challenging refusal of bail:* If bail is withheld, counsel should advise the defendant (and, later, communicate this advice to the instructing solicitor) on any steps which can be taken to increase the chance of bail being granted (eg, the provision of a surety) and/or whether an application for bail should be made to the Crown Court.

The role of the prosecutor is rather more limited. He or she simply makes a speech opposing the grant of bail. In doing this, the prosecutor will usually have to rely on notes contained in the CPS file; those notes are based on information supplied by the police. The police officer in charge of the case is unlikely to be present at the bail application.

There may occasionally be some scope for negotiation between defence counsel and the prosecutor. It may be that the prosecutor will agree not to oppose the grant of bail if the defendant agrees that the grant of bail should be subject to certain conditions.

If the first bail application is unsuccessful, the defence may make a second application to the magistrates a week later. This is so even if the second application says nothing different from the first application (although the person making the application will normally try to find something different to say). Once the magistrates have heard two fully argued bail applications, they can only hear a further application if there is a material change in circumstances (ie, the defence can put forward an argument which has not been put forward already).

Where bail has been refused by the magistrates following the second fully argued bail application, it may be appropriate to make a further bail application in the Crown Court. The procedure in the Crown Court is very similar to that in the magistrates' court (that is, the prosecutor sets out the reasons for opposing the grant of bail and defence counsel then replies to those submissions). However, the defendant will not be present and the CPS will usually be represented by counsel.

If the offence is triable only in the Crown Court, the case may be transferred to the Crown Court after the first appearance in the magistrates' court. If the magistrate refuses bail, any further application for bail will be made in the Crown Court.

13.6.2   Mode of trial

Where the defendant is accused of an offence which is triable either way (that is, triable in either the magistrates' court or the Crown Court), counsel may be asked to advise the client on which court should try the case. This advice will almost always be given orally, and will generally be given just before the mode of trial hearing itself (unless it was given at an earlier remand hearing).

At this stage (if not before) the client may well need advice on plea, since the mode of trial hearing in court begins with a 'plea before venue' hearing. The defendant is asked to indicate whether he or she intends to plead guilty or not guilty to the 'either way' offence(s) with which he or she is charged. If the defendant indicates an intention to plead guilty, then he or she is regarded as having pleaded guilty. At that point the magistrates will either proceed to sentence (if necessary, after an adjournment for a pre-sentence report to be prepared) or else commit the defendant to the Crown Court for sentence (the Crown Court having greater sentencing powers than the magistrates' court). If, on the other hand, the defendant either indicates an intention to plead not guilty, or gives no indication as to the intended plea, the magistrates then proceed to determine the question of mode of trial.

At the mode of trial hearing the magistrates have to decide whether the case is suitable for summary trial. The key question is whether, in the event of the defendant being convicted, their sentencing powers would be adequate to deal with the case. If the magistrates decide that the case is not suitable for summary trial, only trial in the Crown Court is possible. If the magistrates decide that the case is suitable for summary trial (ie, they 'accept jurisdiction') the defendant is asked where he or she wishes to be tried. This is because, in the case of an offence which is triable either way, the defendant has an inalienable right to be tried on indictment (that is, at the Crown Court).

During the mode of trial hearing, the prosecution and the defence both have the right to make representations regarding the appropriate mode of trial. These representations should be based on the criteria set out in Pt 51 of the *Practice Direction (Criminal: Consolidated)* [2002] 3 All ER 904. If the defendant wishes to elect trial on indictment, there is little point in the defence making any representations, because of the defendant's right to choose Crown Court trial. If, on the other hand, the defendant wants to be tried in the magistrates' court but the prosecution are seeking trial in the Crown Court, counsel for the defendant will have to try to persuade the magistrates that the case is suitable for summary trial.

In advising the client on whether to elect Crown Court trial or not in the case of an 'either way' offence, counsel will need to be aware of the various arguments for and against the two types of trial. Jurors tend to be less 'case-hardened' than magistrates, which may explain why the acquittal rate is much higher in the Crown Court than in the magistrates' court. Where it is likely that the defence will seek to have some of the prosecution evidence (such as a confession) ruled inadmissible, Crown Court trial is preferable because matters of admissibility are dealt with by the judge in the absence of the jury; this separation of functions is not possible in the magistrates' court, where the justices are triers of both law and fact. On the other hand, trial in the magistrates' court is a little less formal (and so maybe a little less daunting for the accused) than jury trial; and trials in the magistrates' court tend to be considerably shorter than trials in the Crown Court. Another advantage of magistrates' court trial is said to be that there is a cap on the sentencing powers of the magistrates; this is correct, but the power of the magistrates to commit the defendant to the Crown Court for sentence after they have convicted him or her effectively negates this supposed advantage.

13.6.3   Advising the prosecution

Counsel who has been briefed to prosecute in a forthcoming Crown Court trial may be asked by the CPS to advise on the evidence (and sometimes to redraft the indictment) before the trial takes place. This involves examining the witness statements made by the prosecution witnesses in order to see how strong the prosecution case is; counsel has to consider if the case can be improved (eg, advising that the police take further statements from existing witnesses, to fill gaps or clarify ambiguities, or advising that further investigations be made).

The advice given must be both realistic and practicable. It must be remembered that the police do not have limitless resources (and are not endowed with psychic powers!).

Where the trial is to take place in a magistrates' court, these matters will almost invariably be considered by a Crown Prosecutor, not by a barrister in private practice.

13.6.4   Advising the defendant

Counsel for the defence may be asked to advise on evidence prior to a Crown Court trial. This advice will often be given orally, during a conference with the client, rather than in writing; such conferences usually take place in counsel's chambers or in a prison where the defendant is in custody. Sometimes, however, the only opportunity for a conference is at court, shortly before the start of the trial. Whenever it is given, the advice must be realistic and practicable: where the defendant is represented through the Criminal Defence Service, further enquiries involving considerable expense are unlikely to be covered by public funds. (See **17.3** for an example of a written advice in the case of *R v Costas Georgiou*.)

Prior to a magistrates' court trial, it is very rare for defence counsel to have a conference in chambers or to give written advice. The conference usually takes place in the court building, shortly before the trial is due to begin.

The function of the pre-trial conference (whether held in counsel's chambers or, just before the trial is due to start, in the court building) may include some or all of the following elements:

(a) *Taking instructions from the client (that is, gathering information):* By the time of the trial, counsel will be in possession of a proof of evidence from the defendant which sets out the client's version of events. However, it is still useful to get the client to go through his or her side of the story: the solicitor may have missed something, or the defendant may remember something new. Whilst it is unethical, and therefore forbidden, for counsel to 'coach' the defendant (that is, to suggest evidence which the defendant might give), there is no objection to counsel questioning the client closely on the evidence he or she will be giving. It is helpful for the defendant to rehearse the evidence he or she will be giving in court and to prepare for cross-examination by the prosecutor.

Where counsel is in possession of the witness statements made by the prosecution witnesses, the defendant should also be asked to comment on what those witnesses say (so that counsel can decide what questions to ask them by way of cross-examination). It may be that the solicitor has already performed this task, so that the defendant's proof of evidence contains comments on the prosecution evidence; even then, it can be helpful to ask the defendant if there is anything he or she wishes to add to those comments.

(b) *Advising the defendant on plea and tactics:* Where the client has not received full advice on plea (from the solicitor, or from counsel on a previous occasion) it may be necessary for counsel to advise the defendant (based on what the client has said about his or her side of the story) on plea. It may be, for example, that the defendant has indicated an intention to plead guilty but then says something which amounts to a defence (eg, a person accused of theft says that he or she did not realise that the property belonged to someone else).

It may also be necessary to advise on tactics, for example, what lines of cross-examination to pursue and what evidence to call.

(c) *Taking instructions on matters relevant to sentence:* Counsel should be careful to have all the information needed to make a plea in mitigation. Instructions should therefore be taken on matters which would be relevant to a plea in mitigation. This is so even where the client is going to plead not guilty, since (in the event of the defendant being convicted) there may not be time for a further conference between the defendant being convicted and the moment counsel has to start the plea in mitigation.

(d) *Advising on sentence:* Whether the defendant is going to plead guilty or not guilty, it will almost always be necessary to give advice on the sentence which is likely to be imposed in the event of conviction.

Counsel representing a defendant at an early stage of the proceedings should always be prepared to give advice about later stages of the case. On occasions, for example, counsel may be instructed to attend the magistrates' court to make a bail application, or for the mode of trial hearing, and may be asked for advice then by the defendant. Provided counsel is sufficiently well acquainted with the background to the case, there is no objection to such advice being given (although a short note setting out the advice given should be endorsed on the brief, so that the instructing solicitor, and any barrister involved in the case at a later stage, knows what was said). However, where the advice is given without full knowledge of the prosecution case and the defence response to that case, it should be made clear to the client that the advice is only provisional and may change if new information comes to light.

13.6.5 Pre-trial disclosure

A particularly important aspect of advising on evidence concerns the rules which govern pre-trial disclosure. The rules which apply to the prosecution are different from the rules which apply to the defence. The disclosure rules are contained in the Criminal Procedure and Investigations Act 1996. Further details can be found in the Criminal Litigation and Sentencing Manual. As regards disclosure by the prosecution, a further distinction has to be drawn between material that the prosecution will be using as part of their case and material which they will not be using.

13.6.5.1 Pre-trial disclosure by the prosecution

If an offence is triable either way, the prosecution must (if the defence so request) supply the defence with a summary of the prosecution case or with copies of the statements made by those persons to be called as prosecution witnesses. Guidelines from the Attorney-General suggest that the defence should normally receive the witness statements rather than just a summary. This must be done (assuming the defence request advance information) before the mode of trial hearing (see **13.6.2**) takes place. If the case is to be tried in the Crown Court, copies of the statements made by the witnesses whom the prosecution intend to call at the trial must be supplied to the defence (if this was not done prior to the mode of trial hearing). The effect of these rules is as follows: if an offence is triable either way but is to be tried in a magistrates' court, the defence may have the prosecution witness statements prior to the trial, or they might just have a summary of the prosecution case; however, if an offence is to be tried in the Crown Court, the defence must have copies of the prosecution's witness statements before the case can be sent to the Crown Court for trial. Where the offence is triable only on indictment, the prosecution serve their witness statements on the defence after the case has been transferred to the Crown Court.

Where a case is to be tried in the Crown Court and the prosecution wish to use a witness whose statement has not already been served on the defence, a 'notice of additional evidence' (including a copy of the witness statement) must be served on the defence prior to the trial.

The prosecution are also under a statutory duty to disclose material other than the statements of the persons they will be calling as witnesses. Under the Criminal Procedure and Investigations Act 1996, the prosecutor must disclose to the accused any prosecution material which might reasonably be considered capable of undermining the case for the prosecution against the accused or of assisting the case for the accused. This applies to all trials (whether in the Crown Court, the magistrates' court or the youth court).

It follows that by the time of the pre-trial conference (at the latest) counsel for the accused should be aware both of the case to be met and of any material that has come to the attention of the prosecution and which undermines their case or supports the defence case.

13.6.5.2   Pre-trial disclosure by the defence

The Criminal Procedure and Investigations Act 1996 imposes a compulsory duty of disclosure on the defence, but this compulsory duty applies only to trials in the Crown Court. This disclosure takes the form of a 'defence statement'. This has to:

(a) set out the nature of the accused's defence, including any particular defences on which he or she intends to rely;

(b) indicate the matters of fact on which the accused takes issue with the prosecution;

(c) set out, in the case of each such matter, why the accused takes issue with the prosecution; and

(d) indicate any point of law (including any point as to the admissibility of evidence or abuse of process) which the accused wishes to take, and any authority on which he or she intends to rely for that purpose.

Where the accused wishes to rely on an alibi, the defence statement must give full particulars of the alibi and of any witnesses the accused believes are able to give evidence in support of the alibi. The defence must also supply the prosecution with details of any witnesses they propose to call and details of any experts who have been instructed by the defence (whether or not the expert is to be called a defence witness). The accused is required to serve an updated defence statement prior to trial (or a notice saying that there are no changes to the original statement).

In the case of summary (ie, magistrates' court or youth court) trials, the Act enables the defence to make voluntary disclosure of their case.

If the defence fail to comply with the compulsory duty of disclosure prior to Crown Court trial, or if the defence case at trial differs from that disclosed to the prosecution (whether the disclosure was compulsory or voluntary), then adverse inferences can be drawn by the jury or magistrates as the case may be.

The General Council of the Bar has given guidance on the involvement of counsel in the drafting of defence statements. The guidance makes the point that it will normally be more appropriate for instructing solicitors to draft the defence statement, since counsel will generally have had little involvement in the case at this stage. Nonetheless, there is no reason why a barrister should not draft a defence statement. However, counsel must ensure that the defendant:

- understands the importance of the accuracy and adequacy of the defence statement; and
- has had the opportunity of carefully considering the statement drafted by counsel and has approved it.

13.6.6 Preparatory hearings and pre-trial hearings

The Criminal Procedure and Investigations Act 1996 requires preliminary hearings to take place before all Crown Court trials. The nature of the hearing differs according to whether or not the trial is likely to be lengthy or complex. However, in both cases, the object of the rules is that the issues in the case should have been defined before the trial and to reduce the number of cases where the defendant was due to be tried on a 'not guilty' plea but then pleads guilty at the start of the trial (giving rise to what is sometimes called a 'cracked trial').

13.6.6.1 Complex or lengthy trials

Under the Criminal Procedure and Investigations Act 1996, s 29, which applies to Crown Court cases which are likely to be complex or lengthy, the judge may order a preparatory hearing to take place. The purpose is to identify the issues in the case, to see how the jury can be assisted to understand those issues, to expedite the trial, and to assist the judge's management of the trial.

To this end, the judge can make rulings on the admissibility of evidence or other questions of law likely to arise in the trial. The judge can also order the prosecution to prepare a document setting out the principal facts of the Crown's case, the witnesses who will speak to those facts, and any propositions of law the Crown will rely on. The prosecution can also be ordered to prepare the evidence in a form that is likely to aid comprehension by the jury. Finally, the prosecution can be ordered to provide a written notice detailing any documents the truth of which the prosecutor believes the defence should admit.

The judge can then order the defence to give written notice of any points of law they will be raising and to state which of the documents referred to in the notice from the prosecutor the defence are prepared to admit; where the defence are not willing to admit the truth of any such documents, they must explain why this is so.

13.6.6.2 Other cases

In the case of Crown Court trials other than those which are likely to be complex or lengthy (in other words, the majority of cases) s 39 of the 1996 Act enables a pre-trial hearing to take place. This gives statutory effect to the system of plea and directions hearings which preceded the enactment of the 1996 Act.

At this hearing, the defendant is asked to enter a plea. If he or she pleads 'guilty', the judge proceeds to the sentencing stage (if necessary with an adjournment for a pre-sentence report). If the defendant pleads 'not guilty', a date is fixed for the trial.

Where the defendant pleads 'not guilty', prosecuting and defence counsel are expected to inform the court of matters such as: the issues in the case, the number of witnesses to be called, any points of law likely to arise (including questions on the admissibility of evidence), and whether any technical equipment (such as video equipment) is likely to be needed. It follows that it is very important that, by the time of this hearing, the factual and legal issues in the case should have been identified. (See **17.3.1** for the issues in *R v Costas Georgiou*.)

At this hearing, the judge is empowered to make rulings on the admissibility of evidence and on any other questions of law which are relevant to the case. These rulings are binding for the whole of the trial unless there is an application for the ruling to be altered, but such an application can only be made if there has been a material change in circumstances since the ruling was made.

When Schedule 3 of the Courts Act 2003 comes into force, a magistrates' court will be able to make pre-trial rulings on the admissibility of evidence or any other question of law relating to the case, and those rulings will be binding on the bench that eventually tries the case.

13.6.7   Trial

Defence counsel and the prosecutor may attend court expecting a trial to take place. However, a trial will not take place if either the defendant pleads guilty to the charge(s) or the prosecution accept a plea to a lesser offence. In the Crown Court any negotiations with the prosecution regarding the acceptance of a plea of guilty to a less serious offence than that charged will usually take place at the plea and directions hearing. Such negotiations will usually take place just before the trial where the case is to be heard in the magistrates' court.

We have already seen that counsel for the defence may have to give advice to the defendant at the conference which takes place immediately before the trial.

During the trial itself, counsel is involved in three main tasks:

(a) *Making speeches:* In the magistrates' court the prosecutor usually makes an opening speech but no closing speech whereas counsel for the defence will usually make a closing speech but not an opening speech; in the Crown Court both the prosecution and the defence are usually entitled to make both an opening speech and a closing speech (although the defence often forgo the right to make an opening speech). As well as these speeches, it may be necessary for counsel to address the court on the admissibility of certain evidence or to make (or, if prosecuting, to respond to) a submission that there is no case to answer.

The purpose of the prosecution opening speech is to prepare the jury or magistrates for the evidence they are about to hear. The prosecution case is summarised so that the jury or magistrates can put the evidence they are about to hear in context.

The purpose of the closing speech is to highlight the strengths of one's case and, where possible, to minimise the impact of any weaknesses. The defence, for example, will stress any doubt in the prosecution evidence and any explanation which the defendant has given for apparently incriminating evidence.

A submission of no case to answer may be made by the defence at the end of the prosecution case. The essence of the submission is that the evidence adduced by the prosecution is so weak that no reasonable tribunal (jury or bench of magistrates) could convict the defendant on the basis of that evidence.

(b) *Examination-in-chief:* This means getting the witness to tell the story (answering questions such as 'Who?', 'When?', 'Where?'). Care must be taken not to 'lead' the witness (that is, to suggest answers to the questions being put or to ask a question which can be answered with a simple 'yes' or 'no'). Before going into court, counsel must have decided what he or she hopes to achieve with the particular witness, since the examination-in-chief should only bring out evidence which is relevant to the case. Counsel will always be in possession of a written statement from the witness (which obviously forms the basis of the questions which will be put to the witness). Counsel should also be alert to any inadmissible evidence which is contained in the witness's written statement (eg, references to previous dealings between the defendant and the police) so that those areas can be avoided in the questioning.

Examination-in-chief can also be used to anticipate questions which may be put to that witness in cross-examination. For instance, in a case involving identification evidence, prosecuting counsel would, in examination-in-chief, ask a witness who claims to have identified the defendant as the perpetrator about the circumstances of that identification (eg, distance, lighting, obstructions to view etc). The answers to these questions may well make it more difficult for counsel for the defence to cross-examine effectively on the matters.

The defendant has been present in court throughout the trial and so has heard the evidence of the prosecution witnesses. The defendant may be asked, in examination-in-chief, to comment on what he has heard (for example, 'You heard Miss Jones say ... What do you say about that?').

(c) *Cross-examination:* This means probing the story told by the witness. In the Crown Court counsel for the defence will be in possession of the written statements made by the prosecution witnesses; in the magistrates' court counsel for the defence may have sight of the prosecution witness statements if the offence is one which is triable either way. In any event, the prosecution never have sight of the written statements made by witnesses for the defence. Obviously, it is easier to prepare a cross- examination if one has advance notice of what the witness is going to say.

Cross-examination essentially focuses on inconsistencies and on the probing of weaknesses:

(i) inconsistencies between what the witness is saying now and what he or she has said in the written statement;

(ii) inconsistencies in the evidence which the witness has given to the court (eg, in the course of the witness's testimony, the colour of the getaway car changes from dark blue to black);

(iii) inconsistencies between what this witness has said and what another witness says;

(iv) inconsistencies between what this witness is saying and the theory which counsel has formed about the case he or she is presenting;

(v) inconsistencies between what the witness is saying and what common sense suggests actually happened (eg, a witness who says that a car was travelling at 70 mph and that it braked sharply and stopped within a distance of 15 metres cannot be correct);

(vi) exposing weaknesses in the other side's evidence (eg, establishing that the witness was some distance from the scene of the crime and that there were obstructions to the observation). Does the witness have a motive for misleading the court?

It is important that in cross-examination you 'put your case'. In other words, if a witness called by your opponent may be able to comment on part of your case, the witness should be given the chance to do so. In the case of counsel for the defence, this will include putting to the witness those parts of the witness's evidence which differ from, or are inconsistent with, the defendant's account of what happened.

The fact management process is discussed in detail in the next chapter. Many practitioners have in mind their closing speech from the moment they start to prepare the case (but note that, in the magistrates' court, the prosecutor does not have the automatic right to make a closing speech). In thinking about your closing speech, you are asking yourself how you are going to persuade the jury (or magistrates) to come to the result that you want them to come to. In other words, how will you persuade them to accept your 'theory of the case'. This will determine what evidence you put before the court through the examination-in-chief of your witnesses, and what questions you ask in cross-examination of your opponent's witnesses.

Much of the case analysis process involves consideration of strengths and weaknesses: the strengths and weaknesses of your case, and the strengths and weaknesses of your opponent's case. Your task is to think about ways of emphasising or maximising the strengths of your case and ways of improving, or minimising the effect of, the weaknesses of your case; also, to see if you can reduce the effect of the strengths, and increase the impact of the weaknesses, of your opponent's case.

This process can be expressed as a series of questions:

Strengths of your case

- What evidence supports your case?
- How might your opponent try to undermine the evidence that supports your case?
- How might you be able to prevent your opponent from undermining the evidence that supports your case?

Weaknesses of your case

- What evidence weakens your case?
- How might you reduce the impact of the evidence that weakens your case?
- How might your opponent try to prevent you from undermining the evidence that weakens your case?

Strengths of your opponent's case

- What evidence supports your opponent's case?
- How might you try to undermine the evidence that supports your opponent's case?
- How might your opponent try to prevent you from undermining the evidence that supports their case?

Weaknesses of your opponent's case

- What evidence weakens your opponent's case?
- How might you increase the impact of the evidence that weakens your opponent's case?
- How might your opponent try to prevent you from increasing the impact of the evidence that weakens their case?

13.6.8   Plea in mitigation

A plea in mitigation is required if the defendant pleads guilty or is found guilty. Sentence is usually passed, either immediately or after an adjournment for preparation of a pre-sentence report, by the court which convicted the defendant. However, if the defendant was convicted by a magistrates' court of an offence which is triable either way, the magistrates may (if they decide that their sentencing powers are insufficient to deal with the case) commit the defendant to the Crown Court to be sentenced (the Crown Court having greater sentencing powers); in that case, the plea in mitigation is delivered in the Crown Court. It should be borne in mind that in the magistrates' court, the Bench which sentences the defendant will probably not be the same Bench that convicted him.

If sentence is passed immediately after the defendant has been convicted following trial (ie the defendant pleaded not guilty but was convicted), the prosecutor will simply tell the court about any previous convictions recorded against the defendant. If the defendant pleaded guilty, or the defendant is being sentenced at a hearing after the trial at which he or she was convicted, the prosecutor will also have to explain to the court precisely what the defendant did.

The next step is for defence counsel to make a plea in mitigation on behalf of the defendant. The essence of a plea in mitigation is to emphasise personal mitigating circumstances relating to the offender and to draw the court's attention to any mitigating factors relating to the offence itself.

The plea in mitigation will be based on information gathered from the client (in the proof of evidence and in things said by the client prior to the hearing) and, in many cases, on information contained in a pre-sentence report prepared by a probation officer. A list of the client's previous convictions (if any) should be in the brief; if not, the list can be obtained from the prosecutor. Counsel should check that the defendant agrees that the list of previous convictions is correct and that the defendant is happy with the comments made by the probation officer in the pre-sentence report. Counsel should be prepared to probe the client for details of mitigating factors relating to the offence itself or to the client's personal circumstances.

Before advising the client on likely sentence or presenting a plea in mitigation, counsel should ensure that he or she is familiar with the approach taken by the courts to sentencing for the particular offence(s) of which the defendant has been convicted. If the 'entry point' (ie, the type of sentence taken as a starting point) is a custodial sentence, counsel should indicate that he or she is aware of this before trying to persuade the court to impose a lesser sentence. The Sentencing Guidelines issued to magistrates by the Magistrates' Association are particularly helpful in this regard, as are the guideline judgments handed down by the Court of Appeal in respect of particular offences. This guidance can be found in *Blackstone's Criminal Practice*.

13.6.9   Appeals

13.6.9.1   Appeals from the magistrates' court

Most appeals from the magistrates' court are heard by the Crown Court. An appeal against conviction takes the form of a complete rehearing of the case. The prosecution will usually be represented by counsel instructed by the CPS. Counsel for the defence may or may not have represented the defendant in the magistrates' court.

Leave to appeal is not required and grounds for the appeal do not have to be stated. Because the appeal takes the form of a rehearing, the Crown Court is not concerned with what happened in the magistrates' court; one corollary of this is that a witness who was not called in the magistrates' court can be called in the Crown Court and a witness who was called in the magistrates' court need not be called in the Crown Court. This means that counsel for the appellant may reconsider any tactical decisions (regarding which witnesses to call) which were taken prior to the trial in the magistrates' court.

Similarly, the hearing by the Crown Court of an appeal against sentence imposed by the magistrates' court takes the same form as the original sentencing hearing in the magistrates' court, with a prosecution summary of the facts followed by a plea in mitigation by the defence advocate.

When advising the defendant whether or not to appeal to the Crown Court, counsel should warn the defendant that the Crown Court has the power to increase the sentence imposed by the magistrates' court, up to the maximum which the magistrates could have imposed; this is so even if it is only the conviction (and not the sentence) which is the subject of the defendant's appeal. Thus, if the defendant was convicted of an offence which is triable either way and the magistrates imposed a sentence of three months' imprisonment, the Crown Court could increase the sentence to six months (the maximum the magistrates could have imposed for one either-way offence).

Alternatively, in a case which involves a point of law or jurisdiction, the defendant may appeal instead to the High Court. This can be done in two ways. The first is to ask the magistrates to state a case for the opinion of the High Court ('appeal by way of case stated'); the magistrates duly summarise their findings of fact and their rulings on the law and the High Court considers whether the magistrates reached the correct conclusion. The second way is to apply for judicial review of the decision of the magistrates' court; this method is particularly appropriate where the magistrates exceed their powers in some way or behaved unfairly. The prosecution can also appeal to the High Court by way of case stated, or seek judicial review, on a point of law or jurisdiction.

13.6.9.2   Appeals from the Crown Court

Appeals from the Crown Court against conviction and/or sentence lie to the Court of Appeal (Criminal Division).

Sometimes the appellant is represented by the same barrister who represented him or her in the Crown Court, sometimes a different barrister is chosen. In any event, counsel for the appellant has to examine the notes which were taken during the trial by counsel for the defence to see if any errors occurred during the course of the trial. Particular attention has to be paid to any rulings made by the judge during the course of the trial (eg, rulings on the admissibility of a piece of evidence) and to the judge's summing up of the case to the jury. As far as the latter is concerned, counsel should consider whether the judge stated the law correctly and whether the judge summarised the case for the prosecution, and the case for the defendant, accurately and fairly. Similarly, the comments made by the judge when passing sentence should be scrutinised with care, to ensure that the correct sentencing principles were applied.

If errors were made in the course of the trial and/or in the summing up, or when sentence was passed, grounds of appeal have to be drafted; these grounds are attached to an advice by counsel in which the errors are identified and any relevant case law set out. This is an important document, since it forms the basis of the decision by a Court of Appeal judge whether to give leave to appeal or not.

Once an application for leave to appeal against conviction has been lodged, a transcript of the summing up and any other rulings made by the trial judge will be sent to the barrister who drafted the grounds of appeal; counsel then has the chance to 'perfect' the grounds of appeal (that is, to relate those grounds to the transcript).

If leave to appeal is granted, counsel has to submit a 'skeleton argument' to the court prior to the hearing of the appeal.

The hearing of the appeal itself takes the form of argument by counsel for the appellant and counsel for the respondent; no evidence is heard except in exceptional cases.

14

The fact management process

14.1 Introduction to the fact management process

At the heart of the practitioner's work are facts: an incident has occurred or must be prevented from occurring, a person injured, property damaged or likely to be damaged, and loss threatened or sustained. From the first moment of receiving a brief until the last stage of trial it is the facts of a case that will be the basis of the practitioner's work. 'Facts' are the basis of any evidence given, any speeches made and any questions asked. It is the barrister's ability to manage the facts, to understand their implications and to use them as the basis of argument, which will be crucial to the success of a case.

The majority of cases involve disputes of facts, not, despite the emphasis in academic training, disputes about questions of law. The ability of barristers to carry out the task of managing facts has in the past been developed by experience, and until the development of the vocational course for the Bar, very little attempt had been made to consciously define and develop this skill. Very few texts have sought to unravel the fact management process in order to teach others how to carry it out on a step-by-step basis. However, it is generally recognised that the ability to prepare a set of papers effectively depends on:

- the need to have a clear picture of what you are preparing for;
- being able to identify what is relevant to your task;
- identifying what the issues are;
- recognising what can and cannot be proved;
- evaluating the strength of the case accurately; and
- putting together, from the information available, the most compelling argument on your client's behalf.

The working approach advocated in this chapter, the C.A.P. approach (Context, Analysis, Preparation), applies these intellectual skills in a practical and structured process to case preparation. The C.A.P. method of preparing a case demonstrates, on a step-by-step basis, every stage in the process — from initial understanding of the legal and factual context, to detailed analysis of issues and evidence, and finally the construction of persuasive and pertinent arguments to present to a tribunal, a client or, in negotiation, an opponent. The chapter also illustrates some of the techniques which can be used to aid analysis and the presentation of a case. Thorough case preparation can be achieved by many different working methods and it is usual for these to develop and change with time and experience.

While some may think of this as an objective science, the process involves more than applying a logical method of analysis and presentation. Resourceful barristers also use lateral thinking to identify alternative interpretations of the facts. One's own perception of how witnesses see and describe events and their effectiveness as witnesses will influence a decision about whether they should be called at trial or how to question them. Finally, the ability to use different methods to communicate information in a clear and persuasive way calls for creativity and thought about how to present the facts in the best light. These qualities are part of the practical aspects of fact management which cannot be separated from the more objective tasks of collecting facts.

You will find that your own ability to analyse and evaluate factual situations, and to use the results to communicate persuasively, develop best through conscious application and reflection on how effective the results were. You will have regular opportunities to do this in the practical training exercises on which you will work while studying the Bar Vocational Course. If you are able to take the opportunity of giving advice through pro bono schemes, or to undertake representation through organisations such as the Free Representation Unit you will develop further and faster. You will also find yourself developing your abilities further when you move into practice or any other legally-related career.

14.2   Starting from scratch — defining basic terms

14.2.1   'Agreed' facts

Every problem will contain 'facts': who the parties are, the history of the situation, what transpired on certain dates etc. *'Agreed facts'* are those facts which are conceded by your opponent and are not therefore issues in the case. In criminal cases they may sometimes be set out in a 'formal admission' (see **Chapter 1** of the *Evidence Manual*). More often, practitioners simply tell the court, 'It is not in dispute that . . .'. In civil cases the statements of case will disclose what is agreed between parties. Put simply, if a fact is 'admitted', that fact is not in issue and no evidence has to be adduced to prove it.

It is important to note down what facts are agreed between the parties. It helps to narrow down the issues of a case and will be likely to shorten the length of a trial. It may also assist in a negotiation situation to be able to start from some common ground between the parties.

14.2.2   Facts and evidence

When a 'fact' has been agreed, or can be proved by a witness or document, that fact is then considered to be 'evidence' in the case, and can be taken into account in determining the strengths and weaknesses of the case. The distinction is important: some facts are incapable of proof and (if not agreed) should not be relied upon as part of the case.

14.2.3   Disputed facts and facts in issue

If a fact is in dispute between the parties, that is, the opponent does not 'agree' it, it is deemed to be a *'disputed fact'* in the case. In civil cases you can determine what the 'disputed facts' are by looking primarily at the court papers, although documents and correspondence may bring up other facts that are not agreed. The statements of case (particulars of claim and defence) will show which facts are 'denied' or simply 'not admitted'. If a fact is 'not admitted', the party seeking to prove the fact will have to adduce evidence. By stating 'no admissions are made as to...', the other party is saying 'I will not adduce evidence to contradict this fact but I reserve the right to cross-examine your witnesses to test their evidence on this point'. If a fact is 'denied', the party relying on that fact will have to adduce evidence to prove it and the opponent will probably bring evidence to contradict it.

It is easy to confuse '*disputed facts*' and '*facts in issue*'. First, bear in mind that it is common for a case to contain many disputed facts. Of these, there will be some that are crucial in the sense that they support points that must be proved in law in order for the case to be successful. It is these facts, ie, the facts which are not agreed by the opponent, and which must be proved in law, that become the 'facts in issue'. For example, D is accused of assaulting the owner of a public house after D and his friend asked to play a game of pool. D's story is that he arrived at the bar 15 minutes after his friend on the evening in question; the prosecution say that he arrived sometime before his friend. The time and sequence of arrival are 'disputed facts' between the parties in the sense that there is no agreement as to who arrived first and at what times they arrived. But bringing evidence of the truth of one version or the other is not relevant to proving the elements of the criminal offence of assault, and will not affect a successful outcome. Therefore it is not a 'fact in issue'.

The facts in issue will be determined by what legal elements (in a criminal case) or prima facie requirements (in a civil case) apply. For example, in a contract case where C is suing D for breach of contract and resulting loss, the parties may agree that a contract was made, and the terms of that agreement. However, D disputes that a breach occurred, and naturally disputes causing losses. As breach and causation are two of the prima facie requirements for a successful action in contract (and the facts on these two matters are disputed), these become the 'facts in issue' in the case. C will only win the case by producing evidence on these issues to prove that his version of the facts was correct, and is therefore entitled to judgment in his favour.

It is important to bear in mind that 'facts in issue' (sometimes called 'factual issues') can be a general heading containing several separate issues. For example, in a criminal case, the identity of the defendant might be in issue. One element of the identification evidence concerns the colour of his hair. One witness says that he had fair hair, another that he had brown hair. The colour of the hair is therefore a fact in issue. Its proof will affect whether the prosecution have proved their case in that identification of the defendant as the offender is an element of the offence. It will assist in identifying all the factual issues to divide the case into fairly broad factual issues first, and then look at the facts which are in dispute within each of those main issues. This is covered in more detail later on in the chapter.

14.2.4   Legal issues

These are the questions of law which will have to be answered in the case:

- What are the potential causes of actions or offences?
- What are the potential defences?
- What are the potential legal outcomes?
- What procedural and evidential questions arise?

In tort and contract cases, there are established frameworks to work from, eg, elements that the claimant must prove in order to establish a prima facie case. In criminal cases, the prosecution must prove the elements of an offence, and in some cases, the absence of a defence. Of the host of legal issues that apply to a case, only some will need to be formally proved since often there will be no dispute between the parties on some of the relevant issues. Later on in this chapter we look at establishing legal frameworks, and defining the issues to be resolved.

14.2.5   The 'theory' of the case

After the barrister has identified a framework of the legal and factual issues in a case, and done the necessary legal research, a picture should start to emerge. For each case, it is necessary for you to consider a 'theory' of the case, that is, your explanation of how the events of the case are likely to have happened. The 'theory' of the case will influence the nature of the evidence that will be required for a successful resolution, and will also be the base for the advocacy in the case. For example, in the civil brief of *Lowe* v *Mainwaring* in **Chapter 16**, the claimant (tenant) alleges damages were caused by the failure of the defendants (also tenants) to keep an external pipe in good order. In representing the defendants, one theory might be as follows.

The duty was owed by the landlord (not the defendants) under the lease. If any duty was in fact owed by the defendants, there was no breach of the duty as the pipe was properly insulated and, in any event, the damage which the claimant suffered, if proved, was not caused by the flood of water from the pipe but from the pre-existing financial difficulties.

In a straightforward case, the theory may be fairly clear, and based solidly on legal and factual certainties. But often the law may not be clear, all the facts may not be available, or there may be gaps in the evidence. In those cases, you will need to develop arguments which link the facts and evidence which are available into a persuasive explanation of your client's version of events.

Developing a 'theory' is covered in more detail later in this chapter.

14.3   The C.A.P. approach

Having identified the intellectual elements of fact management skills in **14.1**, there are a number of practical techniques which barristers may use to produce a well-prepared case. Regardless of the task which a barrister might be asked to undertake — to advise on the merits, appear in court, or advise in conference — it is crucial to absorb and analyse the facts of the case. Without a uniform approach and structure to this process, thoughts and theories can become confused. Adopting a logical yet flexible framework will not only minimise the chances of missing important pieces of information, but will maximise productivity in terms of your time and effort.

The C.A.P. approach is a step-by-step method of preparing and analysing a case. All barristers develop their own practical styles of working, with or without attaching formal names or titles to their working methods. In order to study the necessary stages, the C.A.P. approach sets out the three main stages involved in efficient preparation:

- Context;
- Analysis;
- Presentation.

Each stage contains tasks and questions which must be answered before moving on to the next stage. The time necessary for each step depends on the complexity of the case, and the specific task you are instructed to do. The advantage of taking an overview of the preparation process is that it enables the student to see how the process develops from the first reading of the facts, through to the analysis of evidence needed in order to present a successful case. As you gain experience, it is hoped that the C.A.P. framework will allow you to selectively determine what is required by means of thorough preparation for any given case.

In **Chapter 16**, the C.A.P. approach is applied to the civil case of *Lowe* v *Mainwaring* to illustrate the process at different stages in the life of a case when a barrister might become involved, ie, giving advice on merits, drafting, and appearing in an interim application.

The C.A.P. approach is applied to a criminal action in **Chapter 17**, based on the brief for the defence in the case of *R v Costas Georgiou*.

It should be remembered that the C.A.P. approach is only one method of achieving a well-prepared case as discussed in **14.1**. Even while following the C.A.P. approach, the tasks within each stage can be done by using any number of techniques, eg, lists, charts, mind-maps, graphs. As examples, a set of proforma charts which can be used as part of the C.A.P. approach are included at **14.8**. While their use is by no means prescriptive, they may be helpful in clarifying the various steps involved in thorough case preparation.

14.3.1   The three stages of C.A.P.

Stage 1: The context of the case

(a) Understand the stage of the proceedings: your role and instructions, and the objectives.
(b) Understand the problem: eg, the history of the situation, nature and cause of the problem.
(c) Collect the 'facts'.
(d) Identify the agreed facts and facts in dispute: ie, those facts which are disputed between the parties, for example, by use of a chart to set out the facts, queries, and each party's version.
(e) Identify the legal framework: in a criminal case this would be the elements of the offence, possible defences, sentence, jurisdiction and procedure. In a civil case, this would be the elements required to obtain or refuse the remedy sought.

Stage 2: Analysis of issues and evidence

(a) Analyse the issues:
    (i) Identify the factual issues: ie, those disputed facts which are not agreed by the opponent and which must be proved in law for a successful outcome.
    (ii) Identify the legal issues by applying the facts to the legal framework.
    (iii) Identify a potential 'theory' of the case.
    (iv) Identify the gaps and ambiguities in the facts.
(b) Analyse the evidence:
    (i) Analyse the strengths and weaknesses of your case and that of your opponent.
    (ii) Establish 'proof' — turning facts into 'evidence'.

Stage 3: The presentation of the case or argument

(a) Revisit the chosen theory and select a theme.
(b) Consider how to support the legal framework.
(c) Consider how to carry out your instructions.
(d) Consider the intended audience: eg, who will be reading your work or listening to you, and the best method of conveying information.
(e) Ensure that this process enables you to carry out your client's instructions.

14.4 Stage 1: context

14.4.1 Introduction

When you receive a set of papers, they will contain varied information. The first task is a simple one of comprehension. Specialist terminology may be used in a report (for example, to describe a part of a machine used in factory production) and you may need to consult a glossary or trade manual for a full understanding of the term. This occurs frequently with medical terms used in expert reports, eg, diagnosis of a condition, and practitioners must understand the meaning of the term and its application in the particular context. There is a glossary covering medical terms in **Appendix 1** to this Manual.

Increasingly, information is presented in numerical form and you will need to be able to analyse bank statements, sets of accounts, and possibly graphs or statistics. It is likely that you will be expected to verify any figures you have been given. Indeed, in planning for a negotiation or considering a proposed settlement package you would be expected to make accurate calculations without the need to call for an accountant except in fairly complex cases. (See **Chapter 18** on dealing with figures.) Understanding a variety of information is only part of the task. It is also important that you develop an ability to present that information to others using various modes, and for a variety of purposes (see **Chapter 19**).

14.4.2 Understanding the stage of the proceedings, your instructions, role, and the objectives

Just as the facts in a case must be viewed in the context of all the surrounding information, they can be and are interpreted differently according to the standpoint of the interpreter. Before beginning a factual analysis, it is important to understand the stage that the case has reached, what you have been instructed to do and why, and what your client is hoping to achieve.

Your view of the past and present situation will be influenced by whether you are representing the claimant or defendant, prosecution or defence, employer or employee, a consumer or a manufacturer. As you read the papers, it is important to approach them with an objective frame of mind. In some cases proceedings may have already begun before you become involved in the case. In other cases, the 'present' situation is one where there is a threat of future harmful events and the 'future' solution will be some type of preventative action.

14.4.2.1 The stage of the proceedings

Fact management skills cannot be divorced from civil and criminal procedure and require a thorough knowledge of the legal process. **Chapter 16** provides an overview of the stages of a civil case and **Chapter 17** gives an outline of a criminal case. Ascertaining what stage of the process a case has reached is a crucial starting point and it is wise to make a written note of when proceedings were issued, served, previous court orders made etc prior to embarking on further analysis of the case.

Your approach will differ according to your instructions and the development of the case to date. For example, it is common for barristers to be instructed to write an advice on evidence. This is the particular 'task' which is requested, but it can occur at different stages in the life of a case. In a civil case, advice is often requested when a solicitor is preparing for trial and wishes to know if there are any gaps in the evidence or whether to call for further evidence. It is also common for such an advice before disclosure of documents occurs or after an initial wave of disclosure has been completed, or both (see *Civil Litigation Manual* on disclosure). Advice may be requested prior to any proceedings being issued, to ascertain whether there are sufficient grounds to support a claim, and if so, the appropriate parties to be sued. In this case, you will be advising only on the evidence available at that particular time. Advice on evidence may be requested at any time before the trial.

Understanding the procedural and factual history will assist you to appreciate the task requested, define successfully your objectives for the task and to resolve the problem.

14.4.2.2   Your instructions, role and objectives

It is perhaps stating the obvious to point out the necessity of understanding the parameters of your instructions to ensure that the advice sought is in fact given, and the requested performance completed to the letter. However, the fact is that in the process of digesting a multitude of facts, documents, events and statements, particularly in a complex case, it is easy to lose sight of the specific task that has been requested.

Is your role to be the sole counsel who will see the case from beginning to end? Or are you one of several counsel who will represent the client on a variety of ancillary matters? As a junior barrister, it is common to find that you are briefed to appear on a bail application in a criminal case, or an interim hearing in a lengthy and complex civil case. The task involves one small part in the process, and it may be difficult or even impossible in the time available to understand fully the 'past' of the case. While spending hours reading through files in preparation for a hearing is laudable, two points should be remembered.

First, unless you recognise where in the litigation process you (and the court hearing) are, you will be reading the papers with the wrong purpose. A legally-qualified sponge, soaking up facts without a reference point achieves nothing. Time would be better spent analysing the arguments that may be made, both for and against, at the hearing.

Secondly, you will often find that these arguments (particularly in protracted cases) will have already been considered as part of the general strategy for the case. The senior barrister with overall responsibility may have specific thoughts about the hearing for which you have been instructed. In these cases, it would be unwise to decide that the brief is yours to handle independently; the hearing may not achieve its real purpose (either long-term or short-term). The danger lies in highlighting the wrong areas, or giving away points unnecessarily because your involvement prevented you from seeing their long-term significance. In short, determine your role properly in the context of the size of case and the stage it has reached. Consultation with the instructing solicitors and the senior barrister (if there is one) is advised.

In answering 'Why are you instructed to do this task?' you will need to identify your objectives, which you should realise by now may differ from those of the client. Superficially your objective may be to win the case, or succeed at a particular hearing. Of the several aims that you might have, the most obvious is not necessarily the only one or even of primary importance. In carrying out your task, be it written work, or attending hearings, there may be latent as well as manifest reasons for your working methods. For example, when a barrister in court asks his or her own witness, 'What is your name and address?', the manifest purpose is to put on record who the witness is and his or her residence. The latent purpose is usually to settle the witness in the witness box by asking easy and comfortable questions. There may be other latent purposes, for example, to show the judge or jury that the witness comes from a deprived part of the city (if this is part of your theory or theme of the case).

One further point about objectives borrows a page from advocacy skills. Be sure that in clarifying your objectives and expectations, you have considered your audience. It is common for barristers to speak in front of magistrates, judges, juries, administrative or employment tribunals. Thought should be given to their expectations, agenda, and what methods of persuasion will produce the most successful results.

14.4.3   Understanding the problem

To understand the context of a case, it is essential to understand fully the history of the parties (civil), or background information about the client (criminal), and how the situation arose. For every client and fact situation, there is a past, present and future. Once you see how and why the problem arose, it will assist you in identifying how to deal with the present problem, and possible solutions for the future. In the civil context, parties may have enjoyed a good business relationship in the past which one or both parties wish to continue in the future. In a criminal case, the defendant's financial situation leading up to the alleged offence may provide an insight into the circumstances.

14.4.3.1   Looking at the cause of a problem

A crucial part of understanding a problem is appreciating the cause. Why has it occurred? What circumstances led to the problem? If an effective solution is to be found, what circumstances must be avoided to prevent recurrence? For example, your client has asked that a court order be obtained allowing him to have contact with his children on a Sunday, rather than the present arrangement on a Saturday. You will need first to investigate why this issue has arisen between the parties. More specifically you would wish to know:

- whether Saturday contact had been agreed or was the subject of a court order;
- whether the agreement or order had worked well, and the history of any difficulties;
- what the nature of any problems had been;
- whether changing the day is considered by the client and/or child carer to make arrangements easier or more difficult;
- how the children have responded;
- whether the children wish to maintain contact;
- why your client wants to see the children on Sundays, eg, to go to church, because of a work schedule etc;
- whether the children want to change to Sunday — any conflict with their activities or school projects;
- if the proposal has been refused, the possible reasons;
- whether there are any other difficulties between the parties which may be masked by this dispute.

Once this information has been digested, you will then be in a position to understand fully the problem and consider appropriate ways of solving it which will meet the client's objectives.

The process of 'understanding' a problem is achieved by a combination of using your individual sense of perception and intellect. Just as the results of computer output are only as accurate as the data which has been put in, the range and accuracy of facts fed into the human mind will affect the conclusions made from them. You will find that developing an approach or structure for posing generic questions (Who did what to whom, when, where and with what result?) will focus your mind on collecting the crucial facts and appreciating how and why a problem has arisen, thus paving the way to reaching a solution that is appropriate on the facts and desired by the client.

14.4.3.2   The client's objectives

One may wonder why, in a study of fact analysis, the client's objectives, or even those of the barrister, are a part of the process. Simply put, understanding the client's objectives impacts the way the problem-solving process is managed and influences the way facts can be interpreted. As you read the papers, a mental picture emerges of the appropriate ways to resolve the problem. The client's objectives may or may not be reflected in the papers. Alternatively, you may find after a conference that the client holds different or additional objectives that will require a rethink on the best method of resolving or presenting the case.

The barrister's day-to-day contact with the legal system and the constant approach to problems solely from a legal standpoint can easily allow his or her own objectives to influence the understanding of the problem and the client's objectives. For example, you may decide that the best course of action would be to negotiate a settlement or seek arbitration to avoid a court hearing. However, your client may want a public investigation (or a day in court) and/or be opposed to settlement where no commercial benefit can be seen in settling the case, for example, where the client is a supplier of faulty goods but has already received full payment. Your task is to identify your client's values and interests, to know the extent to which your own objectives may affect a proposed resolution, and base your factual analysis on the strengths and weaknesses of the case.

It should be remembered that clients may have non-legal as well as legal objectives; these may or may not be articulated. Some stated objectives may eclipse the true interests that the client has but, for whatever reason, has not verbalised. Rather than taking statements at face value, strive for more thorough questioning which may reveal additional reasons for their objectives, and which may improve the strength of their position.

It is not too soon, even at this stage of reading the papers, to bear in mind possible resolutions to the problem. In civil cases, while some disputes will ultimately go to trial for final resolution, this may not be in the client's best interest. Various forms of alternative dispute resolution (ADR), such as arbitration and mediation are becoming more popular as costs escalate and the delays of bringing an action to trial increase and are actively encouraged by the Civil Procedure Rules. Arbitration is common in construction cases and is increasingly used in commercial and civil cases. Mediation, the process where a mediator attempts to bring the parties together into an agreed resolution is often preferable to a contested trial in family and child cases and neighbour disputes. Further, there are other remedies that might be suggested by the facts including use of internal employee complaint procedures, filing formal complaints with an agency such as the Commission for Racial Equality, or with the local authority. In criminal cases, the client's circumstances may indicate that the best solution would be long-term medical treatment and you may wish to raise with the solicitor the possibility of investigating this option on behalf of the client.

14.4.4   Collecting the facts

The next stage is to collect all the relevant facts in the case. In practice, this work is divided between the barrister and the solicitor. The degree of factual information included in the instructions to counsel will vary according to the type of case (civil or criminal), the size of the case, the stage in the proceedings and the task which you are asked to do. In the early stages, you may have only a proof of evidence from the client, and possibly a few witness statements. In civil cases, this may be sufficient to provide an advice on the merits, although it would be insufficient for providing, eg, an advice on evidence and quantum.

Where you are briefed to appear at an interim hearing and have been sent copies of the drafts and relevant witness statements, there may be no need to acquire further information, unless the facts require clarification. In defending a criminal case, the defendant is likely to be best placed to provide more information about witnesses, particularly about potential alibi evidence. Prosecuting counsel often request additional information from eg, police who were at the scene or otherwise involved in the matter.

In some cases your written instructions to counsel may be minimal. You may need to ask what has taken place in previous conferences between the client and solicitors. If so, you will want to ensure that you understand exactly what was said or done, as different interpretations can easily arise when discussions are relayed second-hand. If the need for information or clarification can best be met by requesting a conference with the client, this is appropriate, but you will want to bear in mind that conferences increase the costs in a case and should only be requested when the information cannot be obtained by other, less expensive means.

Once you have understood the contents of your brief, and held a conference (if necessary), you can begin to clarify in your own mind precisely what is said to have occurred. It is crucial to develop a critical and questioning approach to all information which you receive. Remember that the information that is missing is as important in the context of the situation as what has been said or written. It is not sufficient merely to identify the gaps in the information or inconsistencies in the facts. You must attempt to fill the gaps by acquiring more information and ask, 'Why might these inconsistencies exist?'

It is also important to remember that fact-finding is an ongoing process. New facts will become available at different stages in a case, for instance, on disclosure of documents. As new facts emerge you must keep an open mind; your view of the case may need to be reconsidered and your original conclusions reassessed and possibly modified. You may never possess all the facts in a case.

14.4.4.1 Methods of collecting facts

Rather than start with a group of assorted facts, which at this stage may not bear a great degree of logical order, it is more helpful to approach collection with a structure or framework of main questions to be answered. The facts that are presently available can then be filled in, and the areas where more information is needed, or ambiguities exist are highlighted. Regardless of what task is requested, eg, to advise, draft, or appear as an advocate, you will find that most practitioners undertake several routine steps in preparing a case. These preparatory steps are important because they assist in understanding the events and problem generally, and the schedules and charts produced as a result (if the information they contain is agreed) are often given to the court in hearings and at trial to assist the court's understanding of the case. As there is always that possibility, strive for accuracy, clarity and neatness as you prepare them. There are several methods which can be used, though the purpose of all of them is the same: to ensure that every aspect of the problem is explored thoroughly and from every angle. As you gain experience you will no doubt devise your personal methods of asking these important questions of who, what, where, why and how?

14.4.4.2 Construct a chronology and dramatis personae

Listing the people involved and the events in the order in which they occurred clarifies what happened, assists understanding and can be invaluable as the basis of an opening speech. Increasingly, an agreed chronology is handed up to the judge at the start of both civil and criminal trials which provides a structure for the presentation of the case.

14.4.4.3 Draw a plan of the locus in quo

The *'locus in quo'* simply means the place where the events occurred. It can be represented by maps, floor plans, or other types of drawings. The first plan which you prepare should be entirely uncontroversial: either delete any points which are in dispute or, if they are included, ensure that they are clearly identified as in dispute. The rationale for this is that, where a plan is produced that makes assumptions about facts which are yet to be proved, the plan tends to become fixed in the mind as the true factual scenario and may prevent you from keeping an open mind to consider other possible explanations. An 'undisputed' plan can also be useful in a client conference where asking the client to explain his or her version of events will test the credibility of the client's evidence.

You also need to devise ways to represent in the plan the areas about which you do not yet have enough information to present the data accurately. For example, in the plan of a bank robbery, you are told that a witness was on the opposite side of the road, but at this stage of the case you do not know precisely where. Guessing the position and marking it on the plan is inaccurate and could lead to subconsciously assuming its truth without obtaining further factual information. Mark it in a way that shows there is doubt, or delete it until further facts are known. Until the location is certain, it is impossible to assess the witness's line of view, obstructions etc.

It may also be helpful to draw a series of plans. Following the first which is uncontroversial, additional plans may then show various alternative explanations of what might have occurred.

14.4.4.4 Organise by sorting

This method, based on the five basic questions of who, what, why, where and how, will assist you to categorise main areas. In Table 14.1, column 1 contains main categories of questions; column 2 lists possible answers (or possibilities which may lead to answers). You will note that the suggestions in column 2 are appropriate to different factual situations.

Table 14.1 **Sorting method**

Column 1	Column 2
1. Who did what to whom?	Names, addresses of parties, witnesses.
2. With whom does problem occur?	Friend, employer, supplier.
3. When does the problem occur?	Date, time, season.
4. Where does it occur?	Work, home, public place.
5. In what situation?	Drunkenness, anger, lack of funds, lack of supplies etc.
6. Is there a pattern?	When contact is refused, when maintenance is unpaid, when supplies are scarce.
7. What triggers it?	Smell, noise, rain?
8. What result from the problem?	. . .

14.4.4.5 Flowcharts

Some practitioners prefer to use general-style blank flowcharts which provide an overview of the case as well as prompt heads of information which will be needed. The chart shown in Figure 14.1 is an overview of a civil case. It could be used in its present form in fairly straightforward cases. More complex cases will require a more extensive system of collection and organisation of the facts.

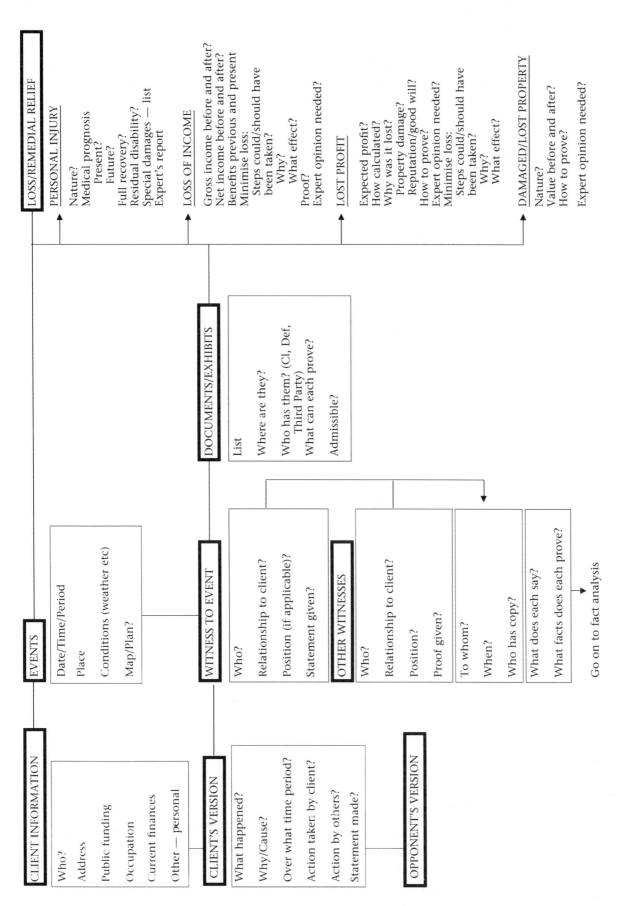

Figure 14.1 Flowchart

14.4.4.6   Checklists

Finally, you may prefer to develop checklists of the information which you will need when you prepare your cases. With experience, you will be able to amend and update your lists to home in on the crucial information, cover new legal developments and avoid spending time and effort on sorting through information which is not relevant to the issues as hand. Of course there may be times when papers are received at the last minute and there is not sufficient time to prepare copious checklists. However, if you have developed this structure as part of your working approach, your mind should automatically take you through the generally relevant areas, using the little time which you have to best advantage.

EXAMPLE

An example of the questions that would be included in a checklist in a civil action based on the flowchart illustrated in Figure 14.1 is as follows:
Personal:
1. Who is your client?
2. Where does he or she live?
3. Occupation?
4. Other personal details?
Event:
5. When and where did event happen?
6. How does your client say it happened?
7. What did your client do or say at the time?
8. Who heard or saw what your client said or did?
9. Who witnessed it? What do the witnesses say happened?
10. Can they give evidence?
11. What points could each prove? Are they consistent with the client's story?
Exhibits:
12. What exhibits are there?
13. Where are they? Who has them?
14. What can each prove?
15. Who will produce them in court?
Loss or damage:
16. Type of loss suffered?
17. If PI, nature of injury?
18. Medical prognosis?
19. Will there be full recovery?
20. If no, to what extent is disability permanent?
21. What experts have given or should give evidence?
22. What other losses are there, eg, lost income, lost profit, lost or damaged property, pain and suffering etc?
If income lost:
23. What is/was client's gross and net income?
24. What payments were/are being received from State?
25. What steps could/should have been done to minimise loss?
26. Why should they have been taken?
If profit lost:
27. What profit should have been made?
28. How calculated?
29. Why was it lost?
30. What steps could/should have been taken to minimise loss?
31. Why should they have been taken?
If property lost or damaged:
32. What was its value before and after the event?

33. What is its value now?
34. Can it be repaired? If so, what is the cost?
35. What could/should have been done to minimise loss?
36. If so, why should they have been taken?

Insurance:

37. Does client have insurance? With whom?
38. Does the policy cover this loss?
39. Has a claim been made? If so, when?
40. Does the other party have insurance?
41. Does that insurance cover this loss if liability can be proved?
42. Has a claim been made?

14.4.5   Identify agreed facts and disputed facts

Once the basic facts have been digested, you will begin to identify the facts which are agreed between the parties and those which are disputed. It is necessary to crystallise these issues and ascertain, for each disputed fact, both your client's version and that of your opponent. This is an important preliminary analysis which should be recorded in a practical form which can be used later in the fact management process. The way in which this information is presented is a matter of style although its usefulness may be increased if it is neat and can be used, for example, in discussing the case with the solicitor. A suggested format can be found in Table 14.8 at the end of this chapter.

EXAMPLE

In the civil case of *Lowe v Mainwaring* (see Chapter 16), the defendants are the tenants of the first and second floors of a property. The claimant is the tenant of the ground floor and uses the space to run the Topspin Snooker Hall. A flood occurred from a water pipe outside the building at about the first-floor level causing damage to the claimant's property. The claimant alleges that the defendants were responsible for the water pipe and their negligence caused the damage. The facts might be recorded as in Table 14.2.

Table 14.2 **Record of facts**

A/D	Claimant	Page/ref	Defendant	Page/ref
A	At the time, C was tenant of ground floor, and D were tenants of the 1st and 2nd floors of 83–87 Leeds Road.	XX		
A	The pipe located in the 1st floor outside the building burst.	XX		
D	Time: it burst between 23 and 30 December 1998	XX	Pipe was repaired within a few hours of bursting on finding it on the 30th	XX
D	D responsible for repairing and maintaining the pipe	XX	Under lease with M. Pike, D *not responsible* for repair or maintenance	XX
D	Pipe was not properly insulated	XX	Properly insulated	XX

This table is further developed at 16.1.1.

There may be many disputed facts in a case and though it may be a tedious job, it is important that all of them are recorded. From this information you will be able to determine which of these disputed facts will actually be 'facts in issue' in the case, ie, facts which are not agreed and which must be proved in law in order to win the case. This will be covered in more detail in Stage 2 of the C.A.P. approach in 14.5.

14.4.6   Identify the legal framework

Having started with facts, you will need to identify a possible legal framework to which the facts will ultimately be applied. This applies equally whether you are determining the best legal basis for bringing a case, or the best defence. At this stage, the aim is to identify all the legal possibilities which may lead to a resolution of the problem. Later in the analysis process, the framework will be developed and any necessary legal research done.

The process of identifying the legal possibilities may be difficult, particularly where the area of law is an unfamiliar one or several potential legal frameworks are suggested. To start, you will need to list all the possible legally relevant factors which are present. You cannot afford at this point to make snap judgments about the best legal framework or settle for a quickly identified clever answer which may have weaknesses or be less appropriate than another legal basis for bringing or defending the case.

14.4.6.1   List the potential legally relevant factors

Having taken a preliminary view of the facts, it may be tempting to place them into familiar pigeon-holes, eg, contract, misrepresentation, mistake, theft etc. While this may assist in providing initial focus, it can be restrictive; the best legal solution may not always come from a textbook framework.

First, list all the factors of the case which may possibly have a legal ramification. The index of *Halsbury's Laws of England* or *Halsbury's Statutes* can be a source for ideas. The general categories in Table 14.3 have legal relevance in most cases.

Table 14.3 **Relevant factors**

Categories	Legally relevant factors
People and partes	Eg, minor, spouse, joint owner, limited company, professional.
Places	Eg, occupier's liability, Factories Act, waterways, party resident in France, leased premises.
Objects/items	Eg, animals, children's toy, car window, machine part, stereo (consumer).
Documents	Eg, contract, will, bill of lading, deed.
Acts	Eg, negligence, intentional, reckless act.
Omissions	Eg, failure to act or deliver or mitigate.
Words	Eg, inducement, fraud, misrepresentation.
Dates	Eg, limitation.

In making this list, you should include everything that underlies or surrounds the facts, as well as actual words that appear in the papers. For example, in a case that concerns a jam jar, even though there is no Jam Jars Act, you will still need to enter 'jam jar' on the list. There are laws relating to the manufacture of jam jars, filling jars either in a factory or at home (if the contents are for sale to the public), labelling them (including EC regulations), not dealing with jars negligently to cause injury to another etc. The more comprehensive your list of potential factors, the more pieces are available for choosing a framework.

The completed list of factors can then be organised and grouped together into 'legal frameworks'. The following headings might be used as general categories for grouping factors in a civil case:

- parties;
- cause(s) of action;
- defence(s);
- remedy sought.

Some factors on the list in Table 14.3 may apply to more than one heading. For example, under 'Acts' you may have: 'Piano owned by client wrongfully taken away from his home'. This factor suggests a possible cause of action (tort of conversion) and also the relief sought (return of piano).

Some potentially relevant factors may not fit easily within one of the headings above but should not be ignored. Retain them in a general category at the end. They may prove useful, for example, by revealing a gap in the case you are preparing.

EXAMPLE

An example of how factors might be grouped in chart form is shown in Table 14.4. In this case example, the claimants have suffered loss and damage as a result of their neighbour (D1) who is burning industrial waste from a machine-shop business operated on the property. The neighbour rents the property from the landowner (D2) who is aware of D1's activities. Column 1 lists the facts which carry a legal implication. Column 2 contains general issue headings. The space in column 3 is for legal frameworks suggested by the facts; in this case nuisance and a possible breach of statutory obligation. This procedure is the same in criminal cases to explore bases for the offences which might be charged, and potential defences. While many methods can achieve this analysis, the benefit of the tabular form is the visual analysis on a single page.

Table 14.4 **Grouping legal factors**

Example of grouping legal factors towards developing a full legal framework. In this example, the clients (Mr and Mrs C) are suffering from the burning of industrial waste by a neighbour (D1) who lives on adjoining property and runs a small business. D1 leases the property from a freehold landlord (D2).

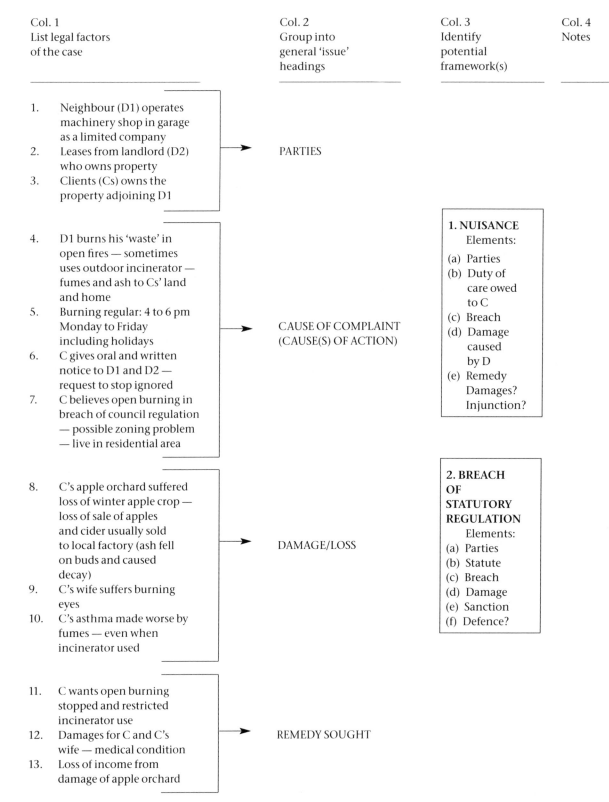

Col. 1 List legal factors of the case	Col. 2 Group into general 'issue' headings	Col. 3 Identify potential framework(s)	Col. 4 Notes
1. Neighbour (D1) operates machinery shop in garage as a limited company 2. Leases from landlord (D2) who owns property 3. Clients (Cs) owns the property adjoining D1	PARTIES		
4. D1 burns his 'waste' in open fires — sometimes uses outdoor incinerator — fumes and ash to Cs' land and home 5. Burning regular: 4 to 6 pm Monday to Friday including holidays 6. C gives oral and written notice to D1 and D2 — request to stop ignored 7. C believes open burning in breach of council regulation — possible zoning problem — live in residential area	CAUSE OF COMPLAINT (CAUSE(S) OF ACTION)	**1. NUISANCE** Elements: (a) Parties (b) Duty of care owed to C (c) Breach (d) Damage caused by D (e) Remedy Damages? Injunction?	
8. C's apple orchard suffered loss of winter apple crop — loss of sale of apples and cider usually sold to local factory (ash fell on buds and caused decay) 9. C's wife suffers burning eyes 10. C's asthma made worse by fumes — even when incinerator used	DAMAGE/LOSS	**2. BREACH OF STATUTORY REGULATION** Elements: (a) Parties (b) Statute (c) Breach (d) Damage (e) Sanction (f) Defence?	
11. C wants open burning stopped and restricted incinerator use 12. Damages for C and C's wife — medical condition 13. Loss of income from damage of apple orchard	REMEDY SOUGHT		

14.4.6.2 Basic legal frameworks

While it would be unwise to conclude at this stage that a particular framework is the only applicable one, it is often a helpful starting point to consider established frameworks which are suggested from the facts, eg, contract, tort, a specific criminal offence. For a specific criminal offence, you would focus on the following headings:

- *Offence*: What are the elements of the offence?
- *Defence*: Applicable common law and statutory defences.
- *Penalty*: Sanctions on summary trial, on indictment.
- *Jurisdiction*: Type of offence, eg, can be tried by magistrates or in the Crown Court; financial threshold eg, if amount less than £5,000 to magistrates' court.
- *Procedure*: Relevant procedural steps.

Table 14.5 shows how this information could be set out in relation to s 18 of the Offences against the Person Act 1861.

Table 14.5 **Identifying the legal framework: example in a criminal case: Offences against the Person Act 1861, s 18**

Heading	Framework
Offence	Unlawfully and maliciously wound with intent to do grievous bodily harm.
Defences	Factual denial of elements including claiming lawfulness of wounding by reason of self-defence, prevention of crime, protection of property or other persons.
Penalty	Imprisonment up to life. Usual bracket 3 to 8 years. Provocation factor which can be taken into account. Deportation. See EC Treaty, Article 48 and Directive 64/221, arts 3 and 9.
Jurisdiction	Indictable offence. Crown Court only. Class 4 offence.
Procedure	Magistrates commit/transfer to Crown Court. Plea taken at plea and directions hearing. If not guilty, date fixed for jury trial.

For civil cases, the facts may suggest a tort and/or a contract claim. The following preliminary frameworks set out the elements which would be considered in determining whether a prima facie case is established.

Table 14.6 **Preliminary framework: civil case**

Tort	Contract
Parties.	Parties.
Accident or cause of complaint.	The contract.
Cause(s) of action (causation).	The terms.
Damage or loss.	Performance.
Remedy sought.	Breach.
	Damage and causation.
	Remedy sought.

Even where an established framework fits the facts well, you should in any event investigate other legal bases to ensure that your chosen framework not only applies to the facts but offers the best opportunity to achieve the client's objectives. In civil cases, it may be wise to plead alternative causes of action, join causes of action or bring in additional parties for the most effective legal solution.

14.4.6.3 Identify areas for legal research

Additional research may be necessary to determine whether the framework is the most appropriate, for example, to determine whether the specific act complained of is covered by statute or constitutes criminal activity. By stepping back and taking a critical view of the framework, it should be possible to see all the strengths and weaknesses within it, and to take decisions where there are options.

If additional research is undertaken, notes of it should be recorded for later use, possibly at trial. At a minimum, the following should be recorded:

- *sources*: including the relevant page or paragraph numbers of textbooks, and full citations of case law;
- *short summary of the relevant legal point*;
- *your view of the answer to the question*: indicating how the point found in research will support a specific fact or issue in the case.

See **Chapters 8** and **9** above.

14.4.6.4 How to choose the best legal framework

Surrounded by a myriad of legal possibilities, it is sometimes difficult to know what particular legal framework should be chosen and why. Having an understanding of alternative ways of assessing the case, as well as using your professional judgment in filling gaps will help you to make the best decision.

14.4.6.5 Which framework makes the best use of the legal and factual strengths? The 'best-fit' approach

If the framework does not provide a single obvious answer, it should nevertheless take you some distance down the road. At a minimum it should define where there are legal and factual certainties and, if options exist, what the options appear to be. One way to proceed is simply to make an objective valuation of all the legal requirements and relevant facts. The solution that 'best fits' the framework — the one which makes the best use of the legal and factual strengths of the case while placing least reliance on its weaknesses — would be the preferred one. This approach is not suggesting that superficial analysis will do so long as it gives a roughly right answer, but that, on critical analysis of the law and facts, a particular framework would make the best use of the elements in the case.

Even in the 'best-fit' method, the elements which do not sit well with the rest of the framework should not be ignored. They may have some use in reviewing the case at a later stage, or in looking for options for a settlement.

14.5 Stage 2: analysis of issues and evidence

14.5.1 Introduction

Thus far, the potential legally relevant factors have been identified and loosely grouped to suggest a possible legal framework or 'legal basis' to the problem. More than one framework may be suggested. The best legal argument has no point in a court if it is not soundly based on the facts. Equally, the facts of the case need the best legal argument to achieve the best result. Although an analysis of a case should start with consideration of the facts, as the case progresses, the role of law and fact is equally important, and the two are closely interrelated. More than that, they are interactive; one moves with the other as more legal or factual input is provided for a case.

14.5.2   Analyse the issues: identify the 'factual issues' and analyse the legal issues by applying the facts to the legal framework

By this stage you will have identified a possible legal framework and noted what facts are agreed and disputed. From the elements or legal requirements of this framework, you must then determine the 'factual issues' (also called 'facts in issue') of the case. The factual issues will be those disputed facts which, according to the legal framework chosen, must be proved in law for the case to be successful. Where statements of case have already been served, these will specify what issues have to be proved. For example, in a contract case where the claimant (landlord) is suing the defendant (tenant) for failure to maintain a gas boiler under the lease, which exploded causing damage to the claimant's property, the analysis might look like Table 14.7.

Table 14.7 **Analysis of the issues**

Framework	Facts of client	Disputed/agreed
Parties	Landlord: Mr X, Tenant: Ms Y	Agreed
Contract	By lease dated . . .	Agreed
Terms	Tenant had obligation to maintain	Agreed
Performance	Tenant in occupation, rent paid	Agreed
Breach	On XYZ date, boiler not in order	Denied
Causation	Caused explosion	Agree: explosion Deny: causation
Loss	Damaged property	Loss not mitigated

From this analysis you will see that the legal and factual issues will be breach, causation and loss. (The loss is a factual issue as the defendant's case is that the claimant's loss is due to his failure to mitigate.) Each of these factual issues must be formally proved by evidence. Thus each issue must be fully analysed to determine which facts can be proved and by what means. This information should be recorded for clarity and use later in the case.

The aim is to identify, for each factual issue, the name of the witness who can prove the fact, whether oral or documentary evidence is available, on which party the burden of proof lies, and in a civil case whether it is specifically raised in the court documents. There are various methods of recording this information and provided the relevant analysis is done, the choice is left to the practitioner. One chart which can be used for this purpose appears in Table 14.9 at the end of this chapter.

In finding the factual support for a framework, remember that every disputed fact will need to be proved. As the evidence is gathered, you will need to update the chart or list of all facts for which evidence is still required. Some of the possible frameworks identified early on may prove unworkable. While you can normally expect to have enough factual information for a preliminary determination, it is rare to have all the relevant facts before starting work on a case. As more information comes to light, your view on the most appropriate framework may change.

One final word on the interrelation of law and fact. It is vital to select relevant law with a sound knowledge of the facts, and then also to consider the facts in the light of the law to ensure coherence. Although law and fact become interrelated, never be deceived into thinking the law has become more important — the evidence, or the proven facts will always be just as important as the law. Table 1.1 in **Chapter 1** showed how the correlation of law, fact and evidence could be achieved.

14.5.3   Identify a potential 'theory' of the case

The theory of the case is a convincing and logical account of why and how the events in the case are likely to have happened. It is based on:

- the principles of law that are likely to be used at trial, ie, the legal solution or framework;
- what has to be proved and/or disproved at trial for the case to succeed;
- consideration of which facts are capable of being proved and the inferences which can be made from them.

Formulating a theory, though based on the available facts and evidence, sometimes requires a degree of guesswork to fill in the gaps. In a sense it puts cement between the bricks of the framework to fill in any factual or legal gaps in order to make a cohesive and persuasive story. It is your theory of the case that you hope to convince the fact finder is the true version of events.

The dangers of developing an imaginative theory that is not well founded on the facts cannot be overestimated. The more gaps that are filled by guesswork, rather than proven facts, the weaker the case. It follows that the more that the theory is grounded on persuasive evidence rather than supposition the higher the likelihood that it will be accepted.

In the context of fact management, developing a theory is an important stage in considering the legal and factual basis for the client's version of events and the chance of successfully obtaining a good resolution. Putting forward a theory is also a basis for persuasive advocacy, used in arguing interim applications, and submissions at trial. This is covered more fully in the *Advocacy Manual*.

The 'theory' should be an objective analysis of the events, rather than merely the best theory for the client. The opponent will also put forward a theory, and seek to disprove your account, thus it is wise to consider how the other parties may view your theory. Critically analyse the legal and factual weaknesses of the potential theory. Ensure that it is coherent and as capable of proof as possible.

In considering the theory, bear in mind:

(a) The need for the *best* explanation for the client's position from all the possible alternatives. Although alternative theories are possible it should be remembered that a single explanation is inherently more compelling.

(b) Early in a case it is desirable to develop provisional theories. The 'theory' may need to be altered as more evidence comes to light with regard to the opponent's defence, disclosure, information received in a criminal case etc.

(c) Although the theory must be logical, the ultimate form that it takes will be influenced by the 'theme' of the case, which goes beyond logic and may show that your client should be successful on, eg, moral grounds. Choosing the theme of the case is discussed in Stage 4 (see **14.7**) after factual analysis of the case is completed.

14.5.3.1   Ways to develop the 'theory'

If you are fortunate enough to have a substantial amount of factual information, and sources of proof, it may be possible to identify the best legal framework and develop a theory fairly easily. However, where the factual information is scarce, you will have to construct, either partially or wholly, a theory of the case alongside the consideration of the best legal framework. Thus the phrase 'developing a theory' is sometimes referred to as using theory to identify the most appropriate legal framework, or, as is used here, to fit together how and why the events or problem occurred.

Identifying alternative theories can be difficult, particularly where the area of law is unfamiliar to you. The more experienced you are with an area of law, the easier it becomes to appreciate the range of different theories which may apply. If you are in uncharted waters, there are guidelines to assist you in developing a perspective on the situation.

First, the problem at hand may be analogous to another situation with which you are familiar. In civil cases, consider the basic rights and obligations of the parties; the same legal principles may apply. In criminal cases, consider how analogous conduct is treated by the law and whether defences in those situations may be applicable to the case at hand. Secondly, consider whether the conduct or acts are of a nature that may be covered by statute. Research in one of the legislation sources may suggest other legal solutions and alternative theories for the case. Finally, bear in mind that there is no need to reinvent the wheel. You may find that merely asking whether someone in your chambers or firm has experience in the area enables them to point you in the right direction. It will very likely save time, may prevent you from going down the wrong path, and also give you a different perspective on the case.

14.5.3.2   Logical and lateral thinking

Many of you have played the game where one word is given and the object is to think of all the different words that can be formed from this one word. There are many variations but the challenge remains the same: to brainstorm, or to use another phrase, to use logical thinking to come up with all plausible answers. In this context, you are presented with a proposition that X happened or did not happen. The challenge is to think logically about all the evidence that exists to support that conclusion, even if purely circumstantial. Your analysis must be based on proved — or provable — facts as far as possible. Beware of emotion, intention and knowledge elements which are particularly difficult to prove. Remember too the weakness of logical thinking: the danger of assuming because a theory is logical, it is actually true.

Lateral thinking asks, not how events are most likely to have happened, but what are all the possible ways in which they *could* have happened, logical or otherwise. It looks for explanation from different, and often unexpected, angles to a problem. An example of reaching a solution by lateral thinking follows:

EXAMPLE

Problem

John states that when he came home, he went into the living room of his house and saw immediately that Victoria was lying naked on the floor, and that she was dead. There was broken glass on the floor, and a small pool of water. The window was open, but John could not remember if he had forgotten to close it before he went out.

Logical assumptions and focus for questioning

It is natural to assume and concentrate on:

- Victoria has been murdered or has died from natural causes such as a heart attack.
- Why was Victoria naked?
- Broken glass — if the window had been closed, an intruder could have broken a window or door for entry.

Logical thinkers would pursue more about Victoria, eg, how she died and why, and about John, eg, how long he had been gone, whether Victoria was very familiar to him etc. Stimulate lateral thinking by putting the problem in the centre of a diagram as in Figure 14.2. Follow the 'dos and don'ts' around the path and think of new lines of questioning.

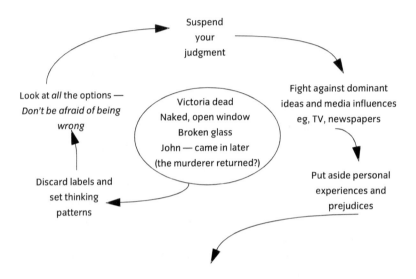

Figure 14.2 Lateral thinking

New lines should include where Victoria lived, whether she was usually clothed and in what type of clothes, who lived with John including any animals, what objects in the room were made of glass, eg, vases, ornaments, drinking glasses.

The answer

Victoria is in fact a fish and has died naturally after John's cat knocked the bowl over and ran out through the window!

This, of course, is an extreme example but does illustrate the trap of simple faith based on assumptions that something is true because it outwardly appears so.

Information rarely arrives in a sequential manner. A piece of information coming in early does not signify that it is particularly important, nor should it prejudice the importance of the other facts arriving later or from unexpected sources.

14.5.3.3　Mind-mapping

Another technique for developing a theory of a case is mind-mapping. When you receive information, your mind processes it in key concepts, interlinking thoughts with other ideas. Each word is received in the context of the words surrounding it, integrating the ideas and concepts to communicate certain meanings. Mind-mapping is a physical picture of the process that is occurring in the mind. Although it can take some time to become proficient at drawing them, the rewards are many as they visually present the structure of the case, and indicate where the weaknesses lie.

To start a mind-map, place the main theme or event in the centre. The branches coming out from the centre outline the main characters and events, with descriptive detail forming smaller branches. The more important elements are placed near the centre; the less important ones nearer the edge. There is an example in Figure 14.3, which suggests how you might use this technique in preparing a bail application for your client, Costas Georgiou (see **17.1**).

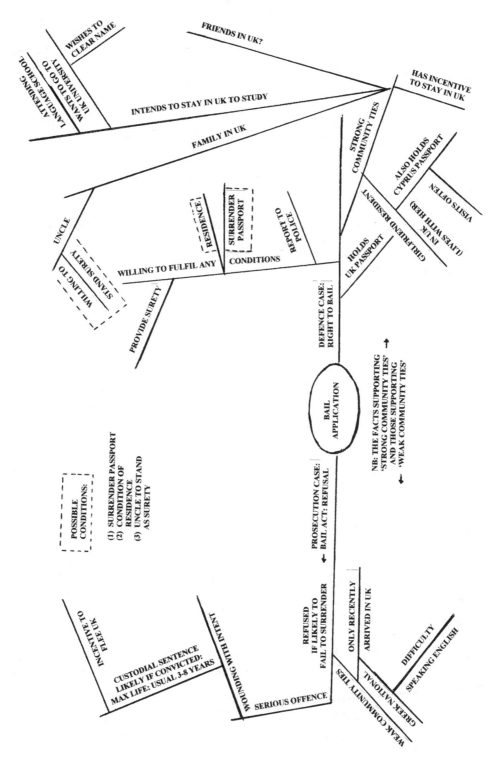

Figure 14.3 Mind-map or concept map of facts for bail application in the case of R v Costas Georgiou (see **Chapter 17**)

14.5.4 Identify the gaps or ambiguities in the facts

The advantage of adopting a methodical approach to analysis and recording is that it tends to highlight any gaps or ambiguities in the fact scenario. Sometimes these are fairly obvious, as where some invoices in a regular pattern of trading are missing which are relevant to the disputed fact. More commonly these are spotted by putting yourself at the scene — try to picture the story and ask yourself what pieces are missing or unclear. For example, in a fact scenario about a bank robbery, there may be a witness to the robbery. Before the picture can be completed you will need to know where the witness was standing, the direction he or she was facing, any obstructions to a clear view such as cars, signs, weather conditions, personal visual disabilities etc.

In some cases, the client is able to supply missing information and the most cost-effective way of obtaining this may be by requesting a conference. In civil cases, it may be necessary to serve a request for further information on your opponent (see the *Civil Litigation Manual*). Information may be needed from a third party and you will need to ask your instructing solicitor to take a proof of evidence if the identity of the witness is known or seek further witnesses who can provide evidence on a particular issue.

14.5.5 Analyse the evidence: importance of analysing the strengths and weaknesses

The question which most clients ask their barristers is 'Will I win my case?'. The answer will depend on the strength of the evidence, ie, on what facts can be proved. Before you are in a position to answer the client's questions, you will need to assess:

- what facts must and can be proved by whom;
- from the facts which can be proved (the evidence), the admissible evidence in support of each proposition which must be proved;
- the degree of conflicting or contradictory evidence;
- whether the evidence is sufficient to satisfy the standard of proof required.

In a civil case, it will be clear from the claim and defence which facts are in issue and therefore must be proved. By identifying which side carries the burden of proof on each issue, and assessing the witness statements and documentary evidence which support your case, as well as the contradictory evidence, you will then be in a position to comment on the likelihood of successfully establishing your client's case. While this information can be collated in a number of ways, you may wish to try using the chart in Table 14.10. This gives an overview to ascertain easily the strengths and weaknesses of a case. The importance of this assessment process, often called 'assessing the strengths and weaknesses' of the case cannot be overestimated. It is not only the key result of the fact analysis process, but is also essential before you can competently:

- give sound advice on the likelihood of success at trial;
- negotiate effectively on your client's behalf;
- advise on whether to accept a Part 36 payment (payment into court);
- advise on whether further evidence is necessary, and if so, the nature of that evidence; and
- plan the presentation of the case at the trial.

In a criminal case, the prosecution must prove the commission of the offence beyond reasonable doubt. Whether you are briefed for the prosecution or the defence, an analysis will still be required to assess whether the facts, or inferences drawn therefrom, can be established to the required standard of proof for each and every element of the offence. As in civil cases, this evidence must be balanced against the opposing evidence which may weaken the prosecution case.

14.5.6   From facts to evidence — establishing 'proof'

By this stage, you should have identified from the information which you have, the facts which are agreed and disputed, their source, ie, who or what will (may) be able to prove the proposition, and, where available from the claim or defence and disclosure, the facts which your opponent will be putting forward. Facts become evidence when they are proved. There are various methods of 'proving' a fact: by direct evidence, inferences and generalisations. Regardless of which form the evidence takes, each required element of the case must be proved.

It is at this point that careful thought will have to be given as to whether, by reason of the rules of evidence, any facts will be (or are likely to be) excluded at trial.

14.5.7   Direct facts versus inferences

Direct evidence is evidence which proves the truth or falsity of a fact, and does not need an inference for proof. Evidence by inference, sometimes called circumstantial evidence, allows proof by virtue of the inference of another fact. The inferred fact may be a required element in the case or, as is more common, may prove a secondary fact which can in turn infer proof of the required element. The chain of facts which can be inferred before finally proving the required element is not limited, that is to say, a court is unlikely to reject evidence simply because several inferred facts were needed to prove an element. However, where the inferred facts are so remote from proving the element that an extensive chain is needed, there is more risk that little probative weight will be given to the evidence.

The importance of the distinction between direct evidence and evidence proved by inference is significant, but not because one is necessarily more persuasive than the other. A group of inferences — or for television viewers of courtroom drama, the circumstantial evidence — may carry more probative weight than a single fact of direct evidence. The distinction is necessary to recognise where proof can only be through one or more inferences.

It is not uncommon to find in some cases the legal elements of the action or offence have been proved primarily, if not wholly, by inference (or circumstantial) evidence. In these cases, the strength of the inferences and credibility of witnesses become crucial as each offers a piece of the overall picture. Witnesses on both sides will have conflicting evidence of what was seen, or what happened. Therefore how credible, accurate and persuasive a witness is perceived to be will directly influence the weight which the inferred evidence will have.

14.5.8   Using generalisations to link inferred facts to required elements

Inferences are based on premises assumed to be true. The truth is assumed possibly because it is based on widely accepted knowledge or science. But where this support is lacking it is also possible to rely on a generalisation. Generalisations are based on general life experience which permit a conclusion that something is more likely to be true. As explained by Binder, D. A., and Bergman, P., *Fact Investigation: from Hypothesis to Proof*, West Publishing Co, 1984, at p 85, the generalisation becomes the premise which enables one to link the specific evidence (inference) to the final elements which are required to be proved:

A generalisation is, then, a premise which rests on the general behaviour of people or objects. How does one formulate generalisations? Usually, one adopts conventional wisdom about how people and objects function in everyday life. All of us, through our own personal experiences...through knowledge gained from books, movies, newspapers and television, have accumulated vast store houses of commonly-held notions about how people and objects generally behave in our society.

EXAMPLE

To illustrate a case example of how inferences and generalisations operate, take the criminal case of Cassie Charnel who has been charged under the Theft Act 1968, s 1, with stealing a bottle of whisky from Super.Stores plc. To establish the case, the prosecution must prove several elements which make up this specific offence. These are:

- Cassie took a bottle of whisky;
- the whisky belonged to Super Stores plc;
- she did so dishonestly;
- at the time, she intended to deprive Super Stores permanently of the whisky.

Suppose the Super Stores detective has made a statement to the police and that part of it reads as follows:

I saw the defendant take a bottle of whisky from the spirits display. She did not put it in the store's wire basket which she was carrying but instead she put it in an inside pocket in the coat which she was wearing. She went to a checkout and paid for the goods in the basket but made no attempt to pay for the bottle of whisky. She then left the store. I followed her and stopped her in the street outside.

Concentrating on proving the elements of the offence, the crucial facts contained in the detective's statement are that she took the whisky from the display at Super Stores plc, put it in her coat instead of her basket, failed to pay for the whisky at the checkout, and left the store with the whisky. However, there is no direct evidence of this. Rather they are inferences from the detective's statement to this effect.

The move from the detective's statement to the inference that what he stated was in fact true involves several generalisations:

- in the absence of a motive to lie or opportunity for erroneous observation, a person's account of what he or she has seen is likely to be true;
- the detective had no known motive to lie;
- he had no known opportunity for erroneous observation.

In analysing the evidential support for your case, you will need to consider each fact, whether its proof is by direct evidence or inferences, and what evidence or inference exists to challenge or weaken the proposition. This should highlight where the proof is weak and requires further evidence to strengthen the proposition. It is important in carrying out the analysis that facts do not take on a theoretical superiority, if in reality they cannot be proved to exist, or for evidential purposes they would clearly be inadmissible. Tabulation can be helpful to do this and is illustrated in Table 14.11.

14.5.9 Wigmore analysis charts

Another method of analysing evidence is by drawing a chart based on a scheme originally proposed by Wigmore (see Wigmore, J.H. 'The Problem of Proof', *University of Illinois Law Review*, 1913, vol 8, p 77). The aim of this method is to identify the chain of proof, including inferences which strengthen or weaken the main proposition to be proved. This method is explained in more detail in **Appendix 2** along with examples. While it can be a time-intensive exercise, many people find it beneficial to produce a visual analysis in this way.

14.6   Stage 3: the presentation of the case or argument

14.6.1   Introduction

The last stage in the C.A.P. approach is to prepare the presentation of the case in light of the task which you have been instructed to do. Presentation is a generic term which in practice means:

- making a final decision on the theory and theme of the case;
- determining how you will support the legal framework;
- considering your task, and its intended audience;
- preparing the results of your analysis for that task.

14.6.2   Revisiting theories — selecting a theme

After the fact analysis process is completed, you will need to consider the theory chosen earlier, and be prepared to amend it as required up until the end of the trial. Having chosen the theory, you will need to select a theme (or themes) to fit the theory of the case. The theme may be defined as the part of the 'story' presented in court which is used because of its persuasive effect.

In an essay entitled 'Lawyers' Stories' (originally presented at the Seminar on Narrative in Culture, University of Warwick, in 1987) in *Rethinking Evidence, Exploratory Essays* (Blackwell, 1990), Professor William Twining defines theme in the following way:

Sometimes it is used to refer to the overall characterization of the situation or story or some element of it that appeals to a popular stereotype. For example: 'This is an example of a grasping landlord exploiting a helpless tenant'; or 'this is a case of property developers needlessly desecrating the countryside'. Another, more precise usage . . . refers to any element that is sufficiently important to deserve emphasis by repetition. An English barrister (Patrick Bennett QC) gives a vivid account of what he calls 'the mantra', as follows: 'In almost all cases there will be a key factor which has played a dominant role in the case from your point of view. It may be stupidity, fear, greed, jealousy, selfishness. Pick your word, inject it into your opening. Put it on a separate piece of paper. Repetition will have a lasting effect. If you have hit the right note and have repeated it often enough, it will echo in the jury's mind when they retire. It will be the voice of the 13th juror. Try to hit the note as soon as possible in opening.'

The theme will be used in opening and closing speeches, and will underpin the questions put to the witnesses. The 'story' should include the items of evidence which support it and exclude any matters that undermine its persuasiveness. Good themes are often very simple. They extend logic and have been defined as the soul or moral justifications of the case, put forward in such a way as to maximise the appeal to the judge or jury.

The theory and the theme must be consistent with each other. The experienced advocate can make the two so consistent that they are virtually indistinguishable. This is done because the better the theme fits with the theory, the greater the moral force of the theory and likelihood of persuading the tribunal of fact to find in your favour. Take, for example, a contested careless driving case in the magistrates' court: a pedestrian steps out on to a zebra crossing, causing the motorist to brake hard and skid. The only substantial dispute on the facts is whether the pedestrian looked to the right before stepping on to the crossing. The defence theme may well be that there is a limit to the care and foresight to be expected of the ordinary competent motorist, especially when faced with a jay-walker.

If, at the trial it emerged that the pedestrian was late for an appointment, another defence theme might be 'more haste, less speed', and so on.

14.6.3   Supporting your legal framework and reasoning

Whether the law on which your case is based derives from established legal principles or is unsettled, eg, because previous precedents conflict, a firm basis of legal sources will be required, including any legal research that is necessary to support the chosen legal solution. You may have referred to key statutes or cases in your advice or opinion. You will generally be required to submit a written 'skeleton argument' prior to the hearing. These outlines of the case and the arguments will require legal support for your key propositions. You will be expected to provide your opponents and the court with a list of authorities (eg, statutes, cases, reports) on which you will rely. Legal research is covered elsewhere in this Manual but a few considerations are included here for thought.

Statute law

If a statutory section is relevant to the legal argument, consider its real role in the case:

- Does the entire section apply to the case, or merely a part?
- Is its effect clear or is its interpretation open to challenge? If so, how could it be challenged?
- What are the relevant principles of statutory interpretation?
- Are there cases interpreting the words of the statute?

Case law

If a case supports your argument, you will want to defend its precedent value; if it does not, you will want to find points on which to challenge or distinguish it, eg, on the facts, or the application of the principle involved. A case is rarely directly on point and you should consider its real value in constructing the legal arguments supporting the framework. For example:

- On what facts was the decision made?
- What precisely was the ratio as opposed to obiter dicta?
- Did all the judges agree? (Which judge gave the principal judgment; what is his or her standing?)
- What was the level of the court making the decision?
- When was the case decided?
- And finally of most importance — has the case been subsequently reviewed or over turned?

There is rarely a single case on a particular point. It is more common to find a variety or line of cases. The whole line of cases should be reviewed, not simply to make coherence of the decisions, but also to consider what pattern of thinking can be seen through them and how this will fulfil your purpose.

If appropriate, note the procedural basis on which the decision was made. In some cases it is not open to the judges to review the facts and their decision is limited to whether the lower decision was properly reached.

Textbooks

While some of the leading textbooks can be quoted in court, and indeed judges have been known to adopt passages within their judgments, the support for the legal framework in a case should be based on original sources, rather than textbook comment.

14.6.4   Consider your task and the intended audience

Whether there are any preliminary matters which must be dealt with before you are able to carry out your instructions will depend on the nature of the task requested; the present stage in the proceedings; and the result of your analysis of the case.

In a sense this is a chicken and egg situation for it is only after you have completed an analysis of the case that it can be determined whether, on the basis of the papers, witness statements etc that have been sent by the solicitor, the instructions can be carried out. In some cases, no further information will be needed, save for clarification of confusing points arising in the papers. An example is where you are asked for advice on the merits based on existing facts (which can be proved).

Sometimes it may be difficult to know what further information to ask for from the solicitor. You should consider the stage of proceedings as this will influence the degree of detail and range of relevant documents which may be required. Where you are briefed to appear at an interim hearing, you will, of course, require support for the arguments to be used at the hearing, and the relevant court documents. However, it would be unreasonable to ask the solicitor to produce documents which are not relevant to the present hearing. An exception might be where the document or evidence to prove a proposition would eventually be needed in any event, and preparation for trial is inevitable. Then, it may be prudent to discuss the matter with the solicitor. The point is that requests for further information should only be made where necessary to enable you to carry out your instructions.

Where you have been asked to provide an advice on evidence, it may also be difficult in some cases to know precisely what to advise, particularly if the area of law is an unfamiliar one. By this time, however, the legal framework and factual issues will have been identified, and usually a 'theory' of the case developed. These will provide you with a focus to concentrate on what evidence will be needed to bring out the strengths of the case or highlight the weaknesses in the opponent's case. You will also want to consider the nature of the evidence, whether it is consistent in itself and with your client's story, and where more detailed facts may be needed to fill gaps. For example, the history of parties and disputes are often found in more than one medium, eg, letters, memos, reports and faxed communications. Many disputes develop over months or years and the client's position will be strengthened if there is supporting evidence over the entire relevant period rather than patchy samples. Even at the stage of preparing for trial, it may be necessary to embark on further disclosure, where, for example, it comes to light that important evidence is in the custody of a third party and previously unseen.

Finally, it may be necessary for counsel to have a site view or product sample in order to appreciate fully the circumstances or how an injury was alleged to have occurred. This is often the case in complex or technical matters, such as engineering, manufacturing or property damage cases. Additional briefing may also be needed in cases involving complicated experts' reports and counsel must prepare the examination of expert witnesses for the hearing.

The manner of 'presenting' your analysis and the case also depends on the intended audience. When you are asked to write an advice or opinion, the audience will likely be limited to your client, the solicitors, and possibly other counsel who may become involved in the case. The knowledge that your written work will not be seen by your opponent (in most cases) allows more flexibility in how you present it. On appearances in court, however, your 'audience' will be the judge whom you are trying to persuade, and, unless it is an application without notice, the opponents and their counsel.

Careful thought must be given not only to the content of presentation, but the best methods of relaying facts and evidence in light of the audience. In studies of how people receive information it has been shown that the majority of human beings are 'visual', meaning that material shown to them using a visual medium, as opposed to, eg, an aural medium, has the highest degree of impact and influence. A smaller number of people react more favourably to 'hearing' the information. Therefore, consider whether it might be appropriate to use charts, graphs or other visual aids in presenting the case.

14.6.5   Preparing the results of your analysis

Your final task will to be make sure that you have everything you need to help you carry out your instructions in a form which will support your presentation. It may be useful to present some of the work you have done in preparation to your opponent or to the court itself. Agreed chronologies, summaries of facts, schedules or plans of the *locus in quo* are frequently handed up before a case begins and can be very compelling and certainly make you appear well prepared and efficient. It is now usual for civil courts to require that lists of issues, skeleton arguments and lists of the authorities which will be relied on should be submitted before a case begins. The Civil Procedure Rules governing civil cases provide for skeleton arguments to be used in most cases.

If you are instructed to hold a conference or to negotiate it will help you to have some notes with you so that nothing relevant is forgotten. If you are appearing at court, notes about the points you wish to make on each issue will be helpful. **Chapter 4** of the ***Advocacy Manual*** contains suggestions of the kind of notes you might find useful to prepare for your own use.

Everyone adopts a method of organising information to suit his or her own needs. Many barristers use blue notebooks for all their work done on preparing a case, from notes of conferences with clients, to preparations for trial. One particular form of organising information for trial, described as a 'trial book' is explained in detail in Anderson and Twining's *Analysis of Evidence*, chapter 5.

14.7   The client's choice — acting on instructions

At the beginning of the C.A.P. approach, you became familiar with the client's objectives and what they hoped to achieve. These should not be forgotten as you proceed with your fact analysis and assess the strength of the case. You may be asked for an advice on the merits, or other task which will result in the client needing to take an immediate decision. Your task may alternatively be part of the overall case management. Apart from your client's overall objectives, other criteria such as costs, time efficiency, the desire to avoid stress or risk, the impact on family or business, and the desire to be exonerated may be factors which determine what decision is made. You will need to bear this in mind and ensure that you present the possible solutions to your client in such a way that all the consequences of a particular course of action are highlighted, thus aiding your client to make an informed decision about the next steps.

14.8   Suggested charts

We have seen that the C.A.P. approach identifies the stages necessary for efficient case preparation and that there are varying techniques which can be used to achieve those tasks. The following four charts can also be used to aid understanding and analysis. The titles refer to the stages in the C.A.P. process.

Table 14.8 **Stage 1: Context of the case: identifying agreed and disputed facts**

(Note: This form may be used for either civil or criminal cases. 'Ref/page' refers to the source of the statement, e.g., witness statement of J. Bloggs, page 6, para. 2.)

A = AGREED
D = DISPUTED

	CLAIMANT'S VERSION OR PROSECUTION VERSION	REF/ PAGE	DEFENDANT'S VERSION	REF/ PAGE	QUERIES/ NOTES
[A]					
[D]					

Table 14.9 **Stage 2: Analysis of issues and evidence: identifying issues and relating evidence to issues**

(Note: This form can be used in criminal cases by changing the reference to the claim and defence.)

Ref	Issue	Para of particulars of claim	Para of defence	Para of reply	Burden of proof	Name of witness	Available oral evidence	Available documentary evidence	Notes/ comments eg, procedure, evidence, gaps

Table 14.10 **Stage 2: Analysis of issues and evidence: analysing the strengths and weaknesses**

(Note: This form can also be used as the basis for examining and cross-examining witnesses.)

Issue	(a) Evidence in support of C's version	Witness	Page	(b) Evidence which contradicts/undermines C's version	Witness	Page	(c) Evidence which contradicts/undermines (b)	Witness	Page

Table 14.11 **Stage 2: Analysis of issues and evidence: analysing the evidence proving the case**

ISSUE/ELEMENT:

FACTS IN SUPPORT	WITNESS	INFERENCE IN SUPPORT	CHALLENGE/ WEAKNESS	NOTES

The C.A.P. approach in action

15.1 Introduction to Chapters 16 and 17

Once the various stages of the C.A.P. approach have been identified and understood, they should be applied routinely to the preparation of every case until you have developed your own effective methods of preparation. Obviously the context of every set of instructions will highlight particular aspects and not every stage may be required to be considered for every piece of work.

The following chapters demonstrate through worked examples how using the C.A.P. approach can ensure that you are able to carry out your instructions effectively. **Chapter 16** deals with a civil case, *Lowe v Mainwaring*, **Chapter 17** with a criminal case, *R v Costas Georgiou*. The contents of each chapter are set out on the title page. Each chapter contains a series of instructions in the case at various stages of the legal process at which a barrister is commonly instructed. Each set of instructions is followed by notes entitled '**C.A.P. in action**' which have been prepared as an example of how a barrister might apply each stage of the C.A.P. approach in preparing to carry out his or her own instructions in the context of a civil and a criminal case (see, for instance, **16.1.1** and **17.1.1**).

15.2 Instructions to counsel

Each set of instructions would include a back sheet similar to that shown at **16.1**. After the instructions have been carried out, the back sheet should be returned endorsed to instructing solicitors together with the completed work (if any). Each subsequent set of papers in the same case in addition to any new documents would also contain all the papers previously before counsel together with a copy of any opinion or case statement previously settled by counsel. For reasons of space, papers have only been duplicated where there is good reason for doing so, for instance in each case one back sheet is shown before and after endorsement. Not all back sheets have been printed. The contents of any set of instructions are set out in the 'Instructions for Counsel' prepared by instructing solicitors. These should always be checked to ensure that nothing has been inadvertently omitted.

15.3 The civil brief: *Lowe v Mainwaring*

In this case counsel is instructed for the defendants on three occasions. The first set of instructions at **16.1** are to draft the defence and a request for further information. The second set of instructions at **16.2** are to advise on the merits of the case and the last set at **16.3** are to make an application for specific disclosure.

15.4 The criminal brief: *R v Costas Georgiou*

In this case counsel is instructed for the defence on three occasions. The first set of instructions at **17.1** are to represent the defendant at an application for bail. The next set of instructions at **17.2** are to advise on evidence some months later. Lastly counsel receives the brief to appear at the plea and directions hearing and to represent the defendant at trial at **17.3**.

15.5 C.A.P. in action notes

The notes, prepared after each set of instructions in **Chapters 16** and **17**, show how every stage of the C.A.P. approach to preparation can be put into practice. The particular technique used in the examples is in no way prescriptive. A variety of methods could be used and everyone will want to develop the method which best suits them. What is important is that preparation should be methodical and accurate so that it is complete and exact and nothing is overlooked which might assist the client, or the presentation of his or her case. There is no 'right' way to prepare a case: the test is whether the preparation is effective.

The notes show examples of small chronologies, lists and tables which can be used to help master the facts and law and identify the issues and evidence in a case using the techniques suggested in **Chapter 14**. You should also refer to the other skills Manuals for further assistance in preparing to carry out particular skills.

The majority of barristers keep the notes they prepare in blue books so that a complete record of a case from beginning to end is maintained. If counsel is subsequently instructed the previous notes can be referred to and built upon thus saving valuable preparation time.

15.6 Practising the skill

All skills require practice. When you have worked through the examples of the use of the C.A.P. approach in **Chapters 16** and **17** you should try to apply it for yourself. **Chapter 20** contains a number of self-assessment exercises, including a civil and a criminal brief, which you can use to practise your own skills in applying the C.A.P. approach until they become second nature and you find that you automatically consider each stage as you get to grips with each new set of papers. Once this level of expertise has been reached you will no longer need to articulate the stage by stage process but can concentrate on whether you have acquired the ability to carry out your preparation effectively. This can best be achieved by self-consciously reflecting on your preparation of each case presented to you on the course.

15.7 Criteria by which you may assess your own performance

When you have completed your preparation of any set of papers you may find it useful to review the list of criteria below to consider which fact management skills you have demonstrated by your preparation and which still require improvement. As these skills are required in all the work you undertake, your performance of other skills will be affected by the level of your fact management skills.

Effective preparation entails the ability to:

- understand data presented in a variety of ways;
- identify gaps, ambiguities and contradictions in information;
- identify and prioritise the objectives of the client both in terms of practical outcomes and legal remedies;
- place the information in context;
- identify and prioritise the factual issues;
- identify and prioritise the legal issues raised by the facts;
- select possible solutions to the client's problem;
- recognise the interaction between law and fact;
- assess the strengths and weaknesses of a case;
- organise information in a variety of ways:
  - to aid understanding;
  - to prove propositions of law;
  - to assist at trial;
- distinguish between relevant and irrelevant facts;
- distinguish between fact and inference;
- construct an argument from the facts to support the client's case:
  - by developing a theory of the case;
  - by selecting a theme to fit that theory;
- evaluate the issues in response to new information and in the light of tactical considerations.

The civil brief

Contents of chapter	Page

Stage 1   The Context of the Case
    (1) The stage of the proceedings
    (2) Understanding the problem
    (3) Collecting the facts
    (4) Agreed/disputed facts: gaps and ambiguities
    (5) Legal framework
Stage 2   Analysis of Issues and Evidence
    (a) The Issues
        (1) The factual issues
        (2) The legal issues
        (3) The potential theory
        (4) Gaps and ambiguities
    (b) The Evidence
Stage 3   Presentation
    (1) The chosen theory
    (2) Carrying out instructions
        A. Preparing to draft the defence
        B. Planning the request for further information

16.2.1 **C.A.P. in action**   **221**

Stage 1   The Context of the Case
    (1) The stage of the proceedings
    (2) Understanding the problem
    (3) Collecting the facts
Stage 2   Analysis of Issues and Evidence
    (a) The Issues
        (1) The legal and factual issues in the case
    (b) The Evidence
        (1) The strength of the case on each issue
        (2) Gaps and ambiguities
Stage 3   Presentation
    (1) The chosen theory
    (2) Supporting the legal framework
    (3) Carrying out instructions

16.3   **Brief for application**   **223**

16.3.1 **C.A.P. in action**   **245**

Stage 1   The Context of the Case
    (1) The stage of the proceedings
    (2) Understanding the problem
    (3) Collecting the facts
    (4) The legal framework
Stage 2   Analysis of Legal and Factual Issues and Evidence
Stage 3   Presentation of the Case

16.1 Drafting the defence and request for further information

Claim No. WF04 048972

IN THE WAKEFIELD COUNTY COURT

BETWEEN:-

ANTHONY MALCOLM LOWE

<u>Claimant</u>

-and-

(1) HENRY GEORGE MAINWARING

(2) ELSA ANN MAINWARING

<u>Defendants</u>

INSTRUCTIONS TO COUNSEL

Counsel: Mr BRIAN BARRISTER

Godfrey & Co
27 Cressey St
Wakefield
West Yorks
WF5 3SL

Ref: BB

Date: 29.10.04

IN THE WAKEFIELD COUNTY COURT   Claim No. WF04 048972

BETWEEN:-

ANTHONY MALCOLM LOWE   <u>Claimant</u>

-and-

(1) HENRY GEORGE MAINWARING

(2) ELSA ANN MAINWARING   <u>Defendants</u>

INSTRUCTIONS TO COUNSEL

Counsel has herewith:

1. Particulars of Claim;

2. Defendants' Lease (only relevant parts reproduced);

3. Relevant correspondence.

Counsel is instructed on behalf of the Defendants, the Tenants of the First and Second Floors of 83–87 Leeds Road, Wakefield. As Counsel will see from the Particulars of Claim, the Claimant is the Tenant of the Ground Floor of this property, which he uses to run a snooker hall business called the Topspin Snooker Hall. It appears that a flood occurred at the premises during the period between the 21st and 29th December 2003, while the building was empty for the Christmas holiday.

The flood came from a water pipe on the outside of the building at about First Floor level. It was discovered by Mr Mainwaring when he went to his premises early in the morning to open up. He immediately switched off the water and called a plumber. Obviously, the flood caused damage to our clients' property as well as to that of the Claimant. The damage to our clients' property was relatively minimal. However, the Claimant is claiming very extensive damages, including not only costs of repairs said to be in excess of £8,000, but also loss of profits and loss of what he claims to be the value of the business. Our clients inform us that the snooker hall has been in operation since the flood, and this would seem to be consistent with our clients' evidence that the flood caused them only a small amount of damage. Nevertheless, the Claimant is claiming £45,000, said to be the value of the business which he appears to be alleging has been totally lost as a result of this flood. Regardless of whether or not the business has closed down, Counsel will also see from the papers that in any event the snooker hall appears to have been in financial difficulties before the damage from the flood happened. Indeed, bailiffs called on our clients some time last year mistakenly calling on them instead of Mr Lowe.

Those Instructing are still making inquiries into the facts of this matter, but the Solicitors for Mr Lowe have refused an extension of time for filing the Defence. Clearly most of the information relating to this claim will be in the hands of the Claimant. Counsel is requested to draft a Defence based on the information to hand, and also to draft a Request for Further Information if so advised to obtain such further information as can be obtained by this means.

Should Counsel have any questions on anything raised in these Instructions, please do not hesitate to contact Miss Pemberton of Instructing Solicitors.

Counsel is instructed to settle
the Defence and Request for
Further Information.

IN THE WAKEFIELD COUNTY COURT   Claim No. WF04 048972
BETWEEN:-

ANTHONY MALCOLM LOWE   Claimant

-and-

(1) HENRY GEORGE MAINWARING
(2) ELSA ANN MAINWARING   Defendants

_____

PARTICULARS OF CLAIM
_____

1. At all material times the Claimant has been the Tenant of the Ground Floor (the 'Ground Floor') of a building known as and situate at 83–87 Leeds Road, Wakefield, West Yorkshire, WF4 1AP (the 'building'), where he has traded as the proprietor of a snooker hall.

2. At all material times the Defendants have been the Tenants of the First (the 'First Floor') and Second Floors of the building, where they are and have been trading as upholstery manufacturers.

3. Between 21st December 2003 and 29th December 2003 the Ground Floor sustained severe flood damage when a pipe located at the First Floor level at the rear of and outside the building (the 'pipe') burst.

4. At all material times the Defendants were responsible for maintaining and repairing the pipe.

5. At all material times the Defendants knew or ought to have known that the pipe carried mains water at mains pressure, was not insulated and was not protected against the elements. In the circumstances the pipe was at all material times in a dangerous state of repair. The Defendants knew or ought to have known of the state of the pipe because it was open to view and readily capable of inspection from a fire escape located at the rear of the building.

6. The flood was caused by the negligence of the Defendants, their employees or agents.

PARTICULARS OF NEGLIGENCE

The Defendants, their employees or agents were negligent in that they:

(a) Failed to insulate or otherwise protect the pipe against the elements whether by lagging or otherwise adequately or at all.

(b) Failed to inspect, maintain or repair the pipe whether adequately or at all.

(c) Failed to identify that the pipe was a source of danger to the building and in particular to the Ground Floor of the building.

(d) Failed to eliminate the danger to the building presented by the pipe by relaying it inside the building.

(e) The Claimant will further rely upon the doctrine of res ipsa loquitur.

7. By reason of the matters set out above the Claimant has been deprived of his use and enjoyment of the Ground Floor and has suffered loss and damage.

PARTICULARS OF LOSS AND DAMAGE

(a) Flooding damage to the Ground Floor   £9,503.40

(b) Before the flood the Claimant's snooker hall business that he ran from the Ground Floor was worth £45,000. That business has ceased trading as a result of damage caused by the flood and now is of no value. Loss of the value of the business   £45,000

(c) Before the flood the Claimant's snooker hall business generated profits of £6,500 per annum. As a result of the flood the Claimant's business has ceased trading and the Claimant claims loss of profits from the 29th December 2003 to the date of issue of this claim at the rate of £6,500 per annum equivalent to £17.76 per day. Loss of profits for 295 days   £5,239.20

(d) Continuing loss of profits at £6,500 per annum.

8. Further, the Claimant claims interest pursuant to the County Courts Act 1984, section 69 at the rate of 8% per annum on such sums and for such periods as the Court thinks fit.

9. The value of this claim exceeds £15,000.00.

AND the Claimant claims:

(1) Damages

(2) Interest thereon pursuant to the County Courts Act 1984, section 69 to be assessed.

ALISON COUNSEL

Statement of Truth

I believe that the facts stated in these particulars of claim are true.

Signed   A. M. Lowe

Claimant

DATED this 20th day of October 2004

Messrs Fraser & Co, of Bank Chambers, Ripon Road, Wakefield, WF1 9GR, Solicitors for the Claimant who will accept service of all proceedings on his behalf at the above address.

To: The Defendants

and to the Court Manager.

THIS LEASE is made the 17th day of October One thousand nine hundred and ninety eight BETWEEN

MARGARET PIKE of Grange House, Cleaver Street, Keighley, West Yorkshire, BD21 6EM (hereinafter called 'the landlord') of the one part and HENRY GEORGE MAINWARING and ELSA ANN MAINWARING both of 18 Conniston Road, Wakefield, West Yorkshire, WF6 2UN (hereinafter called 'the Tenant') of the other part

WHEREAS:

In this Lease where the context so admits:

(1) 'the Landlord' shall include the person for the time being entitled in reversion immediately expectant on the term hereby created and 'the Tenant' shall include the successors in title of the Tenant

(2) in the event of the Tenant being at any time more than one individual 'the Tenant' shall be deemed to include also a reference to any of them and any covenant on the part of the Tenant shall take effect as a joint and several covenant

(3) 'the demised premises' means the premises (including the Landlord's fixtures and fittings) more particularly described in the Schedule hereto and all alterations and additions to such premises

(4) 'the conduits' means all ducts cisterns tanks radiators water gas electricity and telephone supply pipes wires and cables sewers drains soil pipes waste water pipes and any other conducting media under or upon the demised premises

(5) 'the Building' means the building of which the demised premises form part

NOW THIS LEASE WITNESSETH as follows:-

1. IN consideration of the rents covenants and conditions hereinafter reserved and contained and on the part of the Tenant to be paid observed and performed the Landlord hereby demises unto the Tenant ALL THOSE premises more particularly described in Part I of the Schedule hereto (hereinafter called 'the demised premises') TOGETHER WITH the rights set out in Part II of the Schedule hereto EXCEPT AND RESERVING unto the Landlord as stated in Part III of the Schedule hereto TO HOLD the same unto the Tenant for the term of twenty one years commencing from the 17th day of October One thousand nine hundred and ninety eight

YIELDING AND PAYING therefore during the said term:

(1) the yearly rent of Four thousand pounds (£4,000.00) (subject to the provisions for revision contained in Clause 5 hereof) such rent to be paid by equal quarterly payments in advance on the usual quarter days the first of such payments or a proportionate part thereof to be made on the signing hereof . . .

2. The Tenant HEREBY COVENANTS with the Landlord as follows:

(1) To pay the yearly rent and any increased rents as hereinbefore reserved on the days and in manner aforesaid without any deduction . . .

(6) At all times during the said term to keep the whole of the demised premises and the conduits and all Landlord's fixtures and fittings, plant, machinery and equipment therein and all additions and improvements thereto in good and substantial repair and condition (notwithstanding that any want of repair may be due to normal wear and tear) damage by any of the insured risks excepted unless payment of the insurance monies shall be withheld in whole or part by reason solely or in part of any act or default of the Tenant or the Tenant's servants or agents.

3. The Landlord HEREBY COVENANTS with the Tenant as follows:

(1) That the Tenant paying the rents hereby reserved on the days and in the manner aforesaid and performing and observing the several covenants and conditions on the Tenant's part herein contained shall quietly hold and enjoy the demised premises during

the said term without any interruption by the Landlord or any person rightfully claiming under or in trust for the Landlord.

(2) To insure and keep insured the demised premises (including all the Landlord's fixtures and fittings plant machinery and equipment now or hereafter in or about the same) subject to such reasonable and usual exclusions and limitations as may be imposed by the Insurers in some insurance office of repute or with Underwriters or through such agency as the Landlord shall from time to time decide in the name of the Landlord with a note of Tenant's interest and that of any mortgagee of the Tenant from time to time notified to the Landlord to be endorsed on the Policy if required by the Tenant in such sum as shall represent the full reinstatement value thereof including Architects' and Surveyors' and other professional fees and incidental expenses against loss or damage by fire and such other reasonable risks which the Landlord shall reasonably consider necessary and against the public liability of the Landlord arising out of or in connection with any accident explosion collapse or breakdown being referred to in this Lease as 'insured risks'. . .

IN WITNESS whereof the parties hereto have set their respective hands and seals the day and year first above written

THE SCHEDULE above referred to

Part I

The Demised Premises

ALL THAT first and second floors of the Building situate at and known as 83–87 Leeds Road, Wakefield, West Yorkshire, WF4 1AP including the floorboards on the first floor but not the joists on which the flooring is laid.

PART III

Exceptions and Reservations out of the Demise

There are excepted and reserved out of this demise all rights and privileges now enjoyed over and against the premises and the particular rights following namely:

(1) The right of the Landlord her successors in title and assigns and all persons authorised by her during the term hereby granted on prior reasonable notice to enter with or without workmen into or upon the premises for the purpose of executing repairs upon the exterior structure of the Building and such installations thereon the proper repair of which is necessary for the protection of the Building.

FRASER & COMPANY
SOLICITORS

Bank Chambers
Ripon Road
Wakefield
WF1 9GR
Tel: 01924 782364
Fax: 01924 807243
Ref: TBC/DH/04.0247

Date: 19th April 2004

Dear Sir,

Re: TOPSPIN SNOOKER HALL, 83–87 LEEDS ROAD, WAKEFIELD
Our Client: Mr A. LOWE

We have been instructed by Mr Lowe, the proprietor of the Topspin Snooker Hall at the above address. The property has been unusable since it suffered severe flooding damage in late December 2003. The cost of repairing the damage to the property and three tables damaged by the flood has been put at £9,503.40. In addition there is an element of continuing loss of profits.

Everyone is denying responsibility for this occurrence, and, if anything is clear, the blame does not rest with our client. We are instructed that the flood emanated from a mains pipe located in your property, and it is our view that the flood would not have occurred in the absence of negligence on your part. We have been instructed to commence proceedings against you without further warning if we do not hear from you in the next 14 days with sensible proposals for settling our client's claim.

A Legal Services Commission certificate was granted on the 6th April 2004 to our client to commence proceedings and the relevant notice is enclosed herewith.

Perhaps we should suggest that you pass this letter to your insurers without delay.

Yours faithfully,

Fraser & Co

Mr and Mrs H. Mainwaring,
18 Conniston Road,
Wakefield,
West Yorkshire,
WF6 2UN

18 Conniston Road,
Wakefield,
West Yorkshire,
WF6 2UN

27th October 2004

Dear Miss Pemberton,

Thank you for agreeing to take on our case, and it was good to speak to you this morning. We don't have many papers relating to this case, but what we have we are sending you with this letter.

My husband runs an upholstery business from the upper floors of 83–87 Leeds Road. Downstairs on the ground floor there is a snooker hall run by Mr Lowe. During Christmas week there was a flood when a water pipe burst at the back of the property. My husband found it when he went in on the 29th. He noticed as soon as he went in through the front door that the place was very damp, and when he investigated he found a pipe on the rear of the building had burst. He immediately telephoned the plumber, who arrived about two hours after he telephoned. In the meantime he stopped any further damage being done by turning off the mains. I arrived at the workshop at about 10 am. The plumber was still working at the back on the pipe. It had happened on the back wall of the first floor, so our property took the brunt of the damage. A lot of water had got in and a fair amount of stock was soaking wet where it had been stored near the rear wall. The floor was awash, and, together with Paula I set to with buckets and mops in drying the place out.

I don't know how Mr Lowe comes to say he suffered such a lot of damage that the repairs will come to over £9,000. Our soiled stock came to about £800, of which we salvaged about £300. Although the back wall and floors were soaked, and you have to remember that the pipe was immediately outside our part of the building, after a few days they were back to the same condition they were beforehand, and you would never know that anything had happened. Henry asked the plumber when he arrived how long the water had been escaping, and he was told that it could have been only a few hours.

About six months ago the bailiffs came to our property trying to get arrears of rent. They had called on us by mistake, because when we read the warrant we saw that it was for the ground floor where Mr Lowe's snooker hall is. My understanding is that his business has not been doing at all well for some time, and that, in addition to problems with his rent, he has also had problems with other creditors. I think that most of his claims as set out in the court documents are an excuse for a failing business, and not too much store can be placed on them.

My husband tells me that all the pipes on the outside of the building are insulated, so we don't understand why Mr Lowe is saying that this one was not. Fraser & Co seem to be unsure whether we are in fact responsible for the pipes at the back of the building. Surely they come under the landlord's responsibility as common parts of the building?

As we discussed, we have no insurance against this sort of claim, and we enclose the £1,000 you asked for on account of your costs.

Yours faithfully,

H. & E. Mainwaring.

16.1.1   C.A.P. in action

Notes for drafting the Defence and Request for Further Information.

STAGE 1   THE CONTEXT OF THE CASE

(1) THE STAGE OF THE PROCEEDINGS

    (a)   What steps have been taken?
           Particulars of Claim filed at Wakefield County Court 20.10.04

    (b)   Your Instructions
           Draft Defence and Request for Further Information in order to:

- Clarify issues between parties.
- Protect clients' position.
- Show strength of clients' case.
- Highlight weaknesses of Claimant's case.

(2) UNDERSTANDING THE PROBLEM

    (a)   Cause of the problem
           Claimant's business on ground floor at 83–87 Leeds Road, Wakefield, in financial difficulties. He blames financial difficulties on damage to premises caused when water escaped from burst pipe at first floor level on outside of building.

    (b)   Clients' objectives
           Resist claim by Claimant. Put Claimant to proof of loss and damage.

(3) COLLECTING THE FACTS

    (a)   Dramatis personae

- Anthony Lowe the publicly funded Claimant and Tenant of Ground Floor and proprietor of snooker hall
- Henry (Harry) Mainwaring 1st Defendant, Joint Tenant of First and Second Floors where he runs an upholstery business on premises
- Elsa Mainwaring 2nd Defendant, joint tenant with husband Harry
- Margaret Pike Landlord of the premises
- Topspin Snooker Hall business carried on by Claimant on Ground Floor
- Fraser & Co Solicitors for the Claimant
- Godfrey & Co Instructing Solicitors for Defendants (Miss Pemberton)
- Paula: helped to dry out Defendants' premises.

    (b)   Chronology of events

17.10.98	Lease of First and Second Floors of 83–87 Leeds Road, Wakefield, granted to Defendants by Margaret Pike, Landlord Lease of Ground Floor of building to Claimant
29.12.03	Burst external water pipe discovered at First Floor level of premises and repaired
April 04	Distress Warrant for arrears of rent re Ground Floor premises issued
19.4.04	Letter of Claim sent to Defendants
20.10.04	Date of Particulars of Claim
27.10.04	Defendants Instructed Solicitors

(4) AGREED/DISPUTED FACTS: GAPS AND AMBIGUITIES

Para. No	Particulars of Claim	Defendants' Version	Notes/Queries
1.	C tenant of ground floor of 83–87 where ran snooker hall	admitted — see Instructions admitted — see letter of 27.10	
2.	Ds tenants of 1st and 2nd floors trading as upholsterers	admitted — see lease admitted — see letter of 27.10	
3.	22–29/12/03 Ground floor damaged by flood from external pipe at 1st floor level	Burst pipe on exterior 1st floor found 29.12. Probably burst on 29th see letter 27.10	Effect on ground floor? letter suggests that brunt of damage to 1st floor and that minimal
4.	Ds responsible for maintaining and repairing pipe	Landlord's responsibility? See lease preamble cl (4) Tenants' covenants cl 2(6) Schedule 'demised premises' and Landlord's right of entry to repair	Legal basis for allegation? Further legal research needed
5.	Ds knew/ought to have known that pipe carried mains water, not insulated/protected thereby in dangerous state of repair	all outside pipes insulated — see letter of 27.10	No particulars given on why D should have known the pipe carried mains water
6.	Flood caused by Ds' negligence in that failed to: protect against elements, inspect, maintain, repair, identify as danger to building, eliminate danger by relaying pipe inside building	Pipes adequately insulated	
7.	As result C lost use/enjoyment of ground floor suffered loss and damage Flood damage £9,503.40 Loss of value of business £45,000 Loss of profits since 29/12/2003 £5,239.20	Other cause of losses — snooker hall in financial difficulties before flood Snooker hall in operation since flood — see letter of 27.10	Level of alleged damage very high. Compared with Ds' damage. What was damaged? How has this figure been calculated? When did business stop running? Net or gross? How were profits calculated?
8.	Interest		

(5) LEGAL FRAMEWORK

(a) Checklist for Claim in Negligence:
   Was duty owed by Defendants? Has there been a breach? Has any breach caused the incident? Has the loss and damage been suffered? Has any breach caused the loss and damage? Is the loss or damage suffered recoverable?

(b) Areas for Legal Research:
   Tortious liability of landlords/tenants towards tenants of building in respect of burst pipes (Clerk and Lindsell *On Torts*, Charlesworth *On Negligence*). Repairing covenants in leases (*Woodfall*).

STAGE 2   ANALYSIS OF ISSUES AND EVIDENCE

(a)   THE ISSUES

(1) THE FACTUAL ISSUES

See Stage 1(4) above and Particulars of Claim paras 3, 4, 5, 6, and 7.

(2) THE LEGAL ISSUES

(i)   Duty: Whether Defendants responsible for maintaining and repairing external water pipe?

(ii)   Breach: Whether outside pipes insulated?

(iii)   Knowledge: Whether Defendants knew or ought to have known of condition of the pipe; whether Defendants knew or ought to have known the pipe carried mains water?

(iv)   Causation: Whether burst pipe caused by negligence of Defendants?

(v)   Causation of loss and damage: Whether any loss or damage suffered by reason of the flood from the burst pipe?

(vi)   Heads of damage: What heads of damage can be proved by the Claimant?

(vii)   The amounts of each head of damage?

(3) THE POTENTIAL THEORY

Duty owed by Landlord, not Defendants under the lease; in any event no breach because pipe insulated, and pipe did not burst because of negligence of Defendants. Further, any loss suffered by Claimant, if it is proved, not caused by flood but by pre-existing financial difficulties.

(4) GAPS AND AMBIGUITIES

See Stage 1(4) above.

(b)   THE EVIDENCE

At this stage the only evidence available is the lease and the letter of Mrs Mainwaring. Other sources of information are Instructions to Counsel, Particulars of Claim, letter from Claimant's Solicitors.

STAGE 3   PRESENTATION

(1) THE CHOSEN THEORY

See Stage 2(3) above.

(2) CARRYING OUT INSTRUCTIONS

A. Preparing to draft the Defence (see Drafting Manual).

(i)   Parties — Paragraphs 1 and 2 — Admit.

(ii)   The Incident — Paragraph 3 — Admit bursting of pipe, do not admit effect. Clarify date.

(iii)   Duty — Paragraph 4 — Deny. No duty under lease.

(iv)   Knowledge — Paragraph 5 — Deny. Allege pipe insulated.

(v)   Negligence/Causation — Paragraph 6 — Deny. If anyone's fault Landlord's.

(vi)   Causation/Loss and Damage — Paragraph 7 — Deny causation. Require C to prove loss and damage.

B. Planning the Request for Further Information (see Drafting Manual).

(a)   Re Paragraph 3 — How was ground floor damaged?

(b)   Re Paragraph 4 — Why does Claimant think Defendants responsible for repair etc?

(c)   Re Paragraph 5 — Why should Defendants have known that the pipe carried mains water?

(d)   Re Paragraph 7 — Insufficient detail of how loss calculated.

(See **16.2** for completed Statements of Case.)

16.2 Advice on merits

<u>IN THE WAKEFIELD COUNTY COURT</u>   Claim No. WF04 048972

BETWEEN:-

ANTHONY MALCOLM LOWE   <u>Claimant</u>

-and-

(1) HENRY GEORGE MAINWARING

(2) ELSA ANN MAINWARING   <u>Defendants</u>

INSTRUCTIONS TO COUNSEL TO ADVISE

Counsel has herewith the papers previously before Counsel [only backsheet reproduced] together with:

4. Defence and Request for Further Information as settled by Counsel;

5. Response to the Request for Further Information;

6. Notice of Allocation;

7. Surveyor's Report prepared for the Claimant;

8. Legal Services Commission Certificates for the Defendants [extract only reproduced: both certificates are in substantially the same terms].

Counsel will recall this claim having drafted the Defence and a Request for Further Information. The Claimant's response to the Request appears at enclosure 5. The Defendants' business has not flourished in recent years, and their bank called in their loans some time ago. The effect has been to close down their business as they have been unable to pay their staff. It is hoped that the bank will be paid off more or less in full from sale of stock. The present litigation is a great worry to the Defendants, not least because if there is a substantial judgment against them the likelihood is that it will be enforced against their home, which has a substantial equity of redemption.

Counsel will see that public funding by the Legal Services Commission has been granted to the Defendants subject to a limitation. Counsel is asked to Advise on the Merits in this case for the purpose of removal of the limitation on the Certificate and to advise generally. Instructing Solicitors apologise that it has not been possible to arrange a conference with the Defendants as yet due to the ill-health of Mr Mainwaring.

There has been some slippage in the timetable, and the case management conference has been adjourned. A new date has not yet been fixed.

Counsel is instructed to Advise

Claim No. WF03 048972

Herewith:

(1) Defence

(2) Request for Further Information

B. Barrister

17.11.03

IN THE WAKEFIELD COUNTY COURT

BETWEEN:-

ANTHONY MALCOLM LOWE

Claimant

-and-

(1) HENRY GEORGE MAINWARING
(2) ELSA ANN MAINWARING

Defendants

_____

INSTRUCTIONS TO COUNSEL

_____

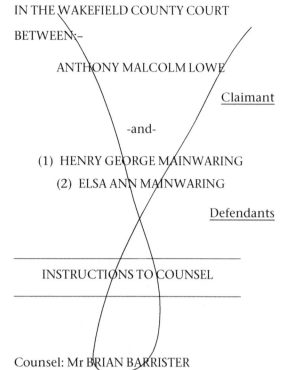

Counsel: Mr BRIAN BARRISTER

Godfrey & Co
27 Cressey St
Wakefield
West Yorks
WF5 3SL

Ref: BB

Date: 29.10.03

IN THE WAKEFIELD COUNTY COURT   Claim No. WF04 048972

BETWEEN:-

ANTHONY MALCOLM LOWE   <u>Claimant</u>

-and-

(1) HENRY GEORGE MAINWARING

(2) ELSA ANN MAINWARING   <u>Defendants</u>

DEFENCE

---

1. Paragraphs 1 and 2 of the Particulars of Claim are admitted.

2. Save that it is admitted that the pipe burst, the Claimant is required to prove paragraph 3 of the Particulars of Claim. The First Defendant arranged for the pipe to be repaired within a few hours of the occurrence of the burst.

3. Paragraphs 4 and 5 of the Particulars of Claim are denied. The pipe was at all material times properly insulated. Further, under their Lease with Mrs Margaret Pike dated the 17th October 1998 the Defendants had no obligation to repair or maintain the pipe. A true copy of the Lease is served with this Defence.

4. For the reasons set out in paragraph 3 above it is denied that the Defendants, their employees or agents were negligent as alleged in paragraph 6 of the Particulars of Claim or at all. It is further denied that the flood was caused by the alleged or any negligence on the part of the Defendants, their employees or agents.

5. Further or alternatively, the flood was caused by the negligence of Margaret Pike.

PARTICULARS OF NEGLIGENCE

(a) Failing to insulate or otherwise protect the pipe against the elements whether by lagging or otherwise adequately or at all.

(b) Failing to inspect, maintain or repair the pipe whether adequately or at all.

(c) Failing to identify that the pipe was a source of danger to the building.

(d) Failing to eliminate the danger to the building presented by the pipe by relaying it inside the building.

(e) The Defendants will further rely upon the doctrine of res ipsa loquitur.

6. The Claimant is required to prove the loss and damage particularised in paragraph 7 of the Particulars of Claim, and the Claimant is required to prove the amounts claimed. Damage sustained by the Defendants as a result of the flood was to a value of about £800, and it is estimated that the Claimant's loss would have been at about the same level.

BRIAN BARRISTER

Statement of Truth

The Defendants believe that the facts stated in this Defence are true. I am duly authorised by the Defendants to sign this statement.

SIGNED   *F Godfrey*

Defendants' Solicitor

DATED the 19th day of November 2004.

Messrs Godfrey & Co, of 27 Cressey Street, Wakefield, West Yorkshire, WF5 3SL, Solicitors for the Defendants.

To: The Claimant

and to the Court Manager

IN THE WAKEFIELD COUNTY COURT   Claim No. WF04 048972
BETWEEN:-

ANTHONY MALCOLM LOWE   <u>Claimant</u>

-and-

(1) HENRY GEORGE MAINWARING

(2) ELSA ANN MAINWARING   <u>Defendants</u>

DEFENDANTS' REQUEST FOR FURTHER INFORMATION AGAINST
THE CLAIMANT PURSUANT TO THE CPR, 1998, PART 18
DATED 19 NOVEMBER 2004

Note: This request must be answered by 4 pm on 10 December 2004.

Paragraph references in this Request for Further Information are references to paragraphs in the Particulars of Claim.

<u>Under paragraph 3.</u>

Of: '. . . the Ground Floor sustained severe flood damage . . .'

<u>REQUEST</u>

1.   Please give full information on all the damage alleged to have been sustained to the Ground Floor by reason of the alleged flooding.

<u>Under paragraph 4.</u>

Of: '. . . the Defendants were responsible for maintaining and repairing the pipe'

<u>REQUEST</u>

2.   Please state whether it is alleged the Defendants were responsible for maintaining and repairing the pipe by reason of contract or otherwise.

3.   If by contract, state the contract relied upon, the parties to the contract, its date and the clauses relied upon.

4.   If otherwise than by contract, state the basis of the Claimant's contention that the Defendants were responsible for the repair and maintenance of the pipe.

<u>Under paragraph 5.</u>

Of: '. . . the Defendants knew or ought to have known that the pipe carried mains water at mains pressure . . .'

<u>REQUEST</u>

5.   State every fact and matter relied upon by the Claimant in support of the contention that the Defendants knew, alternatively ought to have known, that the pipe:

  (a)   carried mains water; and

  (b)   carried water at mains pressure.

<u>Under paragraph 7.</u>

Of: '(a) Flooding damage to the Ground Floor £9,503.40'

<u>REQUEST</u>

6.   Please specify how the alleged loss of £9,503.40 is made up.

Of: '. . . the Claimant's snooker hall business that he ran from the Ground Floor was worth £45,000 . . .'

<u>REQUEST</u>

7.   Specify each and every fact and matter relied upon in support of the contention that the business was worth £45,000.

Of: 'Before the flood the Claimant's snooker hall business generated profits of £6,500 per annum.'

<u>REQUEST</u>

8.   Specify how the figure of £6,500 is made up.

9.   State the period used in calculating the figure of £6,500.

10. State whether the figure of £6,500 is:

   (a)   before or after trade expenses;

   (b)   net of tax.

BRIAN BARRISTER

DATED the 19th day of November 2004.

Messrs Godfrey & Co, of 27 Cressey Street, Wakefield, West Yorkshire, WF5 3SL, Solicitors for the Defendants.

To: The Claimant

and to the Court Manager.

IN THE WAKEFIELD COUNTY COURT   Claim No. WF04 048972
BETWEEN:-

ANTHONY MALCOLM LOWE   Claimant

-and-

(1) HENRY GEORGE MAINWARING

(2) ELSA ANN MAINWARING   Defendants

CLAIMANT'S RESPONSE TO THE REQUEST FOR FURTHER
INFORMATION OF THE PARTICULARS OF CLAIM
DATED 19 NOVEMBER 2004

Under paragraph 3.

Of: '. . . the Ground Floor sustained severe flood damage . . .'

REQUEST

1.   Please give full information on all the damage alleged to have been sustained to the Ground Floor by reason of the alleged flooding.

ANSWER

1.   The matter requested has already been sufficiently set out. Full particulars will be given in a surveyor's report which will be mutually exchanged in accordance with directions.

Under paragraph 4.

Of: '. . . the Defendants were responsible for maintaining and repairing the pipe'

REQUEST

2.   Please state whether it is alleged the Defendants were responsible for maintaining and repairing the pipe by reason of contract or otherwise.

3.   If by contract, the contract relied upon, the parties to the contract, its date and the clauses relied upon.

4.   If otherwise than by contract, the basis of the Claimant's contention that the Defendants were responsible for the repair and maintenance of the pipe.

ANSWER

2.   Contract.

3.   Lease between the Defendants and Mrs Margaret Pike dated the 17th October 1998. The Claimant cannot identify the requested provision thereof until after disclosure of documents.

4.   Not applicable.

Under paragraph 5.

Of: '. . . the Defendants knew or ought to have known that the pipe carried mains water at mains pressure, was not insulated . . .'

REQUEST

5.   State every fact and matter relied upon by the Claimant in support of the contention that the Defendants knew, alternatively ought to have known, that the pipe:

    (a) carried mains water; and

    (b) carried water at mains pressure.

ANSWER

5.   The pipe is and was at all material times located on the outside of the building and is and was open to view. Access to and viewing of the pipe can and could be achieved by way of a nearby emergency escape staircase on the outside of the building and from a flat roof over the rear of the Ground Floor. The Defendants or their employees or agents viewed the pipe and thereby its condition and the fact that it was a mains pipe, or should have viewed the pipe and ought to have known of its condition and that it was a mains pipe carrying water at mains pressure.

Under paragraph 7.

Of: '(a) Flooding damage to the Ground Floor £9,503.40'

REQUEST

6.   Please specify how the alleged loss of £9,503.40 is made up.

ANSWER

6.   The loss of £9,503.40 comprises the following:

Repairs and refelting of snooker tables	£2,760.00	
VAT at 17.5%	£483.00	
Sub-total		£3,243.00
Replastering ceilings	£1,835.00	
Repairs to floors	£1,110.00	
Repairs to electrics	£1,437.00	
Redecoration	£946.00	
VAT at 17.5%	£932.40	
Sub-total		£6,260.40
Total		£9,503.40

Of: '. . . the Claimant's snooker hall business that he ran from the Ground Floor was worth £45,000 . . .'

REQUEST

7.   Specify each and every fact and matter relied upon in support of the contention that the business was worth £45,000.

ANSWER

7.   The matter requested has already been sufficiently stated. Full particulars will be given in an accountant's report which will be mutually exchanged in accordance with directions.

Of: 'Before the flood the Claimant's snooker hall business generated profits of £6,500 per annum.

REQUEST

8.   Specify how the figure of £6,500 is made up.

9.   State the period used in calculating the figure of £6,500.

10.   State whether the figure of £6,500 is:

(a)   before or after trade expenses;

(b)   net of tax.

ANSWER

8.   Full particulars will be provided in the accounts disclosed on disclosure of documents.

9.   1st August 2002 to 31st July 2003.

10.   (a)   After trade expenses

(b)   Yes

ALISON COUNSEL

Statement of Truth

The Claimant believes that the facts stated in this response to the request for further information dated the 19th November 2004 are true.

Full name: Graham Harding

Name of Claimant's solicitor's firm: Fraser & Co

Signed: *G Harding*

Claimant's Solicitor

DATED the 8th day of March 2005.

Messrs Fraser & Co, of Bank Chambers, Ripon Road, Wakefield, WF1 9GR, Solicitors for the Claimant.

To: The Defendants

and to the Court Manager.

Notice of Allocation
to the Multi-track

Claim No. WF04 048972
Claimant ANTHONY MALCOM LOWE
(including ref) TBC/DH/04.0247

To [Claimant's] [Defendants'] Solicitor
Godfrey & Co,
27 Cressey Street
Wakefield
West Yorkshire
WF5 3SL

Defendants HENRY GEORGE MAINWARING
(including ref) ELSA ANN MAINWARING
JTG/AP

Date 10th January 2005

Seal

District Judge Hodges has considered the statements of case and allocation questionnaires filed and allocated the claim to the multi-track.

The District Judge has ordered that:—

1.   Any request for further information based on another party's statement of case shall be served no later than 4.00 pm on Friday 4th February 2005.
Any such request shall be dealt with no later than 4.00 pm on Friday 4th March 2005.

2.   Each party shall give to every other party standard disclosure of documents by list. The latest date for delivery of the lists is 4.00 pm on Friday 18th March 2005.
The latest date for service of any request to inspect or for a copy of a document is 4.00 pm on Friday 25th March 2005.

3.   Each party shall serve on every other party the witness statements of all witnesses of fact on whom he intends to rely.
There shall be simultaneous exchange of such statements no later than 4.00 pm on Friday 22nd April 2005.

4.   A case management conference shall be held at 2.00 pm on Tuesday 3rd May 2005.

5.   Costs in the claim.

The claim is being transferred to the [Civil Trial Centre at   County Court]

[Division of the Royal Courts of Justice] where all future applications, correspondence and so on will be dealt with.

[The reasons the judge has given for allocation to this track [is] [are] that the value of the claim exceeds £15,000 and the multi-track is the normal track for the claim.]

Notes:

You and the other party, or parties, may agree to extend the time periods given in the directions above provided this does not affect the date given for any case management conference, for returning the pre-trial checklist, for any pre-trial review or the date of the trial or trial period.

If you do not comply with these directions, any other party to the claim will be entitled to apply to the court for an order that your statement of case (claim or defence) be struck out.

Leaflets explaining more about what happens when your case is allocated to the multi-track are available from the court office.

The court office at The Crown House, 127 Kirkgate, Wakefield, W. Yorkshire WF1 1JW is open between 10 am and 4 pm Monday to Friday. Address all communications to the Court Manager quoting the claim number.

CHRIS HODGES FRICS
CHARTERED SURVEYOR

43 High Street, Wakefield WF1 6YM

Facsimile: 01924 412020   Telephone 01924 412019

Solicitor's Ref: TBC/DH/04.0247

11th March 2005

Our Ref: GH/AMT

Court's Ref: WF04 048972

Wakefield County Court
The Crown House
127 Kirkgate
Wakefield
WF1 1JW

Dear Sirs,

Re: 83–87 Leeds Road, Wakefield: Mr T Lowe

I have been instructed on behalf of Fraser & Co, the solicitors for Mr Lowe, to inspect the above premises and to report on their condition and the damage which is alleged to have occurred as a result of a flood caused by a burst water pipe at the end of December 2003. I carried out all inspections personally.

SITUATION AND DESCRIPTION:

The premises form part of continuous shopping parades built 80 years ago or thereabouts. It comprises the whole of the ground floor of a three-storey terrace unit generally of substantial stock brick construction under a pitched slated main roof with iron guttering.

In respect of the shop front and return display, these are of old timber with large windows mainly sheeted over. Decorations are fair and condition of woodwork is generally reasonable for its age. There is a dwarf tiled stall riser. There is a lead flashing above the fascia box projection probably replaced and an illuminated fascia board to the front corner and side. Immediately to the rear is a door and entrance and iron staircase leading to workrooms on the upper floors.

INTERNALLY:

GROUND FLOOR:

Front lobby (carpeted). Main snooker hall 32 6 wide by 39 9 long rear bay, false ceiling, parquet floor.

Bar area to side (number 87) leading to store rooms (both with linoleum flooring) and office. Office 15 by 14 2 and carpeted.

Small back addition Rear lobby 2 WCs & washbasins.

REAR:

The rear external staircase presumably part of Landlord's liability is somewhat poor with various rusted sections. The rear main wall is of solid stock brickwork with a metal casement window to the ground floor of the subject property and modern concrete lintel over. Directly above is part of the old iron fire escape landing which has a bearing into the wall. Rust expansion of the steelwork going into the brickwork has caused flaking to pointing and slight gaps underneath the steel landing.

Gerald Walker MA FRICS (Consultant)   VAT Reg No. 405 189622

I enclose copy sketch of the rear showing the staircase and landing and the external half-inch mains water pipe with a brass compression fitting which I understand was replaced as this was the source of the burst. The upper section of the pipe has been partly lagged but not to a good standard and the section below the iron staircase still remains unlagged to this day! Below the joint are streaks to the paintwork where water has washed down. A certain amount of water does drip from the staircase but not directly against the wall. It appears to me that the source of water damage was indeed this defective pipe as I could see no other water pipes to the ground floor and clearly there was a considerable amount of water in the ground floor causing sporadic lifting and damage to the parquet flooring.

There is a flush backdoor to the subject property which appears to be in fair order.

INTERNALLY:
GROUND FLOOR:

Lobby Section

Ceiling	— false plaster ceiling with a few holes where fitments have been removed and otherwise satisfactory.
Floor	— carpet — generally satisfactory.
Walls	— wallpapered and generally in satisfactory condition. 9-light glazed double doors leading to:

Main Area

Ceiling	— plasterboard painted black — from limited view appears generally satisfactory. More recent false ceiling under with sive water streaking with many panels bowed and expanded by water.
	Above the false ceiling towards the rear near the source of dampness there are a few cracks and small holes in the ceiling where water has percolated through. Behind the bar area are beer pumps and cooling apparatus with mains water supply for glass washing.
Walls	— Papered and painted — condition generally good.
Floor	— whole area parquet flooring about a quarter of an inch thick probably on sheet material. Clearly this was affected by a considerable volume of water as there are various sections dotted all over which are lifting and parquet material has become loose or is missing.
	Decorations to the main area are generally reasonable but in reinstating the floor, checking electrics etc, a certain amount of disturbance would need to be made good.

Store rooms

Ceiling	— generally satisfactory
Walls	— plastered but patches of blown plaster from inherent dampness to the front and partly to side adjacent to number 89.
Floor	— old linoleum probably on sheet material, lifting in places as a result of old dampness. This area is used mainly for storage. No apparent damage from the burst water pipe.

Office

Ceiling	— plaster painted white — condition generally satisfactory.

Walls	— wallpapered. Condition generally satisfactory and no apparent water damage.
Floor	— carpet on concrete floor. Worn in places.
Decorations	— fair only with some evidence of wear and tear.

Small Back Addition

Rear lobby

| Ceiling | — plasterboard — some of this is missing as a result of water damage, also damaged plaster above the flush door and frame leading to the middle section and this area will need to be hacked off, rendered and set. Allow for renewing ceiling to this area and treating timbers above. Right-hand party wall covered with wall boarding. Bottom section rotted away clearly from recent water damage and the boards are noticeably warped from water damage and will need to be renewed. |
| Floor | — blue tiles on sheet material — water damaged in places, therefore allow to take up and renew. |

Ladies' lobby/wash basin and WC

Ceiling	— plastered — surface lifting in places — allow for repair and redecoration.
Walls	— stained by water and need redecorating
Floor	— water damage in places to PVC tiles on concrete — strip and relay.

Gents' lobby/wash basin and WCs

| Ceiling | — plaster on concrete — make good where cracked and damaged by water ingress and redecorate. |
| Walls | — the WC areas are fully tiled and various sections are lifting as a result of water damage. Wall plastering at low level has blown as a result of dampness and the plaster between the WC doors has partly washed away as a result of dampness also extending between the lobby door and WC door — therefore allow 100% strip, render, set and fully tile WCs together with new splashback to wash basin and renew enclosure to wash basin which is water damaged. |

Redecorate the whole of this area.

| Floor | — quarry tiles on concrete — appears satisfactory. |
| Electrics | — there is some damage and disturbance to electrical wiring to the lobby and gents' WCs which will need to be renewed and to the ladies' lavatory where there was extensive water damage — it is likely that electrics may be affected and would need to be checked and properly reinstated where necessary. |

I understand my duty to the court and have complied with that duty in compiling this report.

I confirm that insofar as the facts stated in my report are within my own knowledge I have made clear which they are and I believe them to be true, and that the opinions I have expressed represent my true and complete professional opinion.

Should you require any further information or advice, please do not hesitate to let me know.

Signed: CHRIS HODGES F.R.I.C.S.

GROUND FLOOR

GROUND FLOOR

83-87 LEEDS ROAD, WAKEFIELD

NOT TO SCALE

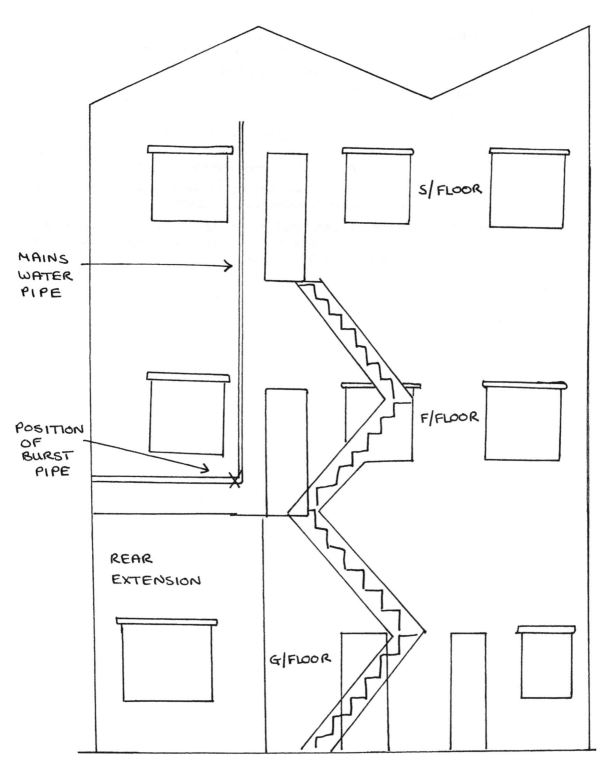

MAINS
WATER
PIPE

POSITION
OF
BURST
PIPE

REAR
EXTENSION

S/FLOOR

F/FLOOR

G/FLOOR

SKETCH OF REAR ELEVATION
83-87 LEEDS ROAD, WAKEFIELD

NOT TO SCALE

EXTRACT

LEGAL SERVICES COMMISSION

COMMUNITY LEGAL SERVICE CERTIFICATE

Assisted person: Mr Henry George Mainwaring

Level of service: Full representation

Description:	To defend a claim in negligence brought by Anthony Malcolm Lowe seeking damages arising from an alleged flood at 83–87 Leeds Road, Wakefield, West Yorkshire, WF4 1AP between 22nd and 29th December 2003.
Conditions:	It is a condition that the solicitor shall report to the area office if profit costs disbursements and counsel's fees exceed £2,500.
Limitations:	Limited to all steps to track allocation, disclosure and asking Part 35 questions to experts, and to obtaining written advice from an independent advocate with higher rights of audience on merits.

12.12.04

16.2.1 C.A.P. IN ACTION

Notes for advice on merits

STAGE 1   THE CONTEXT OF THE CASE

(1) THE STAGE OF THE PROCEEDINGS

    (a) What steps have been taken?
Particulars of Claim, Defence, Request for Further Information served.
Copy Surveyor's Report prepared for Claimant.
Limited Community Legal Service Certificate granted to Defendants on 12.12.04.

    (b) Your Instructions
To advise on merits and quantum in order to:

- Advise on prospects of success.
- Identify further information necessary.
- Remove limitation from Community Legal Service certificate.
- Fulfil Bar Council's Guidelines. (See Code of Conduct: Miscellaneous Guidance.)

(2) UNDERSTANDING THE PROBLEM

Defendants' business now closed down. Main remaining asset is their home. They are anxious that if they cannot defend claim at trial, any award of damages may be enforced against their home. Certificate limited to steps to disclosure and exchange of witness statements.

(3) COLLECTING THE FACTS

Only new sources of information are the Response to the Request for Further Information and the report of the Claimant's Surveyor. See below at 2(b)(1).

STAGE 2   ANALYSIS OF ISSUES AND EVIDENCE

(a) THE ISSUES

(1) THE LEGAL AND FACTUAL ISSUES

See Particulars of Claim, paragraphs 3, 4, 5, 6 and 7 and Response to the Request for Further Information, and Defence, paragraphs 2, 3, 4, 5 and 6. See also **16.1.1** above and (b)(1) below.

(b) THE EVIDENCE

(1) THE STRENGTH OF THE CASE ON EACH ISSUE

Note: Claimant bears burden of proof on each issue.

    (a) Issue (i) Responsibility for maintaining pipes: Depends on construction of lease: Claimant will rely on fact that no express covenant to repair on part of landlord. However, case law favours construction in support of Defendants (implied covenants to repair, *contra proferentem*). Terms of lease ambiguous (clause 2(6) of the tenants' covenants, paragraph 4 of preamble, Schedule Part I and Part III).

    (b) Issue (ii) Insulation of the pipes: Dispute between C. Hodges' report and statement of Mr Mainwaring reported by wife. Report of CH not contemporaneous and difficult to interpret. *Need to get further statement from Mr Mainwaring and plumber called to repair pipe on 29.12. Need to refer CH's report to Mr Mainwaring to confirm location of burst pipe or identify it.*

(c) Issue (iii) Knowledge of Defendants: Claimant's allegations in Response to the Request for Further Information need answering by Defendants, further information needed from Defendants as to knowledge of state of pipes, access to pipes, etc.

(d) Issue (iv) Causation of pipe bursting: Claimant will need to establish why pipe burst, ie, because of failure to insulate?

(e) Issue (v) Effect of flood on Claimant's premises: Report of C. Hodges shows water damage on ground floor but inconclusive on causation of this. Several potential weaknesses, eg, entry point of water, alternative reasons for damage. Defendant will need to instruct own surveyor to report.

(f) Issue (vi) Heads of damage: No evidence/detail of losses given. Possible alternative reason for closure of business — financial difficulty. In any event Claimant cannot claim both lost profits and lost value (double recovery).

(g) Issue (vii) The amounts of each head: Need to await disclosure for Claimant's accounts. Will also need inspection of Claimant's financial books and records, and to consider instructing an expert accountant to form an opinion on the value of the Claimant's business. Alternatively, could wait for the Claimant's accountant's report to see if it can be agreed without incurring the expense of a report on behalf of the Defendants. A further alternative would be to apply for an order that the Claimant answer Request No. 8. Details of the £9,503.40 damage to property claim need to be sought on disclosure, or should be given in exchange of witness's statements or expert reports. *Need to consider seeking permission or an order for an expert (builder or surveyor) to inspect the ground floor for the purpose of giving evidence on the damage, cause and cost of repairs.*

(2) GAPS AND AMBIGUITIES

Defendants should be asked to confirm position of burst pipe identified by C. Hodge. Further Information identified at 2(b)(1) above needed from Defendants, also witness statement from Plumber and report from Surveyor on behalf of Defendants. Unclear whether Paula, who helped dry out Defendants' premises, can assist on any of these issues, so a witness statement should be taken from her to find out what she knows.

Details of Claimant's losses etc should be received on disclosure, if not may need to consider alternative options to secure information.

STAGE 3   PRESENTATION

(1) THE CHOSEN THEORY

Claimant overstating events, hoping to solve present financial crisis by blaming Defendants. Defendants not to blame and Claimant will not be able to establish either fault or loss. See **16.1.1**, Stage 2(3) above.

(2) SUPPORTING THE LEGAL FRAMEWORK

List of Authorities.

Construction of Lease: *Cockburn v Smith* [1924] 2 KB 119

Construction of Lease: *Hope Brothers v Cowan* [1913] 2 Ch 312

Quantum: *C. R. Taylor (Wholesale) Ltd* v *Hepworth Ltd* [1977] 1 WLR 659

(3) CARRYING OUT INSTRUCTIONS

Plan opinion. See *Opinion Writing Manual*.

(See **16.3** for completed Opinion.)

16.3 Brief for application

<u>IN THE WAKEFIELD COUNTY COURT</u>   Claim No. WF04 048972

BETWEEN:-

ANTHONY MALCOLM LOWE   <u>Claimant</u>

-and-

(1) HENRY GEORGE MAINWARING

(2) ELSA ANN MAINWARING   <u>Defendants</u>

BRIEF TO COUNSEL TO APPEAR ON CASE MANAGEMENT
CONFERENCE, 2.00 pm, Tuesday 3rd May 2005

Counsel has herewith the papers previously before Counsel [not reproduced] together with:

9.   Counsel's Opinion dated 14th April 2005;

10. Claimant's List of Documents;

11. Defendants' List of Documents [not reproduced];

12. Documents disclosed by Claimant on Disclosure;

13. Application Notice;

14. Witness Statement in support, and exhibits thereto;

Instructing Solicitors have settled the Application for Specific Disclosure and for an Order granting access to the Claimant's premises for the Defendants' surveyor. The Claimant has been very uncooperative on the questions of disclosure and obtaining access, and Counsel is asked to press not only for the Orders sought but also for suitable Costs Orders against the Claimant.

This application has been listed to be heard at the same time as a case management conference.

If counsel has any questions prior to the hearing, please do not hesitate to contact Miss Pemberton of Instructing Solicitors.

<u>Lowe v Mainwaring</u>

OPINION

1.   I have been asked to advise Mr and Mrs Mainwaring, who are tenants of the first and second floors of 83–87 Leeds Road, Wakefield, on their prospects of successfully defending the claim brought against them by Mr Anthony Lowe (the Claimant), a tenant of the ground floor of the same building. Mr and Mrs Mainwaring have been granted public funding by the Legal Services Commission to continue to defend this claim. However, at present, the grant of public funding is limited to proceedings up to asking Part 35 questions to experts, and to obtaining my advice on merits.

2.   The claim arose as a result of a burst water pipe situated on the outside of the building on the first-floor level and which it is alleged caused water to flood in and onto the ground floor premises in December 2003, thereby allegedly causing considerable damage. The Claimant is alleging that Mr and Mrs Mainwaring are responsible for the upkeep of the pipe and that the pipe burst as a result of their negligence and that they are therefore responsible for the damage. I have not as yet seen Mr or Mrs Mainwaring in conference due to the ill-health of Mr Mainwaring but I have read a letter from Mrs Mainwaring explaining the relevant circumstances and the report of Mr Chris Hodges, the Claimant's surveyor.

3.   In my opinion Mr and Mrs Mainwaring have good prospects of successfully defending this claim. However, an initial question is to identify precisely where the burst pipe was located. Mr Mainwaring discovered the burst, so he should be asked to confirm that the location of the burst as identified by Mr Hodge in his report is correct. For the purpose of this opinion I have assumed this is so. The Claimant has provided very little evidence on quantum, so I am only able to give limited advice on the damages aspect of the case at this stage.

<u>The Duty to Repair</u>

4.   Responsibility for the condition of the external water pipe in this case depends on the terms of the lease between the Mainwarings and their landlord, Margaret Pike dated 17 October 1998. I am however unable to give definite advice on whether the Mainwarings are responsible for the pipe, because the terms of the lease concerning who is responsible for the condition of the external water pipes are ambiguous.

5.   By clause 2(6) of the lease the Mainwarings, as tenants of the first and second floors, covenanted 'to keep the whole of the demised premises and the conduits . . . in good and substantial repair and condition'. Conduits are themselves defined in paragraph (4) of the preamble as including supply pipes 'under or upon the demised premises'. The definition of the demised premises in Part 1 of the Schedule refers to 'all that first and second floors of the Building'.

6.   On this wording it is unclear whether:

(a)   Paragraph (4) of the preamble includes pipes upon the outside of building as well as those within the premises.

(b)   The demised premises as defined in the Schedule includes pipes fixed to the exterior of those premises.

(c)   The landlord has retained the exterior of the Building and/or the pipes and other installations upon it.

7.   In my opinion, a court is likely to construe clause 2(6) in favour of the Mainwarings and limit their obligation to repair and maintain to those conduits which are within

the demised premises and for the benefit of the tenant. Being an external pipe, the Mainwarings will have no liability for its condition. There are two reasons:

First, terms in a lease are usually interpreted against the grantor and for the benefit of the tenant. Secondly the courts have long held that where the lease contains no express provision as to parts of a building, particularly where those parts are for the common benefit of a number of tenants, those parts will generally not be considered to be included in the demise. They will consequently remain in the control of the landlord who will therefore be under an obligation to take reasonable care of the parts of the premises retained (*Cockburn v Smith* [1924] 2 KB 119).

8. However, a demise of a floor in a building has in the past been held to include the exterior of a wall (*Hope Brothers v Cowan* [1913] 2 Ch 312). A favourable construction of the lease is therefore far from certain, although each lease must be construed on its own wording and case law is of limited value.

9. If the terms of the lease are construed in Mr and Mrs Mainwaring's favour the responsibility for the repair and maintenance of the pipe would be upon the landlord, and the Mainwarings as tenants would not be responsible for any damage that occurred when the pipe burst.

Breach of Duty

10. If it were established that the Mainwarings had any responsibility to insulate or repair the pipe, the Claimant would need to adduce convincing evidence to establish that they had in fact been negligent and that it was their negligence which caused the pipe to burst.

11. The allegation that the pipe was not insulated adequately or at all is disputed by the Mainwarings. However, the surveyor's report prepared for the Claimant states that on the date of his visit, the upper section of the water pipe at the rear of the property, was only partly lagged and not to a good standard, and that 'below the iron staircase' there was no lagging at all. As the report refers both to an iron staircase at the rear and an old iron fire escape, and the only staircase on the attached plan seems to extend over the whole height of the building, I have found it difficult to identify the area 'below the iron staircase' from the plan.

12. As requested above, could my Instructing Solicitors ask the Mainwarings to clarify the position of the pipe which burst and also the position of the staircase or staircases at the rear of the building? Obviously it is of the utmost importance to be absolutely clear where the burst pipe was located.

13. Mr Mainwaring's witness statement will need to describe in detail the insulation on the pipes at the rear of the building on 29 December 2003. He had apparently told his wife that all the pipes were insulated. This should also be covered in the witness statement from the plumber who repaired the pipe. Mr and Mrs Mainwaring should also be asked to comment on the ease of access to the pipe. A witness statement should also be taken from Paula (I have not been given her full name), who I see assisted in drying out the Mainwarings' premises.

14. If satisfactory answers are given to the points above I think it will be possible to refute the allegations of any negligence on the part of the Mainwarings in the event that they are held to have any responsibility for the condition of the pipe.

Causation

15. To date it has not been possible to obtain further details of the claim for loss and damage from the Claimant, but it seems very unlikely that he will be able to prove that these losses arose as a result of flood damage from the burst pipe.

16. The plumber who was called to fix the pipe on 29 December told the Mainwarings that he considered that the water may not have been escaping for more than a few hours. Further, Mrs Mainwaring was of the view that their premises took the brunt of the flood.

17. The extensive claim made by the Claimant seems strangely in contrast with the Mainwarings' statement that the total loss they suffered from the flood was some £500 (taking into account the £300 salvaged). It is also difficult to reconcile the surveyor's plan with the presence of water inside the Mainwarings' premises.

18. Mr Hodges' report, on the other hand, does describe considerable water damage to the ceiling and to the floor of the snooker hall. There appears from the report to be no water damage to the walls even at the point water from the burst pipe would be expected to have entered the hall, ie, from the flat roof of the extension. The rear addition which includes a rear lobby and ladies' and gents' WC's appears to be badly affected by water damage. Mr Hodges has given his opinion that the water damage must have been caused by the defective pipe as he could see no other water pipes to the ground floor. There must, however, be a water supply for the WCs in the back addition. A survey of the ground floor on behalf of the Defendants will be necessary to try to discover accurately the condition of the Claimant's premises and whether the condition of the premises is consistent with any cause other than water penetration from the burst pipe.

19. It will in due course be necessary for a detailed statement to be obtained from the Mainwarings and the plumber about these matters. As yet, not having seen Mr and Mrs Mainwaring in conference, I am unable to comment on the reliability of their evidence, but the only issues on which this may be relevant are on whether the pipe in question was lagged, whether Mr Hodges has identified the correct pipe and certain aspects on the Claimant's damages claim (see below). The report of Mr Hodges, however, leaves a number of matters uncertain. It is my opinion that the Claimant has a number of difficulties in establishing that the various alleged losses were caused by negligence on the part of the Defendants.

Loss and Damage

20. The Claimant's claim for loss and damage is in the sum of about £60,000 together with some continuing loss. Of this sum only some £9,503.40 is for damage to the premises themselves. The remainder is alleged to arise from loss of profits and the lost value of the business. It is alleged that the Claimant has ceased trading as a result of the damage from the flood.

21. The Mainwarings assert, contrary to the Claimant's pleaded case, that the snooker hall on the Claimant's premises has been in operation since the pipe burst. This would suggest that the 'flood' was not as extensive as the Claimant alleges and indeed that the reason the business ceased trading was not because of water damage from the flood. In support of this, Mrs Mainwaring has reported that a bailiff called to serve a distress warrant for arrears of rent which does suggest at the least that other factors may have been operating which affected the financial viability of the business.

22. The lost value claim would include the profit-making potential of the business, and there is therefore a measure of double recovery in the Claimant's claim. The Claimant

will not succeed in recovering all the heads of claim and will instead have to choose between the cost of cure together with the loss of profits while the property is being repaired, or the diminution in value of the business.

23. The court will in general choose the measure of damages which provides fair compensation for the Claimant for any loss suffered but which results in the least damages being payable (*C.R. Taylor (Wholesale) Ltd v Hepworth Ltd* [1977] 1 WLR 659). At the present time it is uncertain whether, by the time of trial, the claim for lost profits would exceed that of lost value, but it is likely that the lost value claim of £45,000 would be taken as the maximum amount of the potential claim.

<u>Public Funding</u>

24. I consider that the prospects of the Defendants in successfully defending themselves from all liability to the Claimant are Good (Category B). Even if the issue of liability were to be found against them I consider that on the limited information now before me there are serious issues as to quantum. The claim as formulated in the Particulars of Claim has a present value of £65,000 odd (including one year's alleged continuing loss of profits). That is considerably more than double the estimated costs of defending (see below). The cost-benefit criteria for public funding therefore appear to be satisfied, and I recommend the continuation of Legal Services Commission assistance for both Mr and Mrs Mainwaring.

25. Once witness statements have been exchanged and disclosure has taken place, it will be necessary to reassess whether the Claimant will be able to adduce evidence in support of his sizeable claim for loss. In my view the limitation on the certificates should be altered to cover the exchange of witness statements and filing of pre-trial checklists, and it would be sensible to increase the financial condition to (say) £7,500 or £10,000.

14th April 2005   BRIAN BARRISTER

Temple Court

<u>IN THE WAKEFIELD COUNTY COURT</u>   Claim No. WF04 048972
BETWEEN:-

ANTHONY MALCOLM LOWE   <u>Claimant</u>

-and-

(1) HENRY GEORGE MAINWARING
(2) ELSA ANN MAINWARING   <u>Defendants</u>

List of Documents

Standard Disclosure

Notes:
The rules relating to standard disclosure are contained in Part 31 of the Civil Procedure Rules.
Documents to be included under standard disclosure are contained in Rule 31.6. A document has or will have been under your control if you have or have had possession, or a right of possession, of it or a right to inspect or take copies of it.

Disclosure Statement

I state that I have carried out a reasonable and proportionate search to locate all the documents which I am required to disclose under the order made by the court on 10th January 2005.

(I did not search for documents—
1.   Pre-dating 1998
2.   Located elsewhere than my office and that of my solicitors
3.   In categories other than the lease of the premises, repairs arising out of the flood, and papers relating to the conduct of this claim.)

I certify that I understand the duty of disclosure and to the best of my knowledge I have carried out that duty. I further certify that the list of documents set out in or attached to this form, is a complete list of all documents which are or have been in my control and which I am obliged under the court order to disclose.

I understand that I must inform the court and the other parties immediately if any further document required to be disclosed by Rule 31.6 comes into my control at any time before the conclusion of the case.

(I have not permitted inspection of documents within the category or class of documents (as set out below) required to be disclosed under Rule 31.6(b) or (c) on the grounds that to do so would be disproportionate to the issues in the case.)

Signed: Date: 3rd March 2005
Claimant

I have control of the documents numbered and listed here. I do not object to you inspecting them/producing copies.

1.	Lease Claimant and Margaret Pike [not reproduced]	17.10.1998
2.	Estimate Snooker Restorers Ltd	3.1.2004
3.	Letter Claimant to WY Property Management Ltd	15.1.2004
4.	Copy letter WY Property Management to Belsize Loss Adjusters	19.2.2004
5.	Copy letter Belsize Loss Adjusters to WY Property Management	26.2.2004
6.	Copy letter Claimant's solicitors to WY Property Management	5.3.2004

7. Letter WY Property Management to Claimant's Solicitors	19.3.2004
8. Copy Letter Belsize Loss Adjusters to WY Property Management	23.3.2004
9. Letter WY Property Management to Claimant's solicitors	2.4.2004
10. Correspondence common to both parties [not reproduced]	Various
11. Statements of case, orders [not reproduced]	Various

I have control of the documents numbered and listed here but I object to you inspecting them:

Communications between the Claimant and his solicitors for the purpose of obtaining or giving legal advice, communications between the Claimant's solicitors and third parties in relation to this claim, instructions to, opinions of, and statements of case settled by Counsel.

I object to you inspecting these documents because they are protected by legal professional privilege.

I have had the documents numbered and listed below, but they are no longer in my control.

Originals of copy documents listed as items 1 to 11 above which were last in my control before being posted to their respective addressees.

SNOOKER RESTORERS LIMITED

48 Shaftsbury Road, Leeds, LS3 9IW

Tel: 0113 2879872

ESTIMATE

To:

Repairs and refelting Table 1	£1,350.00
Repairs and refelting Table 2	£850.00
Refelting Table 3	£560.00
Sub-total	£2,760.00
VAT at 17.5%	£483.00
Total	£3,243.00

Date: 3rd January 2004.

Mr Lowe

83–87 Leeds Road

Wakefield

West Yorkshire

WF4 1AP

Topspin Snooker Hall
83–87 Leeds Road
Wakefield
WF4 1AP

Mrs Bainbridge
WY Property Management Limited   15th January 2004

29 Commerce Street
Wakefield
WF1 8FJ

<u>FOR THE ATTENTION OF MRS BAINBRIDGE</u>

Dear Madam,

<u>Re: TOPSPIN SNOOKER HALL, 83–87 LEEDS ROAD, WAKEFIELD</u>

I enclose my insurance claim form together with the two builders' estimates you asked for. I also enclose an estimate from a specialist snooker table repairer with the estimated cost of repairing the felts on the three tables damaged in the flood.

Please pass the claims form and estimates on to the insurance company as quickly as possible. The snooker hall is in a shambles, and I cannot open for business with the place in this state. Could you please impress on the insurance company that this claim is urgent.

Yours sincerely,

Tony Lowe

W Y Property Management Ltd
29 Commerce Street, Wakefield, WF1 8FJ
Tel: 01924 433692

Our ref:	DB/4327
Your ref:	9328721
Date:	19th Feb. 2004

Mr D Beddoes
Belsize Loss Adjusters Ltd
8 Grovelands Road
London
EC4M 6YL

Dear Sirs,

Re: 83–87 Leeds Road, Wakefield

I refer to our telephone conversation this morning.

As I mentioned to you on the telephone, there are two matters arising out of that letter which I find quite extraordinary. The first is that there is a suggestion that if a pipe bursts outside then it is not covered by insurance, and the second is the suggestion that 'the escape of water has served only to bring to light the maintenance problem with the premises'. These suggestions are quite extraordinary and I wonder whether your surveyor has addressed his mind to this claim in any meaningful way.

A great deal of money has been spent in the last 3 years on maintenance of the exterior of the property, and whilst I would not suggest that problems might have arisen, I really cannot accept the proposition that the property had not been adequately maintained.

This is a valid claim, having resulted from an insured risk. Damage caused by a burst pipe is an insured risk.

Also covered under the policy is loss of rent and in that connection we are chasing the tenant for the quarter's rent due 25th December and the tenant is saying, probably quite rightly, that the rent should be paid by the Insurers until reinstatement of the property has taken place. He is also saying that in the event that the Insurers do not meet the claim, then he will be looking to the landlord to meet the claim as she should have had the property adequately maintained and insured.

It seems to me that my Client did have the property adequately maintained and insured, but if the Insurers wish to maintain their present stance and the tenant takes action against my client, then she will be making a claim to the Insurers under the Property Owner's Liability section of the policy. One way or the other therefore the Insurer will have to meet this claim and it seems to me that the claim can best be mitigated if dealt with quickly.

In the circumstances, therefore, can I ask you to take this matter up direct with the Insurer so that a satisfactory conclusion can be arrived at without further delay.

Yours faithfully,

Donna Bainbridge (Mrs) FRICS

Belsize Loss Adjusters Ltd
8 Grovelands Road
London EC4M 6YL
Telephone: 0207 631 2971   Facsimile: 0207 631 3111

Date: 26th February 2004

Our ref: 9328721   Your Ref: DB/4327

Mrs Bainbridge
WY Property Management Ltd
29 Commerce Street
Wakefield WF1 8FJ

Dear Madam

Re 83–87 Leeds Road, Wakefield

We acknowledge receipt of your letter of 19th February 2004 and comment on its contents as follows.

We have in fact given serious thought to this claim. We confirm that a burst pipe is an insured peril covered by the policy and have never suggested otherwise. For a valid claim to arise, it must be shown that an insured peril had operated to bring about the damage for which the Insured is claiming. This gives rise to two points.

The first is that the Insured must take reasonable care to maintain his property and to prevent loss. From the information provided regarding this incident, it would appear that the pipe located externally to the premises had burst due to lack of insulation and protection against the elements and the Insured was thus in possible breach of her policy in failing to take reasonable care in the maintenance of her property by failing to insulate the two external main pipes which led to the escape of the water.

Secondly, the policy does not cover damage caused by wear and tear, general weathering or gradual deterioration. Much of what we were shown by way of 'damage' did not appear consistent with having been damaged by water escaping from a burst pipe. In point of fact, there were several areas shown to our representative by Mr Lowe that were clearly by wear and tear.

We would only be too happy to make available a selection of photographs taken by our representative of the premises which in our view shows clear signs that the premises occupied by Mr Lowe are suffering from lack of maintenance. By this we are not suggesting in any way that the Landlord is not performing her repairing obligations or not adequately maintaining her premises but by way of illustrating the problem as we saw it at the time of our visit.

As regards the claim for loss of rent, it is our understanding from Mr Lowe that the reason why he has been unable to trade from the premises is not solely due to the water ingress and in any event, the policy will only respond to indemnify the Insured for loss of rent if the Insured had taken all reasonable steps to mitigate her loss.

To date we have yet to receive the Insurer's instructions as to how to proceed with this claim and until then we are unable on behalf of Insurers to accept or deny liability and trust this letter has addressed fully your concerns.

Yours faithfully

Belsize Loss Adjusters

FRASER & COMPANY
SOLICITORS

Bank Chambers
Ripon Road
Wakefield
WF1 9GR
Tele: 01924 782364
Fax: 01924 807243
Ref: TBC/DH/04.0247

Date: 5th March 2004

Dear Sir,

Re: TOPSPIN SNOOKER HALL, 83–87 LEEDS ROAD, WAKEFIELD
Our Client: Mr A. LOWE

We have been instructed on behalf of Mr Lowe.

What progress has been made concerning our client's insurance claim in respect of the flooding on the 22nd to 29th December 2003? Pending receipt of funds in respect of the claim our client is unable to reinstate the premises which are not fit for use at the present time.

Yours faithfully,

Fraser & Co

Mrs Bainbridge
WY Property Management Limited
29 Commerce Street
Wakefield
WF1 8FJ

W Y Property Management Ltd
29 Commerce Street, Wakefield, WF1 8FJ
Tel: 01924 433692

Our ref:	DB/4327
Your ref:	TBC/DH/04.0247
Date:	19th March 2004

WITHOUT PREJUDICE

Messrs Fraser & Co
Bank Chambers
Ripon Road
Wakefield
WF1 9GR

Dear Sirs,

Re: 83–87 Leeds Road, Wakefield

We thank you for your letter of the 5th March 2004.

We have heard further from the Loss Adjusters regarding the matter and, without going into too much detail at this stage, it does appear that what they are in fact saying is that the items of damage which your Client is claiming are the result of the lack of his maintenance rather than having been damaged by any water penetration.

However, we are arranging a meeting on site with the Loss Adjusters in an endeavour to get to the bottom of the situation and we hope therefore to be able to write to you more comprehensively following that meeting.

Yours faithfully

Donna Bainbridge (Mrs) FRICS

Belsize Loss Adjusters Ltd
8 Grovelands Road
London EC4M 6YL
Telephone: 0207 631 2971   Facsimile: 0207 631 3111

Date: 23rd March 2004

Our Ref: 9328721   Your Ref: DB/4327

Mrs Bainbridge
WY Property Management Ltd
29 Commerce Street
Wakefield
WF1 8FJ

Dear Mrs Bainbridge,

Re 83–87 Leeds Road, Wakefield

I refer to the above matter and our meeting on Tuesday, the 13th March at 2.30 pm.

I have to advise regretfully, as per my conversation with you, that I was unable to see for myself from my external examination that there has been any real damage to this property.

I have seen both pipes which are alleged to have been the cause of the damage and from my examination cannot see that there is evidence of a burst nor can I see that there has been a recent repair.

I noticed that above the window where the suspended ceiling is alleged to have been damaged by water ingress there has been a recent fitting of a concrete lintel. There is also evidence of recent re-pointing above the lintel.

It does appear to me from the photographic evidence I have in my possession that a lot of the reinstatement works being claimed for by Mr Lowe are of a maintenance nature.

The Lease agreement is clear inasmuch as it places the responsibility upon the tenant to maintain the property and I fear that this has not been done properly.

Yours sincerely,

Belsize Loss Adjusters

W Y Property Management Ltd
29 Commerce Street, Wakefield, WF1 8FJ
Tel: 01924 433692

Our ref:	DB/4327
Your ref:	TBC/DH/04.0247
Date:	2nd April 2004

Messrs Fraser & Co
Bank Chambers
Ripon Road
Wakefield
WF1 9GR

Dear Sirs,

Re: 83–87 Leeds Road, Wakefield

I refer to my letter dated 19th March and enclose a copy of correspondence received from Insurers' Loss Adjusters dated 23rd March 2004.

The contents are not very promising but whilst at the moment they are not prepared to agree to a compromise settlement, we are entering into further discussions in an effort to try and obtain some form of payment here.

As soon as there is any better news to report, I will contact you.

Yours faithfully

Donna Bainbridge (Mrs) FRICS

Application Notice	IN THE WAKEFIELD COUNTRY COURT	
You must complete Parts A	Claim No.	WF04 048972
and B and C if applicable	Claimant	ANTHONY MALCOM LOWE
Send any relevant fee and the	(including ref)	TBC/DH/04.0247
completed application to the	Defendants	HENRY GEORGE MAINWARING
court with any draft order,	(including ref)	ELSA ANN MAINWARING
witness statement or other		JTG/A
evidence; and sufficient copies	Date	5th April 2005
of these for service on each		
respondent		

You should provide this information for listing the application

1.   Do you wish to have your application dealt with at a hearing?

Yes   No   If yes, please complete 2

2.   Time estimate   0 hours   30 mins

Is this agreed by all parties?   Yes   No

Level of Judge   District Judge

3. Parties to be served   Claimant

Part A

We, Godfrey & Co, on behalf of the Defendants intend to apply for an order that:

(1) The Claimant do within 14 days of the date of service of such Order file and serve evidence stating whether the documents specified in the Schedule to this Application are or have at any time been in the Claimant's possession, custody or power, and if not now in his possession, custody or power, when he parted with the same and what has become of them.

(2) Unless the Claimant gives access to the Defendants' surveyor to the Claimant's property at the Ground Floor, 83–87 Leeds Road, Wakefield by 4 pm on the 14th day after the hearing of this application, the Claimant's claim be struck out and judgment entered for the Defendants with costs.

(3) The costs of this application may be provided for.

SCHEDULE

1.   Accounts for the years ending 31.7.02; 31.7.03 and 31.7.04
2.   Tax returns since 1.1.2002
3.   VAT returns since 1.1.2002
4.   All accounts books and financial documentation and invoices since 1.1.2002
5.   All bank statements since 1.1.2002
6.   Insurance claim form about January 2004
7.   Builders' estimates (two) about January 2004

because the Claimant has not given full standard disclosure of documents, and has failed to allow the Defendants' surveyor access to the Claimant's premises for the purpose of reporting on the alleged damage to those premises.

Part B

We wish to rely on: tick one box

the attached (witness statement)(affidavit)   my statement of case
evidence in Part C overleaf in support of my application

Signed:

Applicant's Solicitor

Address to which documents about this claim should be sent (including reference if appropriate)
Godfrey & Co, 27 Cressey Street, Wakefield, West Yorkshire, WF5 3SL
Ref. JTG/AP

The court office at The Crown House, 127 Kirkgate, Wakefield, W. Yorkshire WF1 1JW is open between 10 am and 4 pm Monday to Friday. Address all communications to the Court Manager and quote the claim number.

Made on behalf of the Defendants
Witness: H.K. Jones
1st Statement of witness
Exhibits: HJK 1
Signed: 5.4.2005
Filed: 2005

IN THE WAKEFIELD COUNTY COURT   Claim No. WF04 048972
BETWEEN:—

ANTHONY MALCOLM LOWE   Claimant

-and-

(1) HENRY GEORGE MAINWARING
(2) ELSA ANN MAINWARING   Defendants

1. My name is Helen Katherine Jones. I am a Solicitor of the Supreme Court and employed as an Assistant Solicitor by the firm of Godfrey & Co of 27 Cressey Street, Wakefield, West Yorkshire, WF5 3SL. I have conduct of this claim on behalf of the Defendants. I am duly authorised to make this statement in support of the Defendants' application for specific disclosure.

2. I have read a copy of the List of Documents served in this claim on behalf of the Claimant dated the 3rd March 2005. It is my belief that this List does not disclose all the documents that are or have been in the Claimant's custody relating to the matters in question in this claim.

3. In my belief the Claimant has or at some time has had in his custody the various documents and classes of documents specified or described in the Schedule to the present Application Notice (referred to below as 'the Schedule').

4. My belief is based on the following matters. It is common ground that the Claimant was running a business at his premises, and the Claimant alleges this business has been damaged by the alleged flood. Anyone running a business will keep accounts (item 1 in the Schedule) and will keep books, invoices and other documentation (item 4 in the Schedule). He will be required to file tax returns and in all probability VAT returns (items 2 and 3 in the Schedule). Unless the business is very small (and the Claimant alleges that it generated profits, not turnover, of £6,500 per annum) it will need to operate a bank account, not least for paying in cheques. Therefore item 5 in the Schedule is likely to apply. The insurance claim form and estimates (items 6 and 7 in the Schedule) are expressly referred to in the letter dated 15th January 2004 referred to in the List of Documents at item 3. I refer to the bundle of correspondence marked 'HKJ 1' and a true copy of that letter appears at page 1 of the exhibit.

5. The documents and classes of documents sought in this application all relate to matters in question in this claim. Items 1 to 5 of the Schedule relate to the Claimant's claim for lost profits and the loss of the value of his business, item 6 relates to the issue of liability and is also relevant to the claim on quantum, and item 7 relates to the claim for the cost of putting right the alleged damage.

6. At pages [2] to [4] of my exhibit are letters to the Claimant's solicitors requesting the disclosure sought in this application and access for the Defendant's surveyor, and the Claimant's solicitor's response.

7. I ask the Court to grant the orders sought in this application.

Statement of truth

I believe that the facts stated in this witness statement are true.

Signed: *Helen Katherine Jones*

Date: 5th April 2005

Exhibit HKJ 1
Topspin Snooker Hall
83–87 Leeds Road
Wakefield
WF4 1AP

Mrs Bainbridge
WY Property Management Limited

15th January 2004

29 Commerce Street
Wakefield
WF1 8FJ

FOR THE ATTENTION OF MRS BAINBRIDGE

Dear Madam,

Re: TOPSPIN SNOOKER HALL, 83–87 LEEDS ROAD, WAKEFIELD

I enclose my insurance claim form together with the two builders' estimates you asked for. I also enclose an estimate from a specialist snooker table repairer with the estimated cost of repairing the felts on the three tables damaged in the flood.

Please pass the claims form and estimates on to the insurance company as quickly as possible. The snooker hall is in a shambles, and I cannot open for business with the place in this state. Could you please impress on the insurance company that this claim is urgent.

Yours sincerely,

Tony Lowe

[1]

GODFREY & Co,

27 Cressey Street, Wakefield, West Yorkshire, WF5 3SL
Tel: 01924 985579   Fax: 01924 985877

Our Ref: JTG/AP
Your Ref: TBC/DH/04.0247
Date: 17th February 2005

Messrs Fraser & Co
Bank Chambers
Ripon Road
Wakefield WF1 9GR

Dear Sir,

Re: TOPSPIN SNOOKER HALL, 83–87 LEEDS ROAD, WAKEFIELD

When compiling your List of Documents we would be grateful if you could provide full documentation in support of your client's claims for loss of profits and loss of the value of your client's business. These should include tax and VAT returns, bank statements and accounts.

Our expert surveyor needs to inspect the interior of your client's premises for the purposes of preparing his report, and we should be grateful if you could provide us with dates when this would be convenient to your client.

Yours faithfully,

[2]

FRASER & COMPANY
SOLICITORS

Bank Chambers
Ripon Road
Wakefield
WF1 9GR
Tel: 01924 782364
Fax: 01924 807243

Ref: TBC/DH/04.0247
Your ref: JTG/AP
Date: 21st February 2005

Dear Sir,

Re: TOPSPIN SNOOKER HALL, 83–87 LEEDS ROAD, WAKEFIELD

Further to your letter of the 17th February 2005, we are taking our client's instructions on the second paragraph of your letter. Our List of Documents is currently being prepared, and we hope to be able to serve this in the near future.

Yours faithfully,

Fraser & Co

[3]

GODFREY & Co,

27 Cressey Street, Wakefield, West Yorkshire, WF5 3SL
Tel: 01924 985579   Fax: 01924 985877

Our Ref: JTG/AP
Your Ref: TBC/DH/04.0247
Date: 10th March 2005

Messrs Fraser & Co
Bank Chambers
Ripon Road
Wakefield WF1 9GR

Dear Sir,

Re: TOPSPIN SNOOKER HALL, 83–87 LEEDS ROAD, WAKEFIELD

We acknowledge receipt of the copy documents from your List. We consider your List to be defective in that it does not include the accounts, returns and bank statements that we referred to in our letter of the 17th February 2005. It also does not include the insurance claim form nor the two builders' invoices that your client submitted to the landlord's insurer in about January 2004. Kindly provide us with these documents within the next 7 days, failing which we will be making an application to the Court for an order for specific disclosure.

We still have not heard from you regarding access for our surveyor. Please may we hear from you on this also within 7 days, failing which we will be making an application to the Court.

Yours faithfully,

[4]

16.3.1   C.A.P. in action

Notes on brief for application

STAGE 1   THE CONTEXT OF THE CASE

CHECKLIST

(1) The stage of the proceedings

A.   What steps have been taken:

- Statement of case served/filed including request for further information. C's Expert Report served.
- Exchange of lists. Copies of documents exchanged.
- Directions re exchange of expert reports?

APPLICATION FOR HEARING ON 3.5.2005

B.   Your Instructions:

- Appear at case management conference and obtain:
  Order for specific disclosure: of specific documents relating to C's loss.
  Order for inspection (for purposes of Ds' expert report).

(2) Understanding the problem

A.   Cause of the problem:

- Why not get documents? C failed to disclose in list.
- Why not get access? C failed to allow.

B.   Client's objective

- Purpose of Disclosure: to enable proper preparation, encourage settlement and full argument on all issues, eg, here on what losses actually suffered.
- Purpose of access: to enable Ds' expert to do survey and do report to ascertain damage done by flood and ensure C does not have an unfair advantage by depriving Ds of their own expert evidence.

(3) Collecting the facts

A.   Application for disclosure

- Chronology:

10.1.05	Direction requiring disclosure
17.2.05	Letter D to C — requesting full disclosure of documents in support of financial claim
21.2.05	Letter C to D — consider List served by D
3.3.05	C's list of documents
10.3.05	Letter D to C — asks for additional documents
5.4.05	Application Notice

- Documents sought:
  Financial Info from 1.1.02: accounts, tax returns, VAT returns, accounts, books, documents, invoices, bank statements (to show loss of profit/value)
  Insurance Claim Jan 04: see letter 15.1.04 in List
  Two estimates: see letter 15.1.04 in List

B. Application for inspection

- Chronology:
  17.2.05   First request on behalf of D for access for surveyor C's survey done
  11.3.05   C's surveyor's report
  5.4.05   Application Notice

(4) The legal framework

A. Disclosure: CPR, Part 31

- Procedure: application on notice supported by evidence
- Grounds: party not disclosed document(s) which leads applicant to conclude that documents exist, are disclosable, and within control of C.

B. Inspection: CPR, Part 25.

- Procedure: application on notice
  'Unless order' (attached to application for inspection): empowers court to strike out unless order obeyed

- Grounds: party has been prevented from inspecting property:
  — which is subject matter of the claim or to which any question may arise AND
  — is in possession of a party to the claim

STAGE 2   ANALYSIS OF LEGAL AND FACTUAL ISSUES AND EVIDENCE

A. Grounds fulfilled — Disclosure:

Application:
— sets out documents sought (schedule)
Evidence — Witness Statement:
— states belief list not complete (para 2)
— states belief C has had in possession, custody or power (para 3)
— states grounds for belief (para 4)
— states relate to matters in question; relate to issues (para 5)
— exhibits relevant evidence/requests (para 4, 6)

B. Grounds fulfilled — Inspection:

Application:
— correct address
— seeks access by surveyor
— to inspect to do report
Evidence — Witness Statement:
— exhibits letters requesting access (para 6)

STAGE 3   PRESENTATION OF THE CASE

A. ORDERS SOUGHT

1. Disclosure: Seek Order: C file/serve written evidence stating whether has docs in schedule in control, if not when parted & what became of them.

2. Inspection: Seek Order: C give access to D's surveyor by 4 pm, 14 days of hearing date to do inspection for survey report. If not strike out.

B. ARGUMENTS

(i) Disclosure: In C's possession etc
  — Docs 1, 4, 5: normal business requirement
  — Doc 2: required by Inland Revenue
  — Doc 3: required by Customs & Excise
  — Docs 1–5: all recent, see para 4 wit statement
  — Doc 6, 7: C's own documents refer to these: see HKJ1 and C's list
  Relate to Issues
  — Doc 1–5: C claim loss of profit/value; these docs give information by which can be calculated
  — Doc 6: insurance claim form; relevant to liability and quantum
  — Doc 7: estimates of repair cost; relevant to quantum
  Failed to disclose see list, correspondence — Exhibit

(ii) Inspection
  Arguments: Have C expert report exchanged
  D request access: see exhibits
  C refuse
  D no access/no report — denial by C serious issue so C suffer serious penalty if fail

17

The criminal brief

17.1   Bail application

IN THE COLCHESTER MAGISTRATES' COURT

THE QUEEN

V

COSTAS GEORGIOU

INSTRUCTIONS TO COUNSEL
TO MAKE A BAIL APPLICATION

Public Funding

Counsel: Ms Nicola Grey

Brown Dingle & Slattery
27 New Buildings,
Chelmsford, Essex

100/NG/15/6/05

IN THE COLCHESTER MAGISTRATES' COURT

THE QUEEN

Vs

COSTAS GEORGIOU

INSTRUCTIONS TO COUNSEL
TO MAKE BAIL APPLICATION
ON 15TH JUNE 2005

Those Instructing apologise for the lateness of the Instructions to Counsel.

The above-named defendant was remanded into custody on 7th June 2005, charged with an offence of Section 18 wounding with intent, following a full bail application having been made by our Mr Johnson. The CPS's objection to bail was on the basis that the client may fail to surrender as he had only recently arrived in this country from Greece and he was charged with a serious offence. We have since then managed to take our client's instructions through the services of an interpreter on matters which might be pertinent to the making of a second bail application — please see proof of evidence enclosed. Furthermore, our client's uncle, Mr Demetri Ionides, who will be at court that morning, has also, since the application made last week, offered to stand surety up to the sum of £1000. Mr Georgiou's girlfriend will also be attending court.

Counsel is instructed to use his best endeavours to obtain bail for the client. Public funding was obtained at the hearing last week and a copy of the Representation Order is enclosed with these instructions.

Brown Dingle & Slattery

COSTAS GEORGIOU

PROOF OF EVIDENCE

I am Costas Georgiou and I live at 27 White Hart Lane Tottenham, N15 OHE. I arrived in this country from Greece at Easter of this year. I am currently studying English at a language school and I hope to go on and study engineering at London Metropolitan University when my English is proficient enough. In order to make ends meet, I help out at my relatives' kebab vans in Colchester on most weekends.

I share the above address with my girlfriend, Anna Constantinou, who holds both a British and a Cypriot passport and who has been living in this country on and off for the past 5 years.

I strongly deny committing this offence. My cousin Alexis Ionides has already told the police that he did it. Given the way that Mr Canning and his friend behaved, it is, in my opinion, hardly surprising that Alexis behaved in the manner that he did.

I have no previous convictions either in this country or in Greece and I have found the past few days in prison to be an awful shock.

Signed: Costas Georgiou   10th June 2005

Colchester Magistrates' Court (Code 12343)

Representation Order No.2656–6088–02

In accordance with the provisions of Section 14 and schedule 3 Access to Justices Act 1999, a right to representation is granted as follows

DATE OF GRANT	10.6.05	DATE OF FIRST HEARING AFTER GRANT (M.C.)	10.6 at 10am
NAME	COSTAS GEORGIOU		
ADDRESS WHERE IN CUSTODY	COLCHESTER POLICE STATION		
NAME AND ADDRESS OF SOLICITOR IF APPOINTED	BROWN, DINGLE & SLATTERY 27, NEW BUILDINGS CHELMSFORD, ESSEX		

TERMS OF REPRESENTATION delete as necessary	**MAGISTRATES' COURTS PROCEEDINGS** (1) ~~SOLICITOR~~ (2) SOLICITOR AND JUNIOR COUNSEL	**CROWN COURT PROCEEDINGS** (1) SOLICITOR & JUNIOR COUNSEL

PURPOSE OF ORDER	(1) ~~Proceedings before Magistrates court in connection with (state nature of proceedings)~~ (2) ~~Appealing to the Crown Court against a decision of the said Magistrates' Court~~ (3) ~~Resisting an Appeal to the Crown Court against a decision of the said Magistrates' Court on~~ (4) Proceedings before (both a Magistrates' Court and*) the Crown Court in connection with (state nature of proceedings) including in the event of a person to whom this order being convicted or sentenced in those proceedings, advice and assistance in regard to the making of an appeal to the criminal division of the Court of Appeal. (5) ~~Other (state nature of proceedings)~~

Distribution **Legal Services** **Commission Copy** **Crown Court** **Solicitor's File** **Court File**	

CRIMINAL DEFENCE SERVICE **Representation order**	**Justices' Clerk** **Officer Designated to Act on Behalf of Justices' Clerk**

17.1.1 C.A.P. in action

Notes for the bail application

STAGE 1 THE CONTEXT OF THE CASE

(1) THE STAGE OF THE PROCEEDINGS

  (a) What steps have been taken?

    Defendant arrested. Police bail refused.

    Defendant remanded in Custody on 7.6.05.

    Representation Order granted on 10.6.05.

    Application for bail made by IS refused by magistrates on 7.6.05.

    (Objection to Bail — likely to fail to surrender to custody, only recently arrived in this country from Greece, charged with serious offence.)

  (b) Instructions: to see Defendant and make Bail Application on his behalf at Colchester Magistrates' Court on 15.6.05 at 10.00 am.

NOTE: Interpreter will be at Court. Query client's understanding of/use of English.

  (c) Objective: to secure release of Defendant on Bail.

    Will need to show that either prosecution objection without foundation or can be overcome.

(2) UNDERSTANDING THE PROBLEM

    Defendant in custody since 7.6.05. Last chance for defence to apply for bail as it is second fully argued application before magistrates.

(3) LEGAL FRAMEWORK

  (i) Offences against the Person Act 1861, s 18. (See **Table 14.5.**)

  (ii) Bail Act 1976.

Refusal of bail — if court satisfied that there are substantial grounds for believing that the defendant, if released on bail (whether subject to conditions or not) would . . . fail to surrender to custody etc (Sch 1, Pt I, para 2).

Matters to be considered by court in deciding whether grounds applicable (Sch 1, Pt I, para 9):

  (a) nature and seriousness of offence,

  (b) character, antecedents . . . community ties of defendant,

  (c) . . .

  (d) strength of evidence of his having committed offence.

Conditional bail — imposition of such requirements as necessary to secure that defendant surrenders to custody etc (s 3), eg, residence at particular address, reporting to police, curfew, surrender of passport, provision of surety, security for surrender to custody.

Unless material change in circumstances, only two fully argued Bail Applications can be made before magistrates. Thereafter Application must be made to Crown Court (Sch 1, Pt IIA).

STAGE 2 ANALYSIS OF ISSUES AND EVIDENCE

(a) The Issues

  (1) LEGAL AND FACTUAL ISSUES

Validity of prosecution objection on basis that Defendant has only just arrived in UK and therefore has limited community ties (and there is therefore a greater incentive to abscond to avoid custodial sentence which is the likely outcome if convicted of such a serious offence). See Figure 14.3 — Mind-map.

(2)   POTENTIAL THEORY

Law abiding, strong community ties, unlikely to abscond, strong incentive to clear name, intention to strengthen links in UK.

(3)   GAPS AND AMBIGUITIES

(a) Points to clarify with Client

When did he arrive in UK? Where is he presently studying? Has he enrolled at University? How many relations does he have in UK? How many close relations in Greece? Details of arrest.

How long has Anna Constantinou lived in Tottenham? Is she likely to return to Cyprus in near future? How long has relationship lasted?

(b) Points to clarify with Mr Ionides

Can he show that he has necessary funds to pay amount promised if defendant absconds, eg, building society passbook?

His suitability to act as surety, eg, his influence over his nephew, whether he has any previous convictions.

(b)   The Evidence

(1) THE STRENGTHS AND WEAKNESSES OF THE CASE

Defendant Greek national, short period of residence in UK, speaks little or no English: inference of risk of return to Greece. Custodial sentence almost certain if convicted.

Has number of close relatives in England, long-term plans to study in England, lives with girlfriend, Anna Constantinou (holder of British passport), in Tottenham: inference that Defendant has strong incentives to remain in UK, stand trial and clear his name — no previous convictions. Probably undesirable to reveal nature of defence to prosecution at this stage.

Likely outcome — Conditional bail. Possible conditions — surrender of passport, condition of residence, Mr D. Ionides to stand as surety.

STAGE 3   PREPARATION OF CASE

(1)   CHOSEN THEORY

See above at Stage 2(**a**)(2).

(2)   CARRYING OUT INSTRUCTIONS

(a) Prepare for Conference

See *Conference Skills Manual*, **Chapter 5.**

(b) Prepare to interview Mr Ionides if Solicitor not present.

(c) Prepare for Hearing

See Advocacy Manual, **Part III.**

Mr Ionides will need to give evidence if acting as surety.

17.2 Advice on evidence

IN THE CROWN COURT, CHELMSFORD No. T 05/0656

THE QUEEN

v

COSTAS GEORGIOU

INSTRUCTIONS TO COUNSEL
TO ADVISE

---

1. Counsel will please find enclosed the following:

    (a) Papers previously before Counsel [only back sheet reproduced]

    (b) Indictment

    (c) Prosecution witness statements

    (d) Prosecution Exhibits

    (e) Unused material disclosed by Prosecution on 14 September 2005

    (f) Defendant's proof of evidence.

2. Those Instructing act on behalf of the Defendant, Mr Costas Georgiou, who was committed to the Crown Court from the Colchester Magistrates' Court on 9th September 2005 under the provisions of Section 6(2) Magistrates' Courts Act 1980. The Defendant is currently on conditional bail, the one condition being to reside with his uncle Mr D. Ionides at 51 Piggott Close, Colchester.

3. The Prosecution, in view of the statements of their witnesses, have taken the decision to proceed against Mr Georgiou despite the admission of Mr A. Ionides, which they consider unreliable.

4. Mr Georgiou is the cousin of Mr Ionides. Mr Georgiou has only recently come to live in the United Kingdom and speaks little English. However, both his interview and the statement he has given to those Instructing have been properly translated.

5. Counsel is instructed to draft Defence Statement and advise those Instructing on what further steps should be taken in preparation for the forthcoming hearing.

Brown, Dingle & Slattery
27 New Buildings
Chelmsford
Essex

IN THE COLCHESTER MAGISTRATES' COURT

THE QUEEN

V

COSTAS GEORGIOU

INSTRUCTIONS TO COUNSEL
TO MAKE A BAIL APPLICATION

Public Funding

Coram: Lay JJ
Ms Smith for CPS
Client attends in custody
Full bail app. made
c/bail granted
Conditions: Residence with
D. Ionides at 51 Piggott
Close, Colchester
R on c/bail to 1.8.05
Crown Court

N. Grey 17/6/05

Brown, Dingle & Slattery
27 New Buildings
Chelmsford
Essex

100/NG/15/6/05

INDICTMENT   No. T 05/0656

IN THE CROWN COURT AT CHELMSFORD

THE QUEEN v COSTAS GEORGIOU

COSTAS GEORGIOU IS CHARGED AS FOLLOWS:

STATEMENT OF OFFENCE

Wounding with intent contrary to section 18 of the Offences against the Person Act 1861.

PARTICULARS OF OFFENCE

Costas Georgiou on the 28th day of May 2005 unlawfully wounded Andrew David Canning with intent to do him grievous bodily harm.

Officer of the Court

Statement of Witness

(CJ Act 1967 s 9; MC Act 1980 ss 5A(3)(a) and 5B; MC Rules 1981 r 70)

STATEMENT OF   ANDREW DAVID CANNING

Age of Witness (date of birth)   Over 18

Occupation of Witness   Casual Labourer

This statement (consisting of 2 pages each signed by me), is true to the best of my knowledge and belief and I make it knowing that, if it is tendered in evidence, I shall be liable to prosecution if I have wilfully stated in it anything which I know to be false or do not believe to be true.

Dated the 1st day of June 2005   Signed: Andrew David Canning
                                      Signature Witnessed by: Richard Jones

1.   I am Andrew Canning and I live at the address overleaf. I have never been in any very serious trouble with the police before.

2.   At about 7.45 pm on Friday 27th May 2005, I arrived at the Nine Bells Public House in the Oakridge Centre, Colchester, having walked from my home address. I was met there 20 minutes later by my girlfriend Jackie Perry. We stayed in the pub until 9 pm where I had drunk 1/2 bottles of Budweiser. I think that Jackie had a mineral water or an orange juice because she was driving.

3.   At 9 pm we got into Jackie's car, which is a white Nissan Micra, V36 YYT, and we drove to the Haven Public House at Thorpe to celebrate the landlord's (Mr Patrick du Pont) birthday. We had met a friend of mine at the Nine Bells and he travelled to Thorpe with us. His name is John Archer.

4.   We stayed at the Haven until about 10.30 pm and I had drunk about 3 or 4 bottles of Budweiser whilst there. John was drinking pints of lager. Jackie still drank non-alcoholic drinks. We then drove to the Rabbit Public House at Kirby, arriving at about 10.45 pm where I chatted to Lee, the landlord's son. John was chatting to the landlord. We stayed there until just gone midnight where I drank another 2 bottles of Budweiser and a large vodka. John had another pint of lager and a large whisky.

5.   We then drove back towards Colchester. I felt fine, John seemed fine and we decided to get something to eat. I was sat in the back of the Nissan and I fell asleep. I had already given my food order and I knew that we were going to the Shetland Road kebab van in Colchester for a chicken kebab.

6.   The next thing I remember is being woken up by Jackie. We were parked right next to the van. Jackie looked panicky and said, 'The geezer's threatening John with a knife'. I got out of the passenger side, got onto the grass and walked up to the kebab van.

Signed: Andrew David Canning   Signature witnessed by: Richard Jones

CONTINUATION OF STATEMENT OF ANDREW DAVID CANNING

7.   I saw John stood at the right-hand front of the van, backing away. Inside the van I saw 3 people. Directly in the front of the van was a male who I'd seen working there before. I would describe him as a Greek male, about 5'10" to 5'11", with a muscular build, about 16 years looking. He was wearing a shirt with his arms showing. He was waving an orange-handled knife with about a 12" blade. He appeared to be threatening John with the knife. Both he and John were shouting abuse at each other. It was a slanging match but I could not understand what it was all about. The Greek kept saying 'I'm going to cut you'.

8.   Also in the van was a Greek female who was positioned just to the side of the young male. She appeared to be hysterical, and was grabbing the young male by the arms and by the neck. She appeared to be trying to pull him away from the front of the van. The young man kept trying to throw her off.

9.   There was a second Greek male in the van, and he was stood at the back, to the left of centre. He was about 25 years old, about 5'9", and with a wiry build. He had stubble on his face, and eyes that made him look older. His face was drawn. He wasn't involved at this point and I didn't take much notice of him.

10. I went to the front of the van just left of centre, and started remonstrating with the younger Greek. I rested my left arm on the front of the counter, and waved my right arm towards the young Greek, and was saying, 'Look there's no fucking need for this, put the knife down', and I looked towards the older Greek saying, 'Look, fucking sort him out'. This carried on for less than 30 seconds, and I was concentrating mostly on the young bloke with the knife.

11. I then saw the older Greek move. He was carrying a large knife in his right hand, the one they use for cutting the meat, with a blade about 16" long. He moved around to my left, and I felt a pressure on my left arm just above my elbow. I didn't see the blow, and I thought he had hit me with the handle or the back of the knife. I moved to try and grab him with my left hand, but he pulled back.

12. I was then pulled back from the front of the van by one of my friends. At this point I was very angry, and I punched the perspex at the front of the van 4 or 5 times with the right fist, causing a graze to my knuckle. The three in the van were standing back by this point, and the girl was screaming.

13. I realised I was bleeding from my left arm at this point, but I didn't realise how bad it was. I asked for the car keys off Jackie, and I stormed to the back of the Nissan to fetch the wheelbrace to hit the perspex with. Once at the back of the car I was approached by John and Jackie, and I could see how bad the cut was. I was then taken in the car up to the North Essex Hospital at Colchester. In Accident and Emergency I realised that my jeans and shirt were soaked in blood. I was treated in casualty and then moved up to the ward. I underwent emergency surgery to stitch up the arteries and was later informed that the cut was to the bone. I was discharged on Monday 30th May in the evening. I can't remember any of the doctors' names. My arm is now in a sling and I have no feeling in my lower arm. I am on painkillers and I am likely to be off work for about two months.

14. On the Friday I was dressed in blue jeans, a cream and red T-shirt and red shoes. John was dressed in blue jeans, a shooting jumper with two dogs on it and a denim jacket. Jackie had boots, ski pants and a beige waistcoat.

Signed: Andrew David Canning   Signature witnessed by: Richard Jones

Statement of Witness

(CJ Act 1967 s 9; MC Act 1980 ss 5A(3)(a) and 5B; MC Rules 1981 r 70)

STATEMENT OF   JOHN FREDERICK ARCHER

Age of Witness (date of birth)   Over 18

Occupation of Witness   Self-employed Roofer

This statement (consisting of 2 pages each signed by me), is true to the best of my knowledge and belief and I make it knowing that, if it is tendered in evidence, I shall be liable to prosecution if I have wilfully stated in it anything which I know to be false or do not believe to be true.

Dated the 2nd day of June 2005   Signed: John Archer
Signature Witnessed by: Richard Jones

1. I am John Archer and I live at the address overleaf. I have been in trouble with the police before but that was some time ago.

2. At 8.10 pm on Friday 27th May 2005 I went to the Nine Bells Public House in the Oakridge Centre, Colchester. Inside I met Andrew Canning, a friend from the pub. After 10 or 20 minutes, Andrew's girlfriend Jackie arrived. I had a pint of light and Kronenburg and Andrew had a bottle of Budweiser. I'm not sure what Jackie was having.

3. The pub was quiet, and the three of us decided to travel to the Haven Public House at Thorpe. We travelled in Jackie's car and arrived there between 9 and a quarter past. Andy knows the landlord and it was his birthday. We stayed there until about 10 or 10.30 pm. I drank 3 pints of Stella lager, Andy had 3 bottles of Budweiser. Jackie was on soft drinks and she also had a meal.

4. We left and went to the Rabbit Public House at Kirby. I know the landlord, Roger Mates. He used to be a gamekeeper. We stayed there until about half past midnight, talking to the landlord and friends. I drank 2 pints of Lowenbrau and a large whisky and coke. Andy had another couple of bottles of Bud, and a couple of large whiskies. Jackie stayed on soft drinks.

5. We left and got into Jackie's car and we decided to go and get a kebab. I sat in the front passenger seat and Andy was sat in the back. We drove to the kebab van in Shetland Road, Colchester, which is the one that we usually use. We parked up next to the kebab van and myself and Jackie got out. I think Andy was asleep in the back at this stage.

6. I went to the front of the kebab van, and I could see that there were 3 people inside. There was a male, about 18 or 19 years old, smooth skin, standing just right of centre, from whom I was to order. I've seen him working there before. Behind him was a girl, sat on the bar at the back, young looking, wearing an orange T-shirt and jeans. I've seen her working there before as well. The third person was standing to the left, next to the kebab on the spit. He looked about 25ish, with stubble on his face, about the same height as the younger one, and the same build. He was carrying a large knife and was cutting meat.

Signed: John Archer   Signature witnessed by: Richard Jones

CONTINUATION OF STATEMENT OF JOHN ARCHER

7.   I stepped up and said, 'I'll have a small chicken kebab'. Jackie asked for a large mixed.
      I spoke to the younger Greek, who then spoke to his mate by the meat, who then
      started cutting up the chicken. The younger Greek was carrying what looked like a
      steak knife, with an orange handle and a twelve-inch blade. The older Greek had a
      wooden-handled knife with a two-foot blade.

8.   After I'd ordered, the younger Greek turned to the girl and spoke to her in a foreign
      language. I thought that they were talking about me and I said, 'If you've got any-
      thing to say about me, say it in English'. With that he said, 'I wasn't fucking talking
      to you, I was talking to the girl'. He turned to me and brandished his knife in his right
      hand. He waved it around in front of my face, and I stepped back. He was shouting
      and abusive and I was abusive back.

9.   During the slanging match I noticed Andrew had arrived. By this time the young girl
      was trying to hold the young Greek back, and she was hysterical. Andrew leant on
      the van with his left arm, and started pointing at the young Greek who was arguing
      with me. He said, 'Put the knife down, you're not going to use it, so you might as well
      put it down'.

10.   All of a sudden, I saw the older Greek move forward from the left-hand side, and
      chop down on to Andrew's left arm with the large knife. I saw it strike just before his
      elbow, and I saw the flesh open up. It started bleeding almost immediately. I saw
      Andy punch the van twice with his right fist as I went across to pull him away. We
      tied some clothing around his arm, and got him in the car, and took him straight up
      to hospital.

11.   That night I was wearing a pair of black jeans, Doc Marten shoes and a blue woollen
      jumper with two dogs and a man embroidered on the front. I am of stocky build and
      at the time was sporting a day's growth of stubble.

Signed: John Archer   Signature witnessed by: Richard Jones

Statement of Witness

(CJ Act 1967 s 9; MC Act 1980 ss 5A(3)(a) and 5B; MC Rules 1981 r 70)

STATEMENT OF	JACQUELINE ELIZABETH PERRY
Age of Witness (date of birth)	Over 18
Occupation of Witness	Trainee Hairdresser

This statement, (consisting of 2 pages each signed by me), is true to the best of my knowledge and belief and I make it knowing that, if it is tendered in evidence, I shall be liable to prosecution if I have wilfully stated anything which I know to be false or do not believe to be true.

Dated the 2nd day of June 2005   Signed: Jacqueline Perry
Signature witnessed by: Richard Jones

1. I am Jackie Perry, and I live at the address overleaf. I am the girlfriend of Andrew Canning, and we have a two and half month old son. I have no previous convictions.

2. At 1945 hrs on Friday 27th May 2005 I drove to the Nine Bells public house, Oakridge, Colchester, where I met Andrew and a friend called John Archer was also there. I was driving a white Nissan Micra, index number V36 YYT, and I was wearing black ski pants and a cream waistcoat. I had an orange juice. Andrew drank one or two bottles of Budweiser. John had one Kronenberg top whilst I was there.

3. We left at about 8.45 pm and I drove to the Haven public house at Thorpe. We were going to have a meal there, and it was Patrick, the landlord's birthday. I had something to eat, but Andrew and John didn't. Andrew had one or two bottles of lager, I think, and John about the same.

4. We left the Haven about 10 or half 10, and I drove us to the Rabbit public house at Kirby. John said that it was a good pub and he knew the landlord. I played on the fruit machine while Andrew and John spoke to the landlord. I think both had a pint of lager each, followed by a short each. We finally left the Rabbit shortly after midnight and got back into the car. Andrew got into the back. As we travelled back we decided to go for a kebab at the van in Shetland Road, Colchester. I drove into the road and pulled up next to the van.

5. Andy didn't want anything to eat, and he offered me his shirt to put on because it was cold. It was a denim shirt which was mine anyway. He then tried to go to sleep, while myself and John got out. There were 3 people just getting their kebabs in front of us before they walked off. I think there were 2 girls and a boy.

6. There were 3 people in the caravan. The first was about 5'11", clean shaven, about 18 to 20 years old, wearing a T-shirt and jeans. I've seen him working there before. The second male was shorter, about 5'8", about 24 years old. He had stubble, and was wearing a pastel vest. The third was a female, wearing a yellow T-shirt.

7. John ordered a large kebab from the younger man, who then turned to me, and I asked for a large mixed kebab. I was standing on the grass waiting. The younger man then turned to the girl and started talking in a foreign language. They were laughing and looking at John.

    John said, 'What was that mate?'

Signed: Jacqueline Perry   Signature witnessed by: Richard Jones

CONTINUATION OF STATEMENT OF JACQUELINE PERRY

The younger man replied, 'Private conversation'

John said, 'What are you talking about?'

He replied, 'It's none of your business'

The argument then escalated, and both began swearing at each other, and then I saw the man pick up an orange-handled knife with a 14" blade, which he held high in his right hand, and said, 'Just fuck off mate, just leave'.

8.   John laughed when he picked the knife up, and I could see that the girl was now crying, seated in the corner. The older man was still stood over by the meat and looked upset. I got scared and went to get Andrew. I banged on the window and he got out. Andrew walked across to the left-hand side of the van, and I stood about six feet behind him, just to the left. John and the younger man were still arguing with each other to the right-hand side of the van. By this time the young girl had got up, and was trying to pull the young man back from behind, and I think he pushed her off. She became more hysterical.

9.   Andrew tends to use his arms to talk, and they were on the ledge as he talked to the older man. The older man was now holding a large knife in his hand. It was the long one that they use for cutting the kebab. Andy said, 'You're not going to use that, just put it down'. I don't know who he was talking to. The next thing I could see was blood coming from Andrew's left arm. The older man was just in front of him. I could see a deep gash across Andrew's arm. I grabbed hold of John and pulled him towards Andrew. John grabbed Andrew, and as he pulled away, he punched the van.

10.   I took off my shirt, and it was wrapped around Andy's arm. He then went to the back of the car, where I persuaded him to get into the car, and drove him to Colchester Hospital.

Signed: Jacqueline Perry   Signature witnessed by: Richard Jones

Statement of Witness

(CJ Act 1967 s 9; MC Act 1980 ss 5A(3)(a) and 5B; MC Rules 1981 r 70)

STATEMENT OF   P.C. 250 RICHARD JONES

Age of Witness (date of birth)   Over 18

Occupation of Witness   Police Constable

This statement, (consisting of 1 page signed by me), is true to the best of my knowledge and belief and I make it knowing that, if it is tendered in evidence, I shall be liable to prosecution if I have wilfully stated in it anything which I know to be false or do not believe to be true.

Dated the 1st day of June 2005   Signed: Richard Jones
                                           Signature witnessed by: Thomas Bright

1.   At 1.25 am on Saturday 28th May 2005 I was on uniformed duty in a marked police car with PC 807 Smith, when we responded to an assault allegation, the location being given as the kebab van at Popley Way, Colchester. At 1.32 am we arrived at the kebab van which was in fact in Shetland Road. The shutters on the kebab van were up, and the occupant of the van could be clearly seen in the street lighting and interior lighting of the van.

2.   I went to the front of the van and spoke to one of the occupants, a man I now know to be Alexis Ionides. Also in the kebab van were a female crying, Sophia Ionides, and a second male, Costas Georgiou. The female, who was standing on the right-hand side of the van as I looked at it, by the door, was very upset. Alexis Ionides stood next to her, but nearer to the front counter and he spoke to both myself and PC Smith. The male Costas Georgiou stood on the left side of the van next to the kebab meat. I did not speak to this male, as Alexis Ionides told me that he could not speak English.

3.   Alexis Ionides was very excitable and told me that he had an argument with a customer some 15 minutes earlier. He stated that 3 to 4 males approached the kebab van, and a fat male, quite tall, about 30 years old, with a beard, who was drunk, began telling him not to talk with Sophia Ionides in their own language. Mr Ionides refused to serve the fat male, and as a result says that the fat male punched him on the nose, but did not cause him any injury. He then said that the fat male tried to climb into the kebab van through the serving hatch area.

4.   He then showed a long kebab knife, with which he stated that he cut the fat male's arm. I seized the knife as an exhibit, which I now produce as Exhibit RJ/1. Alexis Ionides stated that he warned the fat male that he would cut him if he didn't withdraw, but he claims that the fat male carried on trying to climb into the van, and ended up cutting his arm with the knife. I saw that there was fresh blood on the top of the counter on the left hand side of the counter, directly in front of where the kebab spit was situated, and where Costas Georgiou stood.

5.   As a result of enquiries that I made, Alexis Ionides and 2 juvenile female witnesses agreed to accompany us back to the Police Station, at Colchester. At the Police Station PC Smith arrested Alexis Ionides on suspicion of s.18 grievous bodily harm at 2 am. Alexis Ionides was booked into the custody area, but continued to behave in an excitable manner, making comments to the effect that he meant to take the fat male's head off with the knife.

Signed: Richard Jones   Signature witnessed by: Thomas Bright

Statement of Witness

(CJ Act 1967 s 9; MC Act 1980 ss 5A(3)(a) and 5B; MC Rules 1981 r 70)

STATEMENT OF	JOHN GOLDSTEIN
Age of Witness (date of birth)	Over 18
Occupation of Witness	General Surgeon, Fellow of the Royal College of Surgeons

This statement, (consisting of 1 page signed by me), is true to the best of my knowledge and belief and I make it knowing that, if it is tendered in evidence, I shall be liable to prosecution if I have wilfully stated anything which I know to be false or do not believe to be true.

Dated the 3rd day of June 2005   Signed: John Goldstein
                                        Signature witnessed by: Richard Jones

1.   At 2 am on Saturday 28th May 2005, Mr Andrew David Canning was admitted to the Casualty Department of the Colchester Hospital. I had to be called out because of the seriousness of the injuries that he had suffered.

2.   On examination at 3 am I noticed that he had a deep cut to his left arm just above the elbow. The wound required some 21 stitches to close. A small piece of bone had actually got knocked off the distal humerus and this was replaced back with some periosteal sutures and the wound closed. He was placed in a plaster at this stage to help splint the muscles whilst they healed. He was discharged on the following Monday, 2nd June, to be seen in clinic some 4 weeks later.

Signed: John Goldstein   Signature witnessed by: Richard Jones

Statement of Witness

(CJ Act 1967 s 9; MC Act 1980 ss 5A(3)(a) and 5B;

MC Rules 1981 r 70)

STATEMENT OF	SCOTT LESLIE
Age of Witness (date of birth)	Over 18
Occupation of Witness	Police Photographer

This statement, (consisting of 1 page signed by me), is true to the best of my knowledge and belief and I make it knowing that, if it is tendered in evidence, I shall be liable to prosecution if I have wilfully stated in it anything which I know to be false or do not believe to be true.

Dated the 30th day of May 2005   Signed: Scott Leslie

Signature witnessed by: Richard Jones

1.   I am a civilian photographer employed by the Essex Constabulary, stationed at Colchester Police Station.

2.   At 4 p.m. on Saturday 28th May 2005, I attended Ramsey Close, Colchester where I photographed a kebab trailer. In total I took 2 photographs which I produce as Exhibit SL/1.

Signed: Scott Leslie   Signature witnessed by: Richard Jones

Statement of Witness

(CJ Act 1967 s 9; MC Act 1980 ss 5A(3)(a) and 5B; MC Rules 1981 r 70)

STATEMENT OF	STEPHEN JOHN CAREY
Age of Witness (date of birth)	Over 18
Occupation of Witness	Detective Constable

This statement, (consisting of 1 page signed by me) is true to the best of my knowledge and belief and I make it knowing that, if it is tendered in evidence, I shall be liable to prosecution if I have wilfully stated in it anything which I know to be false or do not believe to be true.

Dated the 10th day of June 2005   Signed: Stephen J. Carey

Signature witnessed by: Thomas Bright

1.   At 12.16 pm on Saturday 28th May 2005, together with DC Dingwall, I interviewed Alexis Ionides at Colchester Police Station in the presence of his solicitor Mr Melville-Walker. The interview was tape recorded and a copy of the tape is produced as Exhibit SJC/1. A summary of the interview is produced as Exhibit SJC/1A. The interview concluded at 1 pm.

2.   On Monday 6th June 2005, Mr Costas Georgiou attended Colchester Police Station by pre-arranged appointment at 12.30 pm. At 12.33 pm. I attended the front desk and arrested and cautioned Mr Georgiou on suspicion of unlawfully wounding Andrew David Canning on 28th May 2005. He made no reply to the caution.

3.   At 1.42 pm on 6th June 2005, together with DC Johnson, I interviewed Costas Georgiou, in the presence of an interpreter, Mrs Dorothy Hove. The interview was tape recorded and I produce a copy of the tape as Exhibit SJC/2 and a summary of that interview as Exhibit SJC/2A. The interview concluded at 2.26 pm.

4.   I was present the same day (6th June 2005) when at 7.49 pm Georgiou was charged with wounding with intent contrary to section 18 Offences Against the Person Act 1861.

Signed: Stephen J. Carey   Signature witnessed by: Thomas Bright

THE QUEEN

Vs

COSTAS GEORGIOU

EXHIBITS

---

(1)   Exhibit SL/1 (photographs)

(2)   Exhibit SJC/2A (summary of interview)

(3)   Exhibit SJC/2 (interview tape) is available if required

(4)   Exhibit RJ/1 (knife) can be viewed by arrangement.

RECORD OF TAPE-RECORDED INTERVIEW

Person Interviewed:	Costas Georgiou
Place of Interview:	Colchester Police Station
Date of Interview:	6/6/05 Time commenced: 1.42 pm Time concluded: 2.26 pm
Interviewing Officers	DC Carey DC Johnson
Other Persons Present	Mrs Dorothy Hove (Translator)

PERSON SPEAKING	TEXT
	Introduction and caution. Rights explained. Mr Georgiou explained that on the night in question he was working in the kebab van in Shetland Road, Colchester. They had opened up for business at approximately 8 pm. He was cutting the kebabs and cooking chickens and was assisted by Alexis Ionides' sister-in-law, Mrs Sophia Ionides. As he speaks no English, he was not able to take orders from the customers and this was done by Alexis. He explained that there were 3 knives in the kebab van on the night in question, namely a salad knife, a knife with which to cut the chickens and the kebab knife.
DC Carey	Right, at about 1 o'clock in the morning, a large man who's been described as having a beard but in fact has got stubble came to the kebab van and ordered two kebabs. Does he remember that?
Translator	He remembers being asked by Alexis to prepare 2 kebabs and then an argument developing between Alexis and this man who was enormous over Alexis speaking to Sophia in Greek. He remembers this man punching Alexis on the nose and then Alexis picking up the salad knife and threatening the man with it.
DC Carey	And then what happened?
Translator	The girl that the fat man was with ran and got another man from the car. That man came up to the van and he was angry. During that time he was holding the knife that he uses to cut the chickens and the man thumped the back window of the van and he thumped the glass and he tried to take the knife away from him.
DC Carey	And what did Alexis do at this point?
Translator	Alexis picked up the kebab knife which was by the spit and then he didn't actually see the cutting taking place, but he knew that the man had been cut. The man continued to be violent and aggressive even after he was cut.
DC Carey	How did Ionides manage to get past you in the small confines of the kebab van to pick up the kebab knife?
Translator	He doesn't know how he managed it but he just did. The man had been holding on to his arm in which he was holding the chicken knife and he had just broken free of the man's grip when Alexis picked up the kebab knife. The interview concluded at 2.26 pm.

CROWN PROSECUTION SERVICE

UNUSED MATERIAL DISCLOSED UNDER

Section 3 Criminal Procedure and Investigations Act 1996

THE QUEEN

v

COSTAS GEORGIOU

(1)   Statement Tracey Collins

(2)   Exhibit SJC/1A — Interview with Alexis Ionides

(3)   Exhibit SJC/1 (interview tape) is available if required

Statement of Witness

(CJ Act 1967 s 9; MC Act 1980 ss 5A(3)(a) and 5B; MC Rules 1981 r 70)

STATEMENT OF	TRACEY COLLINS
Age of Witness (date of birth)	26th January 1988
Occupation of Witness	Schoolgirl

This statement, (consisting of 1 page signed by me) is true to the best of my knowledge and belief and I make it knowing that, if it is tendered in evidence, I shall be liable to prosecution if I have wilfully stated in it anything which I know to be false or do not believe to be true.

Dated the 1st day of June 2005   Signed: Tracey Collins

Signature witnessed by: Richard Jones

1.   I am the above named person. At approximately 1 am on Saturday 28th May 2005 I was with my friends Kelly Longyear and Aaron Constantine at the kebab van in Shetland Road, Colchester.

2.   I noticed behind me in the queue for kebabs a white male, approximately mid to late thirties. He was of very big build and at least 6' tall. He had a beard and dark hair. My friend Kelly spoke to this man briefly and offered him a piece of her kebab, but the male refused.

3.   Inside the kebab van was a man I know as 'Smiles' who is of Greek appearance. Smiles was putting the meat into the kebabs and taking orders from the customers. There was also another Greek male inside the kebab van who is known as 'Rambo', and a Greek woman.

4.   We were served our kebabs and left the van and walked up Popley Way towards the local infants' school. Aaron and I were together but my friend Kelly had to run back to the van as she had left her purse on the serving counter.

5.   I heard shouting and looked around to see a man punching and kicking the screen of the kebab van and trying to get inside. I had not seen this man before. He was probably in his early 20s, blond hair, wearing a white top with jeans. He was shouting, 'C'mon then, I'll give you a fight, I'll have you'. Kelly was already within the vicinity of the van as myself and Aaron started walking back towards it. The large man who was originally behind me in the queue was trying to rock the van.

6.   I then saw 'Smiles' come out from the back of the kebab van carrying a long knife with about a 2' blade. The knife looked to be the same one that they use to slice the meat for the doner kebabs.

7.   I saw the white man with the blond hair, who had been banging on the van, holding his right arm to his body and he was bent over. He was being helped by the man who was originally behind us in the queue and a woman who was with them. At the time we were queuing for our kebabs, this woman was sat in a car near the van.

Signed: Tracey Collins   Signature witnessed by: Richard Jones

<u>RECORD OF TAPE-RECORDED INTERVIEW</u>

Person Interviewed:	Alexis Ionides
Place of Interview:	Colchester Police Station
Date of Interview:	28/5/05 Time commenced: 12.16 pm Time concluded: 1 pm
Interviewing Officers	DC Carey
Other Persons Present:	David Melville-Walker (Solicitor)
	DC Dingwall

PERSON SPEAKING	TEXT
	Mr Ionides recounted how they had just served two regular customers (2 teenage girls) when an enormous man came up to the van together with a female and placed an order. He described how the argument started and how the female went and got another male with blond hair who came and remonstrated with him. He described how violent and aggressive they were and how scared they all were inside the van, in particular his sister-in-law, Sophia Ionides. He arrived at the point where the blond-haired male was holding on to Georgiou's arm with his left arm and Georgiou in turn was holding on to the knife that they use to cut the chickens.
DC Carey	Where were you at this point and what knife did you have in your hand?
Ionides	I was on the left-hand side of the van facing out and I had the salad knife in my hand.
DC Carey	Then what did you do?
Ionides	I rushed over to where the kebab spit is and picked up the big kebab knife. I told the blond man to let go but he would not. I then rested the knife on his left arm and he continued to pull at my friend's arm and therefore was cut. He only let go of Costas's arm when his friends told him that he was bleeding.
DC Carey	So you cut him with the big kebab knife?
Ionides	Yes, but it was in self-defence.
	General discussion then ensued with regard to reasonableness and self-defence and the interview concluded at 1 pm.

COSTAS GEORGIOU

PROOF OF EVIDENCE

1. I, Costas Georgiou (date of birth 12th August 1980) of 27 White Hart Lane, Tottenham, London N15, deny the charge of wounding with intent which has been laid against me.

2. The incident in question took place in the early hours of the morning of Saturday 28th May 2005. That evening, I had been assisting my cousin Alexis Ionides in his kebab van in Colchester.

3. At approximately 1 am, we had just finished serving 2 young girls and a boy when an enormous man with a beard came up to the van and placed an order. He was accompanied by a young woman.

4. He started an argument with Alexis because (so I was later told) he objected to Alexis speaking to Sophia (his sister-in-law) in Greek. The argument escalated with the man raising his voice and banging and thumping the kebab van. After he'd punched Alexis on the nose, Alexis picked up the salad knife and threatened the fat man with it saying, 'Go away or else I will cut you'.

5. At this stage, the woman who the fat man was with went to their car and fetched a blond-haired man who came out and leant on my side of the van (the right-hand side of the van looking out). He was being just as aggressive as the fat man, and fearing for my safety, I picked up the chicken knife in my right hand and gestured to the blond man to go away.

6. The blond man then grabbed hold of my arm with his left hand, and seeing this, Alexis came behind me and picked up the big kebab knife that was to my right. I'd managed to free myself from this man's grip by the time that Alexis had picked up the kebab knife. I did not actually see the man being cut but I did see him holding his arm afterwards.

7. I have no previous convictions either in this country or in Greece.

8. I am very concerned to avoid a conviction as I have recently become engaged to a Greek girl from a very respectable family who might not consider me a suitable fiancé if I were convicted.

Signed: Costas Georgiou

Date 15th September 2005

17.2.1 C.A.P. in action

Notes for advice on evidence

STAGE 1   THE CONTEXT OF THE CASE

(1)   THE STAGE OF THE PROCEEDINGS

    (a) What steps have been taken?

        Bail application 15.6.05

        Defendant on conditional bail — residence with D. Ionides

        1.8.05: 1st appearance — Chelmsford Crown Court

        Charge — Offences against the Person Act 1861, s 18

        Primary Prosecution disclosure 14.9.05.

    (b) Your Instructions: to draft defence statement and to advise on further steps before trial.

    (c) Objectives: Meet defence disclosure obligations, evaluate strength of defence case and identify any further evidence necessary.

(2)   COLLECTING THE FACTS

    (a) Dramatis personae

Costas Georgious (CG)	The Defendant, inside the kebab van on 28.5.05
Alexis Ionides (AI)	Cousin of Defendant, inside van on 28.5.05, arrested on 28.5.05
Sophia Ionides (SI)	Sister-in-law of AI, inside van on 28.5.05
Andrew Canning (AC)	Injured in incident
John Archer (JA)	Friend of AC and with him when AC injured
Jackie Perry (JP)	Girlfriend of AC and mother of his child. Drove AC and JA to van
Tracy Collins (TC)	Schoolgirl, gave witness statement to police
Kelly Longyear (KL)	Friend of TC, with her at kebab van on 28.5.05
Aaron Constantine (AaC)	Friend of TC, with her at kebab van
John Goldstein (JG)	Doctor who treated AC on 28.5.05
Richard Jones (RJ)	PC attended incident on 28.5.05 and arrested AI
Scott Leslie (SL)	Police photographer
Stephen Carey (SC)	DC who interviewed AI, and arrested and interviewed CG

(3)   AGREED AND DISPUTED FACTS

Prosecution Version	Witness	Defendant's Version	Witness	Notes/Queries
AC, JP, JA visited 3 pubs on evening of 27.5.05. Left Rabbit public house by car approx 12.00 midnight and JP drove them to Shetland Rd to get kebabs	AC			Witnesses vary re times and amount drunk.
AC asleep in back of car.	AC			
JP parked car next to kebab van. JP and JA got out.	JA JP			TC says JP did not get out of car with JA.
3 people getting kebabs in front of JP and JA. 2 girls 1 boy.	JP	TC, KL and AaC in front of big man in queue for kebab. Served two teenage girls.	TC AI	Why no statement from KL or AaC?

Prosecution Version	Witness	Defendant's Version	Witness	Notes/Queries
JA went to front of van 3 people in van. Male, 18, to right of centre, girl at back, male on left next to kebab spit about 25, stubble, cutting meat with large knife.	JA	CG was working in the kebab van on 28.5.05, cutting kebabs and cooking chickens, assisted by AI and SI. AI took orders as CG speaks no English.	CG	JA only one to describe two men as of same height and build.
		Smiles was taking the orders, there was another Greek male in the van known as Rambo and a Greek woman.	TC	It seems that Smiles is AI, CG is Rambo?
		3 knives in van — salad knife, chicken knife and kebab knife.	CG	Size of each knife?
JA ordered a chicken kebab from the younger male, older male started to cut up the chicken.	JA	Enormous man with girl came up to van and placed order.	AI	
		CG asked to prepare two kebabs.	CG	
The younger male was holding an orange-handled knife. The older Greek had a wooden-handled knife with a two-foot blade.	JA			Salad/ chicken/ kebab
Young Greek spoke to girl in Greek. An argument ensued between the younger male and JA.	JA JP	Argument between enormous man and AI about speaking Greek. Fat male told AI not to speak in Greek to girlfriend. AI refused to serve him.	CG RJ	
		The argument escalated with the man raising his voice and banging and thumping on the van.	CG	Any damage to van?
		Enormous man punched AI on nose.	CG RJ	
Younger man brandished knife in right hand at JA.	JA JP	AI picked up salad knife and threatened man with it, saying, 'Go away or else I will cut you'.	CG CG	
JP went to get AC	JP			
		Fat male tried to climb into van through serving hatch.	RJ	
		AI warned fat man that he would cut him if he didn't withdraw. Fat man continued to try to climb into van.	RJ	
AC woken by JP. She said, 'The geezer's threatening John with a knife'. AC walked up to van.	AC	Girl with fat man ran and got other man from the car. He came up to van, he was angry.	CG	
During slanging match AC arrived.	JA			
Male 5' 10", muscular build, 16, waving orange-handled 12" bladed knife shouting at JA saying, 'I'm going to cut you'	AC			
Greek girl trying to pull young male from front of van by arms.	AC FA			Why no statement from SI?
Older Greek, 25, to left of centre about 5' 9" wiry, stubble.	AC	CG holding chicken knife.	CG	

Prosecution Version	Witness	Defendant's Version	Witness	Notes/Queries
AC went to front of van, left of centre.	AC	Blond-haired man came and leant on my side of the van (right side looking out). CG picked up chicken knife and gestured to man to go away.	CG	
AC leant his left arm on the van counter and spoke to the young man to get him to put down the knife.	AC JA	Man was very angry and thumped on back window and on glass.	CG	
The older man was holding a large knife in his hand, it was the long one that they use for cutting the kebab.	JP			
		Heard shouting, looked around and saw man punching and kicking the screen of the van and trying to get inside. He had blond hair. He shouted 'C'mon then, I'll give you a fight' etc.	TC	
		The large man who had originally been behind me in the queue was trying to rock the van.	TC	
The older man moved forward carrying knife with 16" blade used for cutting the meat to AC's left	AC	Man tried to get chicken knife away from CG and held on to his arm. CG managed to break away from man's grip.	CG AI CG	Dispute between CG & AI as to when CG freed.
AC felt pressure on arm above elbow.		AI picked up kebab knife from near spit.		
		Told man to let go. Smiles came out from the back of the van carrying a knife with a 22"-blade like the ones they use to slice the kebabs.	CG AI TC	How did AI get behind CG to pick up kebab knife?
		AI rested knife on man's left arm. Man continued to pull on CG's arm and was cut. Man did not let go until he was told he was bleeding	AI	
Older Greek chopped down on to AC's left arm with large knife. Flesh opened up. Started to bleed.	JA	AI cut fat man's arm with long kebab knife. Ex RJ/1.	RJ	
AC tried to grab him with left hand but he pulled back.	AC			
The older man was just in front of AC.	JP			
AC pulled away from the van.	AC JA			
AC punched the van with his right fist as he was pulled away by JA.	AC	Man continued to be aggressive even after cut.	SJCA	Dispute about how often van punched?
AC taken to hospital.	AC			
AC treated in hospital. Piece of bone which had been knocked off distal humerus replaced, 21 stitches required to close deep cut to left arm just above elbow, arm put in plaster.				How hard a blow necessary to chip bone?

Prosecution Version	Witness	Defendant's Version	Witness	Notes/Queries
Police called to van, arrived about 1.32 a.m.	RJ			
Kebab knife seized as Ex RJ/1.	RJ			Any fingerprints?
Fresh blood on top of counter on left in front of kebab spit	RJ			
RJ spoke to AI.	RJ			
AI interviewed by police on 28.5.05	SJC			
Photographs taken of kebab trailer.	SL			
CG interviewed by police on 6.6.05.	SJC			

(4)   LEGAL FRAMEWORK

  (i) The Offence (See **Table 14.5.**)

  (ii) Criminal Procedure and Investigations Act 1996 (as amended by Criminal Justice Act 2003)

  Section 3   Primary prosecution disclosure of previously undisclosed material which might undermine the case for the prosecution or support the accused's defence.

  Section 5   Defence disclosure within 14 days of primary prosecution disclosure by service of written defence statement setting out nature of defence and indicating the matters on which Defendant takes issue with the prosecution and the reasons why.

  Section 7A Continuing duty of prosecutor to disclose.

  Section 8   Defence can apply to court for disclosure of undisclosed material which ought to have seen disclosed.

STAGE 2   ANALYSIS OF ISSUES AND EVIDENCE

(a)   The Issues

(1)   THE LEGAL AND FACTUAL ISSUES

  (i) Identification — Whether it was the Defendant who cut AC?

  (ii) Self-defence — Whether, if it was the Defendant who cut AC, he acted in self-defence?

The witnesses describe a very confused situation — there are a number of discrepancies, eg, JP's whereabouts before and during the incident. Which knife was held by whom? See above at Stage 1(3). The fact that there are discrepancies in the prosecution evidence is of positive benefit to the Defence.

(2)   THE POTENTIAL THEORY

  It was Alexis Ionides, acting in self-defence, not the Defendant who cut Andrew Canning who had been acting in a violent and threatening manner towards those in the kebab van in what was a very confusing situation.

(3)   GAPS AND AMBIGUITIES

  See table at Stage 1(3) above.

No statement from Sophia Ionides, Kelly Longyear, Aaron Constantine. Only prosecution statements from Alexis Ionides and Tracey Collins. No forensic statement on condition of van or examination of knife Exhibit RJ/1.

(b)   The Evidence

(1)   STRENGTHS AND WEAKNESSES OF CASE

(i)   Strength of identification evidence depends on credibility of prosecution witnesses — obvious weaknesses in discrepancies, amount of alcohol consumed, previous convictions. (Check on previous convictions of defence witnesses.) Defence version might be strengthened by statements from other eye witnesses, from site visit to van to view width of van, from viewing knives. Do police have any further evidence pointing to identification, eg, comments of Alexis Ionides/Defendant recorded on custody records?

(ii)   Strong evidence of self-defence — weakness appears to be seriousness of injury and original behaviour of Alexis Ionides. Opinion of Doctor might be sought and proof of evidence from Alexis and Sophia Ionides.

STAGE 3   PRESENTATION

(1)   CHOSEN THEORY

See above at Stage 2(a)(2).

(2)   CARRYING OUT INSTRUCTIONS

(i)   Draft the Defence Statement

(See General Council of the Bar: The Preparation of Defence Case Statements: Guidance on the duties of Counsel.)

Identify nature of defence, indicate matters on which defence take issue with reasons, provide name, address and d.o.b. of each witness.

(ii)   Plan and Write the Advice on Evidence

Identify and explain what further evidence required.

(See **17.3** for completed Advice on Evidence and Defence Statement.)

17.3 Brief for hearing

THE QUEEN

V

COSTAS GEORGIOU

FURTHER INSTRUCTIONS TO COUNSEL

Further to Counsel's written advice, a copy of which is enclosed, together with the Defence Statement, Counsel will also please find enclosed the following documents namely:

(a) Proof of evidence from Sophia Ionides.

(b) Proof of evidence from Alexis Ionides.

(c) Proof of evidence from Aaron Constantine

(d) Previous convictions of Andrew Canning, John Archer, and Tracey Collins. [Reproduced on one page for convenience.]

With regard to the other items requested by Counsel those Instructing can state the following:

(a) Full statement from Tracey Collins. She was contacted by those Instructing but she has nothing further to add to her original statement. Counsel will no doubt take note of her hitherto undisclosed previous conviction.

(b) Statement from Kelly Longyear. Despite exhaustive efforts by those Instructing it has not been possible to trace this witness. It would appear that she left her last address several months ago to travel around Australia and is not contactable in that country.

(c) Viewing of knives. Counsel will no doubt recall the recent viewing of these items. The knives were much as the witnesses have described, the lengths of the salad, chicken and kebab knives being 12", 16" and 24" respectively. The salad knife has an orange handle and both the chicken and kebab knives have wooden handles.

(d) Scientific report on knife. This confirmed that it was in fact the kebab knife which cut Mr Canning on the night in question. The prosecution have informed those Instructing that the report will be included in the prosecution continuing disclosure.

(e) Forensic report on van. Unfortunately, no such report was carried out by Essex Police, although Counsel will no doubt take note of the fact that fresh blood was seen on the kebab van counter by PC Jones.

(f) Expert medical evidence of force needed for injury. Those Instructing discussed this matter with Mr Goldstein and he felt unable to give a conclusive opinion on the subject.

(g) Interview tapes. Those Instructing have requested the tapes and these will be forwarded to Counsel as soon as they are received. We would be grateful if Counsel could inform those Instructing when she has listened to them as to whether the transcript is a fair and accurate summary of same.

(h) Following the recent site visit, the sketch plan is not yet completed. However, the inside of the van is 3' in width and 10' in length. The width of the work surfaces inside the van is 18".

Counsel is now instructed to attend the Plea and Directions Hearing on 21st October 2005, prepare this matter for trial and use her best endeavours to secure an Acquittal at the forthcoming Hearing due to start on 22nd November next.

Brown Dingle & Slattery
27 New Buildings
Chelmsford, Essex.   14th October 2005

IN THE CROWN COURT, CHELMSFORD   T05/0656

THE QUEEN

v

COSTAS GEORGIOU

ADVICE ON EVIDENCE

1.   Mr Georgiou currently stands indicted for an offence that he on the 28th May 2005 unlawfully wounded a Mr Andrew David Canning with intent to do him grievous bodily harm. I would advise that the following steps are taken in readiness for the forthcoming trial on the basis that Mr Georgiou is intending to plead Not Guilty.

2.   Mr Georgiou maintains that he was not the person who wounded Mr Canning on the night in question. Indeed, this version of events is supported by his cousin, Mr Alexis Ionides, who has already confessed to the Police that he was the person who carried out the wounding. Although we have the transcript of interview to hand, it would appear that no proof of evidence has been taken from this person and I would therefore advise that this be done as soon as possible.

3.   Also in the kebab van on the evening in question was Mr Ionides' sister-in-law, Sophia. It is hoped that she would support our client's version of events and therefore a proof of evidence should be obtained from her. I note that Tracey Collins's statement has been disclosed by the prosecution as Unused Material. Although she does not see exactly what happened, her evidence, in my opinion, is useful in demonstrating the unacceptable manner in which Mr Canning and Mr Archer behaved, which might in turn assist any suggestion of self-defence that we make at the trial. She should therefore be contacted, asked if she wishes to add anything further to the statement that she made to the Police, and then requested to attend court and give evidence at the trial.

4.   Miss Collins was with two friends on the evening in question, namely Kelly Longyear and Aaron Constantine. I am particularly interested in any evidence that Kelly Longyear might be able to give as it would appear that she was much closer to the kebab van than her friends when the wounding actually took place. Having said that, I feel that both of them should be contacted and proofs of evidence obtained.

5.   I note that only one of the prosecution witnesses, namely John Archer, allegedly saw our client wounding Mr Canning. Even if the witnesses from whom I have requested proofs of evidence do not support either the defence or the prosecution version of events, they can be used to depict what I am sure was a fairly chaotic situation. The obvious question for Mr Archer would then be, 'How can you be sure that it was Mr Georgiou who wielded the knife on Mr Canning?'

6.   I am sure that it would be of assistance in re-constructing the events of 28th May last, if a site view of the kebab van could be arranged. At the same time we could also take exact measurements of the inside of the van and draw up a floor plan. I am particularly concerned with regard to the question as to how Mr Ionides managed to squeeze past Mr Georgiou in order to pick up the kebab knife. I would therefore be grateful if those Instructing could liaise with my Clerk to arrange a mutually convenient date and time for the visit.

7. The Police currently have in their possession Exhibit RJ/1, the kebab knife. If possible, I would like to have sight of this prior to the trial. There were also apparently two other knives in use on the evening in question, namely the chicken knife and the salad knife. As these were not seized as exhibits, I presume that they are still in the possession of the Ionides family. Perhaps these could be shown to me at the same time as the site view.

8. I note that PC Jones observed fresh blood on the counter of the kebab van when he was called to the scene. Can enquiries be made of the Police as to whether a forensic examination was carried out on the van? At the same time they can perhaps be asked whether a similar examination was carried out on the knife.

9. There can be little doubt that the injury inflicted on Mr Canning was a serious one, it requiring some 21 stitches. Alexis Ionides states that the wound was inflicted by him resting the kebab knife on Mr Canning's left arm. Mr Archer states that the injury was inflicted by a chopping movement. The surgeon, Mr Goldstein, might be able to shed some light on whether or not the wound is consistent with either or both of the above versions.

10. It would appear from their statements that both Andrew Canning and John Archer have previous convictions. Exact details of these should be requested from the Police. Furthermore, all the witnesses from whom I have requested statements should be asked whether or not they have previous convictions.

11. Could those Instructing ask formally for the interview tapes of Mr Georgiou and Mr Ionides to be forwarded to the Defence. We shall also require the custody records of Mr Georgiou and the Computer Aided Dispatch message (CAD) and Crime Report (CRIS) dealing with the incident and I have included a request for these in the Defence Statement. If Prosecution do not serve these under their continuing duty I shall make a formal request for same at the forthcoming Plea and Directions Hearing under s 7A of the Criminal Procedure and Investigations Act 1996.

12. Whilst I have not taken specific instructions from Mr Georgiou with regard to the contents of his Defence Statement, which as those Instructing are no doubt aware, needs to be served on the Prosecution no later than 28th September 2005, I feel that as I have had conduct of this case throughout, I am well acquainted with the nature of our client's defence. I have therefore prepared a draft Defence Statement pursuant to s 5 of the Criminal Procedure and Investigations Act 1996, which should be shown to the client for his approval prior to its service on the Crown Prosecution Service.

13. In summary, therefore, the following steps need to be taken in preparation for the forthcoming trial namely:

   (a) Proofs of evidence to be obtained from:

      (i)   Alexis Ionides,

      (ii) Sophia Ionides,

      (iii) Tracey Collins,

      (iv) Kelly Longyear,

      (v)   Aaron Constantine.

   (b) Site view of kebab van to be arranged.

   (c) Floor plan of kebab van, showing exact measurements, to be drawn.

   (d) Viewing of exhibit RJ/1 and other 2 knives in use on evening in question to be arranged.

(e) Enquiries to be made as to whether a forensic report was prepared on the kebab van and also Exhibit RJ/1.

(f) If possible, expert medical evidence on the force required to inflict the injury, to be obtained. Note that under s 6D CPIA 1996 (as amended) we must provide name and address of any expert witness we instruct, whether or not we call them.

(g) Defence statement to be served on Prosecution.

14.   Please do not hesitate to contact me if you have any queries on this matter.

Nicola Grey   23rd September 2005

IN THE CROWN COURT, CHELMSFORD   T05/0656

THE QUEEN

v

COSTAS GEORGIOU

DEFENCE STATEMENT
PURSUANT TO s 5 CPIA 1996

---

1.   The Defendant admits that he was working at a kebab van in Shetland Road, Colchester during the early hours of the morning of 28th May 2005.

2.   The Defendant denies inflicting any injury on the alleged victim, Andrew David Canning. He asserts that any injuries caused to the victim were as a result of actions taken in self-defence by his cousin, Alexis Ionides.

3.   It is submitted that the above case disclosed by the Defendant might reasonably be assisted by the following documents and a formal request is made for same:

   (a) Incident Report Book of PC 250 Richard Jones.

   (b) Custody record relating to the Defendant.

   (c) CAD message.

   (d) CRIS report.

4.   The Defendant intends to call the following witnesses to give evidence at trial:

   Sophia Ionides; 51, Piggott Close, Colchester CO10 0AU; 10/02/1984.
   Alexis Ionides: 51, Piggott Close, Colchester, CO10 0AU; 26/03/1984.
   Aaron Constantine: 63, Hillside Drive, Colchester CO6 2YP; 16/10/1984.
   Tracey Collins: 17, Starling Walk, Colchester CO4 3NX; 26/01/1988.

5.   This statement has been prepared on the basis of evidence supplied by the Prosecution to date and the Defendant reserves the right to add to or amend his Defence at trial, in the light of any further evidence that might be served by the Crown.

Dated 28th September 2005

Brown Dingle & Slattery,
27 New Buildings,
Chelmsford, Essex.

SOPHIA IONIDES

PROOF OF EVIDENCE

I am Sophia Ionides (date of birth 10th February 1984) and I live at 51 Piggott Close, Colchester CO10 OAU. I have no previous convictions.

On Friday 27th May 2005 I was assisting my husband's brother Alexis Ionides serve customers at our kebab van which was that evening parked at Shetland Road, Colchester. Also present in the van that evening was my husband's cousin, Costas Georgiou.

We opened up for business at approximately 8 pm and everything went smoothly until about 1 am when the van was approached by a big fat man in his late twenties, early thirties, who appeared to be growing a beard. He was accompanied by a girl who I would say was in her early twenties.

After they had placed their order, Alexis turned round to me and said in Greek words to the effect that the gentleman who had just ordered was a bit of a drunken slob. The fat gentleman appeared to take offence at this although I am almost certain that he did not understand what Alexis had said. An argument then developed between Alexis and the fat man. The girl who was with the fat man then went and got a third man who also joined in the argument in support of the big fat man.

I became quite hysterical whilst all this was occurring and for a lot of the time I had my face buried in my hands. I therefore cannot say who cut the arm of the man who joined the argument later on. I saw both Costas and Alexis holding knives whilst the fight was in progress. I can state that the fat man and his friend were both swearing, rocking the van and banging the perspex window whilst the argument was in progress.

Signed: Sophia Ionides

Date: 13th October 2005

<u>ALEXIS IONIDES</u>

PROOF OF EVIDENCE

I am Alexis Ionides (date of birth 26th March 1984) and I live at 51 Piggott Close, Colchester CO10 0AU. I have no previous convictions.

I confirm that all that I said in my interview of 28th May 2005 was true and accurate to the best of my knowledge and belief. In particular, I was the person who cut Mr Canning by means of the kebab knife. I did this by resting it on Mr Canning's left arm when he would not let go of my cousin Costas's right arm. I only did this in self-defence. At the time I felt that I had no other option given the behaviour of Mr Canning and his friend Mr Archer.

I would further add that Mr Archer punched me in the nose fairly soon after he started to argue with me.

Signed: Alexis Ionides

Date: 13th October 2005

AARON CONSTANTINE

PROOF OF EVIDENCE

I am Aaron Constantine (date of birth 16th October 1984) and I live at 63 Hillside Drive, Colchester CO6 2YP. I have no previous convictions.

On Friday 27th May 2005 I, together with my friends Tracey Collins and Kelly Longyear, had been to the Green Man public house and then on to a nightclub. We decided to buy a kebab on the way home. The time must have been approximately 1 a.m. when we ordered our food. I remember that there was a fat man and a woman behind us in the queue although I didn't take much notice of them at the time.

When we were about 50 yards away from the van, I remember hearing a lot of screaming, shouting and banging. I turned around to see the fat man who had been behind us in the queue rocking the van backwards and forwards. I also saw another man whom I'd not seen before banging the perspex windows on the kebab van with his fists. I don't remember seeing any of the Greek occupants of the van holding knives. This might have been due to the fact that my attention was primarily focused on the men outside the van.

On seeing what was happening, we started walking back towards the van. However, by the time that we got there, the people who had caused the disturbance had driven off.

Signed: Aaron Constantine

Date: 14th October 2005

CRO 05/633421

PREVIOUS CONVICTIONS OF
ANDREW DAVID CANNING

DATE	COURT	OFFENCE	SENTENCE
11th June 2004	Colchester Magistrates	Drunk and Disorderly	Bound Over to Keep the Peace — £100 for 12 months
4th March 2005	Colchester Magistrates	Section 5 POA 1986	Fine: £100 Costs: £50

CRO 99/492178

PREVIOUS CONVICTIONS OF
JOHN FREDERICK ARCHER

DATE	COURT	OFFENCE	SENTENCE
5th February 1999	Winchester Crown Court	S.2 POA 1986	CSO 240 hours

CRO 04/305125

PREVIOUS CONVICTIONS OF
TRACEY BERNADETTE COLLINS

DATE	COURT	OFFENCE	SENTENCE
19th November 2004	Colchester Magistrates	Theft (shoplifting)	Fine: £50 Costs: £25

17.3.1   C.A.P. in action

Notes for plea and directions hearing and for trial

STAGE 1   THE CONTEXT OF THE CASE

(1)   STAGE OF PROCEEDINGS

   (a) What steps have been taken?

   Case sent to Crown Court.

   Defence disclosure made. Prosecution disclosure made.

   Defence Witness statements taken from SI and AaC and AI.

   (b) Your Instructions

   (i)   To appear at the PDH on 21.10.05.

   (ii) To prepare for trial on 22.11.05.

   (c) Objectives

   (i)   Of the Plea and Directions Hearing

   Agree and settle plea, issues in case, prosecution witnesses required, number of Defence witnesses, length of trial, further information required, to be inserted on standard form. (*Practice Direction (Criminal Proceedings: Consolidation)* [2002] 1 WLR 2870, Para 41)

   (ii) Of trial

   Represent Defendant on Not Guilty Plea, examine and cross-examine witnesses.

(2)   COLLECTING THE FACTS

   Further information obtained by Instructing Solicitors does not alter significantly the previous position. However, note previous conviction of Tracey Collins, difference in size of chicken and kebab knives (although both have wooden handles) and narrowness of van.

(3)   AGREED/DISPUTED FACTS

   Table in **17.2.1** shows witnesses who can give evidence on issues of identity and self-defence.

   The new information in statements of SI, AI and AaC, obtained by Instructing Solicitors, needs to be included in that analysis but although useful it is not decisive in any way.

(4)   LEGAL FRAMEWORK

   Elements of offence. Prosecution must prove that:

   Andrew Canning was wounded.

   It was Costas Georgiou who wounded him.

   CG intended when he wounded him to inflict really serious harm.

   The wounding was unlawful, eg, not inflicted in self-defence.

   Burden of proof. On Prosecution throughout but note Prosecution do not have to prove absence of self-defence unless the possibility of self-defence has been raised; but note Defence Statement.

   Standard of proof. Beyond reasonable doubt.

(See **17.3** for completed Advice on Evidence and Defence Statement.)

Before trial serve updated defence statement (or written statement that no changes) (CPIA s 6B).

STAGE 2   ANALYSIS OF ISSUES AND EVIDENCE

(a)   The Issues

(1)   LEGAL AND FACTUAL ISSUES

See Defence Statement.

(a) Identity of the person who cut AC. Was it CG or AI?

(b) There is evidence of violence in support of self-defence. Also the Defence might want to raise sufficient possibility of this to necessitate the Judge leaving the matter to the jury but note CPIA 1996, s 11.

(c) *Mens rea* not in issue as such. Defendant denies wounding. If issue of identity decided in Prosecution's favour, ie, on JA's evidence, his statement of nature of blow, ie, a chop, sufficient for jury to infer intent.

(d) No dispute that AC wounded in incident.

(2)   GAPS AND AMBIGUITIES

Further information required — forensic report, interview tapes, custody record, computer aided dispatch (CAD) message/crime report.

(b)   The Evidence

(1)   STRENGTHS AND WEAKNESSES OF CASE

A. Weaknesses of Prosecution case

The Prosecution case relies on the evidence of AC, JA and JP. Their evidence can be undermined by cross-examination of:

(a)   AC, JA, and JP on how much AC and JA drank between 8.00 and midnight, to show that JA and AC's evidence on detail is not reliable.

(b)   AC and JA on previous convictions to show lack of credibility.

(c)   JP on accuracy of statement — delay in joining JA in queue, left to get AC, 6 feet behind AC at time of wounding, and on credibility, relationship with AC (and mother of his child) has motive to withhold full story.

(d)   AC as to behaviour — trying to get into van, punching, kicking van before wounding to show clear vision of what happened unlikely.

(e)   JA about rocking van — how could he have seen what was happening clearly?

(f)   JA about possible confusion between two Greeks, both same build and height.

(g)   AC, JA and JC about knives to show possible confusion — AC sees CG holding 16" knife — chicken not kebab?

(h)   Establish violence and confusion of incident from all witnesses.

B. Strength of Defence case

Independent witnesses support Defence story of attack on van. TC supports D's version that it was AI who was holding the kebab knife.

C. Weaknesses of Defence case

(a)   AI's initial story that it was fat man he cut (ie, JA not AC).

(b)   TC was not close to van (50 yards away according to AaC). Statement does not give description of 'Smiles' or 'Rambo' identifying AI clearly as person holding the kebab knife.

(c)   TC has previous conviction for offence of dishonesty.

(d)   Van very narrow. (But if CG pulled forward by AC, might not be difficult for AI to get behind, when CG breaks away and AI comes forward. AC who has not seen AI's movement thinks it is CG.)

(e)   SI's statement that AI made derogatory remark might, in minds of jury, justify to some extent behaviour of AC and JA.

(f)   Need for interpreter might affect jury's perception of CG as witness.

STAGE 3   PRESENTATION OF THE CASE

(1)   CHOSEN THEORY

CG and young relatives in van in early hours of 28.5.05. Argument developed between large male customer (JA) and AI. CG not involved (English poor). AI tried to get JA to leave. JA became violent. Tried to climb into van, rocked van.

AC joined JA in attack on van. He was angry and aggressive, he thumped on the back window and on the glass and tried to climb in while JA continued to rock the van.

It was very frightening and SI became hysterical.

Costas gestured to AC to go away. AC grabbed his hand in which he was holding the chicken knife. CG tried to pull away. AI moved behind CG, picked up the kebab knife, rested it on AC's arm. AC tried to recapture CG and arm cut in confusion.

(2)   CHOSEN THEMES

Occupants of van in very vulnerable position.

Attack by two angry, violent, drunken lager louts.

Scene of confusion.

(3)   CONSIDER YOUR AUDIENCE

Tactics: Consider how to deal with Tracey Collins's previous conviction.

Best approach to this case in terms of its theory? Self-defence is inconsistent with client's denial of blow and presenting alternative theories reduces persuasiveness and gives rise to inferences under CPIA 1996, s 11.

(4)   CARRYING OUT INSTRUCTIONS

(i) The Plea and Directions Hearing

Plea: not guilty.

Issues: identity, self-defence.

Prosecution witnesses required: all except Dr and photographer.

Defence witnesses: defendant plus 4 (AI, SI, TC, AaC).

Length of trial: 3–4 days.

Make s 8 application if secondary prosecution disclosure not made.

Note: Check with Instructing Solicitor if interpreter needed at Trial.

(ii) Trial

Prepare for Trial (see *Advocacy Manual*).

Desirable to make opening speech in this case?

Prepare to cross-examine Prosecution Witnesses.

Prepare to examine Defendant and Defence Witnesses.

Dealing with figures

18.1 Introduction

Dealing with figures is part of dealing with the facts of a case. This chapter introduces the role of figures in the work of the barrister, and the contexts in which work with figures may be required.

Some people are quite confident in dealing with numbers, others are rather less confident, but in professional terms, no barrister can tell a client or solicitor, 'I never was much good at arithmetic' — the client wants to know what will be recovered in damages, and the solicitor can take briefs elsewhere. This chapter is designed to show you in what ways numeracy is important, and to help you develop your own skills.

18.2 Importance of numeracy

Your immediate reaction to the proposition that you need to be numerate may well be that the law is about words, not figures — and there will in any event be an accountant if necessary. The student who has got a law degree or diploma without doing any addition or multiplication may well express the view that arithmetic was left behind happily at GCSE with no intention of ever returning to it.

Unfortunately, any suggestion that a barrister can get by without a facility with numbers is not true in practice. Although legal textbooks may have few figures in them, they do include substantial coverage of the legal principles for dealing with figures. A contract law textbook may not include figures, but most of the text ultimately relates to how much money you will get if you are successful in a claim for damages, so that when you have a contract case all the principles for the award of damages must be dealt with in terms of figures, not just words. Also, as outlined below, the barrister will most certainly not always have an accountant to help just because there are figures in the brief.

There are many contexts in which a lawyer will have to deal with figures every day. If you are not confident with numbers, now is the time to get to grips with the problem for the sake of your future clients and your career. If you are fairly confident with numbers, you can now start finding ways to develop your numeracy skills in a professional legal context.

In the simplest terms, as a barrister you must be able to tell the client what he or she might hope to get; you need to be able to deal with figures given to you; you need to be able to identify what further figures you need; and you need to be able to talk intelligently about figures to a solicitor or an accountant. Appreciating this is part of the vital move from the academic approach of university or college to the practical approach of the real barrister in practice.

18.3 Relevance of figures in a barrister's practice

18.3.1 Types of practice

Numeracy is going to be important to a barrister in any area of practice from the solely civil to the wholly criminal, albeit in slightly different ways. To provide some examples:

(a) *Commercial practice*. The relevance of figures is obvious in dealing with companies or partnerships, especially as regards a detailed knowledge of accountancy and tax.

(b) *Chancery practice*. The relevance is clear in actions for breach of trust, or for the administration of an estate, including claims for provision from the estate. Again this will specifically require a thorough knowledge of relevant tax provisions and how to read a set of accounts.

(c) *General common law practice*. This has many elements, but to give some basic examples:

(i) *Contract*. You need to be able to deal with all figures relevant to a contract and to damages. Companies and partnerships will often be parties to the contract. Again a good knowledge of accounts and relevant taxation principles will often be required.

(ii) *Tort*. The importance of figures should be equally obvious here — damages assessment can be very complex in cases of severe injury or fatal accident. You should not be deflected from this by the possible complexity of the facts.

(iii) *Employment law*. Many questions relating to pay arise, and in some cases there will be a need to deal with statistics.

(iv) *Family law practice*. Clearly the greatest relevance is to financial provision, both maintenance and capital payments. There is not simply the question of how much to pay, but also of how much is really available, how much a person needs to live on, the tax consequences and so on.

(d) *Criminal practice*. The importance of numeracy here ranges from the complex fraud trial to the small-scale fiddling of the books. Complete understanding is essential for clear presentation to the judge and the jury. There are also other possibilities, from being able to deal with tracing the monetary proceeds from the sale of illegal drugs to simply finding out what fine a defendant may be able to afford.

In addition, there is a pervasive need to deal with figures with regard to costs, interest etc.

18.3.2 Working with an accountant

When dealing with a case that has a substantial financial factor it is possible that assistance will be available from an accountant. An accountant may actually be called in as an expert witness and you will see him or her in conference. If the client employs an accountant you may direct questions to the client's accountant through the client.

An accountant can be of great assistance, but having an accountant to help is not necessarily an answer, it is simply another element. You will still have to talk to the accountant, to know what to ask about, exactly what questions to ask, and you will have to be able to understand the answers.

However, in the vast majority of cases there will be no accountant to help, for the very simple reason that having an accountant costs money and the client either may not be able to afford this, or the financial issues may not be substantial or vital enough to justify the expense of an accountant.

Whenever there is no accountant you will have to deal with all the figures and financial issues personally, finding the figures, analysing them and coming to conclusions that can be communicated to the client and be presented in court. You will personally have to deal with any relevant accounts and tax issues.

18.3.3 Professional ability

A numerical ability is a matter of maintaining good professional standards. When you represent a client you have the duty to do the best you can, which includes not only winning the case if possible, but achieving the best result. You should get the highest figure that you properly can for a claimant.

This relates not just to the issue of damages, but to every arithmetical aspect of a case. If you think it is legally correct for a husband to pay £20,000 to his former wife you need to check with him whether he can afford to raise the sum without ruining his own financial position. If you advise your client that he or she can expect £40,000 in damages it is verging on the negligent not to advise that the money will be liable to 40% tax, if that is the case.

18.3.4 Personal relevance

There is also a personal relevance for the barrister in practice having a reasonable arithmetical ability and a knowledge of the principles of accounting and taxation. The point is simply that as a self-employed person each barrister will be responsible for drawing up a set of accounts each year and will be personally liable for paying his or her own tax.

Again the reaction of those starting to train for the Bar tends to be that this point is in fact not very important — you employ an accountant to do your accounts and you get a good accountant so that you pay as little tax as possible, so why does a barrister need to be personally concerned? Such a reaction again shows a lack of practical appreciation of how things really work. Even if you are going to have an accountant to draw up your annual accounts, you need to keep all the records on which those accounts are to be based. Indeed with self-assessment there is a legal duty to keep such records. You need to know what is taxable and should be entered and what is not. It is also in your interests to know what is tax-deductible so that you know what to keep receipts for. Tax rules mean that there is sometimes a choice of doing things in a tax-effective or a non-tax-effective way, and it is in your interests to know which is which. In addition to income tax, the barrister with sufficient income will be liable for value added tax, with the need to make quarterly returns.

18.4 Stages in a claim when you may need to deal with figures

18.4.1 In a conference

When planning for or carrying out a conference, dealing with relevant facts must of course include all the relevant figures. Any figures that the client provides should of course be noted. In addition you should identify the figures that will be required to pursue the case and ask the client about them. Often the client will not be able to provide the figures personally, in which case you will have to consider with the solicitor how the figure might be obtained.

18.4.2   In preparing a case

Fact management principles cover figures as well as facts. In dealing with the facts of a case the barrister will need to identify:

- in what areas of the case figures will be needed;
- precisely what figures will be needed;
- what figures are already known;
- what figures need to be ascertained;
- how each figure will be ascertained;
- how each figure will be used;
- how each figure can be proved.

18.4.3   In writing an opinion

A good solicitor will send you most of the figures that you need, but even a good solicitor is unlikely to send all the figures you need in the initial brief. At that stage the main issue is whether there is a case and the strength of the case. But figures will still need to be dealt with — the client will want to know not only whether he or she might win but also at least in general terms what damages might be awarded.

In analysing a brief you must consider in what areas figures are relevant. In writing the opinion you should deal with figures as far as possible. All figures that are provided in the brief should be dealt with, and other areas where figures are relevant should be dealt with in outline. You also need to decide on a suitable way to present the figures in the opinion, whether as part of the text or in a tabulated form.

In writing an initial opinion, it is easy to underestimate the numerical and arithmetical side of a case simply because detailed figures are not always provided. This feeling must be resisted — the barrister is not there simply to accept what is provided, it is for the barrister to indicate what information is needed and how the case should progress. Areas where more detailed figures are required should be clearly identified in an opinion.

18.4.4   In drafting

You should always consider carefully how far figures are facts that need to be included as part of a statement of case. Detailed figures or facts relevant to the calculation of damages may need to be included in the body of a draft or added as a schedule. You may need to cover a number of areas, including all heads of damage resulting from an accident, personal injury and financial loss. You may also need to include facts and figures relevant to interest. A summary of damages and interest may also need to be included in the prayer. Examples are provided in the *Drafting Manual*.

An affidavit or witness statement in a case may require figures to be included in great detail, or, for example, a Form E supporting an application for financial relief on divorce. A draft order will of course need to have any relevant figures specifically included. If the figures are complex they should be presented in a schedule.

18.4.5   In advocacy

When presenting a case to a judge or jury it goes without saying that it is vital for the barrister to have total command of any figures in the case, be they sums of money, measurements or anything else. Only if the barrister has personally gathered all the relevant figures and mastered them will he or she have any chance of explaining them clearly, let alone convincing anyone of the strength of the case. Even someone who is confident in dealing with figures in writing may have more difficulty in dealing with them orally.

There are various ways in which a barrister may have to deal with figures in the course of presenting a case in court. First and most simply, figures may need to be dealt with in opening and closing speeches. Secondly, figures will need to be dealt with in offering evidence, whether it be documents or witnesses. Clearly the barrister must be capable of examining or cross-examining a witness on figures. At every stage you need to be able to present any numerical information in a way which really communicates your meaning to the jury and the judge. Even if you understand the figures, helping someone else to understand them can be very difficult.

If you have complex figures to get across you need to find the best way of doing it. The good barrister should always try to look for summaries or clear ways of presentation that will help comprehension. Computers and video display units are increasingly finding their way into court, and this is another area where facility may help with the presentation of the case.

Also, at an interim hearing, you may need to provide and orally present a summary of the costs to date.

18.4.6   In negotiating a settlement

Before attempting to negotiate a settlement you must have all the relevant figures to evaluate the case and identify the most and the least that the client might expect to win or pay. It is important to stress this. Sometimes the settlement is seen as a quick and easy way of avoiding a legal claim, but of course no settlement should be contemplated until one has a sound grasp of all relevant figures.

18.5   Collecting evidence of figures

Figures need to be ascertained just like other matters of fact, and admissible evidence will need to be found to prove them just as much as any other fact in the case. Having identified an area where figures are relevant, you need to sort out precisely what evidence you need and exactly where it may be obtained. Some the client will be able to provide. For others it is for the barrister to indicate to the solicitor what figures are required and for the solicitor to endeavour to find them.

The sources of evidence of figures, are wide-ranging, from a full set of accounts to cash books, vouchers, receipts and even the backs of envelopes. In looking at figures it is important not to be blinded by big figures. The fact that a figure is large is not impressive — large figures can appear in the accounts of a company that is about to go into liquidation. You still need to be able to detect the truth behind the figures.

You also need to be aware of the procedural ways of getting evidence of figures that your client does not have. An obvious possibility is disclosure, but there are many others that you should watch out for during the civil litigation and evidence parts of the course.

You need to be aware of the problems that can arise in presenting such evidence. If you need to take an accountant through his or her evidence you will have to be familiar with all the appropriate terminology. You need to be able to present evidence in a form in which it can be understood. Most important of all, you will sooner or later need to be able to cross-examine on the figures presented by the other side, which requires a most thorough understanding.

Having stressed the importance of figures, it is equally important for the barrister to be able to deal with the lack of figures — you will often come across a case where you need certain figures to advise in detail and they are simply not obtainable. You can only do your best. Try to think of all the sources from which figures might be obtained. If there are no sources, or if the figures are in any event theoretical, you will have to do your best to argue what the figure should be, from common sense, analogy or some other source. This can, for example, be a problem in arguing for loss of future profit in a breach of contract case. If there is a claim for future loss of profits, students tend to think that the claim is weak if it is difficult to assess what the potential profits might have been. This is of course a problem, but it is by no means fatal. The fact that a figure is difficult to assess simply means that you need to set about constructing a good argument for how it might be assessed. Refer to profits over recent years, or profits of similar businesses to construct an argument.

18.6   Typical numeracy issues in practice

Dealing with figures is not just a matter of addition and subtraction. It may require an agile mind. A few practical points to watch out for are summarised here:

(a) *What numerical issues are there in a case?* Never be happy with just the obvious possibility of damages, or simply dealing with the figures given to you. Look out for all the possibilities. For example, there may be tax issues, interest issues, costs, etc.

(b) *What financial resources are there?* If your client is seeking maintenance you need to know not only what your client wants but also how much the other side may have to meet your claim. If you are suing for damages, you need to look not only at what your client hopes to recover but also at what a potential defendant can afford to pay.

(c) *Where has money gone to?* A question you may well wish to ask if your client's money has disappeared in the hands of the other side and you wish to reclaim it.

(d) *What is the relevance of an individual figure?* This may sound a strange question, but it may be important in analysing a case or tax question. What exactly does a particular figure given to you consist of? For example, is it capital or income? Does it include tax?

(e) *Is a particular figure reliable?* Don't accept any figure without question. A figure may not be accurate. How good is the source of the figure?

(f) *What does a figure really mean?* Is a business really strong or weak? Don't be mesmerised by big figures or long lists of figures. Learn to know what each figure means and what figures are most important.

(g) *Be specific about figures.* Even if the figures given to you are vague, this is no excuse for you to be vague.

(h) *Be comprehensive with figures.* You do an inadequate job if you give a figure for damages without saying that interest will be recoverable too. It is no good giving a figure for damages without warning that it is likely to be liable for tax.

(i) *Be realistic about figures.* It is no use settling for a figure for maintenance for a client if you are not sure it will really cover client's needs. It is no good offering a figure to settle a claim if you are not sure that your client can raise it.

(j) *Know what is suspicious in a set of figures.* There can be many factors in a set of accounts that could do with inquiry — a set of accounts is only a basic summary of the position of a business. Learn what may be suspicious and what to look for. Learn to find figures hidden in a set of accounts but which are not clearly labelled for what they are.

18.7   Statistics and graphs

18.7.1   When may the use of statistics be helpful to you?

Statistical methods and statistical terms are used in reporting the mass data of social and economic trends, business conditions, opinion polls and the census. You should get used to reading statistics and utilise them whenever you seek to prove by inference that in your submission a state of affairs exists. Such information is particularly useful when seeking to establish racial or sexual discrimination, risk factors in such areas as sentencing, parole release from mental hospital, danger from chemicals and other environmental pollutants, risk factors in giving informed consent to medical treatment, future profit forecasts, blood test evidence, genetic fingerprinting evidence, etc.

18.7.2   The language of statistics: averages

There are three different kinds of average: the mean, the median and the mode.

The mean is the arithmetic average arrived at by totalling the number of each of whatever it is you want to average and then dividing that by the total number in the sample. For example, you want to know the average (mean) number of cigarettes that Bar students who smoked, smoke on a particular Monday. If 400 of you smoke, and the total smoked by all 400 on the Monday in question was 8,120; the mean would be 8,120/400 = 20.3.

The median, using the same example, is the number of cigarettes which half the smokers smoke more than, and half smoke less than. In this example the figure could be less than the mean, and might be about 19.

The mode, again using the same example, is the number of cigarettes which the largest number of people in the sample smoke, so that if the greatest number of people in the group actually smoked 16 cigarettes on Monday then 16 is the modal number.

If presenting an average to the court always know what kind of average you are using, and if you are confronted with statistical information by your opponent, always ask what kind of average is being used.

18.7.3   The reliability of statistical information

The major difficulty with all statistics is that they may be biased or based on too small a sample to give anything like a reasonable or believable result. Statistical data are generally developed from information collected in questionnaires. It is important to know: how many were sent out, how the respondents were selected, how many were returned, who did not return them and whether the respondents were likely to respond truthfully to the questions posed or whether there may have been a desire to give a pleasing answer. To be valid the sample must be representative and randomly selected.

18.7.4   Sources of statistics

The government's statistics department provides monthly and annual figures which may be of use to you. Such publications as *Social Trends, Home Office Statistical Bulletin, Annual Abstract of Statistics, Regional Trends, Key Data, United Kingdom National Accounts, Economic Trends* and *Monthly Digest of Statistics* may all be of use to you. The *Guide to Official Statistics* will enable you to decide which of the published statistics may be particularly relevant to a case you are pursuing.

18.8   Displaying numerical information

Explaining this kind of information to a court is something you should plan carefully. One way of doing so is to prepare a graph which can be displayed on an overhead projector, or on a large flip chart. Do not be timid in seeking to use presentational methods that will really assist understanding, for example, using computers rather than paper summaries.

18.9   Numeracy areas dealt with on the course

18.9.1   Damages

Methods of assessing damages will be dealt with in the remedies course (see the **Remedies Manual**). The remedies course will give most emphasis to practial points on approaching the assessment of damages, and particularly complex issues in the assessment of damages. You are expected to know the principles for assessing damages in the core subject areas, and this may be an area where you need to do extra work. You will be expected to deal with general principles for assessing damages and with more detailed questions of whether particular heads of damage are recoverable in a particular case.

18.9.2   Interest

The recovery of interest will be dealt with where relevant in the remedies course, the civil litigation course and the drafting course.

18.9.3   Costs

The recovery of costs will be dealt with where appropriate in the civil litigation and criminal litigation courses.

18.9.4   Revenue law

There will be lectures on revenue law for all students (see the **Remedies Manual**). This course will provide a basic grounding in the principles of tax law that are most relevant for the barrister. Students who have already studied revenue law are still advised to take this course because of the practical professional content.

18.9.5   Accounts

Although there will be no lectures on accounts, the **Remedies Manual** contains a section entitled 'The Principles of Accounts'. This should familiarise you with the basic terminology of accounting, the elements of a set of accounts and the principles of and interpretation of a set of accounts. It is not intended that you will actually be able to draw up a set of accounts, simply that you will have enough knowledge to be able to deal with a set of accounts. A set of accounts can be a useful source of information once you know what it may contain. It can, for example, show how many of a man's possessions are actually owned by his company, and whether he is employing relatives in the business.

18.9.6   Options

All the above areas will be developed as appropriate in the option subjects. For example, the **Family Law in Practice Manual** will look at particular tax implications in family cases.

18.10   Helping yourself to deal with figures

Always carry a calculator, be familiar with how to use it, and use it when figures arise. (A calculator may be taken into classes, assessments and examinations and will be expected to be used whenever appropriate.) Also, make sure you have a calendar available. When you are dealing with cases that happened some time ago a calendar covering more than the current year can be valuable.

Many other things can help with numeracy, the particular requirements depending on a barrister's practice. A ready reckoner can help with calculations. Tax tables are available, as are tables of current levels of social security benefits and so on.

In terms of doing personal accounts, the simple expedient of buying suitable business books for records pays dividends, and increasingly good software packages are available to help with the assessment of personal tax.

You will be expected to deal with all numeracy issues whenever they arise on the course. Such issues will not always be obvious but must be spotted in dealing with an exercise, just as they would have to be in practice.

IT use in case preparation and presentation

19.1 Introduction

Information technology has revolutionised the way that barristers work on cases. Almost every aspect of case preparation has been affected by IT developments in one way or another. The practising barrister today now has a wide range of electronic facilities available that only a decade ago could barely be imagined.

There is a downside to this technological advance. The very profusion of information and tools available may lead to 'overload', and it is important for a barrister to be selective if he or she is not to be overwhelmed. Secondly, the nature of the Bar itself means that the use of IT varies enormously between chambers. The most technologically literate barrister may find himself practising from a chambers that has only one web connection through an analogue line — and that is always being used by the clerks. Many established barristers, with successful practices and tried and trusted methods of working, see little benefit for themselves or chambers in the substantial investment required to obtain modern IT facilities. To that extent, over-reliance on IT prior to practice can be just as dangerous as a lack of training or understanding.

Nevertheless, the majority of junior barristers today use IT in one form or another. An overview of the progress of a case demonstrates that modern technology is there to improve and enhance the service a barrister offers.

19.2 Receiving work

19.2.1 Initial contact

Traditionally the initial method of contact between solicitor and counsel has been by a telephone call to the clerks' room, either to book counsel for a hearing or to check that he or she will be able to undertake a piece of written work within a certain time period. There is no doubt that most cases still begin this way, perhaps because (in most chambers) solicitors can be sure that someone capable of answering will answer the phone, and also because at the end of any conversation a definite answer will usually have been given. However, if both solicitor and chambers have the right technology and, probably, a good working understanding, the initial contact can also be made by way of email.

19.2.2 Sending papers

Most papers are sent through the Document Exchange (DX) or post, although in urgent cases they may also be faxed. (In the writer's experience, some solicitors *always* fax, even when the hearing is three weeks away and the documents being sent number the hundreds. It can be difficult to persuade these solicitors away from a method that can clog a fax machine for hours and often produces unreadable documents.)

There are practical reasons why, given the current state of IT, the emailing of papers is not likely to become prevalent. Most cases involve original documents of some kind, and these are not easily reducible to electronic form. (Or if they are, they become very 'bulky' electronically.) In any event, at some point counsel will require a hard copy for use at court, and as a matter of convenience it is usually preferable for the solicitor to be responsible for printing. However, if counsel is being asked to amend an existing document, such as a statement of case or a witness statement, it may well be worth making a quick telephone call (or sending an email!) to the instructing solicitor, asking for the original to be sent by email or on a floppy disk. There is no point in copying someone else's typing, and a busy barrister needs to use as many ways as possible to save time.

19.2.3 Counsel's diary

Traditionally the clerks held a daily diary, subdivided up to show members' names, and whenever a new booking for counsel was made it was written in in pencil, to be re-written in biro once the hearing was confirmed. Inevitably slips of the rubber eraser were occasionally made, and counsel missed the hearing.

The days of paper diaries are ending, if not already effectively over. Most chambers will have electronic diaries, the two main systems being the ACE and Meridian systems. (In November 2002 Meridian agreed to buy ACE.) These systems are being developed to be compatible with laptops and PDAs (Personal Digital Assistants), so barristers can download information from the chamber's system onto their own equipment. This is obviously much quicker and more reliable than 'page-flicking', so long as counsel remembers to update his own equipment regularly, and always bears in mind that the definitive version is the one operated by the clerks.

19.3 Case preparation

19.3.1 Fact management

Even the simplest case will almost certainly require some basic fact management, whether it be a list of witnesses or a chronology. Many barristers will still simply devote a page of their counsel's notebook for this task, but there are advantages to using your computer. Software such as Microsoft Word and Excel allows information to be easily manipulated, for example alphabetically or chronologically. This kind of document may also be of use in court, for the tribunal. The disadvantage of preparing this information electronically is that counsel has a loose piece of paper that is not attached to his notebook, and can be surprisingly easy to lose.

There are more sophisticated tools that can be used for more complicated cases. Microsoft Excel is a spreadsheet programme, primarily used for manipulation of numbers. As such it is excellent for analysing bank accounts, statistics, or any other numerical data. But as stated above it also works well with dates. There are various automatic functions that can be used, such as the AutoSum button (Σ) which allows for totals to be calculated, and which takes into account any changes to the data inputted. Counsel drafting a Schedule of Loss and Damage in a personal injury claim would be well advised to make use of Excel rather than a calculator and a word-processing program. It is a truism of advocacy that a picture is worth a thousand words, and Excel can easily convert most data into charts and diagrams. A coloured pie-chart of your client's monthly expenditure may be far more persuasive to a District Judge than pages of numbers.

There are also various database programs available on the market, which can be used for the storing and processing of information. For larger cases, for example commercial frauds, these may be the best method for counsel to analyse and retain the large amounts of material involved.

19.3.2   Research

One of the most obvious uses of IT for the practising barrister is in conducting preparatory research for the case. This may not just be a matter of using the standard internet or CDROM sources such as Butterworths Direct or Westlaw. Counsel may encounter non-legal issues that he or she doesn't understand, such as checking up the meaning of words on the Oxford English Dictionary website at http://dictionary.oed.com/ or geographical locations on http://www.multimap.com/. A very useful site for 'legal resources in the UK' is www.venables.co.uk which on an initial glance may appear a little homemade, but is in fact full of very useful links.

It is not yet the case that electronic resources hold as much information as a well-stocked library. Many essential textbooks are still only available on paper. However a barrister, with access to the right electronic resources, can undertake almost all necessary research electronically. The two main methods are over the internet, or using a CD-ROM. Most internet resources are based on subscriptions, which can either be purchased on an individual or a chambers-wide basis. CD-ROMs are usually provided in conjunction with a book. See **Chapter 10** for guidance in this area.

For those people practising in chambers with limited or non-existent electronic resources, it is worth bearing in mind that all four of the Inns' libraries have a wide range of material available electronically, and that *any* barrister is allowed to use *any* Inn library. (This is different to the position for students.)

19.4   Producing documents

Both civil and criminal barristers are required to produce written documents. It goes without saying that word-processing software can be used for this, although it is probably the case that most barristers have only a passing acquaintance with the potential of their word-processing programs, and are probably missing many opportunities to speed up their work. As one example, when the writer was producing a large number of similar pleadings related to road traffic accidents, he was able to use Microsoft Word's Mail Merge facility to automate most of the information. It may therefore be very useful for the technologically aspiring barrister to take classes on their preferred word-processing software.

Most forms, for both civil and criminal cases, are available to download from http://www.courtservice.gov.uk/cms/forms.htm. However, most of the time it is probably still better for counsel to produce documents on blank A4 paper and leave the form-filling for the instructing solicitor to complete.

To assist in this, however, many barristers now email their completed documents back to the instructing solicitor. This saves the time of copy-typing a lengthy document. If the solicitors or counsel is not on email an alternative is to include a disc with the returned papers, although this can end up being expensive as the discs have a habit of not returning!

19.5 Before going to court

Although this should really be a task for counsel's clerk, many court listings are now available on the Internet.

Before going to court, there are many useful pieces of information that a barrister can obtain for himself or herself from the internet. Train timetables are available on http:// www. nationalrail.co.uk. Train times and booking facilities are available on www.thetrainline. com. The precise location of the court is obtainable, using the post code which is usually printed on the bottom of court forms, on the www.multimap.com site mentioned above. More information about counsel's opponent may be available through his or her chambers' website, probably best accessed through www.venables.co.uk. Skeletons arguments can be exchanged by email.

19.6 In court

Although the pace of change varies around the country, and even within an individual court centre different judges may place different emphasis on the use of IT, it is generally the case that electronic methods are finding their way into the courtroom itself. At the lowest level most judges are now provided computers by the Lord Chancellor's Department, and it is not unknown for a District Judge to begin typing up his judgment while counsel is still making submissions (this is not a reassuring experience). If counsel has prepared documents using programs such as Excel, it may work to his or her advantage if he or she brings the documents along on a disc, allowing the judge to manipulate the data as he or she thinks fit. Most judges are impressed by counsel who put this amount of thought into the presentation of the case. Not only can this help you win your case, it may also win you a good reputation in the right places.

Counsel is required to take a note of much of what happens in the court room. Most barristers still rely on the blue notebook and the pen, but the use of personal organisers, PDAs and even laptops is usually considered acceptable. It is surprising how quickly you can type when you need to, and it can save a lot of subsequent effort if counsel is asked to provide a transcript of part of the proceedings. Always be aware that counsel is *also* required to store this information somewhere safe, so it is important to ensure that it is regularly and safely backed up.

Generally court hearings are tape-recorded and nothing more, but increasingly different types of transcription facility are being made available. In some of the bigger High Court and criminal cases, live transcription is available, freeing counsel and judge from the necessity of taking a note, and allowing far quicker resolution of issues concerning the precise evidence that a witness has given. Both the Civil Procedure Rules and recent changes in criminal procedure legislation have allowed for a greater use of video links for giving evidence, although they are probably still an inferior option to hearing from a witness live.

At the end of most civil hearings there will be some argument about costs, and frequently interest too. A simple calculator is therefore essential, although most laptops, PDAs and even mobile phones have a calculator function. (Counsel should be careful using a mobile phone, as it may 'go off' even if the purpose of turning it on was only to add some numbers up). If counsel has no calculator, be prepared for some substantial long division calculations.

19.7   After the hearing

Mobile phones mean counsel can be in contact with chambers from the moment his case has finished. Bear in mind, if just one unexpected afternoon case is picked up at the last minute this way, it may pay off the cost of the phone and several months' charges. By the same token, a quick call and then turning the phone off allows counsel some quiet moments of peace before returning to chambers.

All Chambers now use software to issue counsel's fee notes, mostly using either the ACE or Meridian systems mentioned above. These systems can be networked up so that counsel is able to access at any time any information he or she wants about his or her practice, to ascertain his or her aged debt, monthly earnings, and how much work or fees (often not the same thing) that he or she receives from a particular solicitor. Knowing how valuable a part of your practice is worth may indicate what level of marketing is appropriate.

19.8   At home

Many chambers' networks now allow counsel to access the system from home. Telephone lines can be set up to automatically divert to counsel's home address. No-one outside chambers needs to know that counsel is actually dealing with matters from the comfort of home.

19.9   Conclusion

By the time this Manual comes to print, it is likely that some of the information provided in this chapter will be out of date. Links will be dead, websites closed, old technologies superseded. That is not a problem. Hopefully, something even better will have replaced them.

Self-assessment exercises

20.1 Finding a legal framework

Your client is the mother of a nine-year-old child. She took the child on a picnic in the countryside. They ate their picnic at the side of a cultivated field near a stream. After eating their picnic your client fell asleep and was woken by her child crying out as he had fallen into the stream and cut his arm quite badly. It appears that the child had tripped on some rusty wire at the edge of the stream, but it is not clear how he cut himself. The client is worried that the water in the stream did not seem to be very clean. She took the child to hospital but had to wait some time to get attention for him. The child was not well for several weeks after the incident.

Deal with the following:

- list the gaps and ambiguities that you would wish to pursue before trying to identify the possible legal framework;

- make a key list of as many potentially legally relevant factors as you can that might be involved in finding a legal framework.

20.2 Identifying potential theories

A man and a woman who are in the living room of the man's house, are heard arguing by a neighbour. Shortly afterwards two shots are heard. The man shouts for help, and the neighbour rushes in to find the man nursing the woman, who has a severe head wound. A doctor is called and the woman is taken to hospital but she later dies.

You have evidence that a handgun was found in the man's pocket shortly after the incident by a policeman investigating what happened. The man admits that he has owned the gun for several years. You also have evidence that the man and woman had been living together for several years, but their relationship had not been happy recently.

You are acting for the defence of the man on a charge of murder.

Deal with the following:

- list the factual aspects of the case that will require investigation on behalf of the defence;

- construct as many potential theories of the case as possible which may show the man's innocence.

20.3 Lateral thinking

Consider the following:

(a) There are three witnesses who saw a woman running away from the scene of an armed robbery shortly after the robbery occurred. How many different factual reasons might there be for her conduct? How many different legal hypotheses can these factual possibilities lead to?

(b) You are representing Cinderella's stepmother, who has been charged with ill-treating her stepdaughter. Tell the story from the point of view of the stepmother, offering possible lines of defence.

(c) A man believes that he has developed a way of predicting how an individual's career may progress by looking at specific factors. He charges a fee for his service, which is popular with young people. He accepts that he is not infallible, and it is a term of paying for his service that if his prediction is wrong, he will return double the original fee. He makes a lot of money. He has just been arrested. What might he have been arrested for?

20.4 Analysing the evidence

THE CASE OF R v PETER PENNY

Facts:

Report by PC Giles: dated 2 January 2005. In response to a call from a neighbour I visited 26 Acacia Court at 5 pm this afternoon. I spoke initially to John Thorp, the neighbour who called the police. I found the front door ajar. On entering the flat I discovered a body in the living room. I called for assistance and made a thorough search of the flat. There was no one else present. While in the flat I ascertained that there was no rear entry.

PC David Giles, 8.30 pm, 2.1.05

Summary of police report on the body discovered by PC Giles on 2 January 2005. The body has been identified as that of David Star, of 26 Acacia Court, London SE11. Medical evidence suggests that he was strangled between 4 and 5 pm, on 2.1.05.

John Thorp will say: I was in my lounge on the afternoon of 2nd January 2005, watching out of the window. From here I have a good view of the flats opposite. At around 4.30 pm I saw a tall dark-haired man with a moustache run from the flat opposite: 26 Acacia Court. He appeared to be in a great hurry and this made me suspicious, so I telephoned the police. A constable arrived at around 5 o'clock. I told him what I had seen and he entered the flat and found poor David Star dead. I had been watching from my window for most of the time between 4 and 5 pm, and I am sure that no one entered or left the flat apart from the man I have described.

Paula Lyle will say: I am a neighbour of Peter Penny, who lives at 32 Tamarisk Court, London SE11. I was returning to my own flat on 2nd January 2005, when, at 4.05 pm, I saw Peter Penny enter the Flat at 26 Acacia Court. I know Peter and am confident that it was him I saw.

Alice Lion will say: I was at a party to see the New Year in, where I saw two friends of mine, Peter Penny and David Star. They were engaged in a heated argument, but I do not know what it was about as I did not want to get involved.

Police report on Peter Penny: Mr Penny is 6ft 2in tall, has dark hair and a moustache, and walks with a pronounced limp. He lives at 32 Tamarisk Court SE11, a block of flats on the same estate as Acacia Court. He is known to have been an acquaintance of the deceased.

(Acknowledgment

The facts here are based on materials prepared by Professor Twining, which may be seen used in a different way in Anderson and Twining, *Analysis of Evidence*, and in Gold, Mackie and Twining, *Learning Lawyers' Skills*, at p 253. These materials are used with the permission of Professor Twining.)

Assignment

Draw a chart which analyses the evidence in respect of the identification element only of the potential murder charge. The chart should show the facts and inferences leading to the conclusion that it was Peter Penny who killed David Star. It should also show the facts and inferences which weaken that conclusion.

An example of a completed chart in this case is shown in **Appendix 3**.

20.5 Preparing a criminal case

Your pupillage supervisor has asked you to write notes on the case of *R v Juliet Stevens*, which:

- set out the legal framework of the case;
- identify the issues in the case;
- identify what evidence there is on each issue;
- identify any points to clarify with the client in conference.

You may find it useful to review **Chapters 13** and **14** before beginning any detailed preparation of this exercise. Further examples of analytical techniques can be found in **Chapter 17** in the preparation of the criminal brief.

<u>IN THE SOUTH LONDON MAGISTRATES' COURT</u>

THE QUEEN

v

JULIET STEVENS

BRIEF TO COUNSEL FOR THE DEFENCE

Public Funding

Starling & Co
11 West Square
London WC1R 1AB

<u>IN THE SOUTH LONDON MAGISTRATES' COURT</u>

THE QUEEN

v

JULIET STEVENS

INSTRUCTIONS TO COUNSEL TO
ADVISE IN CONFERENCE

Counsel has herewith:

1. Copy of the charge.

2. Witness statements served under the Advance Disclosure rules.

3. Miss Stevens' proof of evidence.

Miss Stevens is charged with causing criminal damage to a motor car. The cost of repair is in excess of £5,000.

The facts appear from the statements of the prosecution witnesses and her proof of evidence.

Miss Stevens is a lady of good character, with no experience of the courts.

Miss Stevens will need advice as to her plea and she is very anxious to know whether it is better to elect trial in the Crown Court or to get the case over with quickly in the Magistrates' Court.

Counsel is instructed to advise Miss Stevens in conference.

CHARGE

Damaging property, contrary to section 1(1) of the Criminal Damage Act 1971

PARTICULARS

Juliet Stevens on the 5th day of August 2005, without lawful excuse damaged a car belonging to James Kirby, intending to damage such property or being reckless as to whether such property would be damaged.

STATEMENT OF WITNESS

(CJ Act 1967 s 9; MC Act 1980 ss 5A(3)(a) and 5B; MC Rules 1981 r 70)

STATEMENT OF	JAMES KIRBY
Age of Witness (date of birth)	Over 18
Occupation of Witness	Stockbroker

This statement consisting of 1 page, signed by me, is true to the best of my knowledge and belief and I make it knowing that, if it is tendered in evidence, I shall be liable to prosecution if I have wilfully stated in it anything which I know to be false or do not believe to be true.

Dated the 8th day of August 2005   Signed: James Kirby

Signature witnessed by: Jane Smart

I live at 23 Arcadia Mansions, Battersea SW11, with my girlfriend Paula Vernon. Until May of this year I had been living with Juliet Stevens. This relationship had lasted several years.

During the course of that relationship I had bought a BMW 323i motor car, index number W564 RGT. We both used to drive it, but it was my car.

Juliet was very bitter when the relationship came to an end. She said I ought to compensate her for the fact that she had to move out and had nowhere to live.

She kept asking me if she could have the car, and I kept saying no. She seemed to be determined to have it.

Feelings between us remained very bad and there were many disputes over various items of property in the flat which we had acquired during the relationship.

In the early hours of Friday 5th August I was woken by a very loud banging in the street outside. My flat is on the ground floor. I looked outside and saw Juliet attacking the car with a sledgehammer.

I went outside to try to stop her, but she seemed to have gone berserk.

She had smashed all the windows and lights. All the body panels were dented.

She was really furious and kept saying, 'You said I could have the car, but all I ever see is the two of you in it. Well, it's mine and no one will drive it again.'

Shortly afterwards the police arrived. As far as I am concerned I had not given Juliet Stevens the car and it was not hers to damage.

I am willing to attend court and give evidence.

Signed: James Kirby   Signature witnessed by: Jane Smart

STATEMENT OF WITNESS

(CJ Act 1967 s 9; MC Act 1980 ss 5A(3)(a) and 5B; MC Rules 1981 r 70)

STATEMENT OF	JAMES KIRBY
Age of Witness	Over 18
Occupation of Witness	Stockbroker

This statement consisting of 1 page, signed by me, is true to the best of my knowledge and belief and I make it knowing that, if it is tendered in evidence, I shall be liable to prosecution if I have wilfully stated in it anything which I know to be false or do not believe to be true.

Dated the 23rd day of August 2005   Signed: James Kirby
                                            Signature witnessed by: Jane Smart

Further to my previous statement, I have now obtained an estimate for repairs to the car. It will need new windows and lights, new body panels and a complete respray. The estimate is £7,500.

Signed: James Kirby   Signature witnessed by: Jane Smart

STATEMENT OF WITNESS

(CJ Act 1967 s 9; MC Act 1980 ss 5A(3)(a) and 5B; MC Rules 1981 r 70)

STATEMENT OF	JANE SMART
Age of Witness	Over 18
Occupation of Witness	Police Officer

This statement consisting of 1 page, signed by me, is true to the best of my knowledge and belief and I make it knowing that, if it is tendered in evidence, I shall be liable to prosecution if I have wilfully stated in it anything I know to be false or do not believe to be true.

Dated 8th day of August 2005   Signed: Jane Smart

Signature witnessed by: Paul Dunn

At 0200 on Friday 5th August 2005 I attended the scene of a disturbance at Arcadia Mansions SW11. On arrival I saw a person I now know to be Juliet Stevens repeatedly hitting a BMW motor car with a sledgehammer. The car appeared to be severely damaged. A man who I now know to be James Kirby was yelling at her and trying to stop her.

She appeared to calm down when she saw me, and I took her to one side to speak to her.

I asked her whose car it was and she replied, 'mine'. I asked her why she was smashing it up and she said, 'When I broke up with James, he said I could have the car since I'd been living with him for years and had lost out on the chance of getting my own place. I kept asking him for it, and he kept putting it off, saying I could have it soon. This evening I saw James and Paula driving around in it — my car — and I just saw red. It's my car'. Miss Stevens was very distressed.

I spoke to Mr Kirby who told me it was his car. He showed me the Vehicle Registration Document which was in his name. A check on the PNC also revealed him to be the registered keeper.

I went back to Miss Stevens and said, 'It appears that it is not your car. I am arresting you for causing criminal damage to that car.' I then cautioned her and she said, 'It's my car'.

She was taken to Battersea police station.

I was present at 7 am when she was charged and further cautioned, to which she made no reply.

Signed: Jane Smart   Signature witnessed by: Paul Dunn

PROOF OF EVIDENCE

Juliet Stevens will say:

I am 25 years old. I am single and I live at 32 Malpas Road SW 11. This is rented accommodation. I am a PR consultant.

I had been living with James Kirby in his flat for six years until May 2005 when we split up, because he met someone else.

During this time we both bought lots of things for the flat, and it was our home. We occasionally discussed what would happen if we broke up, since I had put a lot of money and time into making the flat our home, rather than buying somewhere of my own. He said we wouldn't break up, but if we ever did he would make sure I was all right financially by giving me the car. He bought the car, but we both drove it.

We always referred to it as my car, as a sort of private joke.

When we broke up I expected him to honour his promise to give me the car. I had taken the promise seriously. At first he said he would, but he kept putting it off. He never said I couldn't have it, but said I'd have to wait until he got another one.

I accept I was very bitter about the way he treated me.

In the evening of 4th August I was walking to a friend's house when I saw James and Paula drive past in the car. James hooted and waved. I was furious. By the time I got home I was even more furious. There is building work going on in the house where I am living, and when I saw a sledgehammer I decided I was going to wreck the car — my car.

By now I had decided he was not going to hand it over to me, so I decided if I couldn't have it, they certainly would not drive it.

I walked around to Arcadia Mansions, which is not far, and attacked the car.

I honestly believed it was my car and that I was entitled to do what I wanted with it.

I am worried about my employers finding out about this court case and want it dealt with as quickly as possible.

20.6 Preparing a civil case

Your pupillage supervisor has asked you to write notes on the case of *Norman v Finings Engineering Ltd*, which:

- set out the legal framework of the case;
- identify the issues in the case;
- identify what evidence there is on each issue.

You may find it useful to review **Chapters 12** and **14** before beginning any detailed preparation of this exercise. Worked examples of some analytical techniques can also be found in **Chapter 17**, in the preparation of civil briefs.

<u>IN THE CANTERBURY COUNTY COURT</u>

Claim No. CT4/01306

BETWEEN:

MELVYN NORMAN   <u>Claimant</u>

v

FININGS ENGINEERING LIMITED   <u>Defendants</u>

BRIEF TO COUNSEL ON BEHALF OF THE CLAIMANT

Agreed Brief Fee £600

Blister & Co
Ryder House
Park Lane
Sevenoaks
Kent

IN THE CANTERBURY COUNTY COURT   Claim No. CT4/01306

BETWEEN:

MELVYN NORMAN   Claimant

v

FININGS ENGINEERING LIMITED   Defendants

INSTRUCTIONS TO COUNSEL

Counsel has herewith:

1.   Statements of case.

2.   The agreed trial bundle (paginated [1]–[6]).

Instructing Solicitors act on behalf of the Claimant Melvyn Norman who was injured in an accident at his place of work on 3rd July 2003. The facts of the accident are straightforward. Mr Norman was walking across the press shop floor of the Defendants' premises when he slipped on a patch of oil and fell.

Counsel is asked to appear on behalf of the Claimant at the trial of this claim. Special damages have been agreed in the sum of £1,110. Unfortunately it has not been possible to agree general damages. However, the Claimant's medical report is agreed. The trial bundle contains the only two relevant extracts from the Accident Report Book, ie, the Claimant's accident and one other similar accident in 2003.

It is also agreed that the oil can is to be an exhibit.

IN THE CANTERBURY COUNTY COURT   Claim No. CT4/01306

BETWEEN:

MELVYN NORMAN   <u>Claimant</u>

v

FININGS ENGINEERING LIMITED   <u>Defendants</u>

PARTICULARS OF CLAIM

---

1. At the time of the accident described below the Claimant was employed by the Defendants as a service hand at their works at Eagle Road, Canterbury, Kent, which was at all material times a workplace to which the Workplace (Health, Safety and Welfare) Regulations 1992 ('the Regulations') applied.

2. At about 3.45 pm on 2nd July 2004 the Claimant, in the course of his employment, was walking across the floor of the 'press shop' at these premises when he slipped on a patch of oil and fell.

3. The accident was caused by a breach of statutory duty under the Regulations and/or negligence on the part of the Defendants, their servants or agents.

PARTICULARS OF BREACH OF STATUTORY DUTY

(a) Failing to maintain the press shop floor in an efficient state, contrary to regulation 5(1) of the Regulations;

(b) Failing to keep the floor free from a substance which may cause a person to slip, namely oil, contrary to regulation 12(3) of the Regulations.

PARTICULARS OF NEGLIGENCE

(c) The Claimant repeats the allegations of breach of statutory duty above;

(d) Causing or permitting the patch of oil to be and/or to remain upon the press shop floor;

(e) Failing to carry out any or any adequate cleaning and/or failing to remove the oil from the press shop floor;

(f) Failing to warn the Claimant of the dangers of the oil;

(g) Failing to heed an oral complaint about the danger of oil on the floor made by the Claimant on 25th June 2004 to the Defendants' responsible servant one Andrew Jackson, the works foreman;

(h) Failing to provide a safe system of work;

(i) In the premises, failing to take any or any adequate care for the Claimant's safety and exposing him to the unnecessary risk of injury.

4. By reason of the matters described above the Claimant suffered personal injuries and was put to loss and expense.

PARTICULARS OF INJURIES

The Claimant who was born on 18th March 1973 suffered bruising to and a ligamentous strain of his right knee. He was away from work for 3 weeks during which time he underwent a course of intensive physiotherapy. Pain, swelling and tenderness remained. The Claimant had a further 2-week course of physiotherapy in August 2004. During this 2-week period he was again absent from work. There is still some restriction of movement of the knee joint but this should fully resolve within 18 months from the date of the accident. There is no evidence of osteoarthritis. Full details of the Claimant's injuries are set out in the medical report of Mr Westside of St Hugh's Hospital in Sevenoaks, Kent, dated 1st April 2005 a copy of which is served pursuant to Civil Procedure Rules, PD 16, para 4.3.

PARTICULARS OF SPECIAL DAMAGE

Particulars of the Claimant's loss and damage appear in the statement of special damages served herewith.

5.   Further the Claimant claims interest pursuant to section 69 of the County Courts Act 1984 on such sum as may be found to be due to the Claimant at such rate and for such period as the Court shall think fit.

AND the Claimant claims:

1.   Damages.

2.   The aforesaid interest pursuant to statute to be assessed.

Statement of Truth

I believe that the facts stated in these particulars of claim are true.

Dated the 25th day of April 2005   *M. Norm*

<u>SAINT HUGH'S HOSPITAL, SEVENOAKS, KENT</u>
<u>MEDICAL REPORT ON MELVYN NORMAN</u>

Melvyn Norman aged 32

34 Copping Rise, Sevenoaks, Kent

Occupation: Service Hand at Finings Engineering Limited

Date of accident: 2.7.04

Date of Examination for this Report 25.3.05

Mr Norman tells me that whilst at work on 2/7/04 he slipped on a patch of oil and injured his right knee. He was taken to hospital where X-rays revealed no bony injury. There was severe bruising over the lateral aspect of the knee joint. A ligamentous strain was diagnosed, a supportive bandage provided and analgesics prescribed.

Mr Norman was off work initially for three weeks. During this period he had a course of intensive physiotherapy at Sevenoaks Hospital. At home he was restricted in his activities. He could not play with his two young children. He had difficulty negotiating stairs, his sleep was interrupted and he could not perform his normal household jobs. Mrs Norman therefore had to do more by way of jobs around the house and looking after the children in this period. Mr Norman says that when he returned to work he was still in pain. He worked for a week and then had a further two weeks off. In this period he had another course of physiotherapy. I have had the benefit of reading notes supplied by Mr Norman's GP, Mr Strange, and also from Mr Irwin the physiotherapist. There was an initial reduction in flexion of 40% in the joint, but this has steadily improved. Mr Norman still experiences pain when kneeling at work but this is a dull ache and not severe. He has needed painkilling tablets intermittently since the accident but the instances of need have become less frequent.

<u>Examination</u>

General health: good

Height: 6ft 1. Weight: 12 stone

Mr Norman presented as a pleasant if somewhat absent minded man. On examination his gait was normal. There was a 10% reduction in flexion of the right knee joint. Kneeling is still painful. There is no current bruising but there is a little residual tenderness over the lateral aspect of the joint.

<u>Conclusion</u>

There is a clear evidence of an initially severe ligamentous injury of the right knee joint. There is no evidence of osteoarthritis. I foresee no long-term effects and would anticipate full resolution of the injury within 18 months from the date of the accident.

TIM WESTSIDE
Consultant
1st April 2005

<u>IN THE CANTERBURY COUNTY COURT</u>   Claim No. CT4/01306

BETWEEN:

MELVYN NORMAN   <u>Claimant</u>

v

FININGS ENGINEERING LIMITED   <u>Defendants</u>

SCHEDULE OF LOSS AND EXPENSE PURSUANT
TO CPR PD 16, PARA 4.2

---

5 weeks' loss of earnings	£1,000
Taxi fares to and from hospital	£ 75
Damaged clothing	£ 35
	———
TOTAL	£1,110

Dated the 25th day of April 2005

Blister & Co
Ryder House
Park Lane
Sevenoaks, Kent

<u>Solicitors for the Claimant</u>

To the Defendants:
Finings Engineering Limited
Eagle Road
Canterbury, Kent

And to the Court Manager

<u>IN THE CANTERBURY COUNTY COURT</u>　　　　　　　Claim No. CT4/01306

BETWEEN:

MELVYN NORMAN　　　　　　　<u>Claimant</u>

v

FININGS ENGINEERING LIMITED　　　　　<u>Defendants</u>

DEFENCE

1.　Paragraphs 1 and 2 of the Particulars of Claim are admitted.

2.　It is denied that the Defendants were negligent or in breach of statutory duty as alleged in the Particulars of Claim or at all.

3.　The Defendants aver that they maintained the press shop floor in an efficient state and did all that was reasonably practicable to keep the floor free from oil or any other substance which may cause a person to slip or fall. The Defendants' servant one James Stonehouse was charged with cleaning the floor twice each day and had cleaned the floor approximately 2 hours before the accident.

4.　The accident referred to in the Particulars of Claim was caused solely or alternatively contributed to by the negligence of the Claimant.

<u>PARTICULARS OF NEGLIGENCE</u>

(a) Carrying an oil can with him across the floor in such a manner that oil was dripped on to the floor;

(b) Causing or permitting oil to fall onto the floor;

(c) Failing to look where he was going and slipping on the oil he had dropped;

(d) In the premises failing to take any or any adequate care for his own safety and exposing himself to the unnecessary risk of injury.

5.　Further or alternatively, if, which is denied, the oil upon which the Claimant slipped was not dropped by him immediately prior to the accident, the Defendants will rely upon the failure of the Claimant to look where he was going and thereby avoid the patch of oil upon which he slipped.

6.　The Defendants make no admissions as to the alleged or any injury, loss or damage, or as to the amount thereof.

7.　Save in so far as has been expressly admitted the Defendants deny each and every allegation in the Particulars of Claim as if the same were set out in turn and specifically denied.

<u>Statement of Truth</u>

I believe that the facts stated in this defence are true.

Dated the 27th day of May 2005

D Temple Director

for Finings Engineering Ltd

<u>TRIAL BUNDLE</u>
<u>INDEX</u>

[1]

Claimant
M. Norman
1st
2.9.2005
Claim No. CT4/01306

<u>IN THE CANTERBURY COUNTY COURT</u>

MELVYN NORMAN   <u>Claimant</u>

v

FININGS ENGINEERING LIMITED   <u>Defendants</u>

WITNESS STATEMENT OF MELVYN NORMAN

I, Melvyn Norman of, 34 Copping Rise, Sevenoaks, Kent, service hand, will say as follows:

1.   I am the Claimant in this action. I make this statement concerning the accident that occurred at work on 2nd July 2004.

2.   I am married with two daughters aged 5 and 7. I have worked for the Defendants for two years as a service hand at their Eagle Road works. My job involves me in looking after and adjusting the press machines on the press shop floor. At about 3.40 pm on the day of the accident I was adjusting a B/44 press machine in the press shop when I realised that I needed an adjustable spanner. I decided to go to the tool shop to get the spanner. I had just oiled a B/44 machine and had the oil can in my hand. As far as I can recall I was holding the oil can in an upright position. The can has a long, thin spout that points upwards. I believe that it was pointing upwards at the time of the accident. It is possible that a few drops of oil were dripping from the can as I made my way to the tool shop. If this was the case then they would most likely have dripped on to my overalls rather than the floor as I always carry the oil can very close to me.

3.   I had reached the middle of the press shop floor when I slipped and fell. I had been chatting to workmates as I passed them. Simon Packer was working on a press near to where I fell and saw the whole thing.

4.   James Stonehouse the press shop apprentice had been standing at the door of the press shop, some 20 feet away from the place where the accident occurred. After the accident I remember him coming over and helping me to the sickroom. I remember Simon Packer saying something about there having been a large patch of oil on the floor for some time.

5.   Oil has always been a problem in the press shop. Lately the problem has got worse. On 25.6.04 I actually spoke to the works foreman, Mr Jackson, about it. It was a sort of general chat but I told him I thought the floor was dangerous.

6.   I was in great pain when I fell. My knee was badly bruised. At hospital they said it was ligaments. I had the bandage on for three weeks. I was off work and couldn't play with the kids. Also I had difficulty getting up and down stairs and doing jobs around the house. The wife had to do it all. I went to physiotherapy for 3 weeks then I went back to work. The pain was still bad and after a week I had to have 2 more weeks off work and more physiotherapy.

7.   I like a game of football now and again but I haven't played since the accident. I don't trust the leg. The same applies to the gardening which was one of my favourite hobbies. I was a very keen gardener and kept our front and rear gardens immaculately.

[2]

I was particularly keen on the bedded plants and shrubs and very proud of the way I'd arranged and groomed the flower beds. Since the accident I have had difficulty bending down to do the gardening. My wife has done most of the gardening but she isn't so much of a perfectionist as I am and the garden looks pretty untidy as a result.

STATEMENT OF TRUTH

I believe that the facts stated in this witness statement are true.

M. Nor⁓

Dated the 2nd day of September 2005

[3]

Claimant
S. Packer
1st
2.9.2005
Claim No. CT4/01306

<u>IN THE CANTERBURY COUNTY COURT</u>

MELVYN NORMAN   <u>Claimant</u>

v

FININGS ENGINEERING LIMITED   <u>Defendants</u>

WITNESS STATEMENT OF SIMON PACKER

I, Simon Packer, of 4 Blood Lane, Sevenoaks, Kent will say as follows:

1.   I am employed as a press operator at Finings Engineering's Eagle Road works. I know Melvyn Norman as a fellow employee but we are not friends. On the day of his accident I was in the press shop working on my press. When I returned from lunch at about 2.15 pm I noticed that there was a patch of oil by the side of my machine. The floor of the press shop is often oily. The apprentice is supposed to keep the floor clean but he often forgets. I do not remember him cleaning the floor on the day of the accident.

2.   It is difficult to keep the floor clear of oil. The machines shed some oil and the adjusting and maintenance work involves the use of oil. Really the floors should be inspected and, if necessary, cleaned every couple of hours just to be on the safe side. Even that might not solve the problem.

3.   I remember that Melvyn was carrying a can of oil as he approached my press. I can't say if it was leaking or not. He seemed to be walking in a line that would have taken him wide of the oil but he must have altered his course. When he fell the oil can went flying and Melvyn clutched his right knee in agony.

4.   James Stonehouse helped me to take him to the sickroom. I do remember that there were some oil stains down the front of Melvyn's overalls and on the top of his boots when we picked him up.

<u>STATEMENT OF TRUTH</u>

I believe that the facts stated in this witness statement are true.

S Packer

Dated the 2nd day of September 2005

[4]

Defendant
J. Stonehouse
1st
2.9.2005
Claim No. CT4/01306

IN THE CANTERBURY COUNTY COURT

MELVYN NORMAN   <u>Claimant</u>

v

FININGS ENGINEERING LIMITED   <u>Defendants</u>

WITNESS STATEMENT OF JAMES STONEHOUSE

I, James Stonehouse of 39 Snargate Road, Sevenoaks, Kent, will say as follows:

1.   I am 17 years old and work as an apprentice at Finings Engineering in the press shop. The foreman, Mr Jackson, asked me to keep the floor of the shop clean. I give it a clean twice a day. The problem is that oil gets all over the place and there isn't much you can do. Some of the lads are careless with their oil cans, and the presses spurt out a bit as well.

2.   At about 3.40 pm on 2.7.04 I was standing by the door of the press shop. I saw Melvyn Norman walking across the shop towards the door. I particularly noticed him because he was carrying an oil can in one of his hands, I can't remember which. The spout was facing downwards and oil was leaking out. Melvyn didn't seem to realise. I was about to shout out when he slipped and fell. When we picked him up there was some oil on the front of his shoes. I was surprised that there wasn't more oil on his clothes and shoes. I usually clean the floor at about 1.30 pm at the end of the morning shift, and again at about 4 pm in the afternoon. A few days earlier Mr Jackson, the works foreman, had asked me to clean the floor carefully, that's why I'm pretty sure that I had cleaned the floor at 1.30 pm on 2.7.04.

STATEMENT OF TRUTH

I believe that the facts stated in this witness statement are true.

J. Stonehouse
....

Dated the 2nd day of September 2005

[5]

Defendant
A. Jackson
1st
2.9.2005
Claim No. CT4/01306

IN THE CANTERBURY COUNTY COURT

MELVYN NORMAN   <u>Claimant</u>

v

FININGS ENGINEERING LIMITED <u>Defendants</u>

WITNESS STATEMENT OF ANDREW JACKSON

I, Andrew Jackson, of 5 Rosebush Lane, Canterbury, Kent, will say as follows:

1. I am the works foreman at the Defendants' premises at Eagle Road, Canterbury, Kent. I have worked at those premises for the Defendants since that particular factory opened in 1975. I started as an apprentice press operator and have been works foreman for the last five years.

2. The press shop floor contains 10 presses in all. The maintenance of the presses involves them being regularly oiled to ensure that the moving parts move freely and do not grind causing wear. Any oil spillage from routine maintenance should be minimal.

3. When the presses are operating there is some minimal release of oil. This is the oil used for maintenance which will sometimes escape from the moving parts when a press is working at full capacity. Most of the moving parts are boxed in, but occasionally oil escapes. The amount of oil is small, more in the nature of a few droplets than a pool or puddle.

4. Melvyn Norman is a service hand at the Defendants' Eagle Road works. He is responsible for maintaining the presses on the press shop floor. This involves him regularly oiling the moving parts of the machine.

5. On 25.6.04 he spoke to me about a number of maintenance matters. He mentioned in a general way that he thought that there might have been more oil on the press shop floor in the last few days. He did not say that he thought that this oil was causing a greater hazard than usual. The floor is cleaned twice a day by one of our apprentices, James Stonehouse. Even though Mr Norman had made no mention of a greater hazard being caused by the oil, following my discussion with him on 25.6.04 I told James Stonehouse to clean the floor particularly carefully.

<u>STATEMENT OF TRUTH</u>

I believe that the facts stated in this witness statement are true.

AJackson

Dated the 2nd day of September 2005

[6]

ACCIDENT REPORT BOOK

Date/Time	Location	Details
12/2/03	Press shop	F. Collins. Slipped on oil, Injured elbow and shoulder.
...		
2/7/04	Press shop	M. Norman. Slipped on oil, injured knee.

[7]

20.7 Dealing with figures

Problem 1

Examine the following facts in detail, and identify as many areas as you can where information about numbers must be sought and dealt with.

In each case, identify where information about relevant figures might be sought by yourself or by instructing solicitors.

Mr Duff, aged 59, was injured in April 2005 when he was driving his car and it was hit by another vehicle. His father was a passenger in his car at the time and was killed in the accident. The accident was caused by the driver of the other car, Mr Young, who has since been convicted of dangerous driving with regard to the incident. Mr Duff is suing Mr Young for negligence. As a result of the accident, which broke both his legs and caused serious internal injuries, Mr Duff could not work for six months. In order to be able to return to work as quickly as possible, Mr Duff used a substantial amount from his savings to pay for private medical treatment.

Mr Duff has had particular difficulties in that he is the manager of an interior design business. The business was incorporated in 1999 as Duff Decor Ltd, with Mr Duff as a 60% shareholder and his brother as a 40% shareholder. Business has suffered while Mr Duff has not been able to work. His brother is not good at business, so a manager had to be employed while Mr Duff was not there. In addition, a few months before the accident, £100,000 was borrowed to fund expansion of the business, and there have been problems keeping up with repayments on this loan.

Mr Duff's father left a will appointing Mr Duff and his brother as his executors. The main provisions of the father's will was to leave the residue of his estate in trust for his grandchildren.

Mr Duff left his wife and two children three years ago, and he has since lived in a flat. The wife and children are still in the former matrimonial home, and Mr Duff had been voluntarily paying maintenance to them. However, following his accident he has been unable to make such payments, and his wife is currently in receipt of social security benefits. Mr Duff has heard rumours that his wife has formed a relationship with another man who has done substantial work on the home.

Problem 2

A wife tells you that she needs maintenance from her husband. Both parties have made full disclosure of their financial situation and below you will find each party's schedule of income and expenditure. Is she right?

Wife	£
Gross income	15,708.00 p.a.
Net income, approximately	927.50 per month
National insurance	50.36 per month
Monthly expenditure:	
Gas	25.00
Electricity	15.00
Television licence	8.00
Contents insurance	13.00
Car tax and insurance	24.00
Car maintenance	34.00

Wife	£
Petrol	50.00
Dental treatment	10.00
House repairs, etc	40.00
Investments: life assurance, etc	154.25
Increase in national insurance contribution	68.00
Council tax, water rates, buildings insurance, etc	136.50
Food	200.00
Clothes	100.00

Husband	£
Gross income	34,000.00 pa
Net income, approximately	1,845.00 per month
Monthly expenditure:	
Expenses of former matrimonial home, council tax, etc	136.30
Mortgage	719.00
Endowment policy	198.00
Gas	50.00
Electricity	20.00
Telephone	20.00
Contents insurance	10.00
Ground rent and maintenance charge	12.00
Television licence	8.00
Council tax and water rates	58.00
Hire purchase: car, furniture	135.82
Savings	152.00
Food	200.00
Clothes	20.00
Holidays	150.00

Problem 3

The XYZ Building Society is unwilling to advance money for the purchase of terraced houses without front gardens in an area where members of ethnic minority groups live. Your instructing solicitors have presented you with a copy of a report compiled by the Commission for Racial Equality which states that 86% of ethnic minority families living in that area live in terraced houses without front gardens, and that 46% of white families living there live in terraced houses without front gardens.

Your instructing solicitors believe that their client (a member of an ethnic minority group) can successfully claim that she has been indirectly discriminated against on racial grounds by the Building Society, which has refused to advance her a mortgage to purchase a terraced house without a front garden in the area. Explain how you can use the figures supplied to help to prove discrimination.

Problem 4

The defendant is charged with fraud. The prosecution wishes to prove that in May of a particular year her level of income and expenditure rose significantly, and has obtained copies of her bank statements. Do they bear this out?

BARTLETT'S BANK PLC
27 Old Street
London EC8Y 2HR

Account: J Park
14278693

Date	Details		Withdrawals	Deposits	Balance
					3,018.88
27 Mar		000621	50.00		2,968.88
28 Mar	CHEQUES			321.67	3,290.55
30 Mar		000620	98.27		
	PAYROLL			948.25	
		AC	30.00		4,110.53
3 Apr	HOLT FINANCE	SO	59.28		
	BROADWAY RENTALS	SO	22.90		4,028.35
5 Apr		000622	31.84		3,996.51
6 Apr		AC	75.00		3,921.51
7 Apr	W LONDON CTY CT	SO	100.00		3,821.51
10 Apr		000623	1,260.55		2,560.96
11 Apr		CC		13.60	
		000624	80.00		2,494.56
14 Apr		AC	50.00		
		000627	142.88		2,301.68
17 Apr	WESTLAND B/SOC	SO	392.27		
		000628	50.00		1,859.41
18 Apr		000625	27.00		1,832.41
19 Apr		AC	75.00		
	L. B. LAMBETH	SO	76.82		
		CC		500.00	2,180.59
20 Apr		000626	60.48		2,120.11
21 Apr		000629	100.00		2,020.11
25 Apr	S/ELEC	SO	43.00		1,977.11
26 Apr		000630	5,000.00		3,022.89 OD
27 Apr		CC		142.80	2,880.09 OD
28 Apr	PAYROLL			948.25	
		AC	75.00		2,006.84 OD
2 May	HOLT FINANCE	SO	59.28		
		000632	50.00		2,116.12 OD
3 May	BROADWAY RENTALS	SO	22.90		
	CHEQUES			347.80	1,791.22 OD
5 May		000633	50.00		1,841.22 OD
8 May		AC	25.00		
	W LONDON CTY CT	SO	100.00		1,966.22 OD
9 May		CC		87.30	1,878.92 OD
10 May		000636	32.99		1,911.91 OD
11 May		000635	50.00		1,961.91 OD
12 May	BANK CHARGES		36.80		
		AC	75.00		
		CC		7.21	2,066.50 OD
16 May	WESTLAND B/SOC	SO	392.27		
	P. LANGTON			2,500.00	41.23

Date	Details		Withdrawals	Deposits	Balance
17 May	INTEREST		36.67		
		000634	186.21		181.65 OD
18 May	STAR CLUB	DD	32.00		
		AC	75.00		
		CC		500.00	211.35
19 May	L. B. LAMBETH	SO	76.82		134.53
22 May		000637	75.00		59.53
25 May		AC	75.00		
	S/ELEC	SO	43.00		58.47 OD
26 May		000638	21.95		
		CC		142.80	62.38
30 May	PAYROLL			948.25	
		000639	50.00		
		000640	17.90		
		000641	100.00		
	CHEQUES			338.92	1,181.65
1 Jun		AC	50.00		1,131.65
2 Jun	INTEREST		2.86		1,128.79
5 Jun	HOLT FINANCE	SO	59.28		
	BROADWAY RENTALS	SO	22.90		
		000642	50.00		996.61
7 Jun		000644	250.00		
	P. LANGTON			2,500.00	
	W LONDON CTY CT	SO	100.00		3,146.61
8 Jun		000643	44.99		3,101.62
9 Jun		AC	75.00		3,026.62
12 Jun		AC	50.00		2,976.62
13 Jun		CC		28.50	3,005.12
16 Jun	WESTLAND B/SOC	SO	392.27		
		000645	50.00		2,562.85
19 Jun	L. B. LAMBETH	SO	76.82		
		CC		500.00	2,986.03
20 Jun		000646	60.00		2,926.03
23 Jun		000647	23.90		2,902.13
23 Jun		AC	75.00		2,827.13

Key: SO STANDING ORDER   AC AUTOMATED CASH   OD OVERDRAWN   CC CASH AND/OR CHEQUES
DD DIRECT DEBIT

APPENDIX 1
GLOSSARY OF MEDICAL TERMS

This glossary contains the meaning of certain technical terms commonly found in medical reports.

Abduction: movement away from the mid-line

Adduction: movement towards the mid-line

Amnesia: absence of memory

Analgesic: pain-relieving medication

Ankylosis: obliteration of a joint by fusion, either bony or fibrous

Aphasia: loss of power of speech

Arthrodesis: fusion of a joint by operation

Arthroplasty: production of movement in a joint by operation

Arthroscopy: direct vision inside a joint using a fibre-optic scope

Aspiration: sucking out fluid (eg from a joint or a cavity) through a hollow needle

Ataxia: unsteadiness of gait

Atrophy: wasting of a body part from lack of vascular or nerve supply

Avascular necrosis: death of tissue through deprivation of blood supply; refers particularly to bones — eg head of femur following fracture of neck of femur

Avulsion: wrenching away of a part, eg avulsion fracture, the wrenching away of a fragment of bone by force applied by an attached tendon

Axonotmesis: interruption of conductivity in a nerve by 'physiological' (ie not physical) division of the axons, resulting in paralysis and anaesthesia in the distribution of the nerve; spontaneous recovery can be expected but will take some months (cf. neurapraxia and neurotmesis)

Biopsy: microscopic examination of tissue taken from the living body

Bi-valve: removal of a plaster cast by cutting along each side of its length, permitting replacement if required

Brachial: pertaining to the arm

Brachioradialis: muscle of the forearm

B.S.R. (or E.S.R.): Blood (or erythrocyte) rate — a laboratory test upon the blood to detect the presence of an inflammatory process somewhere in the body

Bursa: a cyst-like sac between a bony prominence and the skin — eg prepatellar bursa, inflammation in which constitutes 'housemaid's knee'

Calcaneal: pertaining to the calcaneus

Calcaneus: the heel bone, or os calcis

Callus: the cement-like new bone formation which produces union of the fragments of a fracture

Cardiac: pertaining to the heart

Cephalic: pertaining to the head

Cervical: pertaining to the neck

Chondral: pertaining to cartilage

Chronic: long-lasting, the reverse of acute

Claudication: lameness; applied particularly to pain in the calf muscles resulting from defective blood supply owing to arterial disease

Comminuted: a type of fracture of a bone in which there are more than two fragments

Concussion of the brain: to establish the diagnosis the loss of consciousness must be immediate and complete though it may be of very short duration

Condyle: a rounded articular eminence

Cortex: the outer layer of a structure — eg the 'shell' of a bone; the surface of the brain

Costal: pertaining to the ribs

Crepitus: a creaking or grating, found in osteoarthritic joints; also in recent fractures and with inflammation of tendons and their sheaths (tenosynovitis)

C.S.F.: cerebro-spinal fluid, which lies on the surface of the brain and spinal cord and inside the ventricles of the brain

Cuboid: a small bone of the foot

Cyanosis: blueness from deficient oxygenation of the blood

Deltoid region: the outer region of the upper third of the arm

Diplopia: double vision

Disarticulation: amputation through a joint

Disc, intervertebral: fibro-cartilaginous 'cushion' between two vertebrae

Distal: farthest point from the centre (opposite to proximal)

Dorsal spine: that part of the spine from which the ribs spring; known also as the 'thoracic' spine

Dorsiflexion: movement of a joint in a backward direction (syn. extension)

Dorsum: back or top — eg back of hand, top of foot

Dupuytren's contracture: thickened fibrous tissue in the palm of the hand causing contracture of the fingers

Dys-: prefix meaning difficult, defective, painful — eg dyspnoea, meaning shortness of breath

-ectomy: suffix meaning surgical excision — eg patellectomy, removal of the patella

E.E.G.: electro-encephalogram (graph of electric impulses in the brain)

Effusion: extravasation of fluid in a joint (or any cavity) — eg 'water on the knee' (ie synovitis)

Embolism: blockage of blood vessel by a clot which has migrated

Emphysema, surgical: collection of air in the tissues through puncture of the lung by a fractured rib

E.N.T.: ear, nose and throat

Epiphyseal line: the cartilaginous plate near the end of a bone at which the bone grows in length

Epiphysis: the end of a bone during the period of growth

Erythema: superficial blush or redness of the skin — eg as from a very slight burn or scald

Erythrocyte: red blood corpuscle

Eschar: crust of dead skin

Extension: moving a joint into the straight position (opposite to flexion)

External: outer side, syn. lateral (opposite to medial)

Fascia: a fibrous membrane

Femoral: pertaining to the femur

Femur: the thigh bone

Flexion: moving a joint into the bent position (opposite to extension)

Flexor: a muscle that bends or flexes a part

Fossa: anatomical term for a depression or furrow

Gangrene: total death of a structure through deprivation of blood supply

Genu: the knee joint

Gluteal: pertaining to the buttock

Haemarthrosis: effusion of blood in a joint

Haematoma: localised collection of blood

Hallux: the great toe

Humerus: the bone of the upper arm

Hyper-: prefix meaning increase above the normal

Hypo-: prefix meaning decrease below the normal; anatomical term for below

Ileum: the lower half of the small intestine

Ilium: the main bone of the pelvis

Induration: hardening of a tissue

Infarct: a wedge-shaped haemorrhagic or necrotic area produced by obstruction of a terminal artery

Inguinal: pertaining to the groin

Intercostal: between the ribs

Interosseous: between bones

Intracranial: within the skull

Intubation: insertion of a breathing tube through the vocal cords

Ischaemia: reduction of local blood supply to a structure

-itis: suffix meaning inflammation — eg osteitis, inflammation of a bone

Keloid: a scar which is thickened and deep pink in colour

Kyphosis: posterior convexity of the spine

Laceration: physical tearing of a structure, eg lacerated skin

Lateral: outer side, or external (opposite to medial)

Leg: that part of the lower limb between the knee and ankle

Lesion: a structural change in a tissue caused by disease or injury

Leucocyte: white blood corpuscle

Ligamentous: pertaining to a ligament

Lipping: ridge of adventitious bone at joint edges in arthritis (syn. osteophytic formation)

Lordosis: anterior convexity of the spine

Lumbar: the 'small' of the back — ie situated between the dorsal (thoracic) and sacral levels

Lumen: the cavity of a tubular structure

Macro-: prefix meaning abnormally large size

Malar: pertaining to cheek

Mallet finger: inability actively to straighten the terminal joint of a finger

Mandible: the lower jaw

Maxilla: the upper jaw

Medial: inner side, or internal (opposite to lateral)

Medullary cavity: the soft interior of a bone

Meniscus: the semilunar cartilage of the knee

Metacarp-phalangeal: pertaining to the joint between the fingers and the bones of the palm of the hand

Micro-: prefix meaning abnormally small size

Motor: pertaining to movement (applied particularly to peripheral nerve function)

Myelo-: prefix meaning pertaining to the spinal cord

Myo-: prefix meaning pertaining to muscle

Necrosis: death of tissue

Neurapraxia: interruption of conductivity in a nerve owing to pressure thereon, resulting in temporary paralysis and anaesthesia in the distribution of the nerve; full recovery will take place spontaneously in a matter of days or very few weeks (cf. axonotmesis and neurotmesis)

Neurotmesis: interruption of conductivity in a nerve by anatomical division causing permanent paralysis and anaesthesia in the distribution of the nerve; recovery cannot take place unless the nerve is surgically repaired (cf. axonotmesis and neurapraxia)

Nystagmus: oscillatory movement of the eyes

Oedema: accumulation of fluid in the tissues

Oesophagus: the gullet, the muscular tube connecting the back of the mouth and the stomach

Olfactory: pertaining to the sense of smell

Oligo-: prefix meaning lack of

Optic fundi: optic disc, where the optic nerve enters the retina

Orthopaedic: pertaining to bony deformity

Os calcis: see calcaneus

Osteitis: inflammation of bone

Osteoarthritis: degeneration of a joint from wear and tear

Osteophyte: ridge of adventitious bone at joint edges in arthritis (syn. 'lipping')

Osteoporosis: loss of mineral salts from bones, the result of lack of use owing to injury or disease and causing softening of the bone

Palmarflexion: moving the wrist in the direction that the palm faces (syn. flexion)

Para-: prefix meaning by the side of, near, through, abnormality

Paramedian: pertaining to a vertical line parallel with the midline, ie a line drawn down through the xiphoid process and umbilicus

Paresis: incomplete paralysis

Patella: the knee bone

Periarthritis: inflammation round a joint, due to infection or injury, causing pain and restricted movement

Phalanx: a finger

Phlebo-: prefix meaning pertaining to a vein

Plantarflexion: flexing the foot — ie 'pointing the toes'

-plegia: suffix meaning paralysis

Plexus: a network of nerves or veins

Pneumothorax: air in the pleural cavity — eg from the puncture of the lung by a fractured rib — and causing collapse of the lung

Poly-: prefix meaning much or many

Prolapse: falling down, or extrusion or protrusion, of a structure

Pronation: twisting the forearm, the elbow being fixed, to bring the palm of the hand facing downwards (opposite to supination)

Proximal: nearest the centre (opposite to distal)

Pulmonary: pertaining to the lung

Quadriceps: the main muscle of the front of the thigh

Recurvatum deformity: bent backwards

Reduction: restoration to a normal position — eg of a fractured bone or a dislocated joint

Renal: pertaining to the kidney

Retro-: prefix meaning behind or backward

Rhomberg's Test: a test of balance — the patient stands erect with toes and heels touching and eyes closed; unsteadiness occurs if test positive

Sclerosis: increased density, eg of a bone, owing to disease or injury

Scoliosis: lateral (ie sideways) curvature of the spine

Sensory: pertaining to sensation (applied particularly to peripheral nerve function)

Sequestrum: a fragment of dead bone

Sinus: a track leading from an infected focus — eg in a bone — to an opening on the surface of the skin

Slough: tissue, usually skin, dead from infection

Spondylosis: degenerative changes in the spine

Sternum: the breastbone

Subscapular: beneath the shoulder blade

Subtalar: beneath the talar bone

Supination: twisting the forearm, the elbow being fixed, to bring the palm of hand facing upwards (opposite to pronation)

Supraclavicular: above the clavicle

Suture: stitch

Synovitis: inflammation of the lining membrane of a joint

Tachycardia: increased pulse rate

Talar: bone of the foot

Therapeutic: pertaining to treatment, the application of a remedy

Thorax, thoracic: the chest, pertaining to the chest

Thrombosis: clotting (thrombus) in a blood vessel or in the heart

Tissue: anatomically a complex of similar cells and fibres forming a structure

Tracheotomy: operative opening into the trachea (windpipe) to assist breathing in certain chest injuries

Traction: method by which fractures, particularly of the femur, are treated — the lower limb is suspended by weights and pulleys and a continously pulling force is applied by means of further weights and pulleys attached to a metal pin (Steinmann pin) passed through the upper end of the tibia

Trauma: an injury, eg physical, emotional

Ulcer: localised destruction, by injury or disease, of a surface tissue (ie skin, mucous membrane)

Umbilicus: the navel

Valgus: outward deviation — eg genu valgum knock knee (the tibia deviates outwards from the knee)

Varicosity: dilation and pouching of the veins

Varus: inward deviation — eg genu valugum bow leg (the tibia deviates inwards from the knee)

Ventilation: the movement of oxygen in and carbon dioxide out of the lungs, mechanical ventilation is ventilation by means of a machine.

Vertebra: one of the backbones

Whiplash injury: strain of cervical structure from the head moving violently in one direction and then bounding back in the reverse direction

Xanth-: prefix meaning yellow

Xiphoid process: the lower most bony part of the sternum

APPENDIX 2
WIGMORE ANALYSIS CHARTS

For an introduction to Wigmorean analysis, see **14.5.5** to **14.5.9**.

The aim of producing a Wigmore chart is to identify the chain of proof, including inferences which stengthen or weaken the main proposition to be proved. The chart is developed according to the purpose for which it is required and the standpoint of the person producing it. While there is often not time to produce this level of sophisticated analysis, for those who persevere it is well worth the effort. To produce a Wigmorean analysis chart:

(a) Identify the ultimate probandum — the proposition ultimately required to be proved.

(b) Identify the penultimate probanda — the matters leading directly to what must be proved.

(c) List the facts in a key list which can include the whole case, or only certain elements in a case. Each proposition is then charted with a specific symbol. A square indicates evidence that can be directly perceived, eg, the detective's statement in the example below. A circle indicates an inference from another source.

(d) Draw the chart from top to bottom and from right to left. One item stands for one proposition and no more.

In the case example in **14.5.8**, the 'ultimate probandum' — the proposition that must be proved — is that Cassie Charnel stole a bottle of whisky from Super Stores plc. Figure App 2.1 shows how this would look on a Wigmorean analysis. Note that items 1–4 represent the 'penultimate probanda', ie, matters leading to the main proposition to be proved. Concentrating on the line of proof for the first item — (item 1 on the key list) that she appropriated a bottle of whisky — items 5, 7, 9 and 11 are only inferences from, respectively, 6, 8, 10 and 12. These last are facts to which you have direct access — the detective's statement — on the assumption that you either have the original statement, or a copy of it. The special nature of these facts is shown by the square, rather than the circle.

Figure App 2.1 Wigmorean analysis

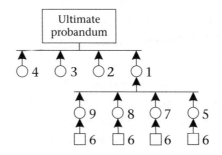

Key list:

1. CC appropriated a bottle of whisky.
2. The whisky belonged to Super Stores.
3. CC appropriated the whisky dishonestly.
4. At the time, she intended to deprive Super Stores of the whisky permanently.
5. CC took the whisky from the display.
6. Store detective's statement to this effect.
7. CC put it in her coat instead of the basket.
8. CC failed to produce or pay for the whisky at check-out.
9. CC left store with whisky.

Strictly speaking, there is another stage of thought which the chart might have shown. The move from the store detective's statement to the inference that what she stated was in fact the case involves a generalisation and could be charted as in Figure App 2.2.

Figure App 2.2 Wigmorean analysis

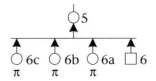

Key list:

5. CC took the whisky from the display.
6. Store detective's statement to this effect.
6a. In the absence of a motive to lie or opportunity for erroneous observation, a person's account of what he has seen is likely to be true.
6b. The store detective had no known motive to lie.
6c. He had no known opportunity for erroneous observation.

The symbol π is used to designate a fact noticed as a matter of general knowledge or inference without evidence being introduced specifically on the point. Here 6a takes the form of a generalisation about the trustworthiness of a particular type of evidence, whilst 6b and 6c may be inferred from the absence of evidence to the contrary.

The objective of the chart is to clarify, and since clarity is likely to be obscured by density of items it may be thought unnecessary to chart all the generalisations on which inferences depend. But care should be taken because some generalisations which are necessary to support an inference are a good deal more questionable than might at first appear. With or without explicit generalisations, the chart should always show the fact that a witness states something to be the case and the inference that that is indeed the case as two distinct items. One of the dangers of the Wigmorean exercise is that it can lead to the production of a rigid pattern of unnaturally solid 'facts', whereas reality is altogether more fragile and elusive.

Strengthening and Weakening Inferences

Suppose the evidence of the store detective's observation is not so clear-cut. There are difficulties because he admits in his statement that the store was crowded and so he did not have the defendant in view for the whole time at the spirits display. But an assistant manager who had been alerted was also observing the defendant and he confirms the detective's account that the bottle of whisky was taken. The appropriate section of the chart will look something like Figure App 2.3.

Figure App 2.3 Wigmorean analysis

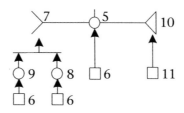

Key list:

5. CC took whisky from display.

6. Detective's statement to this effect.

7. His observation may have been mistaken.

8. Store was crowded.

9. Detective could not have defendant in view all the time at the spirits display.

10. Assistant manager confirms 5.

11. His statement to this effect.

(The numbers of the items shown in Figures App 2.1 and 2.2 will have to be adjusted.) The symbol ⟩— shows something which weakens the effect of another piece of charted information. It appears on the left of the symbol which represents the weakened information. The symbol —◁ shows something which strengthens the effect of another piece of charted information. It appears on the right of the symbol which represents the strengthened information.

The most basic features of Wigmore's system have been shown. It should now be possible to construct a chart and key list either for a whole case or for part of one.

With the task completed you will have a better idea of how your information hangs together. The chart cannot, of course, tell you which propositions are likely to be accepted by the court but your own judgment will be greatly assisted in dealing with that problem by the construction of the chart. Wigmore observed that the use of this method came more readily to some than to others. Experience has shown, however, that initial difficulties disappear if the student persists in trying to make the method work. The best way to learn this technique is to use it.

Wigmore's ideas have since been elaborated by Terence Anderson and William Twining in *Analysis of Evidence*, Weidenfeld, 1991.

APPENDIX 3
COMPLETED CHART FOR R V PENNY

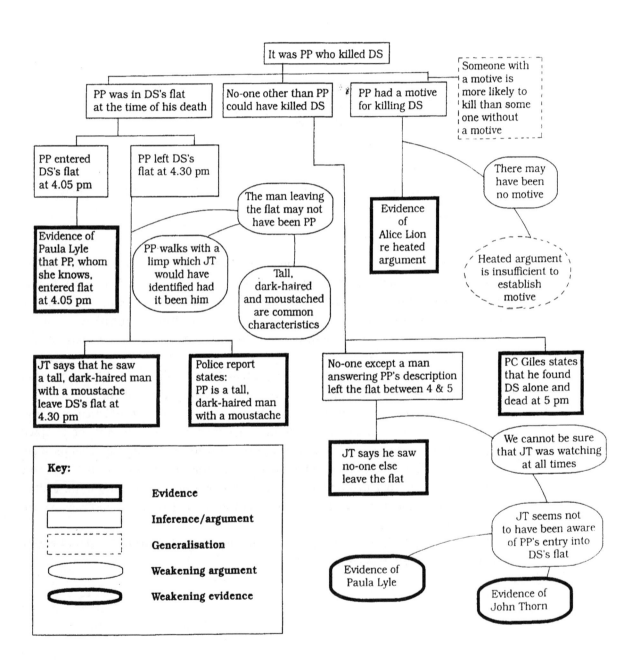

FURTHER READING

Anderson, T. and Twining, W., *Analysis of Evidence*, Butterworths, 1991.

Binder, D.A., and Bergman, P., *Fact Investigation: from Hypothesis to Proof*, West Publishing Co, 1984.

Bono, E. De, *Lateral Thinking*, Penguin, 1990.

Bono, E. De, *New Thinking for the Millennium*, Penguin, 2000.

Bono, E. De, *Six Thinking Hats*, Penguin, 2000.

Bono, E. De, *Teach Yourself to Think*, Penguin, 1996.

Buzan, Tony, *Use Your Head*, BBC Books, 1995.

Constanzo, M., *Problem Solving*, Cavendish Publishing, 1995.

Gold, N., Mackie K., Twining W., *Learning Lawyers' Skills*, Butterworths, 1989.

Moore, A. J., Bergman, D., and Binder, D. A., *Trial Advocacy: Inferences, Arguments and Techniques*, American Case Book Series, West Publishing Co, 1996.

Nathanson, S., What Lawyers Do: A Problem-solving Approach to Legal Practice, Sweet & Maxwell, 1997.

Purver, J. M., *et al.*, *The Trial Lawyer's Book: Preparing and Winning Cases*, Lawyer's Cooperative Publishing, New York, 1990.

Sonsteng, J., Haydock and Boyd, *The Trial Book. A Total System for the Preparation & Presentation of a Case*, West Publishing Co, 1984.

Twining, W., *Theories of Evidence: Bentham and Wigmore*, Butterworths, 1985.

Twining, W., and Miers, D., *How to Do Things with Rules*, Butterworths, 4th edn, 1999.

Wigmore, J.H., 'The problem of proof', *University of Illinois Law Review*, 1913, vol. 8, p 7.

Wigmore, J.H., *The Science of Judicial Proof*, 1937.

INDEX